Social Theory and the Politics of Identity

Social Theory and the Politics of Identity

Edited by Craig Calhoun

BLACKWELL
Oxford UK & Cambridge USA

Preface, editorial matter and organization, copyright © Craig Calhoun 1994

Copyright © for all chapters rests with the authors.

First published 1994

First published in USA 1994
Reprinted 1995

Blackwell Publishers Inc.
238 Main Street
Cambridge, Massachusetts 02142
USA

Blackwell Publishers Ltd
108 Cowley Road, Oxford OX4 1JF
UK

Library of Congress Cataloging-in-Publication Data

A CIP catalogue record for this book is available from the Library of Congress.

ISBNs: 1–55786–472-1; 1–55786–473-X (paperback)

British Library Cataloguing in Publication Data

A CIP catalogue record for this book is available from the British Library.

Typeset in 10½ on 12pt Goudy Oldstyle by Apex Products, Singapore

Printed in Great Britain by T. J. Press, Padstow

This book is printed on acid-free paper

Contents

Contributors

Craig Calhoun is Professor of Sociology and History and Director of both the University Center for International Studies and the Program in Social Theory and Cross-Cultural Studies at the University of North Carolina at Chapel Hill.

Manthia Diawara is Professor and Chair of the Africana Studies Program at New York University.

Gloria D. Gibson is a graduate student in the Department of Sociology at the University of Michigan.

Todd Gitlin is Professor of Sociology and Communications at the University of California, Berkeley.

Charles Lemert is Professor of Sociology at Wesleyan University.

Stephen Mennell is Professor of Sociology at University College, Dublin.

Thomas Scheff is Professor of Sociology at the University of California, Santa Barbara.

Margaret R. Somers is Assistant Professor of Sociology at the University of Michigan.

Loïc J. D. Wacquant is Associate Professor of Sociology at the University of California, Berkeley, and a Visiting Scholar at the Russell Sage Foundation.

Norbert Wiley is Professor of Sociology at the University of Illinois, Champaign–Urbana.

Eli Zaretsky is Professor of History at the University of Missouri, Columbia.

Acknowledgments

No book is ever the product of its authors alone. This one has been helped into print by several people and institutions. It originated as a "miniconference" of the Theory Section of the American Sociological Association, held during the annual meeting in Pittsburgh in 1992. I am grateful to the Section for the opportunity to organize this miniconference during my service as chair. Most of the chapters were originally presented to that miniconference and benefitted from the critical comments of Elizabeth Long and Peter Bearman.

This volume is also the first in a new series of Theory Section Publishers publications with Blackwell. Simon Prosser has proved an able and supportive editor, and his Blackwell's colleagues have been equally helpful. Leah Florence of the Program in Social Theory and Cross-Cultural Studies at the University of North Coralina at Chapel Hill has also been extremely helpful in various aspects of this project, including managing the flow of paper, editing, and proofreading.

Preface

> It is crucial that we not ignore the self nor the longing people have
> to transform the self, that we make the conditions for wholeness such
> that they are mirrored both in our own beings and in social and
> political reality.
>
> bell hooks, *Sisters of the Yam*

There have always been differences among people and tensions within
people. People have always faced issues of figuring out just who they
were, how they might reconcile their different desires and aspirations, and how they ought to relate to others. But something seems
qualitatively new to the problems of both individual and collective
identity and the problem of relating to each other across lines of
difference in the modern world.

While ethnicity and ethnic antagonism are very ancient, genocide
like that of the holocaust and the many, normally more benign
forms of nationalism are distinctively modern. Modern individualism,
modern state structures, the impetus that capitalism has given to
expand the organization of commerce and industry throughout the
world, the mobilization of citizens for total war have all changed the
stakes of issues of collective identity.

In the cosmopolitan capitals of empires and the great merchant
cities on long-distance trade routes, members of different religions
and ethnic groups coexisted in a harmony we find hard to recall.
Istanbul (or formerly Constantinople) was home to different sects of
Christians, Jews, Muslims, for example. So too was Beirut, and the
example of Lebanon — a relatively peaceful, ethnically heterogeneous
state to which people fled from the horrors of Nazi Germany —
should remind us that tolerance is no invention of the modern West.
But the citizens of these cosmopolitan cities could coexist in tolerance

not because they necessarily liked each other, or shared some lowest common denominator of common culture. They could coexist in large part because they were not called upon to join in very many collective projects. They were not called upon to join together in democratic self-government, most crucially, or to share their universities, or their neighborhoods. Though they met each other in commerce, the peace among them was maintained in part because they were otherwise separated into enclaves concerned with their internal affairs. The matters of central government were left with little choice to emperors and sultans.

It was democracy, and more generally the rise of a way of thinking that said governments get their legitimacy from the people and not from divine right, ancient inheritance or sheer power, that transformed relations among the different groups of citizens. Democratic thinking depended on notions such as "the will of the people," which in turn depended on constituting or discovering some such common will. The idea of the nation was invoked early on not just against neighboring peoples, but on behalf of "the people" against kings and emperors. But once it was invoked, citizens could no longer stay so separate in their enclaves, for a common discourse about collective matters of public concern was required. Their various different grievances against each other had to be resolved not by an independent ruler but by some manner of putative representative of all of them, and their grievances against the state became often grievances against each other.

In this context, identity became newly problematic. Issues of collective identity joined, moreover, with the increasing prevalence of ideas that individual identity was a product of self-construction, was open to free choice, and was not simply given by birth, or divine will. In the Protestant Reformation perhaps most importantly, but throughout the early modern era, a revolution in thinking gave individual identity new moral and social weight. It became increasingly an object of personal struggle not merely a premise of action.

Problems of individual and collective identity were joined, both because individual identity was shaped by what Foucault called new disciplines of power, and because the question was raised of what sort of individual identity qualified one to participate in the public discourses that shaped policy and influenced power.

Modern social theory arose in this same context, and with its own problematic relationship to issues of identity. On the one hand, social theory pioneered ways of thinking that emphasized individuals but not the differences among individuals. In early political economy, thinking about the self-regulating market system was paralleled by ideas of individual actors making autonomous decisions in relation to the market, but the ideology necessarily reduced them to equivalent individuals. In social contract theory, the individuals empowered by the opportunity to participate in the implicit contract were so many members of a set of equivalent citizens. In both realms, tacit assumptions about the identities of these individuals privileged certain identities even while they presented themselves as universal. The individuals facing the market were prototypically male, property-owning or labor-selling heads of households; they were free, though the law still recognized slavery. The individuals joining in the social contract, like those joining in the eighteenth-century golden age of public discourse, were prototypically educated, property-owning male speakers of the dominant language of the nation. Thus individualism ironically repressed difference. This was a problem both internally, as some members of each country's dominant nation were subordinated to a vision of proper citizens constituted in the image of others, and externally, as the borders of the state were joined in imagination to those of nation and the accident of inclusion became a reality of moral entitlement that has bedeviled us ever since. Our ideologies of democracy presume boundaries and imply exclusions that we find it very hard to justify internally to the discourse of democracy.

Social theory has been shaped by this repression of certain aspects of the issue of identity. It has long had to deal with a tension between the need to presume identities equivalent enough to allow individuals to be taken as equivalent units of analysis. It has reified notions of markets and elections that presume the equivalence of individuals and render their differences epiphenomenal. At the same time, it has carried on innumerable forms of the argument between nature and nurture, overall committing itself to the claim that identities are constructed but primarily seeing that construction as a matter of the preparation of young people for adult participation. Socialization has thus replaced property-owning as the qualification for citizenship, but identity is still held to be established in advance of participation. Identity formation on most models – including for example Habermas's famous theory of the public sphere – prepares one for entrance into the public arena. It gives one individual strength and individual opinions. Conversely, the public sphere calls on one to put to the side the differences of class, ethnicity, and gender in order to speak as equals. And it thereby makes it all but impossible to thematize those very differences as the objects of politics instead of as obstacles to be overcome before rational political formation of the collective will.

Social theory has had a hard time, thus, coming to terms with the idea that identity itself might be a crucial focus of political struggle. Various new social movements of the post-war era brought this idea to prominence: the civil rights movement in the United States and anti-colonial nationalist movements in the Third World, the women's movement, the gay movement, a range of movements that sought not only various instrumental goals but the affirmation of excluded identities as publicly good and politically salient. I think we are misled by our theories to see these claims as a little more novel than they are. It is not as though identities were settled throughout the preceding 200 years. On the contrary, Americans forged a national identity in both revolution and civil war, workers fought to make their identity publicly salient, neither women's struggles nor those of African-Americans or immigrant ethnic groups began after the Second World War. The problem was more that during the whole earlier era, we had managed to maintain for the most part theories that obscured the importance of identity politics from our analyses. This we can no longer do.

The present prominence of identity politics is linked to an increasing recognition that social theory itself must be a discourse with many voices, not a monological speaking of a simple and unitary truth or its successive approximations. An increasingly transnational sphere of public and academic discourse and increasing roles for women, gay men and lesbians, people of color, and various previously dominated or repressed ethnic groups all press theorists not only to make sense of differences in the "world-out-there," but to make sense of the differences within the discourse of theory. This calls on theory to take culture seriously and to approach it reflexively, not objectivistically.

The chapters in this book take several different approaches to the challenge of putting the problems – and politics – of identity on center stage for social theory. One theme that unites all of them, however, is a sense of the importance of avoiding a sharp split between what have been called "micro" and "macro" perspectives. All chapters explore issues of identities in ways that join rather than severing discourse about the personal and collective.

The introductory essay explores why issues of identity appear so often as political issues, the challenge of moving beyond a constraining, either/or opposition of essentialism to constructionism, and the reasons why dealing with cultural diversity is harder than commonplace relativist rhetorics imply.

Margaret Somers and Gloria Gibson synthesize and probe the implications of the wide-ranging and exciting recent revitalization of narrative. This has special importance for sociology which, they suggest, has taken an image of narrative particularism as a crucial disciplinary "epistemological other." By contrast to this problematic understanding, they develop an account of narrative identities that challenges the common, but misleading and often disempowering, opposition between theory and narrative and that speaks to basic epistemological concerns raised by the dialectics of diversity and identity. Linking narrative identity to relational settings, they also develop a specifically sociological dimension often lacking in recent literary approaches to this theme.

Charles Lemert uses a form of narrative, the case study, to add empirically concrete structure to his account of how social theory misses the complexity of personal identity. He focuses especially on how themes of gender and race are normalized in conventional discourses, obscuring recognition of their deep personal power as well as many dimensions of their embeddedness in power relations. He also problematizes the notion that identity depends on a strong discourse of self, or a strong notion of collective "we." Essentialist thinking, he suggests, undermines much contemporary anxiety about problems of the self and consequent moral debilities.

Norbert Wiley takes a sharply opposed tack, emphasizing universal human nature. He seeks, however, to base an understanding of the politics of identity not on traditional notions of psychological individuality but on a semiotic approach to the self. Wiley explores changing discourses of identity by looking back through American history. In this way, he situates the development of pragmatist approaches (including symbolic interactionism, the branch of sociology that has given the most sustained attention to issues of identity) as an indigenous and explicitly democratic alternative to the "faulty psychologism" of the founding fathers.

Todd Gitlin looks at the consequences of the rise of "identity politics" for politics. More specifically he asks whether the affirmation of difference is being pursued in ways that undermine the potential for affirming broad commonalities − such as those of class − and achieving collective strength in political action. His essay, articulated clearly from the perspective of the political left, questions the self-declared radicalism of many versions of identity politics. His call is not for a return to the search for progress through universalist ideas and putatively all-embracing collective agents. Rather he emphasizes the importance of deep but still limited commonalities and the problems of "group solipsism."

Stephen Mennell takes on directly the contrast between approaches to collective identity rooted in notions of aggregation of individual selves and approaches that see the formation of self-images and we-images as inextricably interdependent cultural processes. Drawing on the notion of "habitus" used by Bourdieu and Elias, Mennell explores the link between understandings of collective identity rooted in the pre-conscious practices and understandings of everyday life and those that depend more on the mediation of discourse and other means of making identity more self-conscious. Looking at the implications of increasing scale of social life, he examines changing forms and extents of mutual identification and the production of many layers of human identities. Mennell counterposes cultural sociology to psychologism — treating the "psychologization" as itself a moment in the historical change in balance between "we" and "I."

Zaretsky also seeks to situate historically the thematization of aspects of psychological and/or individualistic discourse in "identity politics." Most especially, he traces shifts in the role psychoanalysis has played in formulated questions about identity. Unlike conventional narratives of psychoanalytic history, however, Zaretsky's focuses on the reconfiguration of relations between "public" and "private." Zaretsky sees in the production of an increasingly particularized identity politics not just a general trend but a response to a political conjuncture shaped crucially by the end of any separation between capitalist production and personal life. This undermined the traditional Marxist pursuit of a unified project of political liberation as well as changed the meaning of psychoanalytic discourse and paved the way for the "polities of difference" inspired by poststructuralism.

The next two chapters address problems of social theory and the politics of identity in empirical analyses of themes in African-American life and cultural production. Manthia Diawara begins by noting the extent to which some versions of African-American cultural criticism presume a kind of pathology in contemporary black American life — however much this pathology is shown to be caused by external factors. He seeks an approach to African-American identity that does not build in from the start a presumed need for "conversion." With this in mind, he looks at the tension in the first part of The Autobiography of Malcolm X, that focused on Detroit Red, between affirmation of aspects of black culture and calls for conversion *away* from that culture. Diawara shows how this issue of affirmation or conversion relates to broader themes in African-American cultural production, including the standing of black musicians performing primarily for white audiences.

Loïc Wacquant takes up partially related themes with an emphasis on social organization and material factors. He explores the emergence of a "new color bar" and the constitution of certain forms of life in and against the stigmatization of "the ghetto" or "the underclass." Wacquant is concerned to reconstitute the way we pay attention to life in hypersegregated, economically devastated sections of America, focusing on the theme of "institutional abandonment" that makes the ghetto seem a place from which one ought to escape. This in turn blocks recognition of and commitment to the production of social organization in the ghetto and encourages the widespread imputation of pathological disorganization as though this were an internal, primarily cultural phenomenon. The crises of the ghetto come to be presented as a reflection of problematic black identity rather than a challenge to black identity.

The last two chapters take up the theme of nationalism, a very large-scale instance of the politics of identity. Scheff offers a theory of ethnic nationalism and conflict based on the sociology of emotions. Finding fault with accounts that focus only on cultural production of meaning, he stresses the importance of pride and shame as powerful orienting emotions (or, perhaps, two sides of an emotional coin). Particular modern versions of nationalism and ethnic conflict grow out of shame–anger sequences rooted in universal human nature. My own final chapter, by contrast, suggests that it is impossible to pin down any single, substantive source of nationalism as its universal base. Rather, seeing nationalism as a rhetoric in which projects of large-scale collective identity are pursued and challenged, I explore how this figures in relation to democratic theory, first as central to the drawing of boundaries around polities and second as a powerful source of pressures for internal conformity and repression of contrary dimensions of identity politics.

Obviously this book is not a comprehensive guide to social theory useful in understanding the politics of identity nor to issues raised for social theory by the politics of identity. It is, rather, an attempt to create a better intersection between two fields of discourse. It is an attempt to bring serious social analysis into debates over identity politics that sometimes proceed as though cultural production and interpretation fully constituted the field of analysis. Equally, it is an attempt to show how important struggles over identity are for social theory, and how inadequately attended to they have been in many branches of social theory. The eleven authors represented here do not agree on all the questions to ask, much less on the answers. But their disparate contributions do show how widespread is the conviction that this is an important terrain for questioning.

1

Social Theory and the Politics of Identity

Craig Calhoun

THE MODERN DISCOURSE OF IDENTITY

Plurality, as Hannah Arendt (1958) observed, is basic to the human condition. We are distinct from each other, and often strive to distinguish ourselves further. Yet each dimension of distinction is apt at least tacitly also to establish commonality with a set of others similarly distinguished. There is no simple sameness unmarked by difference, but likewise no distinction not dependent on some background of common recognition (C. Taylor 1992a, b).

Concerns with individual and collective identity, thus, are ubiquitous. We know of no people without names, no languages or cultures in which some manner of distinctions between self and other, we and they are not made. Though the concern may be universal, however, the identities themselves are not. Gender and age seem to distinguish people nearly everywhere, pedigree or parentage are of almost equally wide significance. Yet it is no accident that discourse about identity seems in some important sense distinctively modern — seems, indeed, intrinsic to and partially defining of the modern era.

This has to do both with intensified effort to consolidate individual and categorical identities, to reinforce self-sameness, and with social changes that made the production and recognition of identities newly problematic. The modernity of concerns for identity is thus argued as much in Foucault's (1977) analysis of how discipline produces a new sort of individual self as in more conventional treatments of the rise of individualism. A crucial common denominator is recognition of a new kind of stress on identity, that is, on the notion that self is integrally and immediately being and consciousness, name and voice. Descartes' *cogito* is a crucial index of the novel stress on identity: "I think therefore I am." Not only does the person become a disembodied cognitive subject, knowledge is presented as dependent on this subject. In Fichte, the simple equation "I am I" is elevated to a philosophical claim to the self-sufficiency of identity, and in other parts of the German idealist tradition this is joined to an emphasis on the fundamental formative power of will. As the knowing and recognizing self is made to carry this philosophical weight, it is also more commonly seen as fixed, as reflecting itself in simple identity rather than complex relationship. The stage is set for Hegel's dialectical transformation of this tradition and for later thinkers, like Freud, Vygotsky and Bakhtin to rediscover notions of internal dialogue and contestation. Even as they and their successors have questioned simple self-sameness, however, most have retained a focus on identity in a relatively strong sense, on integral individuality.

At the same time, modern selves are called on to carry new sorts of moral weight. This weight was already assigned to the self in Augustine's *Confessions*. Augustine joined Judeo-Christian concerns with an individual god and individual salvation to Greek forms of intellectual exploration and ideas of recognition to create a new sort of morally charged introspection. Not until a thousand years after Augustine, however, did a similar synthesis re-emerge as part of the configuration of modern self-understanding. The same sorts of moral sources informed the crucial movements, largely on Christian motivations, to rethink the nature and significance of subjectivity in the era from the Reformation to the Enlightenment.[1] That this morally charged subjectivity is not in all respects uniquely modern does not stop it from being distinctively modern.

The discourse of self is distinctively modern, and modernity distinctively linked to the discourse of self, not just because of the cognitive and moral weight attached to selves and self-identity. Modern concerns with identity stem also from ways in which modernity has made identity distinctively problematic. It is not simply – or even clearly the case – that it matters more to us than to our forebears to be who we are. Rather, it is much harder for us to establish who we are and maintain this own identity satisfactorily in our lives and in the recognition of others.

Both self-identity and recognition can pose challenges and difficulties. Self-knowledge – always a construction no matter how much it feels like a discovery – is never altogether separable from claims to be known in specific ways by others. But the two dimensions may not always be equally problematic. Many aspects of constructing or achieving identity, for example, can be fraught with obstacles without making the identity itself problematic for others to recognize. Upward mobility, say through the Church from the ranks of the common clergy to the episcopate, has always been hard to achieve and harder for some aspirants than others. But only rarely and intermittently have the identities of bishops been subject to dispute. Moreover, the Church offers – or at least has seemed through much of its history to offer – an all-encompassing scheme of identities. Bishops need not be validated in isolation but are consecrated through ceremony based on tradition and ideology and invested not only with the symbols of their office but with implicit recognition by a range of authoritative others. But this kind of clarity, rooted not only in cultural or ideological consensus but in the reinforcement offered by systematically organized networks of social relations, is precisely what is challenged in the modern era. If it has never been quite perfect, and often characterized by more anomalies, doubts and deceptions than we retrospectively imagine, it has nonetheless commonly underwritten a level of unquestioned acceptance of the apparent order of social categories that we no longer experience. In Bourdieu's (1976, 1990) terms, it has allowed schemes of understanding and normative order to appear as doxic, as simply given, rather than merely *orthodox* or authoritatively defended, let alone *heterodox* and implicitly contested.

Modernity has meant in significant part the breakup – or the reduction to near-irrelevance – of most all-encompassing identity schemes. Kinship still matters to us as individuals; we invest it with great emotional weight, but kinship no longer offers us an overall template of social and personal identities. When we meet strangers in an airport, we are unlikely to be able to place their relationships to us as part of a singular, overall system of kin relations which would offer both clarity about who we are in relation to each other and how we should behave. This distinguishes us from, say, Nuer of the Nilotic region of southern Sudan meeting with their cattle at a watering hole in the 1920s or 1930s (Evans-Pritchard 1940). The Nuer might have faced complexities – they might have shared clanship yet come from rival villages, for example, or been joined affinally while consanguinally opposed – but though they might have had a multiplicity of identities to sort out, and quite actively to manage, they had a minimally disputed set of shared rhetorics for both self-identification and recognition of others. Without attaining perfection, they had a very high level of systematicity to their scheme of identities. This was problematic primarily at the fringes – and of course patterns of migration, intergroup conflict and communication were complex and important throughout the African continent. I do not

mean to suggest that all issues of identity were simply and stably
settled for the Nuer, but rather that most appeared within a
range of activity where a limited range of common rhetorics could
organize the struggles for identity and recognition. Now, of course, as
southerners within an ethnically, religiously and politically diverse
Sudan, members of a tribe implicated within a secessionist rebellion, occasional Christians and widely labeled animists, construction
workers in an increasingly city-centered economy, Nuer no longer can
treat the categories of Nuer identity as doxically given but must face
the modern challenge of deciding how to fit them into projects of
collective and individual identity that presuppose inscription in a
multiplicity of often incommensurable identity schemes.

Kinship systems are not the only kind of all-encompassing identity
scheme the world has known. Within European history, despite the
considerable heterogeneity of institutions and local identities, the
notion of a "great chain of being" long offered a kind of doxic
background to contests over more specific identities. [2] More generally,
the point is not to contrast extremes of all-encompassing systematicity to the illusion of complete absence of pre-established rhetorical
systems of identity but rather to recognize a variable. The modern
era brought an increase in the multiplicity of identity schemes so
substantial that it amounted to a qualitative break, albeit one unevenly distributed in time and space. In the modern era, identity
is always constructed and situated in a field and amid a flow of
contending cultural discourses. In Cascardi's (1992: 3) terms, "the
modern subject is defined by its insertion into a series of separate
value-spheres, each one of which tends to exclude or attempts to
assert its priority over the rest." This formulation perhaps overstates
the extent to which each "value sphere" can be said equally and
completely to claim exclusivity or priority, but the general suggestion
is sound. And as Cascardi goes on to argue, the tension and even
incommensurability among the various discourses – at the extreme
where they claim autonomy – appears not just as an "external"
difficulty for individuals but as a series of contradictions within the
"subject-self."

ESSENTIALISM AND CONSTRUCTIONISM

A sociologist is apt to think that the new, post-structuralist rhetoric
of "subject-positions" and "enactments" is an unnecessary reinvention of the familiar vocabulary of status and role. This is one result
of the fact that so much of the most prominent recent social theory

has been generated outside sociology and too often in ignorance of sociological theory. Nonetheless, while the older sociological approach to "roles" did provide a way to note that individuals bear multiple identities, it commonly obscured the full impact of this. Most versions of role theory tacitly posited a kind of onto-logical independence of the individual from her/his various roles. Individuals, thus, might experience "stress" based on the tensions among their roles.[3] In strong versions of role theory, persons might even be understood as partially constituted by their roles. But even within its own rhetoric, role theory did not adequately address the complexity of the problem of relating multiple roles to each other – or more precisely, of reconciling the expectations (including self-expectations) based on multiple statuses. Attention was focused on how well (or poorly) individuals played socially prescribed roles – doctor, father, etc. There was correspondingly little attention to (1) the discourses which lent value to or withdrew it from various possible role-performances, (2) dissent from or political contestation about those roles, (3) the kinds of performances through which actors went beyond or outside roles and/or created new ones, or (4) the possibility that a kind of fragmentation of self was a com-mon, possibly ubiquitous, by-product of apparently successful role-performance.[4] The sociological analysis of roles was nonetheless a step beyond the essentializing of biological or psychological human identity; it facilitated recognition of the construction of self in social life.

Social constructionism has become extremely widespread, well beyond sociology. It challenges at once the ideas that identity is given naturally and the idea that it is produced purely by acts of individual will. At their best, social constructionist arguments also challenge "essentialist" notions that individual persons can have singular, integral, altogether harmonious and unproblematic identi-ties. And by the same token subtle constructionist arguments challenge accounts of collective identities as based on some "essence" or set of core features shared by all members of the collectivity and no others. Thus, for example, Dyson (1993: xxi) writes of the need to move "beyond essentialism" in "expanding African-American cultural criticism":

> Of course, I don't mean that there are not distinct black cultural characteristics that persist over space and time, but these features of black life are the products of the historical and social construction of racial identity ... These distinct features of black life nuance and shape black cultural expression, from the preaching of Martin Luther

King to the singing of Gladys Knight. They do not, however, form
the basis of a black racial or cultural essence. Nor do they indicate
that *the* meaning of blackness will be expressed in a quality or
characteristic without which a person, act, or practice no longer
qualifies as black. Rigid racial essentialism must be opposed.

Essentialist invocations of races, nations, genders, classes,
persons and a host of other identities nonetheless remain common
in everyday discourse throughout the world. Pointing to the social
and cultural histories by which they have been constructed has
become the main way of trying to challenge the grip these essentialist identities have over us and the problems they create. Thus
Hobsbawm and Ranger (1983) seek to weaken the grip of nationalist
thinking by showing it to be based on "the invention of tradition."
There is some risk, though, that simply showing a process of construction fails to grapple with the real, present-day political and
other reasons why essentialist identities continue to be invoked and
often deeply felt. There is also risk that the "social constructionist"
story will become a social determinism, too easily paired with an
overly fixed, "essentialist" notion of society or culture. Thus sociologists who challenged essentialist approaches to individuals would
willingly speak of "the essence of community" (Hewitt 1989: 127) and
sophisticated role analysts could unself-critically employ terms like
"deviance" to describe persons who did not fit normatively sanctioned
roles (e.g. Merton 1968). Within sociology, as Hewitt (1989: 150) puts
it, "the fundamental reference of identity is social location."

Recent approaches to issues of identity have stressed the incompleteness, fragmentation and contradictions of both collective and personal
existence. They have shown how complex is the relationship among
projects of identity, social demands and personal possibilities. And
in order to do so, they have commonly started with the deconstruction of "essentialist" categories and rhetorics.[5] These discussions
have been widespread and bear the general stamp of what from the
vantage point of Anglophone discourse is called "post-structuralism"
(a more complex and less unitary phenomenon seen from within
France); Derrida's challenge to essentialism is perhaps the most
influential. But the exploration of this theme has been most far-
reaching and sociologically substantive within the discourses of
feminist and gay theory.[6]

This is not because feminists, gay men or lesbians have settled
the issue. On the contrary, each group remains deeply divided, but
the concerns are widely understood to be basic and therefore have
drawn substantial theoretical attention. In a sense, the debate stems

from a collision between the core practical political theme of both movements – claiming, legitimating and valuing identities commonly suppressed or devalued by mainstream culture – and the post-structuralism that emerged as the theoretical discourse of choice for leading-edge feminists and gay or lesbian thinkers. Post-structuralism's attack on essentialism and "decentering of the subject" came into conflict with thinking and politics rooted in the standpoint of women or the experience of gays. This was not simply a conflict between theory and popular political practice, however, for the theoretical discourse was deeply involved in and shaped by political practice, and the practice often fissured along the same lines as the theory. The claim that a standpoint of women "essentialized" gender identities, for example, came not only from abstract or academic deconstructionist critiques, but from women of color and lesbians who argued that presumptions of white, heterosexual (and for that matter middle-class) experience structured both the women's movement and academic feminist analyses.[7] As hooks's (1993: 124) recent restatement of this point reveals, however, the issue runs deeper than simply biasing theory or practice towards one group or excluding others; it strikes at core matters of conceptualization: "The concept "Woman" effaces the difference between women in specific socio-historical contexts, between women defined precisely as historical subjects rather than *a* psychic subject (or non-subject) ... For ... only as one imagines "woman" in the abstract, when woman becomes fiction or fantasy, can race not be seen as significant."

Behind this argument over "essentialism" lie a number of long-standing approaches to identity. Philosophical arguments rooted most importantly in Aristotle, for example, pursued identity in terms of the relationship between "essence" and "appearance," or between the true nature of phenomena and epiphenomenal variations. This appeal to nature was reinforced and transformed with the rise of both modern arguments about the biological roots of human identities and Romantic demands for individuals to express and be true to their inner natures. Psychoanalysis challenged the appeal to nature by making the individual newly complex and showing the ways in which identity had to be achieved in development rather than merely discovered in direct reference to nature. At the same time, psychoanalysis continued a version of naturalizing discourse in its widespread approach to difference as pathology, and of essentialism in its argument that individuals must pursue a project of integral identity – e.g., must work to achieve an essentially coherent gender identity despite the ambiguities of early experience. Functionalist sociology participated in the naturalizing language of "pathology" and even non-functionalists pursued theories of "deviance" that reproduced essentialist notions of both normal and deviant identities. It was a crucial part of Derrida's intellectual project to challenge all such essentializing moves as reproductions of an illegitimate and imprisoning metaphysical tradition which needed to be contested even if it was not quite possible to escape through this contest. [8]

Critiques of aspects of these naturalizing and/or essentializing discourses did not have to wait for Derrida's radical formulation, however, but were developed early on, and in each case the discourse itself was amenable to reformulation away from essentialism. Thus psychoanalysis was reproduced as a theory of social construction of *seemingly* natural identities and characteristics (as in Karen Horney's work and that of interactionists more generally) and later became (especially in "object relations" and Lacanian versions) a theory of fragmented and incomplete selves and one of the principal sources of the feminist critique of essentialism. Even sociologists who continued to use labels like "deviance" often committed themselves to radical social constructionist theories that insisted that unmediated nature had little influence on individual or collective identities, while "socialization" processes were all-important.

Social constructionism was an ambiguous ally in the attempt to oppose the devaluing of various identities. Social constructionist approaches could be just as determinist as naturalizing approaches, for example, when they denied or minimized personal and political agency by stressing seemingly omnipresent but diffuse social pressures as the alternative to biology causation. The emphases on early socialization and on the power of social structure also led many social constructionists to treat identities in terms nearly as "essentialist" as those of biological determinists. The origins of various identities were seen as constructed and therefore potentially mutable, thus, so that in principle socialization processes and social structure could be changed. Boys might not be brought up to be violent, or girls might be brought up to excel at math. But such programs of social change operated only on "sex-roles," rather than on gendered thinking as such. More specifically, one-sided social constructionism suggested variability in the correlates of "male" and "female," "homosexual" and "heterosexual," but did not address whether the people addressed under these labels were essentially similar — i.e., similar to each other in terms of some true underlying identity or standard of equivalence. hooks (1984) made this point sharply in arguing against the term "sexual orientation." By the time she wrote, this was displacing the alternative "sexual preference." [9] But hooks suggested that the notion of a singular sexual "orientation" was a reification. It suggested that individuals were somehow sexually open to or desirous of sexual interaction with all members of one sex or the other, minimizing both the autonomy of the individual and the differentiation of people within genders. [10] Relatedly, theorists like Sedgwick (1980, 1985) would show the implicit narrowing of agency in strong versions of constructionism – those that emphasize not what individual people construct for themselves, nor the histories by which some construct for others, but the massive but diffuse impact of impersonal social processes – and Fuss (1989: xii) would make the claim that "constructionism (the position that differences are constructed, not innate) really operates as a more sophisticated form of essentialism."

Haraway (1991) has also argued brilliantly that the opposition between essentialism and constructionism has often been deployed in such a way as to reinforce a nature/culture division that should instead be deconstructed. Reference to biology was commonly dismissed with the accusation "essentialist." Among other effects, this freed critics from the obligation to learn enough biology to engage it in really serious critique. It presented biology as itself, ironically, an essentialized category, neglecting the internal differentiation of positions, the possibilities for critical intervention and new thinking – including thinking with concepts that had been deployed in essentialist fashion but against the grain of the theories in which they had previously been invoked. Perhaps most incisively, Haraway showed how a rejection of all biological thinking as essentialist contributed to difficulties in taking biology seriously on the part of the very women's movement that played such a large role in returning the body to social and cultural discourse.

Rather than a simple opposition between essentialism and constructionism, it is important to see a field of possible strategies for confronting issues of identity. Several feminist thinkers, for example, have argued that it may sometimes be crucial to "risk essentialism." [11] They do not have in mind a simple return to uncontested categories or uncritical assumptions of the biological determination of true identity. Rather, the point is to see that under certain circumstances – mainly identified as political but I think arguably also intellectual – self-critical claims to strong, basic and shared identity may be useful. At its simplest, the argument suggests that where a particular category of identity has been repressed, delegitimated or devalued in dominant discourses, a vital response may be to claim value for all those labeled by that category, thus implicitly invoking it in an essentialist way. Thus in the early years of the women's movement (leaving ambiguous whether also in later years), it may have been vital for resistance to male domination and even for creative initiatives to construct a standpoint of women as such, to essentialize *écriture féminine*, to appeal to the presumed commonalities in the embodied experience of women. Even the critique of how such usage of the category of "woman" obscured the variations among "women" may depend on the evocation of more specific quasi-essentialist categories – e.g., black women, lesbians, etc. In short, it may not be helpful to allow the critique of essentialism to become a prohibition against the use of all general categories of identity.

It is misleading to see essentialism as simply a historical stage, as though it is an error of seventeenth-, eighteenth-, and nineteenth-century thought out of which all "advanced" thinkers have grown. In the first place, the seventeenth, eighteenth, and nineteenth centuries were more complex than that. The roots of social constructionist arguments, after all, lie in Lockean behaviorism and such nineteenth-century inheritors as Owenite socialism (in which context some of their early applications to gender issues arose; see B. Taylor 1983) and were in many ways extended by nineteenth-century social theory. It is common to speak as though essentialism reigned throughout western history until a new Enlightenment freed us in the post-war era. Sometimes the contrast is narrower – essentialism is seen as modernist and postmodernism has saved us from it. In many cases such views are supported by rather simplistic reflection theories of knowledge suggesting that successive stages of capitalism or of communications technology have unequivocally produced their fitting complements in the realm of knowledge.

A more accurate historical story might start by recognizing the special force essentialist reasoning gained during the modern era as part of several different but related intellectual and practical projects. It reinforced and was reinforced by the rise of individualism, the rhetoric of national identity, and appeals to nature as a "moral source." [12] It participated in both the advance of universalistic moral reasoning – as for example the notion of human rights was grounded on a presumed essential commonality of human beings – and the advance of relativistic social explanation and moral construction – as from Montesquieu on the laws and mores of different peoples were understood as specific to their contexts. But this essentialist reasoning did not disappear. In the current clash between promoters of western democracy and advocates of a neo-Confucian authoritarianism in Asia, the competing essentialisms just mentioned come to the fore again as proponents of democracy are described as "human rights imperialists." Within the women's movement the matter is no clearer. For every critique of liberal "rights talk," there are two defenses of women's choice regarding abortion and childbirth rooted in essentialist claims to rights. [13] There is no easy and clear-cut answer to Fuss's question, "How do we reconcile the poststructuralist project to displace identity with the feminist project to reclaim it?" Her question is addressed most immediately to Luce Irigaray, the French feminist theorist who absorbs much from Lacanian psychoanalysis but who also insists on a distinctive female imaginary rooted in female bodies. Irigaray's materialism has seemed simply an essentialism to many critics. Moi (1985), for example, reads Irigaray as fixing the representation of women in the metaphysical project of defining "woman." Others are troubled by her insistent focus on genital physiology. Yet Irigaray (e.g., 1977) herself argues against an order in which only men have full subjectivity and therefore essential identities while women are defined by their lack and presumed non-self-sufficiency. Her work is full simultaneously of deconstruction of essentialist male logic and qualified, strategic claims to female essence. This can be read negatively for its seeming inconsistencies, or positively for the suggestion that it is not productive to be simply for or against essentialism.

The road forward from the early predominance of essentialist approaches to identity lies not in simple reversal. Rather, it lies – historically in the last hundred-plus years of western thought and prospectively for each of us – in a proliferation of the theoretical and practical tools with which we can confront problems of identity and difference. To essentialist reason we *add* constructionism and to this dualism we add the possibilities of *both* deconstructing and claiming identities. [14] Moreover, we can see that essentialism itself need not be essentialized, that there are a plethora of claims to "basic" or "root" or essential identities that stand on different grounds, that cohabit with different political bedfellows, that open (or foreclose) different insights or coalitions or conflicts.

One implication of this is that the challenges posed by projects of identity cannot be averted simply by asserting that those projects are embedded in essentialist thinking. We cannot really stop thinking at least partially in categories – and therefore in at least something rather like an essentialist manner. Just as Derrida suggests we can never entirely escape from metaphysics however critical of it we may become, our task must be to remain seriously self-critical about our invocations of essence and identity. This means among other things paying attention to the agonistic, fractured, problematic aspects of identity. The politics of identity – politics either starting from or aiming at claimed identities of their protagonists – have to be taken seriously. The struggles occasioned by identity politics need to be understood, however, not as simply between those who claim different identities but within each subject as the multiple and contending discourses of our era challenge any of our efforts to attain stable self-recognition or coherent subjectivity.

IDENTITY POLITICS AND THE PROBLEM OF RECOGNITION

Recognition is at the heart of the matter. No matter when and where one looks, subjectivity is perhaps best understood as a project, as something always under construction, never perfect. In varying degrees for different people and in different circumstances it may be more or less challenging, but it is never automatic. A crucial aspect of the project of subjectivity is identity. Identity turns on the interrelated problems of self-recognition and recognition by others. Recognition is vital to any reflexivity, for example, any capacity to look at oneself, to choose one's actions and see their consequences, and to hope to make oneself something more or better than one is. This component of recognition may be the aspect of identity made most problematic by the social changes of modernity.

Recognition may never have followed immediately on socially derived and/or sanctioned identities. There has probably always been some room for manipulation, some need for management or at least for successful presentation or performance. But with enormous nation-states, international diasporas, wide realms of personal choice, unstable and heterogeneous networks of social relations, mass media for the proliferation of cultural transmission and the sheer multiplicity of discourses attempting to name or constitute persons, the social basis for recognition has come under particular challenge. The sheer scope and complexity of recognizable identities and competing identity schemes makes recognition problematic and in need of specific establishment in various institutional and interactional settings. [15]

Problems involving recognition – or nonrecognition – by others are integrally related to issues in personal self-recognition. This is one of the reasons why the sometimes abused and increasingly criticized feminist slogan, "the personal is political," still merits attention. It is not just that others fail to see us for who we are sure we really are, or repress us because of who they think we are. We face problems of recognition because socially sustained discourses about who it is possible or appropriate or valuable to be inevitably shape the way we look at and constitute ourselves, with varying degrees of agonism and tension. These concerns frequently, though not uniformly, are expressed in and give rise to "identity politics."

These identity pursuits are "politics" for several reasons. These go beyond the general assertion that "the personal is political," even though that slogan helped pioneer the feminist version of these identity politics. The reason is that the slogan accepted the implicit division of personal or private and public or social systemic realms in order to challenge the notion that power and politics did not operate in the family, intimate relations and other aspects of "personal" life. [16] But almost immediately, feminist theorists also began to challenge that very division, showing for example how the distinction of public and private had operated to marginalize women and to distort both the realms it helped to constitute.

The pursuits labeled "identity politics" are collective, not merely individual, and public, not only private. They are struggles, not merely gropings; power partially determines outcomes and power relations are changed by the struggles. They involve seeking recognition, legitimacy (and sometimes power), not only expression or autonomy; other people, groups and organizations (including states) are called upon to respond. Indeed, one of the most problematic effects of the new age, pop psychological and self-help rhetorics with which many identity politics movements have articulated their concerns and programs is a tendency to obscure their necessarily social, political and public character. Finally, identity politics movements are political because they involve refusing, diminishing or displacing identities others wish to recognize in individuals. This is familiar in rethinkings of both gender and racial identities – and made particularly visible in the latter case by the recurrent replacement of collective labels (negro, colored, black, Afro-American, African-American) that had come to impose identities at odds with the identity claims of those labeled. It is given a sharp focus in the difference between critiques of homophobia and of compulsory heterosexism. The former accepts the category "homosexual" and challenges the fears, attacks, and delegitimations visited upon homosexuals. The latter resists the particular version of sexual identity (and for that matter sexualization of identity) that undergirds a host of social practices, opening a space for other practices or sexual orientations (including those often labeled collectively as homosexual) without being rooted in a specific identity-claim. [17]

The issue of resistance to imposed or fixed identities has encouraged in many quarters a shift from identity politics to a politics of difference. This focus on a critique of identity – often extended in post-structuralist and especially Derridian circles through a critique of identity as such rather than merely specifically problematic identities — is sometimes presented as though it marks a transcendence of identity politics. As Christina Crosby (1992: 130) remarks, however, "'differences' work now more or less as 'identity' did before."[18] Or as I have suggested above, the choice between deconstructing and claiming identities (or identity as such) may be one that needs to be shaped by strategic considerations, not dictated by theoretical and normative first principles; to speak of identity is not always simply or only to repress. The operations of deconstructing and claiming coexist only in tension, but they may need nonetheless always to coexist and inform each other.

These various versions of identity politics have shaped and been shaped by a range of specific movements. Among the most commonly cited cases are the so-called liberation and lifestyle movements that have flourished in the relatively rich countries since the 1960s: women's movements, movements of gay men and lesbians, movements of African-Americans, Chicanos, Asians, youth and countercultural movements, deep ecology and so forth. This list of examples is commonly associated with the idea of new social movements (NSM).[19]

The new social movements idea is, however, problematic and obscures the greater significance of identity politics. Without much theoretical rationale, it groups together what seem to the researchers relatively "attractive" movements, vaguely on the left, but leaves out such other contemporary movements as the new religious right and fundamentalism, the resistance of white ethnic communities against people of color, various versions of nationalism, and so forth. Yet these are equally manifestations of identity politics and there is no principle that clearly explains their exclusion from the lists drawn up by NSM theorists.

The NSM idea is rooted in an opposition of various movements that began to flourish in the 1960s to the labor and socialist movements that had putatively previously dominated activism, and which were allegedly governed by a single dominant identity structure rather than allowing for the open play and legitimation of many identities. Whether or not this accurately characterizes the labor and socialist movements of the 1950s and 1960s, it is historically myopic.[20] In the early nineteenth century, labor movements were engaged in identity politics, presenting the case that "worker" was an identity deserving of legitimacy, calling for solidarity among those sharing this identity, demanding their inclusion in the polity, and so forth. At the same time, socialism was dominated by utopian visions, calls for direct action, and attempts to reformulate fundamental ideas about human nature.

The notion that identity politics is a new phenomenon (or one limited to the experience of the relatively affluent – the "post-materialists" as Inglehart [1990] calls them) is equally false. The women's movement has roots at least 200 years old. The founding of communes was as important in the early 1800s as in the 1960s. Weren't the European nationalisms of the nineteenth century instances of identity politics? What of anti-colonial resistance?

In short, identity politics is not new, or limited to "post-materialist" ideologies or stages of development. It has been part and parcel of modern politics and social life for hundreds of years. But it has had to contend with various more universalizing, difference-denying, ways of thinking about politics and social life, and these have shaped the nature not only of our politics but of our academic thinking. Social science has paid only intermittent attention to issues of identity and identity politics. They do not figure in strong ways in classical social theory (though the construction of the generic, identity-bearing individual does). More recently objectivism, systemic determinism, and instrumental, interest-based understandings of motivation have kept social theorists from appreciating the importance of identity and identity politics.

Identity formation is commonly brought into consideration, if at all, as a prior condition of adult participation in social life – e.g. in socialization theory (and note the special place of socialization in, e.g., Parsons's functionalism). This is so even with regard to public life: in conceptualizing the public sphere, Habermas (1989) presumes that the private sphere provides it with fully formed subjects with settled identities and capacities. Upon entrance to the essentially liberal public sphere, these differences of identity must be bracketed rather than thematized. [21] But here Habermas's theory with its famous inattention to difference shares a problem with many forms of identity politics rooted in claims to difference. As Judith Butler (1992: 13) puts it, "for the subject to be a pregiven point of departure for politics is to defer the question of the political construction and regulation of the subject itself." This is a problem with the presumption of woman or women as subject just as with the implicitly male universal subjects of Habermas's public sphere. Social science suffers from this inattention (even incapacity) at all levels of analysis from individuals through such larger units as nations and even the globe or species. There is generally no attention to the constitution of subjects in the discourse of human rights, for example, and although this issue is sometimes problematized for nations, more often they are understood as always already existing in some sense.

The constitution of identities has not only been kept off center stage. It has been presented as a more or less harmonious process resulting in a normally stable and minimally changing identity. Thus we have been led by our theories often to underestimate the struggle involved in forging identities, the tension inherent in the fact that we all have multiple, incomplete and/or fragmented identities (and sometimes resistances), the politics implied by the differential public standing of various identities or identity claims, and the possibilities for our salient constructions of identities to change in the context of powerfully meaningful, emotionally significant events – like many social movements.

Just as conventional social theory misleads us, however, and obscures the importance of identity and identity politics, the contemporary advocates who have brought identity politics into the forefront of our attention often present the phenomenon in misleading and problematic ways. The false novelty of NSMs is an example of this. Many advocates and sympathetic analysts falsely oppose the struggle for identity to the demands of society; they accept far too sharp a separation between the individual as locus of interior feelings that need to be expressed in identity claims and society as the exterior source of pressures for conformity.

This obscures the extent to which social life calls forth or demands identity claims and provides opportunities (albeit biased ones) for their assertion. Among other things, our various claims and resistances to identities make sense only against the background of other identity claims and social valuations. As Charles Taylor (1992a, b) has argued, we need to be wary of a kind of "soft relativism" that suggests that all claims to recognition have the same standing, and that recognition can proceed without judgment. To try to grant *a priori* equal recognition to all identity claims (or deconstructions) amounts to taking none seriously. Or as Rey Chow (1992: 104) puts it, "Since positions are now infinitely interchangeable, many feel that postmodernism may be little more than a recompensatory 'I'm OK, you're OK' inclusion or a leveling attribution of subversive 'marginality' to all." Soft relativism also commonly obscures the extent to which identity claims are socially nurtured and constructed, not merely reflections of each individual's inner (natural) truth. In some versions, it even (and somewhat ironically) reproduces tendencies to radically liberal individualism with its implied universalism. Those making identity claims often present them within a rhetoric implying that everyone is equally endowed with identity, equally entitled to their own identity, and equally entitled to respect for it. But this liberal conception can at best provide a ground for tolerance, not for mutual respect or acceptance, and not for understanding the phenomenon of identity formation itself.

A particularly troubling version of this impulse to find universally acceptable grounds for distinctive identities is the recurrent – and currently resurgent – urge to naturalize. For all the critiques of essentialism that figure in gay theory, thus, many gay men are drawn to research suggesting a genetic foundation for homosexuality and to claims that gays should be accepted not because they are free to choose their own identities, but because they had no choice in the matter.[22] While the naturalizing arguments advanced on the basis of genetic research and examinations of brain structure have been advanced by and I think have appealed mainly to gay men, a number of lesbian thinkers have advanced their own naturalizing arguments. These are more often rooted in phenotypic physiology than in posited underlying genetic or neural structures, and have been advanced with more theoretical sophistication (as for example by Irigaray with her account of natural female auto-eroticism based on the "two lips").[23]

Advocates of identity politics too commonly opt in the same arguments for a "soft relativism," a rediscovery of the philosophy of will that glorifies choice as such, and an exaggeration of difference. Such arguments cannot quite make sense of identity politics, however, since claims for legitimacy or recognition are more than claims for tolerance. It is crucial analytically to recognize that common frames of significance are implicitly claimed even in arguments emphasizing difference and denying shared moral discourse beyond the level of "you do your thing, I'll do mine" (Taylor 1992b). This is so in two senses.

First, the significance of the identity struggled over is almost always claimed not just against other identities but within a particular field of shared relevance – e.g., a polity. Proponents of identity politics offer claims to have difference recognized as legitimate within a field like employment or legal treatment where people with many different identities are making similar claims. This is even so for the identity of nations, which normally involves a rhetoric of cultural difference yet is in large part a claim to equivalent standing with other nations – i.e. to be the same sort of thing that they are (see, among many, Anderson 1991; Chatterjee 1986; Calhoun 1993c).

Second, internal to the various identities on behalf of which political claims are made are various differentiated subgroups. Thus within the gay community there are gay men and lesbians, and many different sorts of communities of each. For identity politics to work, these must not all accentuate their differences but rather adopt a

common frame of reference within which their unity is more salient.
The claim that their shared identity is salient and even somewhat
obligatory – as suggested by those who would "out" others –
thus, cannot be entirely coherent with a tacit relativistic ethics as
an account of how we ought to deal with difference.

MULTIPLE IDENTITIES AND DIVIDED LOYALTIES

Underlying much of the pressure towards repressive sameness and
essentialist identities is a tendency to think in terms of what Harrison
White (1992) has called categorical identities rather than either more
complex notions of persons or networks of concrete social relations.
Most identity politics involves claims about categories of individuals
who putatively share a given identity. This allows a kind of abstraction from the concrete interactions and social relationships
within which identities are constantly renegotiated, in which individuals present one identity as more salient than another, and within
which individuals achieve some personal sense of continuity and
balance among their various sorts of identities. Categorical identities
can be invoked and given public definition by individuals or groups
even where they are not embodied in concrete networks of direct
interpersonal relationships. Indeed, they are quintessentially objects
of such public address. The abstractness of categories encourages
framing claims about them as though they offered a kind of trump
card over the other identities of individuals addressed by them. This
encourages an element of repression and/or essentialism within the
powerful categorical identities.

This struggle to achieve a "trump card" salience for a categorical
identity – in the face of a modern world where there are always
many possible salient identities – often encourages an ironic in-group
essentialism. Such in-group essentialism is implied by the example
given above of claimed biological determination of homosexuality,
and the battles within the gay movement over this argument on
the one hand and "queer theory" on the other would be well worth
research. [24] In-group essentialism – ironically often juxtaposed to
strident attacks on the essentialism of dominant categorizations of
identities – is linked to portrayals of identities as more singular
and/or fixed than they easily can be. Even while pointing to agonism
about identity, in other words, such views often imagine their complete resolution. If only Serbia were autonomous and not subject
to the threats of Croats, Catholics and Muslims, thus, there would
be no identity politics, only the one, true, correct model of Serbian

identity. No Serbian women's movement, no Serbian gay movement, no Serbian debate about being inside or outside of Europe, or about pan-Slavic identities. In the American context too we can see how in-group essentialism is linked to suppression of some identities – like a distinct black feminist voice within black nationalism – and in general to pressures to conform to standard views of the identity in question and often to dependence on expert authoritative sources as to that identity.

As the previous two examples suggest, every collective identity is open to both internal subdivision and calls for its incorporation into some larger category of primary identity. This is not only an issue for alternative collective identities, but for individuals who are commonly treated in this discourse as though they were unitary and internally homogenous. The capacity for an internal dialogicality is erased.

Tension between identity – putatively singular, unitary and integral – and identities – plural, cross-cutting and divided – is inescapable at both individual and collective levels. As lived, identity is always project, not settled accomplishment; though various external ascriptions or recognitions may be fixed and timeless. That is, for example, being Jewish is always a project (or an occasion for resistance) for every modern Jewish individual and community, even if stereotypes about how to be Jewish are maintained or presented as fixed by anti-Semites or the ultra-orthodox. Or, to change the example radically, black unity in South Africa can be understood only as a political project pushed and challenged by the ANC, Inkatha and various factions within each. "Black" is not a settled, pre-theoretical or pre-political position from which to grasp practical affairs or achieve knowledge any more than Zulu is.

Rather than addressing this problem head on, much mainstream sociological theory tries to find a way to fix identity by appeal to some more "objective" underlying variable or factor. The most common candidate is rational self-interest. But identity cannot be collapsed satisfactorily into interest or made to reflect it except as part of a personal and/or political project. In the first place, identities can and to some extent, indeed, always do change. [25] More than merely externally determined change, one can seek to transform oneself – wanting, for example, to have better wants. Whether or not weakness of will hinders such a project, its very possibility necessarily means that we cannot understand individuals well as fixed bearers of interests. Finally, there are always internal tensions and inconsistencies among the various identities and group memberships of individuals. These are not always open to simple averaging solutions (as utilitarianism generally requires) because they often lack common denominators for such quantitative compromises. Thus acting on certain identities must frustrate others.

This is a key reason why the politics of personal identity and the politics of collective identity are so inextricably linked. In many settings it is not possible to make even an expressive, individual choice for the primacy of, say, an independent female identity (let alone to enter into active feminist politics) without running afoul of nationalist assumptions about gender. As Collins (forthcoming) has pointed out with regard to black nationalism, this is painful because many women really understand themselves to be fundamentally – "essentially" – both feminist women and African-Americans. They necessarily experience the hostility of conventional black nationalist discourse not simply as an external constraint but as an internal tension. Similarly, Bosnian Muslim feminists and other advocates of Bosnian women faced in 1993 a horrific version of the way nationalism and gender can collide. Serbian men raped thousands of Bosnian women individually and in large, public groups as part of their project of ethnic cleansing. This was a specifically gendered violation equally specifically deployed against a nationally defined group. Yet Bosnian men added to the calamity by treating the women who were raped as defiled and impure. They were defiled not only in the general sexist discourse of female purity, but in a specifically nationalist discourse in which they had been inscribed in proper roles as daughters, wives and mothers. To think of themselves as either women rather than Bosnian Muslims or Bosnian Muslims rather than women made no sense. They were raped because they were both, and to condemn the Bosnian Muslim culture equally with the Serbian project of ethnic cleansing (as some American feminists have done) is to condemn those very women. Yet the obvious claim to be both women and Bosnian Muslims was available only as a political project (however implicit) to refigure the discourses of gender, religion and nation within which their identities were inscribed and on the bases of which their bodies and their honor alike were violated.

To see identities only as reflections of "objective" social positions or circumstances is to see them always retrospectively. It does not make sense of the dynamic potential implicit – for better or worse – in the tensions within persons and among the contending cultural discourses that locate persons. Identities are often personal and political projects in which we participate, empowered to greater or lesser extents by resources of experience and ability, culture and social organization.

But the puzzles lie not just in invocations of strong collective identity claims. They lie also in the extent to which people (and not only in the West) are not moved by any strong claims of identity – or communality – with others and respond instead to individualistic appeals to self-realization. Moreover, these two are not altogether mutually exclusive in practice. The same unwillingness to work in complex struggles for social transformation may lie behind both a preference for individualistic, psychologistic solutions to problems and a tendency to accept the illusory solutions offered by strong, simplistic identity claims on behalf of nations, races and other putatively undifferentiated categories. In any case, as hooks (1989: 34) puts it:

> Just as Nancy Hartsock's new work urges us to question why we are being asked to surrender a concern with the subject at this historical moment, when women have been struggling to move from object to subject, we must ask why it is women are being seduced by models of individual change that imply that no change has to occur in larger political and social realities.

In other words, rather than being surprised by the prevalence of identity politics and seeking to explain it, should we not consider whether it is more remarkable and at least as much in need of explanation that many people fail to take up projects of transforming shared identities or the treatment accorded them? Should we really be more shocked by those who risk much to be true to high ideals and moral aspirations – by a Dietrich Bonhoeffer, say, or by Chinese students who defy their government – or by those who are complicitous in the myriad daily horrors of banal evil?

Our identities are always rooted in part in ideals and moral aspirations that we cannot realize fully. There is, therefore, a tension within us which can be both the locus of personal struggle and the source of an identity politics that aims not simply at the legitimation of falsely essential categorical identities but at living up to deeper social and moral values. Claims to the priority or dominance of large collective identities, therefore, are not only the stuff of manipulations by the Milosevics and Karadzics of the world, but sources of heroism and self-sacrifice that are as hard to understand in the conventional terms of social theory as in popular ideologies of purely individual self-fulfillment.

REFERENCES

Anderson, Benedict 1991: *Imagined Communities: Reflections on the Origin and Spread of Nationalism*, rev. edn. London: Verso.

Arendt, Hannah 1958: *The Human Condition*. Chicago: University of Chicago Press.

Bourdieu, Pierre 1976: *Outline of a Theory of Practice*. Cambridge: Cambridge University Press.

Bourdieu, Pierre 1990: *The Logic of Practice*. Stanford: Stanford University Press.

Butler, Judith 1991: *Gender Trouble*. New York: Routledge.

Butler, Judith 1992: "Contingent Foundations: Feminism and the Question of 'Postmodernism'," in Butler and Scott, eds, pp. 3–21.

Butler, Judith and Joan W. Scott, eds 1992: *Feminists Theorize the Political*. New York: Routledge.

Calhoun, Craig 1988: "Populist Politics, Communications Media, and Large Scale Social Integration," *Sociological Theory*, vol. 6, no. 2: 219–41.

Calhoun, Craig 1991: "The Problem of Identity in Collective Action," in J. Huber, ed., *Macro–Micro Linkages in Sociology*. Beverly Hills, CA: Sage, pp. 51–75.

Calhoun, Craig ed., 1992: *Habermas and the Public Sphere*. Cambridge, MA: MIT Press.

Calhoun, Craig 1993a: "Civil Society and Public Sphere," *Public Culture*, 5: 267–80.

Calhoun, Craig 1993b: "'New Social Movements' of the Early 19th Century," *Social Science History*, vol. 17, no. 3: 385–427.

Calhoun, Craig 1993c: "Nationalism and Civil Society," *International Journal of Sociology*, vol. 8, no. 4: 387–411.

Cascardi, Anthony J. 1992: *The Subject of Modernity*. New York: Cambridge University Press.

Chatterjee, Partha 1986: *Nationalist Thought and the Colonial World: A Derivative Discourse*. Atlantic Highlands, NJ: Zed Books.

Chow, Rey 1992: "Postmodern Automatons," in Butler and Scott, eds, pp. 117–32.

Cohen, Jean 1985: "Strategy or Identity: New Theoretical Paradigms and Contemporary Social Movements," *Social Research* 52: 663–716.

Collins, Patricia Hill 1991: *Black Feminist Thought*. New York: Routledge.

Collins, Patricia Hill forthcoming: *Fighting Words*. Minneapolis: University of Minnesota Press.

Crosby, Christina 1992: "Dealing with Differences," in Butler and Scott, eds, pp. 130–43.

Derrida, Jacques 1978: *Writing and Difference*. Chicago: University of Chicago Press.

Dyson, Michael 1993: *Reflecting Black: African American Cultural Criticism*. Minneapolis: University of Minnesota Press.

Evans-Pritchard, E. 1940: *The Nuer*. Oxford: Oxford University Press.

Foucault, Michel 1977: *Discipline and Punish*. New York: Pantheon.

Fraser, Nancy 1990: *Unruly Practices*. Minneapolis: University of Minnesota Press.

Fuss, Diana 1989: *Essentially Speaking: Feminism, Nature and Difference*. New York: Routledge.

Fuss, Diana, ed. 1991: *Inside/Out: Lesbian Theories, Gay Theories*. New York: Routledge.

Goffman, Erving 1959: *The Presentation of Self in Everyday Life*. New York: Doubleday.

Habermas, Jürgen 1984: *The Theory of Communicative Action, I: Reason and the Rationalization of Society*. Boston: Beacon.

Habermas, Jürgen 1987: *The Theory of Communicative Action, II: Life-World and System*. Boston: Beacon.

Habermas, Jürgen 1989: *The Social Transformation of the Public Sphere*. Cambridge, MA: MIT Press.

Haraway, Donna 1991: *Simians, Cyborgs and Women*. New York: Routledge.

Hartsock, Nancy 1989–90: "Postmodernism and Political Change: Issues for Feminist Theory," *Cultural Critique* 14: 15–33.

Hewitt, John P. 1989: *Dilemmas of the American Self*. Philadelphia: Temple University Press.

Hobsbawm, Eric and Terence Ranger 1983: *The Invention of Tradition*. Cambridge: Cambridge University Press.

Hollis, Martin 1987: *The Cunning of Reason*. Oxford: Oxford University Press.

hooks, bell 1981: *Ain't I a Woman: Black Women and Feminism*. Boston: South End Press.

hooks, bell 1984: *Feminist Theory: From Margin to Center*. Boston: South End Press.

hooks, bell 1989: *Talking Back: Thinking Feminist, Thinking Black*. Boston: South End Press.

hooks, bell 1993: *Sisters of the Yam: Black Women and Self-Recovery*. Boston: South End Press.

Inglehart, Ronald 1990: *Culture Shift in Advanced Industrial Society*. Princeton: Princeton University Press.

Irigaray, Luce 1977: *This Sex Which Is Not One*. Ithaca: Cornell University Press.

Jardine, Alice and Paul Smith, eds 1987: *Men in Feminism*. London: Methuen.

Lovejoy, A. O. 1936: *The Great Chain of Being*. Cambridge, MA: Harvard University Press.

Melucci, Alberto 1989: *Nomads of the Present: Social Movements and Individual Needs in Contemporary Society*. Philadelphia, PA: Temple University Press.

Merton, Robert K. 1968: *Social Theory and Social Structure*. New York: Free Press.

Moi, Toril 1985: *Sexual/Textual Politics: Feminist Literary Theory*. New York: Methuen.

Negt, Oskar and Alexander Kluge 1993: *Public Sphere and Experience: Toward an Analysis of the Bourgeois and Proletarian Public Sphere*. Minneapolis: University Minnesota Press.

Norris, Christopher 1987: *Derrida*. Cambridge, MA: Harvard University Press.

Rhode, Deborah L. 1990: *Theoretical Perspectives on Sexual Difference*. New Haven: Yale University Press.

Rich, Adrienne 1983: "Compulsory Heterosexuality and Lesbian Existence," in A. Snitow, C. Stansell, and S. Thompson, eds, *Powers of Desire*. New York, NY: Monthly Review Press, pp. 177–205.

Schor, Naomi 1989: "This Essentialism which is Not One: Coming to Grips with Irigaray," *Differences* 1: 2.

Sedgwick, Eve Kosovsky 1980: *Epistemology of the Closet*. New York: Columbia University Press.

Sedgwick, Eve Kosovsky 1985: *Between Men: English Literature and Male Homosexual Desire*. New York: Columbia University Press.

Seidman, Steven 1992: *Embattled Eros: Sexual Politics and Ethics in Contemporary America*. New York: Routledge.

Seidman, Steven, ed. forthcoming Special issue of *Sociological Theory* on "Queer Theory."

Smith, Paul 1988: *Discerning the Subject*. Minneapolis: University of Minnesota Press.

Spivak, Gayatri Chakravorty 1987: *In Other Worlds: Essays in Cultural Politics*. London: Methuen.

Spivak, Gayatri Chakravorty 1992: "French Feminism Revisited: Ethics and Politics," in Butler and Scott, eds, pp. 54–85.

Taylor, Barbara 1983: *Eve and the New Jerusalem*. New York: Pantheon.

Taylor, Charles 1989: *Sources of the Self*. Cambridge, MA: Harvard University Press.

Taylor, Charles 1992a: *Multiculturalism and the Politics of Recognition*. Princeton: Princeton University Press.

Taylor, Charles 1992b: *The Ethics of Authenticity*. Cambridge, MA: Harvard University Press.

Touraine, A. 1985: "An Introduction to the Study of Social Movements," *Social Research* 52: 749–88.

Touraine, A. 1988: *The Return of the Actor*. Minneapolis: University of Minnesota Press.

Warner, Michael 1993: *Fear of a Queer Planet*. Minneapolis: University of Minnesota Press.

Weber, Max 1922: *Economy and Society*. Berkeley: University of California Press.

White, Harrison 1992: *Identity and Control*. Princeton: Princeton University Press.

NOTES

1 This story is traced admirably in C. Taylor (1989).

2 Lovejoy (1936) offered a loving reconstruction of this scheme of identities. It was a crucial background to the medieval world that Weber

(1922) took as an archetype of traditionality. One should note, though, that by taking medieval Europe as his archetype for traditional social organization and orientations to action, Weber failed to recognize the power of kinship in nonwestern societies and in general the much greater capacity for continuous social and cultural reproduction in a number of other settings.

3 See Haraway (1991) on the vocabulary of "stress" as characteristic of functionalist-systemic formulations in biology as well as sociology.

4 This is one reason why Goffman's work (e.g., 1959) stands out as so distinctive, though even Goffman addressed these topics very unevenly.

5 Post-structuralism is certainly not the only source for this argument. It is also, for example, central to bell hooks's (1989, esp. ch. 5; 1993) differently grounded attempts to develop a vision of "self-recovery" that is at once personal, social and political.

6 Though these theoretical discourses have been very sociological in many respects, they have seldom been the product of sociologists. Sociology, especially in the United States, has remained remarkably resistant to post-structuralist cultural discourse and to both feminist and gay theory (as distinct from empirical studies on gender or sexuality). One result of this has been that empirical sociological studies of women and homosexuals have often relied upon essentialist invocations of those categories; it has been exceptional – at least until very recently – for "mainstream" sociologists to participate in or even learn from the rethinking of the category of gender rather than simply relying upon seemingly manifest gender disctintions. If sociology has suffered from its resistance to the largely literary discourse of post-structuralism and cognate developments in feminist and gay theory, it should also be said that these interdisciplinary discourses – and that of "cultural studies" more generally – have suffered from a relatively underdeveloped understanding of the social dimensions of life and a tendency to see – and dismiss – terms like social structure, organization, or integration as always and necessarily reified, totalizing and/or reductionist. Nurturance of a better relationship between sociology and this interdisciplinary discourse is in order for both (or all) sides. For some recent steps in this direction, see Seidman (1992 and forthcoming) and Collins (1991 and forthcoming).

7 Collins (1991) reviews and adds to the arguments developed by black feminists; the most important of which may be those of bell hooks (1981, 1984, 1989). The lesbian critiques are discussed in Fuss (1989), Butler (1991), and several of the essays in Butler and Scott (1992) and Rhode (1990). But it is important to keep distinct the more general post-structuralist decentering of subjectivity from the specific challenges to totalizing accounts of collective subject categories that efface the diversity of more concrete individuals and groups. Nancy Hartsock (1989–90), for example, has questioned the call to surrender a concern with the subject precisely at the historical moment when women have

been meeting with some success in moving from object to subject (see also hooks's 1989: 34 assent).

8 Aspects of this challenge appear throughout Derrida's work; *Writing and Difference* (1978) is perhaps as good a place as any to begin, and this is not the place to try to synopsize Derrida or deconstruction. Norris (1987) strikes me as the best secondary source.

9 "Sexual orientation" was gaining the upper hand largely, I think, because it sounded more scientific and immutable. It fitted with the increasingly normative construction of the experience of being gay as something over which individuals had little or no choice, something they merely recognized in themselves. This in turn was reinforced by the growing sense that convincing the public that homosexuality was not subject to choice would reduce the extent to which it was morally condemned.

10 hooks's argument dovetails with the critique of "compulsory heterosexism," which shows how social norms have involved an implicit assumption that all members of each sex should have some level of sexual openness towards all members of the other. See Rich (1983) and discussion below.

11 See Fuss (1991), Schor (1989), Spivak (1987), Smith (1988) and several of the essays in Jardine and Smith (1987).

12 See C. Taylor (1989) on the idea of "moral sources" and the specific modern importance of appeals to nature as a basis for moral claims and self-understandings.

13 It should be emphasized that the choice of rhetorics cannot be made in isolation from a larger political context in which both "rights talk" and naturalizing essentialism have substantial normative power. Quite apart from the way they figure in discourse about women, consider how they shape the legal treatment of children. There is a highly charged debate about the notion of children having rights *vis-à-vis* their parents, construed by many conservatives as undermining the nuclear family. Both naturalizing assumptions and a history in which children were treated as the property of their parents influence this debate. Both themes figure not just in cases where children are neglected or abused, but in decisions like those in which Iowa and Michigan courts recently affirmed the rights of biological parents to their offspring as taking precedence over those of adoptive parents. That having raised a child since birth gave the adoptive parents no rights indicates that social constructionism has little standing in these courts; that the parental rights of possession took priority over arguments about the welfare of the child indicates the continuing power of thinking in terms of property.

14 And of course in claiming identities, as Collins (1991) has argued forcefully, we are not obliged to make either/or choices. It is often our prerogative and perhaps our best strategy to insist on the option of "both/and."

15 In this paragraph I am broadly following the lead of an argument offered by Taylor (1992b) but qualifying it somewhat. Taylor assumes that

pre-modern and nonwestern social institutional arrangements offered grounds for more immediate, perfect, unnegotiated and conflict-free recognition than seems plausible to me.

16 This was not just a short-term challenge in practical politics but involved a sustained theoretical discourse. Consider, for example, Habermas's famous distinction of system from lifeworld. Habermas (1984, 1987) identifies the lifeworld as a realm of relatively undistorted communicative action, at least potentially free from the instrumentalization characteristic of systemic social organization with its nonlinguistic steering media of power and money. The lifeworld is continually faced with encroachments or colonizations by the system; these make it the crucial site for resistance (thus solving the problem faced by critical theories that attempted to locate the source of resistance in the proletariat or some other concrete social group). This argument grasps a good deal, but as Fraser (1990) has shown most incisively, it is deeply flawed by its presumption of a lifeworld that is (a) separable in principle from systemic organization (e.g., not also constituted and given its specific organization by capitalism), and (b) somehow free from the reign of power and oppression and constituted – even in principle – by pure communicative action. In a world of compulsory heterosexism, family violence and legal, economic and cultural pressures that reduce women's choices about marriage and childbearing, it is hard to see the lifeworld – or the sphere of intimate and family relations that Habermas takes as its archetype – as unambiguously the locus of quality human relationships or to see all the problems of personal life as stemming from colonization by the system. The system–lifeworld tension commonly grounds a sort of "populist" politics that is far from the critical and potentially radical perspective Habermas hopes will grow out of resistance to colonization (Calhoun 1988).

17 As Fuss (1989: 110) has rightly argued, seeing that the critique of compulsory heterosexism grasps something the critique of homophobia does not, is not necessarily grounds for dropping the critique of homophobia. It is also worth noting that the critique of compulsory heterosexism grows out of feminist theory foregrounding lesbian experience (paradigmatically Rich 1983, but also the work of Irigaray and Wittig) and that this division of two stances of theoretical critique has in many cases divided lesbians from gay men.

18 The Butler and Scott (1992) collection in which Crosby's article appears raises this issue in selection after selection, showing the centrality and currency of the problem, however varied the proposed resolutions.

19 See, e.g., Melucci (1989), Touraine (1985, 1988), Cohen (1985).

20 I have argued this in more detail in Calhoun (1993b).

21 See discussion in Calhoun (1993a) and Calhoun (1992). Habermas discusses ways in which the literary public sphere helped to prepare the kinds of subjects needed for public political discourse, but once it has fulfilled its role as precursor to the political public sphere, the literary

discourse drops out of Habermas's picture. He does not consider the continuing transformations of subjectivity wrought not only in literature but in a host of identity-forming public spheres (this is one of the reasons why Negt and Kluge [1993] use an appeal to the "horizons of experience" to criticize Habermas). Neither does he consider how identity might be transformed through public political activity. On the other hand, of course, one of the problems that has led to the emphasis on a politics of the personal is that identity-forming discourses, even when carried out in public spheres of readers, cinema viewers, students, or self-help oriented radio talk shows, often fail to institutionalize attention to their own publicness and to recognize their implicit politics. Many of these discourses are "public" in the sense of being open to a variety of different participants, but not in the sense of thematically constituting themselves as about public matters. This has profound implications for the ways in which they can empower their participants and suggests an important politics about what discourses are either able or inclined to present themselves as being about matters of public significance. In reaching beyond Habermas's narrow conception of the public sphere, however, it is important not to forget that his analysis is about what enables people to make collective political decisions by rational-critical argument and different publics vary widely in the extent to which they are able to maintain such standards of discourse.

22 It is a curious ideological development, and testimony to the power of naturalizing discourse, that so many "mainstream" Americans believe that any natural identity must be good, or at least acceptable, while free "choice" is considered a weak basis for recognition. It is as though the long history of struggles over free choice in a variety of arenas – most notably religion – has been forgotten. Would anyone really want to argue that Jewishness (to focus on a frequently stigmatized religious identity, though one could as well have said Protestantism) is acceptable only if it can be shown to be immutable, and thus that those born Jews must be accepted while converts need not be?

23 Just how essentialist Irigaray's arguments really (essentially?) are is a matter of active contention as noted above. Spivak (1992: 74) has suggested that Irigaray is criticized as an essentialist mainly by those who do not see "the aggressive role of rhetoricity in her prose," while Fuss (1989: 57) suggests that Irigaray uses essentialism as part of "a larger constructionist project of re-creating, re-metaphorizing the body."

24 On possible links between queer theory and social theory more generally, see Warner (1993), Seidman (forthcoming).

25 Among other things this creates a host of problems about how to understand the relationship between present and future selves within rational choice theory. See Hollis (1987). Calhoun (1991) develops a fuller argument on this theme in regard to social movement participation.

2

Reclaiming the Epistemological "Other": Narrative and the Social Constitution of Identity

Margaret R. Somers and Gloria D. Gibson

A Word on Categories

As I write, my editor at Harvard University Press is waging something of a struggle with the people at the Library of Congress about how this book is to be categorized for cataloging purposes. The librarians think "Afro-Americans – Civil Rights" and "Law Teachers" would be nice. I told my editor to hold out for "Autobiography," "Fiction," "Gender Studies," and "Medieval Medicine." This battle seems appropriate enough since the book is not exclusively about race or law but also about boundary. While being black has been the powerful social attribution in my life, it is only one of a number of *governing narratives* or *presiding fictions* by which I am constantly reconfiguring myself in the world. Gender is another, along with ecology, pacifism, my peculiar brand of colloquial English, and Roxbury, Massachusetts. The complexity of role *identification*, the politics of sexuality, the inflections of professionalized discourse – all describe and impose boundary in my life, even as they confound one another in unfolding spirals of confrontation, deflection, and dream...

Patricia J. Williams, *The Alchemy of Race and Rights: The Diary of a Law Professor*

An earlier version of this chapter (by Somers) was presented at the 1992 American Sociological Association Meetings, Pittsburgh. We are very grateful to Elizabeth Long for her comments as the discussant on that panel, and to Renee Anspach, Craig Calhoun, and Marc Steinberg for their useful suggestions on that earlier version.

Introduction

Every knowledge discipline needs an *"epistemological other"* to consolidate a cohesive self-identity and collective project.[1] For the social
sciences, the concept of narrative – with its long association with
the humanities and the historical profession – holds pride of place
in filling that role. Variously formulated in binary terms as "idio-
graphic" versus "nomothetic," "particularistic" versus "generalizable,"
or "description" versus "theory," the contrast between the "mere
narrative" approach of the historians and the more rigorous methodologies of the social sciences has effectively cordoned off narrative
studies from the legitimate "identity-terrain" of social science epistemology.[2] But a small revolution with potentially large consequences is occurring in our contemporary knowledge culture.[3] Over
the last few decades many historians have lost, abandoned, and
even scorned narrative explanation.[4] At the same time, moreover,
a protean *reframing* of the narrative concept is seeping and/or
being appropriated into the central epistemological frameworks of a
spectrum of other disciplines – including medicine, social psychology,
anthropology, gender studies, law, biology, and physics.

The expressions of this narrative reframing are broad and diverse.
One aspect of many of the new works in narrative studies, however,
is especially relevant to our understanding of how identities are
constituted, namely the shift from a focus on *representational* to
ontological narrativity. Philosophers of history, for example, have
previously argued that narrative modes of representing knowledge
(telling historical stories) were representational *forms* imposed by
historians on the chaos of lived experience (Mink 1966; Hayden
White 1984). More recently, however, scholars (political philosophers, psychologists, legal theorists, feminist theorists, social workers,
organizational theorists, anthropologists, and medical sociologists)
are postulating something much more substantive about narrative:
namely, that social life is itself *storied* and that narrative is an
ontological condition of social life. Their research is showing us that
stories guide action; that people construct identities (however multiple
and changing) by locating themselves or being located within a repertoire of emplotted stories; that "experience" is constituted through
narratives; that people make sense of what has happened and is
happening to them by attempting to assemble or in some way to
integrate these happenings within one or more narratives; and that
people are guided to act in certain ways, and not others, on the
basis of the projections, expectations, and memories derived from a

multiplicity but ultimately limited repertoire of available social, public, and cultural narratives.[5]

But there is a paradox. On the one hand, sociologists have by and large kept their distance from these studies of ontological narrativity.[6] Yet on the other hand, sociology has shown an immense interest in theorizing about the very themes these new approaches to narrative are addressing – the study of meaning, social action, social agency, and most recently, collective identity. Indeed the last two decades have been notable for the number of heroic efforts by sociologists to recast social analysis along the central axes of the interaction between *agency* and *structure* – that is, to develop a social theory that allows for human action which is nonetheless bounded and constrained by structural restraints (e.g., Abrams 1982; Alexander 1982, 1988a, 1989; Bourdieu 1977, 1990; Coleman 1990; Giddens 1977, 1985; Habermas 1979, 1984; Hawthorne 1976; Sewell 1986; Smith 1987, 1990a, 1990b; Harrison White 1992b).[7]

There are perhaps two reasons for this paradoxical distancing from the new narrative studies on the part of sociologists. The first is that social scientists overwhelmingly limit their definition of the term "narrative" to that of a representational form/method of presenting social and historical knowledge. And it is in this very methodological terrain, where the debate over what counts as valid explanation has raged, that social scientists have forged their unique identity and distinction from the humanities. As long as this representational definition prevails, then, social scientists – in order to *be* social scientists – must continue to view narrative as the epistemological other and in symbolic contrast to causal explanation. Indeed to the extent sociologists have engaged with narrative studies, the dialogue often recreates the familiar Manichean dichotomy between social science explanation and the narrative other. Whether in favor or disparagement, the encounters between sociology and narrative analysis seem inevitably to result in counterposing narrative to that of causality. Seidman (1991), for example, recently criticized the "foundational obsessionalism" of mainstream sociological theory while demonstrating his support for an understanding of social theory as "narrative with a moral intent." Seidman is a sociologist who strongly endorses the turn to narrative. Nonetheless, in his association of narrative with "story-telling particularism," he straps it into an unnecessary opposition to, and ultimately distancing from, the social sciences.[8]

The second reason for the neglect of the recently reframed narrativism follows directly from the self-identity project of the social sciences. From their inception, the social sciences have been concerned with what one political scientist calls the "primacy of epistemology" (Connolly 1992b), or the eclipsing of discovery and *ontology* by the context of *justification* (Somers 1994a).[9] The latter is comprised of the standards we use to know about the world, the grounds we rely upon to legitimate these foundations of knowledge, the validity of competing methodologies, and the criteria for viable explanations. Discovery and ontology, on the other hand, refer to problem-formation and social being respectively. Both are seen as better left to speculative philosophers or psychologists. The consequences of this division of labor for a sociology of action are significant: (1) Issues of social being, identity, and ontology are excluded from the legitimate mainstream of sociological investigation; and (2) the social sciences focus their research on action and agency by studying primarily observable social behavior – measured variously by social interests, rational preferences, or social norms and values – rather than by exploring expressions of social being and identity. Therefore, precisely to the extent that sociologists are aware that the recent focus of narrative studies is towards issues of identity and ontology, these same studies are defined as beyond and outside the boundaries of appropriate social science concern.[10]

We argue in this chapter that the association of identity and ontology with philosophy or theoretical psychology on the one side, and action with interests, norms, or behavior on the other, is a limited model and deprives sociologists of the deeper analysis that is possible to achieve by linking the concepts of action and identity. To get these benefits, however, we must reject the decoupling of action from ontology, and instead accept that some notion of social being and social identity is, willy-nilly, incorporated into each and every knowledge-statement about action, agency, and behavior. Just as sociologists are not likely to make sense of action without focusing attention on structure and order, it is unlikely we can interpret social action if we fail to also emphasize ontology, social being, and identity.[11] We thus enlarge our analytic focus when we study social action through a lens that also allows a focus on social ontology and the social constitution of identity.[12]

Once we have acknowledged the potential significance of identity, however, we must reject the temptation to conflate identities with what can often slide into fixed "essentialist" (pre-political) singular categories, such as those of race, sex, or gender – a tendency which has characterized a number of recent feminist theories in their efforts to restore the previously marginalized female "other."[13] Anthropological studies of different cultures have often been used to avoid this danger (Mauss 1985; Dumont 1982). But, as P. Williams (1991:

256) illustrates in the quotation with which we begin this chapter, we do not have to resort to cultural "others" to recognize the false certainties imposed by categorical approaches to identity. We can avoid this danger only if we incorporate into the core conception of identity the dimensions of *time*, *space*, and *relationality*. And it is this enlargement that drives us to combine studies of action and identity with what we will be calling *conceptual narrativity*.

Once we have linked identity and action research to narrative analysis, however, we need to remember to focus our attention on the new *ontological* dimension of narrative studies rather than be satisfied with the traditional rendering of narrative as limited to a method or form of representation. The reason why is straightforward. While sociologists worry endlessly over the (unresolvable?) questions of what counts as valid knowledge (should it be pure "science" or "narrative with a moral intent?"), we are meanwhile being distracted from the exciting new developments in which researchers outside of sociology are coming to grips with a new, historically and empirically based, narrativist understanding of social action and social agency – one that is temporal, relational, and cultural, as well as institutional, material, and macro-structural. Engaging with this aspect of narrative studies clearly should be on the agenda for sociological studies of action and agency. After all, if research results are correct, then everything we know from making families, to coping with illness, to carrying out strikes and revolutions is at least in part a result of numerous cross-cutting story-lines in which social actors locate themselves (Somers 1986, 1992).

An energetic engagement with this new ontological narrativity, then, provides an opportunity to connect the long-term interest in a sociology of action with studies of identity formation. The hope is that bringing together narrative and identity can bring a new perspective to some of the seemingly intractable problems contained in social theories of action. For that reason we begin (part I) by exploring the issues and the recursive fault-lines surrounding the sociology of action; part II addresses the new sociology and politics of identity as an important development in the study of agency and structure; and part III discusses in more detail the reframed concept of narrative. In part IV we introduce the concepts of *narrative identity* and *relational setting* as conceptual links between the reframed approach to narrative and some of the enduring conundrums in the sociology of action. We end with part V, which considers the research implications of a conceptual narrativity.

I THE PROBLEM OF ACTION IN SOCIAL THEORY

The problems in the sociology of action are rooted in the development, course, and consequences of the original eighteenth-century social science project – a project which fused together a revolutionary epistemology with a nineteenth-century rendering of historical change to create the great metanarrative of classical modernization. Let us start with the epistemology. [14]

Like the naturalistic fable that inaugurated its birth, the logic of modern social science has elements of the incoherent. Both were built of utopian fictions about society's emancipation from history. In the 1750s William Townsend, the late eighteenth-century English statesman, wrote a social parable about the isle of Juan Fernandez. The island (it had been made famous in England by the mythical R. Crusoe) was populated only by goats and dogs (men and women). According to reigning Hobbesian assumptions, these allegorical people should have had brutish, nasty, and very short lives in the absence of institutional authority. Townsend, however, endowed the island with a perfect harmony through a natural balance of population and food. He did not explain this by what we might today identify as an Orwellian allegory in which order is maintained through bureaucratization or political tyranny. Rather the fable's utopianism was precisely in its inverse postulate: No state or artificial law was necessary to maintain the equilibrium. This mini-society flourished precisely because it was left to its natural laws freed from what he viewed as the chains of state politics, kinship, religion, and "traditional" cultural institutions. Townsend built his case by borrowing a revolutionary new metaphysics – the laws of nature – from a revolutionary new epistemology – that of natural science. He combined these into a new science of society to conceptually liberate the social world from political or social authority and the claims of its most articulate apologists, Hobbesian and Lockean political theory. Classical social science was born of this revolutionary epistemology constructed upon a myth and a metaphor about a unified social system whose parts expressed an inner working autonomous logic. Social thinkers of the late eighteenth century appropriated Townsend's anti-institutional naturalism – the optimistic belief that politics, philosophy, and symbolic meaning had been surpassed by the laws of nature and society – as the core metaphor of a new science of society. Prevailing Hobbesian assumptions yielded to a social utopianism and radical naturalism: for Hobbes, society needed a state because humans were like beasts; for Townsend, it seems that natural law sufficed because humans were beasts. Liberated from the burdensome traditions of the past – elegant in its parsimonious simplicity – the revolutionary *science of society* had arrived. [15]

Complexity, however, made trouble in Eden. A great sociological conundrum was to sprout from this naturalistic fantasia: how to make coherent the meaning of human agency. The detachment of social science from the sphere of moral and political philosophy in favor of the scientific study of society and culture starkly posed the critical problem of whether this systemic notion of society could be reconciled with an intelligible – that is to say, meaningful – understanding of human action. Could a naturalistic law-like representation of society be reconciled with an ontology which still accommodated moral agency rather than mere behaviorism, individualism as well as social holism? Simply put, could there any longer be a place for the beliefs and actions of social actors other than as mere reflections of the deterministic societal laws at the heart of the new paradigm? If society is made up of humans, and humans have free will to act, how is the capacity for agency accounted for in a naturalistic ontology? Alexander (1982: 98) effectively articulates the problem: How [can] sociological theories which do accept the sui generis collective character of social arrangements retain a conception of individual freedom and voluntarism?

From its inception, then, the upstart new science of society has been aggravated with a great thorn of its own making. Devised to solve the problem of how there could be any social order in a society comprised of autonomous individuals (the Hobbesian and rational choice dilemma), the systemic solution created a yet more intractable problem, one best parsed by the circularity of Marx's (1978[1852]) famous statement that "Men make their own history, but they do not make it just as they please ..." To date, the dilemma of how to reconcile the naturalistic logic of social science with human agency – that elusive escape artist which as Abrams (1980: 7) has wryly suggested "is not a new discovery, although from Hobbes onward, people have repeatedly unveiled it as solemnly as though it were" – continues to provide grist for efforts at theoretical renewal in social theory. Arguably, the various solutions, as much as the original problem, have since left the social sciences fundamentally divided over the relative import of action and structure.

In this discussion of the conundrum of action we join with and benefit immensely from the critical energies of many other approaches to social action (e.g., Abrams 1982; Alexander 1982, 1988a, 1989; Bourdieu 1977, 1990; Coleman 1990; Giddens 1977, 1985; Habermas

1979, 1984; Hawthorne 1976; Sewell 1986; Smith 1987, 1990a, 1990b, Harrison White 1992b). Our approach, however, is premised on the assumption that we need to explore it as an *historical* problem and deploy for the task an *historical epistemology* (Somers 1994a). The concept of an historical epistemology is purposefully oxymoronic; it is intended to contradict the assumed foundationalism of epistemology and standards of knowledge. The term defines a way of carrying out social research based on the principle that all of our knowledge, our logics, our presuppositions, indeed our very reasoning practices, are indelibly (even if obscurely) marked with the signature of time. They are "history-laden." [16] The challenge of an historical epistemology is neither to discover nor to invent the past. Rather it is to appropriate and interpret knowledge histories through a reconstruction of their making, resonance, and contestedness over time. [17]

The goal of an historical epistemology is thus to explore the process by which those problems which have such a formative place in theory construction get identified as such – in time and over time. This means examining the historical construction of presuppositional social science concepts and in turn examining the internal logic of their categories and assumptions as they unfolded historically. The goal is not primarily to understand "why" in sense of locating a sociological environment; it is more to understand *how* competing ontologies of identity, political life, society, and so on, gain currency and shape the empirical problems we encounter as sociologists. Much of what we in sociology treat as abstract or presuppositional categories – subject and object, agent and structure for example – carry within them "frozen" historical arguments which have been abstracted into our familiar general categories. To "unfreeze" requires an "undoing" and that requires history. Taking a look at the historicity of apparently presuppositional categories of social thought also involves asking how the historical construction and transformations of a concept shaped and continues to shape its logical dimensions and its social meanings. Hacking (1990b: 359; 1984: 110) calls this level of conceptual analysis looking at "words in their sites." It is another approach to historicizing by locating conceptual problematics not only in time, but in conceptual space. Sites include "sentences, uttered or transcribed, always in a larger site of neighborhood, institution, authority, language" without which ideas would be just words, not concepts. Looking at the rise and fall of moral and social concepts as words in their sites, and in time, reveals their existence as historical – and thus contingent.

Thinking about the problems in a sociology of action through an historical epistemology leads to a different strategy for thinking about the ontological stalemate in the sociology of action – namely, that a theoretical resolution cannot proceed independently of an historical exploration. The metatheoretical attempt to resolve the conundrum of action flounders on the unexplored historicity of its central categories. *We need to look at the encoding of category by history.* The theoretical task is thus at once an historical one: we cannot overcome the impasses of our theories without a new look at the histories they encode. But we cannot reread history without a new conceptual framework – at least tentative. Since each task requires the other, both must proceed at once. [18]

Classical Modernization as Metanarrative

To illustrate: We have seen that the conceptual framework of modern social science has a built-in aporia between actors and society – an aporia in part born of the revolutionary epistemology described in the opening paragraph. But the aporias of agency and system are not only a product of the logic of social science. Even more important, *they rest on the core of an historical "metanarrative" of classical western modernization* embedded in the logic. Social theory is as much history and narrative as it is metatheory. In its very construction all theory presumes a prior question to which the theory is designed to be an answer (Gadamer 1989; Collingwood 1970[1939]) – hence the theory itself is already an intervening moment in a narrative process of knowledge construction. In the form of an "answer," social theory contains a historicity which can be disclosed only by discovering both the original historical problem it was designed to solve and the complex ways in which answer has found its way into the core of our most presuppositional concepts. Modern social theory emerged as the answer to the macro-sociological question by which our social science founders were possessed: namely, how to explain the emergence and the nature of the modern world and its epochal break from "traditional society." To answer this question, the classical founders constructed a social theory based upon an appropriation of the historical and empirical world. Indeed the very power and durability of sociological thought can be explained only by the substantive and historical answers to which it lays claim. [19]

What were the consequences of this inextricable entanglement between the new social scientific naturalism and the historical transformations of modernity? A most unique idea: if the nature of modern society could be conceived as organized according to the systemic laws of nature, the emergence of modernity could be explained by

a self-generated, rational, and progressive logic shed of the constraints of ethics and law, political authority, religion, and kinship.
New concepts were thus unleashed. The social world was now
conceptually bifurcated between "tradition" and "modernity," driven
by the relentless motor of technical rationality which had the power
to remake society, institutions, social life, even the drama of human
intentionality itself, in its own image.

Nothing could have been more ironic and paradoxical. A master-
narrative of modernity was produced through the lens of a self-
consciously, indeed belligerently so, anti-historical, anti-narrative,
naturalistic conceptual frame. The results are the strange hybrid we
unconsciously live with today – a social science sprung from a
utopian vision of escaping the past (history) that is nonetheless
constituted upon a metanarrative framework. Classical modernization theory – the macro-theoretical story aimed at describing and
explaining the making of the modern western world, its structural
and its social dynamics – was the outcome, indeed the great and
lasting invention, of this complex fusion of history and theory. The
foundational story deeply encoded within modern social science had
all the formal components of analytic narrative – causal emplotment
(the engine of industrialization), a beginning (traditional society),
a middle (crisis of industrial revolution), and end (resolution into
modernity), and leading protagonists in action (classes in struggle).
The only thing missing, however, was *conceptual narrativity*. Its conceptual core – classes, society, social actors, social action – were
devoid of ontological historicity. Temporality, spatiality, relationality,
and concrete linkages all gave way to the utopian ideals of social
abstractionism. And in this paradoxical combination can be found
the source of many of the problems of social action.

Modern social theory was thus crafted out of epic moments in
history. Plagues, wars, famines, and revolutions all play their parts;
the Black Death, the English Civil War, the Reformation, the French
Revolution, the Industrial Revolution all figure as shadows in the
heart of the metatheoretical and theoretical framework. Society, social
action, the social actor, causality, and even social change are each
terms carrying within themselves pieces of the great metanarrative
of modernity. But the stories and researches (Lieberson 1992) that
constitute some of our most important and significant theories are
completely invisible; that is, they have been naturalized to the point
where what is in fact a narrative – that is a *constructed* story
– becomes metatheory. The narratives that have so long constituted
social theory are excluded from the very definition of theory and
relegated to the realm of "just history."

But the consequences are ironic. On the one hand, it is their very powers of abstraction which serve to privilege theories over "mere history." Who among us has not been thoroughly convinced by the post-positivist argument that facts are "theory-laden," and that histories are organized by theoretical categories? But, on the other hand, few among us would "accuse" a theory of being "*history-laden*," that is, actually constructed on the basis of a story. The lowly status of history is evident in the scorn "empiricism" is met with. To the extent that empiricism suggests that there is such an activity as the assemblage of raw facts, such derision is well deserved. But the case we are making is something different altogether: Not "raw facts" but constructed *stories* sit in the core of virtually all of our social theories.

We have arrived at one of the reasons for the enduring presence of the ontological impasse between *actor* and *society* in social theory; the terms are themselves creations of a particular historical narrative. It is their unexamined and deeply problematic historicity that reproduces the dilemmas in a sociology of action. If sociology's impasses are in the original fusion of macro-historical analysis and epistemology, and if the concepts we use to describe the world are historicized and limited, it follows logically that we must deconstruct the historicity of the concepts we use by means of an historical epistemology. The challenge this poses for a sociology of action is to develop ways of knowing, exploring, and explaining that can accommodate historically constituted concepts of human agency, institutions, cultures, and social identities. This historical dimension of theoretical practice is one which subjects claims of naturalism to the challenge of competing historical epistemologies.

Historicizing Agency

Recall the epistemological template for the problem of action as expressed in Townsend's fantasia of the goats and the dogs on the isle of Juan Fernandez. This naturalistic epistemology was one moment of the general revolutionary progressivism of eighteenth- and nineteenth-century science and politics in which societal laws of nature – rather than laws of the state – now explained the social world. But naturalism inevitably threatened to annihilate the subject. Faced with this dilemma, sociological theory did not bury a theory of action. Rather, it conjoined its new-found naturalism with the ontological counterpart to social structural progressivism and created the "revolutionary idiom of action" – *the compulsion to individuate* was at once both naturalistic and an historical creation of modernity. Recognizing and naming the revolutionary idiom at the heart of theories of agency are the first steps to understanding the problem the idiom has left us with. The next step is to deconstruct its historicity.

Sociology's discovery of the social actor emerged from a convergence of mushrooms, reason, and revolution. In the first case, the Hobbesian abstraction ("Let us ... consider men ... as if but even now sprung out of the earth ... like mushrooms ... without all kinds of engagement to each other") celebrated the emancipatory vision contained in the idea of the self-interested individual free to create his/her world anew. [20] Second, the Kantian critique positing reason over the naturalism of Hobbes's ontology appealed to progressive minds and lodged the idea of the morally autonomous modern individual on firm grounds. Finally, the French Enlightenment sealed the amalgamation: Voltaire's, Diderot's, and Rousseau's free self was driven naturally to repel the force of political authority, tradition, custom, and institutional bonds – all in the name of freedom from domination.

But the appropriation of the conceptual agent from the philosophers by the social scientists involved a critical transmutation. They moved the foundations from a transcendental to an empirical and historical grounding because social science's individual actor could not, of course, remain a Hobbesian or Lockean pre-social being. Rather, the sociological innovation was to reconceive the social actor as a *developmental product* of the modernizing process of *progressive individuation*. Only this way could a sociology of action dovetail with premises of classical modernization: The process of achieved individuation towards "freedom from ..." was enmeshed within the continuum of societal change – from *traditional to modern* society. Individuation itself could thus be seen along a progressive continuum running from political and/or religious embeddedness to freedom. Authentic social action necessarily meant a facing away from all that "tradition" represented – the past, institutional relations, contingency. From the French Revolution, the triumph of political and economic liberalism, and the German route to modernity, modern social science derived the lesson that the free modern self which comprised the actor of modern society had to be an autonomous self severed from the archaic ties of the past and *others*. Action thus became authentic only when it was striving forward toward individuation and "freedom from ..."

Social science's modern actor was thus conceived through a blending of philosophy with Newton. At a stroke, a philosophy of moral autonomy was refashioned to accommodate the progressive naturalism of modernization theory. This new revolutionary idiom of agency raised to a priori status an abstracted fiction of the social subject. Agency and social action became theoretically embedded in the historical fiction of the individuating social actor whose natural state was moving toward freedom from the past and separation from symbolic association, "tradition," and above all, the constraint of "others." Marx's celebration of bourgeois society as a necessary societal stage in the progression of freedom, Weber's autonomous individual as the only valid subject of action, and the early Durkheim's moral individual freed by the overturning of gemeinschaft all confirmed the sociological appropriation of this revolutionary idiom. [21] They each built their theories on the duality of subject and object, the individual versus society. The identity of the subject was abstracted from history; social relations and institutional practices − even collective memory − would exist as external objects of power and constraint.

Yet herein lies the explanation for why the revolutionary idiom of action generates an incoherent and unintelligible ontology. The sociology of action is rooted in the strange premise that somewhere and somehow between the social and historical production of agential beliefs, needs, even individuality itself on the one side (through modernization, socialization), and on the other, the reception of and acting upon these beliefs by a fully formed subject, the original process of social constitution is lost and the modern social actor becomes a fixed and universal self driven to maintain separation and autonomy from others. No longer ontologically natural as in natural rights theory, the sociological agent becomes an historicist product of modernization. The twist is that social science's discrete individuating actor becomes naturalized by virtue of becoming modernized. For sociological theory − a theory of modernized society − what is modern becomes naturalized; hence presuppositional.

From Freedom in Separation to Constraint by Others

But here the sociology of action confronts a recurring problem. Even sociologists have not failed to note the inconsistency between the postulates of the revolutionary idiom and the abundance of evidence which calls into question the assumption that modern social agency − in the absence of domination − is universally oriented toward and constituted by a naturalized state of individuation. Why, for example, do social agents sometimes act within "traditions?" [22] Why do some people in some places seem to value "relationality" more than separation (Gilligan 1982) and others value autonomy

considerably more than community? Why do so many social movements not try to overthrow the state but work to persuade the
state to meet its promised obligations (Somers 1986)? Why, more
than 30 years after the Civil Rights movement – a movement
for universal rights – are there discussions about whether blacks
should be called African-Americans? Why the interest and controversy around proposals for an Afrocentric approach to knowledge
(Asante 1987)? Why do "moderns" "continue to infuse values, institutions, even mundane physical locations with the mystery and awe
of the sacred" (Alexander 1989: 246)? Why are people willing to
die in situations where there is minimal likelihood of achieving
instrumental goals (Calhoun 1991c)? Why do some families consider neighborhood associations to be more valuable than cash (Stack
1974)? Why did (and do) working classes strike to preserve the
honor of their skills and crafts (Reddy 1987)? Why is social capital
often more valuable than material capital (Bourdieu 1984a; Lamont
1992)?

Faced with such questions there have been two logical choices
for the social sciences: (1) to toss out the revolutionary idiom as
a useless heuristic for explanation – and by implication, call into
question one of the central postulates of sociology and its grounding
in classical modernization theory, or (2) to preserve the revolutionary
idiom by looking *outside* of it for an explanation of anomalousness
from its vision. It is the second course that has characterized sociology's approach to the "meaning of meaning" (Putnam 1975). To
preserve the pristine status of the revolutionary idiom, "deviant"
behavior has been consistently explained by the *power of the social
order to determine social action over and above the naturalized state of
individuation*. For if social action appears to derive meaning in ways
that are incompatible with the revolutionary idiom of action – then
only a phenomenon *external* to the modern actor can explain this
incompatibility. Hence the entity of "society" – the object in a
subject–object duality – becomes the determinant of all constraining action (whether through economic forces, bureaucratic control,
or internalized constraint and shared norms). The most common
sociological understanding of the modern version of this constraint
is "internalized norms" mediated through society's regulative institutions of law, religion, family, community, education, kinship, and
social policy. More radically (from Marx and Weber), constraint
derives from the state itself, now conceived as a dangerous residual
of traditional forms of domination that has been modernized through
capitalist development and class formation (Marx) or through the
rationalizing processes of bureaucratization (Weber).

The Institutional Conundrum

But here we confront the second great problem of social theory — the problem of institutions. The institutional problem exists ambiguously among the shadows of societal determinism. Since research on social institutions has always figured prominently in the social sciences, until recently the problem has not achieved the publicity of that of action (March and Olsen 1984; Powell and DiMaggio 1991). But surely it is as great a conundrum: We have seen how a sociology of action by necessity takes as its universal state a striving for "freedom from ..." And we have in turn seen that in this context acting within the constraints of relationality can be made intelligible only through the notion of societal constraint. But if relationality is embedded in institutions external to the social agent, where do institutions come from? The problem is highlighted by recalling Townsend's fable and the narrative of modernization. Both displaced law, moral authority, and power to peripheral status in a naturalistic societal paradigm. The consequences were that the autonomous societal market would now rule the conceptual terrain where institutions and relationships had once prevailed. But, no less than that of agency, this produced a glaring enigma: On the one hand, power and institutions were reconceptualized as epiphenomena of a naturalistic social system. That made institutions into functions of societal principles writ large — principles which were crystallized in the individuation and analytic autonomy assumed to be characteristic of the modern social actor. But on the other hand, these very institutions were also to serve as the explanation for the sociological conception of relational constraint. How could power and institutions embody *both* the individuating principles of modern action and the expressions of modern relational constraint?

This, then, is the problem arising from the awkward coexistence of naturalism, the revolutionary idiom, and sociology's conceptual confrontation with institutions. Faced with expressions of agency that cannot be located within an analytic state of individuation, sociological logic must rely on institutional domination to explain the deviancy. A dominating state, laws, bureaucracy, the power of ideology and/or social norms, become the mechanisms of explanation for the failure to account for relational social agency. The permutations on this theme can be staggering: tradition, social control, bureaucratic manipulation, institutional rationalization, false consciousness, norms, roles, and values are but a few of the mechanisms assumed to be expressions of societal constraint. The true accomplishment, however, was the conceptual consolidation of what was to become the great agony of modern social theory. The modern agent – freed by modernity from traditional relationality to arrive at a condition of ontological autonomy – coexists in sociology's theoretical universe alongside both the naturalism of a systemically conceived society and a simultaneous notion of domination and control from institutions and others. Marx, Weber, and Durkheim, with different normative premises, each carried forth the dualism of the individuated actor against society.[23]

Thus sociologists relentlessly push human agency into the reductionist cul-de-sac against which we so insistently rail. As long as the social actor is represented as the analytic individual, relational action challenging the postulates of the revolutionary idiom – action organized through patterns of community constraint, for example (whether defined as private – family, church, tradition, or public – economy, state), cannot be considered authentic but rather a result of societal constraint or domination. No amount of willfully pushing and prodding this revolutionary idiom of action will resolve the conundrum; the problem lies in history, not in will.

II THE POLITICS OF IDENTITY: FROM UNIVERSALITY TO CATEGORY

In recent years classical social theory has been confronted with a set of extraordinary challenges – ones that have arisen in part from external political and social transformations and in part from theoretical attempts to make sense of those social developments. The political and social elements are best represented by such factors as the "failure" of western working classes to carry out their "proper" revolutionary (class) interests, the collapse of communist regimes, the radical increase of women in the workforce, and the resurgence of ethnic solidarities and cultural nationalisms throughout the world. Among the responses to these changes are the vast array of "new social movements" that have arisen to prominence in the last twenty years (Green parties, gay and lesbian liberation movements, and so on), the explosion of a feminist consciousness which valorizes female "difference" as much as equality, and the politics of multiculturalism.[24]

Although they takes no universal form (Aronowitz 1992: 12) the various expressions of this new "politics of identity" all share the common feature of being constituted by people who previously felt marginalized from dominant political channels and more mainstream social movements. Similarly, these are also groups and individuals who have been marginalized by our prevailing social theoretical accounts for why people act the way do. Thus, for example, classical theoretical accounts of social movement organizations focus on class interests as a motivating factor for action and/or "instrumental" calculi to achieve specifically power-oriented goals. But rather than emphasize traditional issues of labor and production, the new politics and movements of identity stress "expressive" goals of "self-realization" (Pizzorno 1978, 1985) while they attempt to positively restore previously devalued differences, e.g. female care-taking and "being-in-relations" (Chodorow 1978; Elshtain 1981).

To make sense of these striking developments, new theories of action and agency have emerged. These new theories of "identity politics" have shifted explanations for action from "interests" and "norms" to *identities* and *solidarities*, from the notion of the universalistic social agent to particularistic categories of concrete persons. Based on the assumption that persons in similar social categories and similar life-experiences (based on gender, color, generation, sexual orientation, and so on) will act on the grounds of common attributes, theories of identity politics posit that "I act because of who I am," not because of a rational interest or set of learned values.

Identity politics are relatively new on the agenda of social theory. But when viewed in the context of the perduring conundrum of explaining social action, these new theories of identity are easily recognizable as confrontations with the same intractable problem of agency discussed above: how to formulate viable sociological accounts of moral action which do not resort to external constraint (or "internalized" external constraint) to explain action that "deviates" from the universalistic premises of those concepts that have shaped our theoretical discourses, especially the revolutionary idiom with its emphasis on an individuated ontology. The solution has been to challenge the putative universalism of the modernist ontology itself, for it is only when judged against this alleged norm that women and other "others" have been found wanting. The new theoretical perspectives have argued, therefore, that the putative universal social actor is in fact extremely particularistic – namely, white, male, and western. Most important, they claim that it is only in the context of this theoretical sleight of hand, one which claims universality for the particularistic and androcentric, that the experiences of "others" are suppressed, denied, and devalued in the first place. Thus the theoretical response has been not only to reveal the gendered, racial, or class-specific character of the "general" modern social actor. It has also been to propose and envision a theoretical alternative that transforms those very devalued traits of (female or racial) "otherness" into a newly esteemed ideal of selfhood and normatized social action.

Leading examples of such changes in feminist theory are the well-known works of Nancy Chodorow (1978) and Carol Gilligan (1982). Gilligan began by confronting the fact that for years scholars of moral development had pondered the seemingly unanswerable question of why women did not achieve the highest stages of development allegedly achieved by men. Social scientists and psychologists alike kept asking why women are anomalous to the norm. More specifically, they wanted to know why women were getting "stuck" at a "lower stage" of moral development, while men developed a sense of agency and judgement according to the theoretical social norm – that is, they become increasingly autonomous, individuated, and oriented to rules of abstract justice. Women, by contrast, were believed to be at a lower stage because they were found to have a sense of agency still tied primarily to their social relationships and to make political and moral decisions based on context-specific principles based on these relationships rather than on the grounds of their own autonomous judgements.

Students of gender studies know well just how busy social scientists have been kept by their efforts to come up with ever more sociological "alibis" for the question of why women did not act like men. Gilligan's response was to refuse the terms of the debate. She thus did not develop yet another explanation for why women are "deviant." Instead, she turned the question on its head by asking what was wrong with the *theory* – a theory whose central premises defines 50 percent of social beings as "abnormal." Gilligan translated this question into research by subjecting the abstraction of universal and discrete agency to the concreteness of comparative research into female behavior evaluated on its own terms. The new research revealed women to be more "concrete" in their thinking and more attuned to "fairness" while men acted on "abstract reasoning" and "rules of justice." These research findings transformed female deviance and "otherness" into variation and "difference" – but difference now freed from the normative devaluation previously accorded to it. In so doing, Gilligan contributed not only to a new recognition but to a theoretical and political celebration of the very female identity which prevailing theories had denigrated. [25]

Struggles over identity are thus being framed by the recognition that getting heard requires new theories. Scholars engaged in identity politics, for example, are insisting that there are ways of knowing and defining experience that are different from but equally valuable to those experiences of the dominant discourse. While law professor

Catharine MacKinnon (1989) insists, for instance, that it is difficult for women to stage a revolution using the tools of the oppressor – especially his *words*, cultural analyst Molefi Kete Asante (1987: 165) implies the same when he asks: how can the oppressed become empowered if they use the same theories as the oppressors? In "The Search for an Afrocentric Method," moreover, Asante (1987) not only challenges assumptions about the universality of Eurocentric concepts, he simultaneously restores dignity to the very qualities of "otherness" by which such Eurocentric theories had previously defined and devalued these same non-western identities.

Such theoretical challenges are indeed welcome. They move away from deriving the meaning of action and the definition of self from falsely imputed universalities and toward generating concrete notions of social being which begin from difference. This can only improve the prospects for a sociology of agency. At the same time, however, the virtually simultaneous outcries of "essentialism" directed towards these new identity politics testify to a whole new set of stubborn conceptual difficulties. Among the many questions we must ask, for example, are whether the new theories of identity politics are not creating their own new "totalizing fictions" in which a single category of experience, say gender, will overdetermine any number of cross-cutting other differences. Does this not run "roughshod" over women who might be "ill-served" by replacing all other forms of difference by the singular one of gender (Di Stefano 1990)? Feminists of color charge that feminist identity theories focusing exclusively on gender oversimplify their situation, since gender is just one of a number of other fundamental facets of identity and difference, such as poverty, class, ethnicity, race, sexual identity, and age (hooks 1984; Jordan 1981; Lorde 1984).

Another question we must ask is how it is possible to claim *social* agency for these notions of identity if its putatively motivating force derives from "essential" (that is, pre-political – e.g., "woman," "African-American") or "fixed" categories constructed from given attributes. If identities are fixed there is no room to accommodate changing power relations or history itself as they are constituted and reconstituted over time. One of the most influential of these criticisms has been that directed by Joan Scott against the work of Chodorow (1978) and Gilligan (1982) discussed above. Scott (1988a) pointed out that even with a well-deserved refutation of abstract universalism, Chodorow and Gilligan had only substituted their own ahistorical and essentialist notion of "woman." Why, asked Scott, should we assume that "women" will all act the same under all conditions simply because of their biological sex or even their socialized gender-identities? Does that not open up the possibility for a female version of abstract universal agency and identity against which any number of historically different forms of female moral agency will be held newly "deviant"?

There is also a question about the allegedly stable content of the new categories of identity. To assume that simply because in some places and in some times women appear to be more morally "relational" than men in their sense of agency does not in any way support the more general conclusion that *all* women are more morally relational than men. Even if such a generalization could be demonstrated, however, do we really want to accept that these dichotomous concepts of gender distinction really *reflect* the social world? Is it not just as likely that the theoretical categories of exclusion helped *constitute* those gender differences in the first place? And if it is indeed the case that female identities are the consequence of categories based on false universality and exclusions, should we not *criticize and contest* these categorical identities rather than applaud them simply for their "anti-masculinism"? In short, even assuming the empirical case to be true, is it not a serious mistake to leap from the empirical presence of relational identities to their *normative* valorization? There is too much evidence of the suffocating and negative effects of "being-in-relations" to accept this move uncritically. The underlying argument here is that a gender-centered identity politics does not take on the real challenge of criticizing, contesting, transforming, indeed escaping from the theoretical dichotomies which buttress and hierarchicalize forms of difference in the first place. Instead, the new identity theories merely reify anew what is in fact a multiplicity of historically varying forms of what are less often unified and singular but more often "fractured identities" (Haraway 1991). Thus while some scholars claim that establishing an identity or expressing self-realization is one of the goals of new social movements (Melucci 1989), there are others who consider the newly celebrated but fixed categories of "identity" and "self-realization" to be the problem itself, regardless of the fact that they are newly informed by the traits of the previously excluded. [26]

Finally, and perhaps most worrisome, we must question the slide from the gendered distinction between a moral and normative notion of relationality (women are "relational," men are "self-interested") to a gendered distinction in the degree of *analytic* relationality between men and women. The latter is an impossible conclusion. Even if men can be shown to be less morally oriented towards relationships than women, this in itself is a result of the *social* and *relational* constitution of male identity. That is, *both* men and women

must be conceived analytically as being embedded within and constituted by relationships and relationality. Whether or not the analytic relationality characteristic of both men and women devolves
into a gendered distinction in moral or normative relationality must
not be presumed a priori but can only be explored empirically and
historically.

These questions and concerns usefully highlight the theoretical
dangers contained in the new theories of agency being called identity
theories. In the absence of clearly positive theoretical and epistemological alternatives to the problem of identity, however, such criticisms can have the effect of only tossing theories of social action
and identity back and forth between the abstract universality of the
modern individuating agent who starves in a vacuum of abstraction,
and the essential "woman" (or black, or Serbian, or gay man) who
drowns in a sea of relationality, "experience," and identity. A
number of studies from different approaches have therefore begun
the task of developing positive theoretical and epistemological alternatives to these two mutually reinforcing opposites (Scott 1988a,
1991; Canning forthcoming; Poovey 1988; Minow 1990; Gagnier
1991; Cohen and Arato 1992 are but a few.) Fraser and Nicholson
(1990: 34) offer what seems to us to be one of the best summations
of the challenge at hand. They suggest that alternative theories of
agency – in this case feminist agency – should "be inflected by
temporality, the historically-specific institutional categories like the
modern, restricted, male-headed, nuclear family taking precedence
over ahistorical functionalist categories like reproduction and mothering. Where categories of the latter sort were eschewed altogether,
they would be genealogized, that is, framed by historical narrative
and rendered temporally and culturally specific." Joining the many
others who are struggling to give substance to this directive, we
propose linking the concepts of *narrativity* and *identity to generate a
different approach to theories of social action, agency, and identity.*

III   INTRODUCING NARRATIVITY

We argued above that what we know today as social theory and its
attendant problems are the legacies of historicist fragments distilled
into abstract ontological presuppositions about the modern actor.
Recent challenges to these long-dominant presuppositions, however,
have reified their own culturally and gender-specific identity stories
and in the process created a new shade of universalism that contains its own historicist fragments, and its own inevitable exclusions.

It would be a short leap to suggest simply that new stories need to be written, and perhaps old stories need to be recovered, in the effort to reconstruct a viable sociology of action. But different stories cannot merely be the product of one assertion against another. The classical story of modernity was constructed, like all narratives, through a particular epistemological filter conjoining eighteenth- and nineteenth-century social naturalism with a revamped seventeenth-century ontology of the social agent.[27] Both were epistemological escapes from all we associate with historicity – time, space, relationality. The paradoxical consequence is that the master-narrative of modernity at the heart of social theory is conceptually both anti-narrative and ahistorical. If our new stories are not to sound relentlessly like variations on the old, we need more than historical deconstruction. In the task of rethinking theory and recognizing history we must also reconstruct and rebuild a sociology of action constituted on *conceptual narrativity*.

Reframing Narrativity

The last two decades have been notable for the degree to which historians have debated and increasingly scorned the value of narrative. But to understand why the new developments in narrative studies by other disciplines could proceed quietly uninterrupted, it is important to remember what exactly it was that the historians were rejecting. The conception of narrative that is common to historians is one that is treated as a mode of representation – discursive, rather than quantitative; non-explanatory, rather than conditionally propositional; and non-theoretical, rather than one of the theoretically driven social sciences.[28] The conflict among historians was solely over how to *evaluate* that representational form.[29] For "traditional" historians, narrative was seen as ideal because the accurate representation of history was the essence of the historian's craft; for the social science historians, the traditional narrative representational form was inadequate because it neither explained nor interpreted the past.[30] While the debate over representational narrative was raging among historians, however, others were quietly appropriating the abandoned concept and using it to produce major conceptual breakthroughs in their fields.[31] As stated above, however, the narrative concept employed in these new researches is radically different from the older interpretation of narrative as simply a representational form. The new notion recognizes narrative and narrativity to be concepts of social epistemology and social ontology. These concepts posit that it is through narrativity that we come to know, understand, and make sense of the social world, and it is through narratives and narrativity that we constitute our social identities. They argue, therefore, that it matters not whether we are social scientists or subjects of historical research for all of us come to be who we are (however ephemeral, multiple, and changing) by locating ourselves (usually unconsciously) in social narratives *rarely of our own making.* [32]

From diverse sources [33] it is possible to identify four features of a reframed narrativity particularly relevant for the social sciences: (1) relationality of parts, (2) causal emplotment, (3) selective appropriation, and (4) temporality, sequence, and place. Above all, narratives are *constellations of relationships* (connected parts) embedded in *time and space*, constituted by *causal emplotment.* Unlike the attempt to produce meaning by placing an event in a specified category, narrativity precludes sense-making of a singular isolated phenomenon. Narrativity demands that we discern the meaning of any single event only in temporal and spatial relationship to other events. Indeed the chief characteristic of narrative is that it renders understanding only by connecting (however unstably) parts to a constructed configuration or a social network (however incoherent or unrealizable) composed of symbolic, institutional, and material practices. [34]

The connectivity of parts is precisely why narrativity turns "events" into *episodes*, whether the sequence of episodes is presented or experienced in anything resembling chronological order. This is done through "emplotment." It is emplotment that gives significance to independent instances, not their chronological or categorical order. And it is emplotment which translates events into episodes. As a mode of explanation, causal emplotment is an accounting (however fantastic or implicit) of why a narrative has the story line it does (Veyne 1984[1971]; Ricoeur 1981, 1984–6). Causal emplotment allows us to test a series of "plot hypotheses" against actual events, and then to examine how – and under what conditions – the events intersect with the hypothesized plot. [35] Without emplotment, events or experiences could be categorized only according to a taxonomical scheme. Polkinghorne (1988: 21) implicitly addresses the difference between emplotment and categorization when he notes that social actions should not be viewed as a result of categorizing oneself ("I am 40 years old; I should buy life insurance") but should be seen as emerging in the context of a life-story with episodes ("I felt out of breath last week, I really should start thinking about life insurance"). Similarly, it is also apparent that serious mental confusion or political emotion rarely stems from the inability to place an event or instance in the proper category. Rather we tend to become confused when it is impossible or illogical to integrate an event into an intelligible plot (MacIntyre 1981). To make something understandable in the context of a narrative is to give it historicity and relationality. This makes sense because when events are located in a temporal (however fleeting) and sequential plot we can then explain their relationship to other events. Plot can thus be seen as the logic or syntax of narrative (Ricoeur 1979; Veyne 1984[1971]; Polkinghorne 1988).

The significance of emplotment for narrative understanding is often the most misunderstood aspect of narrativity. Without attention to emplotment, narrativity can be misperceived as a non-theoretical representation of events. Yet it is emplotment that permits us to distinguish between narrative on the one hand, and chronicles or annals (Hayden White 1987), on the other. In fact, it is emplotment that allows us to construct a significant network or configuration of relationships.

Another crucial element of narrativity is its *evaluative criteria* (Linde 1986; L. Polanyi 1985). Evaluation enables us to make qualitative and lexical distinctions among the infinite variety of events, experiences, characters, institutional promises, and social factors that impinge on our lives. Charles Taylor (1989), for example, argues that the capacity to act depends to a great extent on having an evaluative framework shaped by what he calls "hypergoods" (a set of fundamental principles and values) (see also Calhoun 1991b). The same discriminatory principle is true of narrative: in the face of a potentially limitless array of social experiences deriving from social contact with events, institutions, and people, the evaluative capacity of emplotment demands and enables *selective appropriation* in constructing narratives (Somers 1986). A plot must be thematic (Bruner 1986; Kermode 1984). The primacy of this narrative theme or competing themes determines how events are processed and what criteria will be used to prioritize events and render meaning to them. Themes such as "husband as breadwinner," "union solidarity," or "women must be independent above all" will selectively appropriate the happenings of the social world, arrange them in some order, and normatively evaluate these arrangements.[36]

Four Dimensions of Narrativity

So far we have presented the meaning of narrative in its most abstract dimensions. These relatively abstract concepts, however, can also be expressed as four different dimensions of narrative – ontological, public, conceptual, and "meta" narrativity.

Ontological narratives

These are the stories that social actors use to make sense of – indeed, in order to act in – their lives. Ontological narratives are used to define who we are; this in turn is a precondition for knowing what to do. [37] This "doing" will in turn produce new narratives and hence new actions; the relationship between narrative and ontology is processual and mutually constitutive. Both are conditions of the other; neither are a priori. Narrative *location* endows social actors with identities – however multiple, ambiguous, ephemeral, or conflicting they may be (hence the term *narrative identity*; Somers 1986). To have some sense of social being in the world requires that lives be more than different series of isolated events or combined variables and attributes; ontological narratives thus process events into episodes. People act, or do not act, in part according to how they understand their place in any number of given narratives – however fragmented, contradictory, or partial. Charles Taylor (1989: 51–2) puts it this way: "because we cannot but orient ourselves to the good, and thus determine our place relative to it ... we must inescapably understand our lives in narrative form ..." [38]

But ontological narrativity, like the self, is neither a priori nor fixed. Ontological narratives make identity and the self something that one *becomes* (Nehamas 1985). Thus narrative embeds identities in time and spatial relationships. Ontological narratives affect activities, consciousness, and beliefs (Carr 1985, 1986) and are, in turn, affected by them. Like all narratives, ontological narratives are structured by emplotment, relationality, connectivity, and selective appropriation. So basic to agency is ontological narrativity that if we want to explain – that is, to know, to make sense of, to account for, perhaps even to predict, anything about the practices of social and historical actors, their collective actions, their modes and meanings of institution-building and group-formations, and their apparent incoherencies – we must first recognize the place of ontological narratives in social life.

But where do ontological narratives come from? How are people's stories constructed? Above all, ontological narratives are social and interpersonal. Although psychologists are typically biased toward the individual sources of narrative, even they recognize the degree to which ontological narratives can only exist interpersonally in the course of social and structural interactions over time (Sarbin 1986; Personal Narratives Group 1989). To be sure, agents adjust stories to fit their own identities, and, conversely, they will tailor "reality" to fit their stories. But the interpersonal webs of relationality sustain and transform narratives over time. Charles Taylor (1989) calls these "webs of interlocution," others (MacIntyre 1981) call them "traditions," we call them "public narratives."

Public narratives

Public narratives are those narratives attached to cultural and institutional formations larger than the single individual, to intersubjective networks or institutions, however local or grand, micro or macro – stories about American social mobility, the "freeborn Englishman," the working-class hero, and so on. Public narratives range from the narratives of one's family, to those of the workplace (organizational myths), church, government, and nation.[39] Like all narratives, these stories have drama, plot, explanation, and selective appropriation. Families, for example, selectively appropriate events to construct stories about their descent into poverty. The mainstream media arrange and connect events to create a "mainstream plot" about the origin of social disorders. The seventeenth-century church explains the theological reasons for a national famine. Government agencies tell us "expert" stories about unemployment. Taylor (1989) emphasizes the centrality of public to ontological narrative when he states (p. 39):

> We may sharply shift the balance in our definition of identity, dethrone the given, historical community as a pole of identity, and relate only to the community defined by adherence to the good (or the saved, or the true believers, or the wise). But this doesn't sever our dependence on webs of interlocution. It only changes the webs, and the nature of our dependence.

Conceptual narrativity

These are the concepts and explanations that we construct as social researchers. Because neither social action nor institution-building is produced solely through ontological and public narratives, our concepts and explanations must include the factors we call social forces – market patterns, institutional practices, organizational constraints. Herein lies the greatest challenge of analytic and conceptual narrativity: to devise a conceptual vocabulary that we can use to reconstruct and plot over time and space the ontological narratives and relationships of historical actors, the public and cultural narratives that inform their lives, and the crucial intersection of these narratives with the other relevant social forces.[40] To date, few if any of our analytic categories are in themselves temporal and spatial. Rather, our modern sociological use of terms such as "society," the "actor," and "culture" was for social science purposes intentionally abstracted from their historicity and relationality. The conceptual challenge that narrativity poses is to develop a social analytic vocabulary that can accommodate the contention that social life, social organizations, social action, and social identities are narratively, that is, temporally and relationally constructed through both ontological and public narratives. [41]

Metanarrativity

This fourth dimension of narrativity refers to the "master-narratives" in which we are embedded as contemporary actors in history and as social scientists (Jameson 1981; Lyotard 1984; Foucault 1972, 1973[1970]). Our sociological theories and concepts are encoded with aspects of these master-narratives – Progress, Decadence, Industrialization, Enlightenment, etc. – even though they usually operate at a presuppositional level of social science epistemology or beyond our awareness. These narratives can be the epic dramas of our time: Capitalism versus Communism, the Individual versus Society, Barbarism/Nature versus Civility. They may also be progressive narratives of teleological unfolding: Marxism and the triumph of Class Struggle, Liberalism and the triumph of Liberty, the Rise of Nationalism, or of Islam. The example of the master-narrative of Industrialization/Modernization out of Feudalism/Traditional Society, is only one of many cases in which a metanarrative becomes lodged in the theoretical core of social theory.

We have also pointed to what is perhaps the most paradoxical aspect of metanarratives: their quality of *denarrativization*. That is, they are built on concepts and explanatory schemes ("social systems," "social entities," "social forces") that are in themselves abstractions. Although metanarratives have all the necessary components of narrativity – transformation, major plot lines and causal emplotment, characters and action – they nonetheless miss the crucial element of a conceptual narrativity.

IV THE CONCEPTUAL IMPLICATIONS OF THE NEW NARRATIVE

So far, we have elaborated some of the dimensions of narrative analysis and have identified the major types of narrativity. What, then, are the implications of this conception of narrative for social theory? How can narrativity help us understand social life and social practices? If narrative is indeed a constitutive feature of social life as we so claim, our first analytic challenge is to develop concepts that will allow us to capture the narrativity through which agency is negotiated, identities are constructed, and social action mediated (Harrison White 1992b; Taylor 1989; Cohen 1985; Somers 1986, 1992). Although our four kinds of narrativity are relevant to social theory, it is the third that we consider the most important if theories are to adequately account for social action and collective projects. This is because conceptual narrativity is framed by temporality, spatiality, and emplotment as well as relationality and historicity. In this section, we examine the two central components of conceptual narrativity: *Narrative identity* and *relational setting*.

Narrative identity

Recall the trap of the sociology of action. The mythic heroism of the social actor was canonized in a revolutionary idiom, an idea so potent it dissolved classical views of the mutual constitution of the subject and the social world. While the classical view believed autonomy to be conditional upon social and political embeddedness, the new idiom substituted the notion that the freedom of the self was conditional upon an antagonistic differentiation of the individual from his/her cultural and institutional webbing. Social relations and "traditions" became the "object" – the domain of constraint – in a subject–object duality. Social connectiveness became part of the *external* structure alone. It was the object in a subject–object, individual-against-society, antagonism from which the actor was impelled to be free. Theories of identity politics are the most recent response to this theory of action that so frequently cannot account for deviations from its ideal-typical formulation. We have noted, however, that many difficulties arise when these new identity perspectives take those same "deviations" and move them onto newly rerevalorized ontological foundations. Thus, for example, the argument that women are more attuned to "being-in-relations" than to the (male) norm of individuation becomes the grounds for a new theory of fundamental analytic differences between men and women generalized from what is in fact a questionable *normative* affirmation of the moral relationality believed to be characteristic of female identities.

The concept of a narrative identity dovetails with the move to reintroduce previously excluded subjects and suppressed subjectivities into theories of action. At the same time, however, the narrative identity approach firmly rejects the tendencies of identity theories to normalize new categories that are themselves as fixed and removed from history as their classical predecessors. The approach builds from the premise that narrativity and relationality are conditions of social being, social consciousness, social action, institutions, structures, even society itself − that is, the self and the purposes of self are constructed and reconstructed in the context of internal and external relations of *time* and *place* and *power* that are constantly in flux. That social identities are constituted through narrativity, social action is guided by narrativity, and social processes and interactions − both institutional and interpersonal − are narratively mediated provides a way of understanding the recursive presence of particular identities that are, nonetheless, not universal.

The importance of conceptual narrativity is therefore that it allows us to build upon the advances and simultaneously to transcend the fixity of the identity concept as it is often used in current approaches to social agency. Joining narrative to identity introduces time, space, and analytic relationality − each of which is excluded from the categorical or "essentialist" approach to identity. While a social identity or categorical approach presumes internally stable concepts, such that under normal conditions entities within that category will act predictably, the narrative identity approach embeds the actor within relationships and stories that shift over time and space and thus precludes categorical stability in action. These temporally and spatially shifting configurations form the relational coordinates of ontological, public, and cultural narratives. It is within these temporal and multi-layered narratives that identities are formed; hence narrative identity is processual and relational. In this sense, the narrative identity approach shares much with the relational epistemologies most associated with Harrison White (1992a, b; White et al. 1976).

The analytic relationality of the narrative identity concept is thus at odds with the normative relationality of theories of identity politics. Feminist identity politics, for example, see relationality as a normative ontology − that is, women are socialized to be more relational than men. This quality of "being-in-relations" in turn makes women more "caring." In the narrative identity perspective, by contrast, relationality is used only analytically − that is, *all* identities (male and female) must be analyzed in the context of relational matrices because they do not "exist" outside of those matrices. [43] At the same time, this analytic relationality tells us nothing in advance about the value or moral quality of those relationships and relational identities. The meaningful implications of a relationally-embedded concept of identity can be determined only by empirical inquiry, not by a priori assumptions. In other words, to say that identities are forged *only* in the context of ongoing relationships that exist in time, space, and emplotment, is not to say that "being-in-relationship" is somehow "better" or "worse" than the individuating notions of agency. It is, rather, to divest conceptual narrativity of any particular normative implications. The interdependence and connectivity of parts characteristic of narrative analysis makes relationality an analytic *variable* instead of an ideal type or normative stand-in for an unchanging sense of "community." Relationships may be more or less bonded, the experience of them may be more or less constricting or enabling – but again, this is a question of narrative contingency not utopian ideals (see Calhoun 1980 for a similar argument about the use of "community" as a variable rather than an ideal type).

This argument can be exemplified by class-formation theory. Class-formation theory explains action with the concept of interest. Since interest is determined by either the logic and stages of socio-economic development or by universal rational preferences, the social analyst imputes a set of predefined interests or values to people as members of social categories (e.g., traditional artisans, modern factory worker, peasant). Historians commonly argue, for instance, that the decline of traditional domestic modes of production and its (this decline's) concomitant threat to custom, created an "artisanal interest" from which explanations for social movements can at least in part be derived. Although social science historians almost always demonstrate with subtlety how these interests are mediated through intervening factors (culture, gender, religion, residential patterns, etc.), the interests remain the foundational explanation for working-class practices and protests. Making sense of social action thus becomes an exercise in placing people into the right social categories by identifying their putative interests, and then doing the empirical work of looking at variations among those interests (e.g., McNall, Levine, and Fantasia 1991; Wright 1985).

But why should we assume that an individual or a collectivity has a particular set of interests simply because one aspect of their identity fits into one social category? Why should we assume that activist artisans (people who work in a particular way) should be defined above all by their "artisanal" interests simply because they are members of the "declining artisanal mode of production" category? To let "class" stand for a determinative experience is to presume that which has not been empirically demonstrated – namely that identities are foundationally constituted by categorization in the division of labor.

Substituting the concept of narrative identity for that of interest circumvents this problem. A narrative identity approach to action assumes that social action can only be intelligible if we recognize that people are guided to act by the relationships in which they are embedded and by the stories with which they identify – and rarely because of the interests we impute to them. Whereas interest focuses on how we as analysts categorize people's role in a division of labor, the narrative identity approach emphasizes how people characterize or locate themselves within a processual and sequential movement of life-episodes. Whereas an interest approach assumes people act on the basis of rational means–ends preferences or by internalizing a set of values, a narrative identity approach assumes people act in particular ways because not to do so would fundamentally violate their sense of being at that particular time and place. [44] In another time or place, however, or in the context of a different prevailing narrative, that sense of being could be entirely different (Halbwachs 1980 [1950]). What is most significant is that narrative identities are constituted and reconstituted in time and over time – that is, through narrative processes. Calhoun (1991c), demonstrates this in his narrative about how Chinese students, who had initially displayed no interest in politics, formed cohesive political identities during the one month they were thrust into the overpowering drama of Tienanmen Square.

The "narrative" dimension of identity there and elsewhere, thus presumes that action can be intelligible only if we recognize the various ontological and public narratives in which actors plot or "find" themselves. Rather than by interests, narrative identities are constituted by a person's temporally and spatially variable "place" in culturally constructed stories comprised of (breakable) rules, (variable) practices, binding (and unbinding) institutions, and the multiple plots of family, nation, or economic life. Most important, however, narratives are not incorporated into the self in any direct way; rather they are mediated through the enormous spectrum of social and political relations that constitute our social world. People's experiences as workers, for example, were inextricably interconnected with the larger matrix of relations that shaped their lives – their regional location, the practical workings of the legal system, family patterns – as well as the particular stories (of honor, of ethnicity, of gender, of local community, of greed, etc.) used to account for the events happening to them. [45]

It would be hard to find a more compelling illustration of the narrative identity concept than in Steedman's (1987) widely read sociological autobiography of her English working-class childhood in the 1950s. According to the dominant scholarly accounts (e.g., Hoggart 1959; Seabrook 1982), the extreme poverty of mid-century English working-class life was compensated by a robust "independence, pride, and sense of community." Sociologists have long assumed that social experience did in fact conform to this depiction of working-class identity. Steedman's narrative shatters all of our assumptions about the attributes of identity and agency that should normally fit with this form of social categorization. She presents us, instead, with an aching picture of the "class longings," and narratives of envy and desire (that life might be different), which characterized her life of underprivileged exclusion from the dominant culture. Steedman's representations of identities constructed of emotional and material poverty unfold sociologically in the context of the relational complexity in which her life was embedded, and in the narratives she inherited from her mother's life – ones in which gender intersected with class and so utterly challenge the usual attributes assigned to both of those categorical identities. [46]

The narrative contingency of identity is similarly vividly suggested in Davis's (1991) historical sociology of the notorious "one-drop rule" in racial classification. Davis's study demonstrates the numerous conflicts which accompanied the rule of a type of racial classification which failed to take into account the historical intermingling of different races. By declaring that anyone with even a drop of African blood was a "Negro," the burden of proving one's identity – for blacks and whites – made it obvious that such a universal binary classification was too rigid to account for those lives which failed to conform to the dominant public accounts of racial purity and segregation. The irony was that the very people or groups who deliberately created racial classifications in the first place often could not even identify correctly those individuals they wanted to classify; obviously skin color was now a poor indicator of race. The impact of America's imaginative one drop rule, moreover, went beyond public and private struggles over personal identity. By compelling all children of mixed blood to live in the black community, "the rule made possible the incredible myth among whites that miscegenation had not occurred, that the races had been kept pure in the south" (Davis 1991: 174). The problem of who gets to define a person continues even today. One of the key decisions many principal investigators make about research projects concerning race is whether their interviewers should categorize the race of respondents or whether the persons being interviewed should get to choose their race from a preselected category.

An important theoretical distinction needs to be made at this point between two kinds of classifications: Those based on (1) taxonomical categories of identity aggregated from variables (age, sex, education, etc.) or "fixed" entities (woman, man, black), and (2) categories that coincide with a narrative thematic. For instance, it is not hard to classify certain narratives as falling in the category of the "heroic Westerner," or "the virtues of American democracy." This is a classification, however, of the narrative itself: It can still be abstracted from context and its ontological meaning kept intact. By contrast, the classification of an actor *divorced* from analytic relationality is neither ontologically intelligible nor meaningful. In her study of audience responses to western movies, for instance, Shively (1992) appropriately must classify by theme the western movies she shows her audiences. Yet while these thematic classifications of the narratives remain stable throughout the study, her findings reveal that audience identification with and response to those themes depends less on the racial category of the respondent (native American or white) and more on the actors' changing social and historical embeddedness.

Relational Setting

Another challenge of conceptual narrativity is to develop a vocabulary that will allow us to locate actors' social narratives in temporal and spatial configurations of relationships and cultural practices (institutions and discourses). We need concepts that will enable us to plot over time and space the ontological narratives of historical actors, the public and cultural narratives that inform their lives, as well as the relevant range of other social forces – from politics to demographics – that configure together to shape history and social action. We thus need a conceptual vocabulary that can relate narrative identity to that range of factors we call social forces – market patterns, institutional practices, organizational constraints, and so on.

Society is the term that usually performs this work of contextualization in social analysis. When we speak of understanding social action, we simultaneously speak of locating the actors in their "societal" context. But society as a concept is rooted in a falsely totalizing and naturalistic way of thinking about the world. As in Townsend's fable, for most practicing social science research, a society is a social entity. As an entity, it has a core essence – an essential set of social springs at the heart of the mechanism. This essential core is in turn reflected in broader covarying societal institutions that the system comprises. Thus, when sociologists speak of feudalism, for example, we mean at once "feudal society" as a whole, a particular set of "feudal class relations" at the core of this society, a

"feudal manorial economy," and a concomitant set of "feudal institutions" such as feudal political units and feudal peasant communities. Most significantly for historical research, each institution within
a society must covary with each other. Thus in "feudal societies,"
the state by definition must be a feudal state whose feudal character covaries with all other feudal institutions; feudal workers must
all be unfree and extra-economically exploited peasants. And in
"industrial society," a "modern industrial/capitalist" state must be
detached from civil society and the industrial economy, and industrial
workers must be individual and legally free. To be sure, the syn-
chrony is not always perfect. In periods of transition from one society
to another, there occurs a "lag effect" and remnants of the old
order persist against the pressures of the new. But despite these
qualifications, the systemic metaphor assumes that the parts of society
covary along with the whole as a corporate entity.

To make social action intelligible and coherent, these systemic
typologies must be broken apart and their parts disaggregated and
reassembled on the basis of relational clusters. For a social order
is neither a naturalistic system nor a plurality of individuals, but
rather a complex configuration of cultural and institutional relationships. If we want to be able to capture the narrativity of social life
we need a way of thinking that can substitute relational imagery for
a totalizing one. We thus concur with Michael Mann (1986: 2) who
writes: "It may seem an odd position for a sociologist to adopt;
but if I could, I would abolish the concept of 'society' altogether." [47]
Substituting the metaphor of a *relational setting* for "society" makes
this possible. [48] A relational setting is a pattern of relationships
among institutions, public narratives, and social practices. As such
it is a relational matrix, similar to a social network. [49] Identity
formation takes shape within these relational settings of contested
but patterned relations among narratives, people, and institutions.

One of the most important characteristics of a relational setting
is that it has a history (MacIntyre 1981), and thus must be explored
over time and space. A relational setting is traced over time not
by looking for indicators of social development, but by empirically
examining if and when relational interactions among narratives and
institutions appear to have produced a decisively different outcome
from previous ones. Social change, from this perspective, is viewed
not as the evolution or revolution of one societal type to another,
but by shifting relationships among the institutional arrangements
and cultural practices that comprise one or more social settings.

Spatially, a relational setting must be conceived with a geometric
rather than a mechanistic metaphor since it is composed of a matrix

of institutions linked to each other in variable patterns contingent on the interaction of all points in the matrix.[50] A setting crosses "levels" of analysis and brings together in one setting the effect of, say, the international market, the state's war-making policies, the local political conflicts among elites, and the community's demographic practices – each of which takes social, geographical, and symbolic narrative expression. This cross-cutting character of a relational setting assumes that the effect of any one level (for example, the labor market sector) can be discerned only by assessing how it is affected interactively with other relevant dimensions (for example, gender and race). To do so requires that we first *disaggregate* the parts of a setting from any presumed covarying whole and then reconfigure them in their temporal and geographic relationality. In this way, for example, different regions of a single nation-state are no longer cast as variants of a single society, but as different relational settings that can be compared.[51]

V CONCEPTUAL NARRATIVITY AND THEORIES OF ACTION AND AGENCY

Narrative Identity and Social Meaning

A major advantage of the concept of narrative identity is in the challenge it poses to the false dichotomy too often posed between ideal versus instrumental meanings of action.[52] One sociological claim is that action is authentic only when it is expressive rather than instrumental. To enforce the point, material goals – such as bread and wages – are typically called instrumental while ideal activities are usually associated with qualitative concerns in daily life. Weber, for instance, argued that if wages were of secondary importance for German workers that was evidence of the superiority of ideal action.[53] From the same assumptions, neoclassical economists go to equal lengths to provide support for the primacy of self-interest among workers in order to support the concept of rational action. And most currently, it is theorists of the new identity politics who distinguish the new social movements (from the old) by their putatively exclusively ideal – hence, identity – focus (Pizzorno 1978, 1985; Melucci 1989).[54]

Yet from a narrative identity perspective there is nothing self-evident about the instrumental nature of wage demands any more than that of the ideal nature usually attributed to cultural activities. Just as an adequate material life is an essential means of preserving normative relations, so cultural and symbolic relations provide material resources for livelihood (Stack 1974; Berg 1987; K. Polanyi 1977). Similarly, instrumental strategies and identity politics appear to be increasingly linked in research findings about the new social movements (Touraine 1985; Cohen 1985; Cohen and Arato 1992).

Many examples defy attempts to periodize or categorize a transformation from instrumental (material) to ideal (identity) ends. Joyce (1987) has collected an array of studies illustrating the remarkable variation in "the historical meanings of work." It is not just that work signified honor as much as livelihood; equally important, even when money wages were at stake, it was impossible to separate their value from that of the "dignity of the trade" (see also Joyce 1991; Reddy 1987; Sonenscher 1987). Many years ago Smelser (1959) demonstrated that collective movements aimed at factory reform (surely the quintessential "instrumental" object) were motivated by working families' efforts to hold the "traditional" family together against the destabilizing impact of women and children's factory labor. And when nineteenth-century working people demanded the vote on the grounds of their "property in labor," it was not the autonomous workmanship ideal of Locke on which they founded these claims, but on the relational property of apprenticeship – a form of familial cohesion (Somers 1994b).

The meaning imputed to the appropriation of material life should not, therefore, be presumed until historically explored. When we look at wage struggles, for instance, as part of an a priori system of categorization, we inevitably classify them as expressions of instrumental goals. But when we view these same wage struggles through the lens of a narrative identity analysis, we are immediately impressed by the difficulty of classifying them as solely either instrumental or ideal. Wages served every purpose from maintaining social honor, to preserving families, to asserting independence in the face of newly imposed factory regimes. Historical studies demonstrate the vast range of variation in the use of bread and wages. Indeed if there is any common narrative theme that emerges from these studies, it is that wage struggles appear to be most commonly viewed as a form of *provisioning* – a characteristic social activity that defies either ideal or instrumental classification in its focus on maintaining relational continuities over time and within space. [55]

The narrative identity concept allows us to make this shift in the interpretation of action from an a priori categorization to a focus on contingent narratives of meaning. The example of the conceptual shift from ideal versus instrumental agency to the concept of provisioning, for example, strikingly supports the switch from fixed notions of agency to relational analyses of identity formation. If persons are socially constituted over time, and space, and through relationality, then *others* are constitutive, rather than external, to identity; they are simply other subjects, rather than external objects, in the social order. From this perspective authentic social action can readily encompass institutional practices that organize social inclusions and institutional exclusions – such as trade unions or community associations. [56] Historical and contemporary studies indeed suggest that structural autonomy, and sometimes normative, was more often than not contingent upon the grids of social relationality (everything from collective memories, to political power and policies from above, to competing social claims, to pasts and futures of intractable social connections, and public narratives) that variably adhere to the interstices of an individual life. [57] These institutional and symbolic relationships are no mere external set of norms to be "stripped away by the sociologist" to discover the "real processes analytic self" (MacIntyre 1981: 26); they are not "internalized" sets of societal rules residing within the human being. Rather they are constitutive to self, identity, and agency.

Consider the comments of one late eighteenth century English artisan on some of the progressive French notions of liberty that threatened to dismantle regulative welfare policies: "It cannot be said to be the liberty of a citizen, or of one who lives under the protection of any community; it is rather the liberty of a savage; therefore he who avails himself thereof, deserves not that protection, the power of society affords (cited in E. P. Thompson 1971). For this individual, others were not part of the external problem of constraint but constitutive – for good or for bad – of his narrative identity.

Race, Gender, and Power

Although we argue that social action is intelligible only through the construction, enactment, and appropriation of narratives, this does not mean that actions are free to fabricate narratives at will; rather, they must "choose" from a repertoire of available representations and stories. Which kinds of narratives will socially predominate is contested politically and will depend in large part on the distribution of power. This is why the kinds of narratives people use to make sense of their situation will always be an empirical rather than a presuppositional question. It is essential, in other words, that we explicate, rather than assume or take for granted, the narratives of groups and persons. The extent and nature of any given repertoire of narratives available for appropriation is always historically and culturally specific; the particular plots that give meanings to those narratives cannot be determined in advance.

Since social actors do not freely construct their own private or public narratives, we can also expect to find that confusion, powerlessness, despair, victimization and even madness are some of the outcomes of an inability or powerlessness to accommodate certain happenings within a range of available cultural, public, and institutional narratives. Thus in everyday talk we characterize the most incoherent of experiences – and especially those where we feel controlled by a greater power than our own – as "Kafka-esque." [58] And it is for this reason that gender studies and critical race theory have so eagerly argued for the importance of new public narratives and symbolic representations that do not continue the long tradition of exclusion so characteristic of dominant ones.

Patrizia Violi (1992), for example, reminds us how critical the presence or absence of particular narratives have been to the construction of both male and female subjectivity. The archetypical "universal" narrative allows men "to objectivize" themselves and their own experiences in these stories – stories that not only represent maleness, but in effect replicate the metanarratives of classical social theory. In pointing out that women do not have available to them the same normatively valued forms of symbolic representation, Violi notes the difficulties women have constituting social identities. These representational silences are therefore tantamount to keeping invisible not only the differences between men and women but also the very subjectivities of women. Seeing representation, narrative, and subjectivity as part of the same process, Violi (1992: 175) argues that unless female subjectivity is made visible through narrative "it will remain confined within the closed space of individual experience." Choosing narratives to express multiple subjectivities is a deliberate way of rejecting the neutrality and objectivity appearance typically embedded in master narratives. Steedman's (1987) analytic autobiography of her English working-class roots is perhaps the most powerful example we have available to date of the power of alternative public narratives in countering the potential damage to identity formation caused by singular dominant narratives. The public narratives of working-class community she had available as a child omitted women, just as many of the current feminist accounts of identity omit class and poverty (Collins 1990). In this context of narrative silence toward her own experiences, Steedman presents a picture of a self's (her mother) absolute longing and absence. Challenging the silence, Steedman articulates a counter-narrative –

one which joins gender and class, with many other relational complexities of English life – and thus she lays the groundwork for a newly reconstructed process of identity formation.

Struggles over narrations are thus struggles over identity. In an examination of their legal training, for instance, Patricia Williams (1991) and Charles Lawrence (1992) explicitly reject silencing the human voice in order to produce "abstract, mechanistic, professional, and rationalist" (Lawrence 1992: 2286) legal discourse. Embracing the notion of multiple subjectivity, Williams tells us that she does not use the "traditionally legal black-letter vocabulary," because she is "intentionally double-voiced and relational" (1991: 6) Lawrence (1992) calls this kind of multiple consciousness by another name – "dual subjectivity." Either way, these scholars of color contend that writing counter-narratives is a crucial strategy when one's identity is not expressed in the dominant public ones. Furthermore, it is not surprising that the narratives of excluded voices reveal "alternative values" since narratives "articulate social realities not seen by those who live at ease in a world of privilege (Minow 1987: 10). The centrality of ontological narrative in the construction of social identities is also revealed in a story Williams tells about starting law school at Harvard University. With "secretive reassurance," Williams recalls, her mother explained why she knew the young black student would succeed at the prestigious university. "The Millers were lawyers, so you have it in your blood" (1991: 216). Encoded in that story about the white slaveholder (Attorney Austin Miller) who had purchased and impregnated Williams's great-great-grandmother was the proof that a category is neither fixed nor non-relational. If "one drop" of blood could be constructed into a narrative to dominate one sector of the population, could the story not also be inverted so that the single drop of blood is a symbol of status and thus a source of empowerment?

Narrative Identity and Social Class

Conceptual narrativity also allows us to think differently about the relationship between social classes and social action. T. H. Marshall (1964[1949]), for example, in his classic study of citizenship correlated the stages of citizenship's development with epochs of class formation; each stage represented the expression of the interests of an emerging historic class. Underpinning this argument is the assumption that actors within the same category ("the working-class," "the gentry," "capitalist employers," "state bureaucrats") will have shared attributes – hence shared interests directing them to have similar citizenship practices. Naturally this assumption leads us to expect intra-class uniformity throughout each period of citizenship formation: All the members of a single category of actors – the eighteenth-century English "working class," for example – should behave similarly and have the same capacities with respect to citizenship, regardless of other differences such as residence, family, or gender.

But evidence shows otherwise. Even though eighteenth-century English working people certainly shared important attributes – they were propertyless in most respects, exploited by their employers, and working for wages – their conditions and degrees of empowerment with respect to citizenship were not uniform but varied dramatically across the social and geographical landscape. More important, the "same" working class differed radically as to whether they even perceived the laws of citizenship to be rights in the first place (Somers 1993). Neither class nor status divisions could account for these differences since those in similar class situations maintained different degrees of power across regions.

From the narrative identity perspective these same working classes would be seen as *members* of political cultures whose symbolic and relational "places" in a matrix of narratives and relationships were better indicators of action than their categorical classification. From this angle of relational membership, identities are not derived from attributes imputed from a stage of societal development (be it pre-industrial or modern), or by "experience" imputed from a social category (such as traditional artisan, factory laborer, or working-class wife), but by actors' places in the multiple (often competing) symbolic and material narratives in which they were embedded or with which they identified. [59] We would thus no longer assume that a group of people have any particular relationship to citizenship simply because one aspect of their identity fits into a single category known as the "working class." Social action loses its categorical stability, and group embeddedness and cultural representations become more important than class attributes – thus directing us to investigate citizenship identities by looking at actors' places in their relational settings, or what Bourdieu (1977, 1984b, 1985) would call a "habitus." As a general proposition, this would direct us to expect greater contingencies of agency. We would be considerably less concerned with "deviation" and more fascinated by variation.

This shift would in turn allow us to make sense of a situation in which even though a large group of English people could be similarly categorized as "working class" – in that they shared working-class attributes (lack of ownership of means of production, landlessness, and so on) – their political activities varied radically depending upon their settings. [60] In the case of eighteenth-century England the effects usually attributed to proletarianization were in fact over-determined in many instances by particular narrative relationships and institutional practices (including national apprenticeship laws, the participatory rules and expectations of enforcement, the durability of partible inheritance, the local control and symbolic meaning attached to skilled work, and the skilled practices of affiliation). In a context configured by these relationships, certain working communities were able to offset many of the "normal" consequences of propertylessness with a more powerful form of "property" in association and membership (Somers 1994b).

CONCLUSION

We have argued that both an epistemology and a metanarrative of modernity were embedded in the origins of modern social science – that of a naturalistic logic of society and a progressivist "revolutionary idiom" of the modern social actor. But the two coexisted uneasily. In joining naturalism to ontological individuation, the social sciences had welded together a social agent firmly situated in an oppositional relationship to the intersubjective context of which it was an inextricable part. In the now naturalized condition of modern individuation, the social actor was thus *constrained* to enter into social relations with others. In philosophical terms, the subject–subject relationship that had prevailed in traditional political and moral philosophy was replaced by the subject–object one – the individual against society.

We have pointed out that as a result, much of the data of human activity has been inexplicable; by default, it has been explained by recourse to various themes of social determinism. As a result, women, non-westerners, and minorities often are defined in social analysis as "irrational" or "anomalous." Consider the "problem" of those many nineteenth-century working-class movements, for example, that deviated from Marxist predictions of revolutionary class consciousness when they demanded state intervention to protect their rights. All too frequently, these movements have been labeled by historians and sociologists as "reformist," or as victims of "social control" and "false consciousness." This barely conceals a hidden contempt for those putatively duped objects of history who acted differently than would the putatively universal modern actor. Yet as long as we continue to conceptualize others as sources of external constraint – a position logically necessary to the individual/society dichotomy – we are forced to label such relational and institutionally-oriented goals as "backwards-looking," "reactionary," or as evidence of "social control."[61] Action and agency that fail to conform to the postulates of the revolutionary idiom are explained by the external power of order, or internalized institutional constraint – be it norms or social laws, bureaucratic power, or economic forces. Why? Because the dispossessed ghost-like individual self is "less liberated than disempowered" (Sandel 1982: 178). Indeed one could go further; such a person cannot – even heuristically – exist.

This sociology of action thus leads to a puzzling circularity: it strives to assert moral agency against the naturalistic logic of society, but its criteria for authentic action negate the historical weightiness of analytic relationality and narrativity. By aspiring to capture a fiercely individuated notion of behavior all of the time, the revolutionary idiom does not achieve an historical intelligibility of action even some of the time. Its presuppositional claims have consistently been unable to account for the constitution of agency through relationality. The consequences can be dizzying tautologies: Ontologically emptied of relationality, agency can be explained only by recourse to the external social order; deprived of substance, action can only be a response to collective constraint. Social theory has reproduced the very problem it set out to solve – how to find a theory of action in the shadow of a naturalistic determinism.

But reductionism is not the only problem that can result from social theories of action. When agency is explained through internalized social norms or externalized constraint, the meaning of action becomes historicist – a mere reflection of its immanence within the accordant level of the developing social order. In this kind of historicism characteristic of classical theories of the modernizing process, people are detached from historical continuity over time and space while they simultaneously are made and remade by the restless momentum of changing social conditions. This hubris, too, fades under the glare of research. There is considerable evidence for the presence of certain existential themes – death, for example – in all expressions of identity – despite tremendous variation in strategies deployed to tame them.[62] Thus historicism too must give way to explanation that can accomplish what is the *sine qua non* of theory – the capacity to theoretically account for recursive patterns. In this project, tentative claims for circumscribed patterns of social arrangements and human action might be identified, but to arrive at these safely we must immerse ourselves in history as well as theory.[63] If the aim of sociology is to generate explanation that is indeed meaningful, the capacity of its logic to lay the basis for achieving that end will depend on its epistemological principles and categories being informed by time, space, and narrativity. [64]

Bringing the rich dimensions of ontological narrativity to the new identity approaches in social action theory is one way of doing this. It not only addresses the incoherencies of theories of action which leave vast numbers of social actors and social practices thoroughly unaccounted for – redefined as "marginal," "deviant," or "anomalous." It also builds upon the strengths of the recent shift in sociologies of action from universal notions of agency to more particularistic identities – a shift which endows the previously marginalized with a powerful new sense of subjectivity.

In recognizing the importance of these new sociologies of identity, however, we have also tried to call attention to their considerable weaknesses – foremost among which are the conflation of analytic or structural relationality into normative values about "being-in-relations" (e.g., Chodorow 1978; Gilligan 1982), as well as the inadvertent ahistoricism that results from constructing new *categories* of identity. To be sure, there is still a place for the use of categories of identity in everyday social practice. [65] Brint (1992: 196), for example rightly says that the sociological use of categories reflects the "belief that the experience of common conditions of life ... makes people with shared attributes a meaningful feature of the social structure." [66] But it is precisely because this belief is accepted into social analysis too uncritically that new theories of action centered around identity are often empirically confounded. Our argument is that there is no reason to assume a priori that people with similar attributes will share common experiences of social life, let alone be moved to common forms and meanings of social action, unless they share similar narrative identities and relational settings. Bringing narrativity to identity thus provides the conceptual sinews that will allow us to produce a tighter, more historically sensitive, coupling between social identity and agency.

Finally, the concepts of narrative identity and relational setting allow us to reconceptualize the subject–object dynamic of modern social theory. This dichotomous dualism is transformed into numerous matrices of patterned relationships, social practices, and institutions mediated not by abstractions but by linkages of political power, social practices, and public narratives. This simultaneously reconceptualizes social agency away from its unitary status of individuation, and towards an understanding of agency constituted within institutions, structures of power, cultural networks, and, more generally, those *others* who are a central analytic dimension (again, not necessarily normative) of that identity. In this view, institutions (however dominating or constraining) are wholly a product of collective practices rather than of external entities. These conceptualizations are themselves premised on the extensive research, across time and space, which already suggests that social identities are constituted by the intricate interweaving of history, narrativity, social knowledge, and relationality, as well as institutional and cultural practices.

NOTES

1 Discussion of collective projects in the establishment of professional identity include Larson (1977) and Abbott (1988a). For the social sciences in particular, see Zald (1991), Collini et al. (1983), Hacking (1990a), and Ross (1991).

2 Abell (1984, 1987), Abbott (1983, 1984, 1988b, 1990, 1992) have been in the vanguard of challenging this exclusion in the domain of methodology. Lloyd (1986) provides an excellent analysis of the development of these binary oppositions in the social sciences. A recent example of defining sociology by its opposition to "merely" writing history can be found in Kiser and Hechter (1991).

3 The term comes from and is elaborated in Somers (1994a).

4 On historians abandoning traditional notions of narrative or even standard notions of history *per se*, see, e.g., Megill (1989, 1991), Novick (1988, 1991), Towes (1987), Eley (forthcoming), Stone (1979b).

5 See especially Ricoeur (1979, 1981, 1984–6). In law and critical race theory see P. Williams (1991), Lawrence (1992), Geertz (1983), J. B. White (1984); Dworkin (1982); in psychology see Hales (1985), Kemper (1984), Bruner (1986, 1987), Sarbin (1986), Gergen and Gergen (1986); in medicine see G. Williams (1984), Keinman (1988); in psychoanalytic theory see Spence (1982), Schafer (1981, 1983); in education see Witherell and Noddings (1991); in philosophy see MacIntyre (1981), Taylor (1989); in gender studies see Violi (1992), Zerilli (1991), Bell and Yalom (1990), Miller (1991), Personal Narratives Group (1989), Maynes (1989), Gordon (1986), Graham et al. (1989); in anthropology see Daniel (1984), Turner and Bruner (1986), Ortner (1991); in physics, Cartwright (1983); in biology, S. J. Gould (1988, 1989).

6 This is beginning to change, e.g., Alexander (1989), Hart (1992), Sewell (1992), Somers (1992), Steinmetz (1992), Harrison White (1992b).

7 Harrison White (1992b) has broken critical ground by bringing narrativity (stories) into the heart of is structural theory of social action, and see also Bearman (1991). Alexander (1988a, 1989) has also theorized the importance of narrative to social action.

8 And despite their radically divergent evaluation of what counts as theory, the same conceptual polarities between narrative and causality are posited in the work of Abbott (1990, 1992) on the one hand, and Kiser and Hechter (1991) on the other.

9 This and the context of discovery were first formalized by Reichenbach (1947).

10 In his introduction to the special section on "Narrative Analysis in Social Science," Sewell (1992: 479) stresses this point in observing the highly unusual "departure [of the topic] from the usual fare of *Social Science History* and from the vision of social-scientifically informed historical study that has dominated the SSHA since its founding a decade and a half ago."

11 See especially Mauss (1985) and, more generally, Carrithers et al. (1985).

12 Attention to identity formation is slowly gaining ground in sociology. Significantly, the two major sources for these developments are both groups of "outsiders" from the discipline who are at once "marginal" to the theorized social actor: (1) women, people of color, ethnic minorities, and more recently, those who feel nationally excluded, see Collins (1990), Laslett (1992), Smith (1987, 1990a, 1990b), and Yeatman (1990) and (2) the "new social movements" in Europe and America whose goals of "identity expression" have been used to distinguish them from more "instrumental" movements, e.g., Aronovitz (1992), Calhoun (1991a, 1991b, 1991c), Cohen (1985), Cohen and Arato (1992), Melucci (1989), Pizzorno (1985), Touraine (1985).

13 Chodorow (1978), Elshtain (1981), Gilligan (1982), MacKinnon (1989), Smith (1987, 1990a, 1990b), and Belenky et al. (1986) are some examples of the reinterpretation of female "difference" into a form of gender identity. The criticism of categorical fixity is of course the animating impulse behind much of feminist, postmodernist, critical race theory, and the "new historicism." Canning (forthcoming), Chartier (1988), Collins (1990, 1992), Davis (1991), Flax (1990a, 1990b), Fraser (1989), Haraway (1991); Laqueur (1990), Lawrence (1992), Nicholson (1990), Scott (1988a, 1988b, 1991), Smith (1987, 1990a, 1990b), Tavris (1992), and P. Williams (1988, 1991) are among the many contributions that have recently shown that racial and sexual categories cannot be conceived as pre-political and/or outside the bounds of social constitution.

14 The next few paragraphs draw upon Somers (1994a).

15 On the myth, see William Townsend (1979[1786]). The potency of the parable was not dependent on its lack of empirical validity. Malthus and Darwin were both inspired by its message – Condorcet passed it on to Malthus, and Malthus to Darwin. Yet both owed the success of their theories in large part to the impact on actual social policy that Townsend's anti-statist *Dissertation* enjoyed. His injunction that "legal constraint is attended with much trouble, violence and noise; creates ill will, and never can be productive of good and acceptable service: whereas hunger is not only peaceable, silent, unremitting pressure, but, [is] the most natural motive to industry and labor [and] lays lasting and sure foundations for good will and gratitude" spurred the repeal of the English Poor Laws which had long supported the poor in periods of unemployment. From this perspective, the true founder of modern social

science was not Adam Smith who still argued for the moral role of political regulation, but this long forgotten figure of Townsend. See K. Polanyi (1944), especially Chapters 7–10 for an important discussion of Townsend. On the discourse of "society," see K. Polanyi (1944: Chapter 10); Bossy (1982); R. Williams (1976: 243–7).

16 This phrase is meant to evoke, but also to escape, the constricting binary, indeed almost Manichean, dichotomy between "theory-laden" versus "empiricist/positivist" conceptions of science and social science that frames the terms of controversy within most social science theory.

17 This conceptualization shares much with Taylor's (1989) "epistemic gain." See also Calhoun (1991b).

18 See Somers (1986, 1994b) for attempts to carry this out.

19 Lieberson (1992) makes a similar point about modern research.

20 Hobbes (1962: 109).

21 The early Durkheim could also be called here the Parsonian Durkheim since Parsons's reading was the most influential introduction and interpretation of his work. More recently Alexander (1988b) has reassessed Durkheim's contributions by focusing on the later writings. Among the most important findings of this reassessment is Durkheim's conclusive break with what we are calling the "revolutionary idiom" and the formulation of a critique of historicist readings of modernity that are among the most influential in today's cultural studies.

22 Alexander (1989: 246) rightly states: "there seems to be abundant evidence that moderns still seek to understand the contingency of everyday life in terms of narrative traditions whose simplicity and resistance to change makes them hard to distinguish from myths."

23 For interesting secondary discussions that bear on this point see Dumont (1977, 1982), Benhabib (1981), Giddens (1977).

24 For discussion of the new identity politics in theories of social movements, see n. 12 above.

25 See also Elshtain (1981), MacKinnon (1989), and Ruddick (1989) for extremely influential versions of feminist identity politics.

26 These criticisms of identity theories are articulated in many different ways and places. Some of the most useful include Flax (1990a, 1990b), Fraser and Nicholson (1990), Haraway (1991), Lemert (1992), Scott (1988a).

27 K. Polanyi (1944) still presents us with the deepest understanding of the discovery of society. See also Collini, Winch, and Burrow (1983) and Block and Somers (1984), Dumont (1982), Carrithers et al. (1985).

28 This view of narrative as methodology was importantly substantiated by the philosophers and historiographers. Hayden White (1981, 1984, 1987) and Mink (1966, 1978) both argued that despite the representational value of narrative, it had to be seen as a superimposed form that analysts/historians placed over the chaos of "reality" to organize it into coherency. See also Danto (1985) for a complex philosophical discussion of the analytic place of narrative in historical analysis. The major exception to this position, and a major influence on the new narrative

approach, is Ricoeur (1979, 1981, 1984–6).

29 For a sampling of the raging debate among philosophers of history in the 1940s through 1960s over these issues, see Hempel (1959[1942], 1965), Dray (1957), Gallie (1968), Atkinson (1978), and Gardiner (1952).

30 Hempel (1959[1942]) of course initiated a major challenge to this in his theories of scientific narrative.

31 See n. 5 above.

32 Cf. especially the "life-stories" scholarship of Bertaux (1981), Bertaux and Kohli (1984), Freeman (1984), Linde (1986), L. Polanyi (1985).

33 This discussion of narrative draws from Somers (1992). For a range of discussions of narrative theory, see Scholes and Kellogg (1966); Genette (1980); Mitchell (1981); Jameson (1981); Brooks (1984); Barthes (1974)[1966].

34 We are happy with Friedland and Alford's (1991: 243) definition of an institution as: "simultaneously material and ideal, systems of signs and symbols, rational and transrational ... supraorganizational patterns of human activity by which individuals and organizations produce and reproduce their material subsistence and organize time and space ... [t]hey are also symbolic systems, ways of ordering reality, and thereby rendering experience of time and space meaningful."

35 This is indeed a different approach to the concept of explanation that the strictest of analytic philosophers of science would accept – causality as a deductive instance of a generalization. Indeed the very strength and utility of the latter is its valid "denarrativization" or abstraction of instances, elements, or events from time and space into categories. See Somers (1994a).

36 For an especially useful empirical application, see Alexander (1989) for the impressive array of narratives that were deployed to explain action on both sides during the Watergate hearings.

37 This is not to endorse the hermeneutic claim that the actor's intentions or self-understanding are a sufficient condition for a sociological explanation of action. We argue only that analyses of actors' own self-stories are a necessary condition.

38 Samples of different approaches to ontological narratives can be found in Sarbin (1986), MacIntyre (1981), Taylor (1989), Bruner (1987), Bell and Yalom (1990), Bertaux and Kohli (1984), Crites (1986), Ferccero (1986), Freeman (1984), Gergen (1973, 1977, 1985), Gergen and Gergen (1986), Didion (1992), Swift (1983).

39 Organizational theory is one area of the social sciences that has used the narrative concept in particularly creative ways. Cf. DiMaggio (1988), Martin et al. (1983), Meyer and Rowan (1977), Meyer and Scott (1983), Mitroff and Killman (1975), Smircich (1983), Zucker (1991).

40 On narrative methodology in sociology and history, see n. 2; cf. Abell (1984, 1987), Abbott (1990, 1992), Brown (1987, 1990), Isaac and Griffin (1989), Griffin (1991), Quadagno and Knapp (1992), Reed (1989), Sewell (forthcoming), Somers (1994a).

41 We are faced with an even greater problem in thinking about explanatory sociological narrative. Indeed in light of their status as the epistemological "other," constructing narratives would seem to be precisely
what we as social scientists do not want to do. Should we not focus
exclusively on explanation? As we argued above in the general discussion
of narrativity, the presumed incompatibility between narrative and
explanation may well be specious. Of course this raises the question of
what counts as an explanation; there are, after all, competing positions
on the validity capacity of different modes of justification. Rather than
argue the nature of and case for explanatory narrativity which has
been done elsewhere and at some length, e.g., Abbott (1990, 1992), Abell
(1984, 1987), Aminzade (1992), Quadagno and Knapp (1992), Somers
(1992, 1994a), let us make the argument that when we say that sociological explanations entail analytic narrativity, that is not the same as
arguing that social science theory is solely narrative. As Alexander (1991:
149) recently argued, it is also a code (Bernstein 1971). Even more
important, to argue the case for explanatory narrativity is not to argue
that there is no qualitative difference between at least the norms of
analytic narrativity, on the one hand, and those of cultural and ontological narrativity, on the other. The latter attain meaning through
internal integrity alone, that is, they are only partially subjected to
external truth criteria. But as Alexander (1991: 149) has also reminded
us, "science differs from other narratives because it commits the success
of its story to the criterion of truth. For every scientific narrative we
are compelled to ask, 'Do we know whether it is true?'" The strength
of explanatory narrativity, however, is that it steps out of the typically
either/or version of "truth" versus "relativism" and uses criteria for
validity that are outside the extremes of "localism" versus foundational
truth. Narrative explanatory analysis, from this perspective, guides us
to construct and to believe in "the best possible account" at the same
time that we know full well that (1) what counts as "best" is itself historical and (2) that these criteria will change and change again. See
Longino (1990), MacIntyre (1973, 1980), Nehamas (1985), and Taylor
(1991).

42 Thus it is not at all surprising that in his recent book, Harrison White
(1992b) has made stories and identity central aspects of his theory of
social action. A useful summary of the structural approach is offered by
Wellman and Berkowitz (1988: 15): "... mainstream sociologists have
tended to think in terms of categories of social actors who share similar
characteristics: 'women,' 'the elderly,' 'blue-collar workers,' 'emerging
nations,' and so on ... this kind of approach has its uses, but it has
misled many sociologists into studying the attributes of aggregated sets
of individuals rather than the structural nature of social systems."

43 Even an isolated "hermit" is a social actor and must thus be made
intelligible through a relational and narrative approach.

44 Calhoun (1991c) gives an example of how identity politics moved Chinese

students in Tienanmen Square to take risks with their lives that cannot be accounted for in rational or value terms.

45 Fantasia's (1988) study of varying cultures of solidarity is one of the best examples of the empirical power of the narrative identity approach over the interest-based one.

46 All of Steedman's writings (1987, 1988, 1990, 1992) could be seen as elaborations on the theme of narrative identity.

47 See also C. Tilly (1984) for the first of his famous "eight pernicious postulates."

48 See also Bourdieu (1984b, 1985) on social space and the genesis of groups.

49 On the epistemological significance of networks and relational analysis over categories in understanding social structures see Harrison White et al. (1976) and White (1992a, 1992b); for applications in historical sociology see R. Gould (1991), Mann (1986), and Bearman (1993).

50 The epistemological implications of recent work in historical geography have been little noted by sociologists. Exceptions include Aminzade (1992), Giddens (1985), Mann (1986), Tilly (1984).

51 An important view of the value of theoretically disaggregating social reality can be found in Bell (1976) and Walzer (1982).

52 See, e.g., Pizzorno (1978, 1985), Melucci (1989).

53 See Alexander (1983).

54 Cohen and Arato (1992) challenge this point effectively.

55 On the concept of provisioning, see Sahlins (1976). And for the importance of provisioning for gender analysis see Fraser and Gordon (1992).

56 See Parkin (1979) for a sociological elaboration of this basic Weberian and anthropological notion.

57 See, e.g., Stack (1974), Vincent (1981), L. Tilly et al. (1976).

58 Ortner calls this "rupturing of narrativity" in her analysis of Eliot Liebow's *Tally's Corner* where she gives a example of how power relations have ruptured the narrative identities – and thus "normal future-oriented" behavior – of urban African-American men (Ortner 1991). See also Haraway (1991) and Lemert (1992) on "fractured identities."

59 This is of course only an analytic distinction; no narrative can be purely one without the other.

60 This is a situation described in detail in Somers (1986). This of course fits much more with Weber's understanding of class as objective market chances divorced from values.

61 See F. M. L. Thompson (1981) and Reid (1978) for a sense of how pervasive the social control thesis was in social history during the 1970s.

62 For examples see Bell (1980), Laqueur (1981), Needham (1978), Beidelman (1980), Burguiere (1982), Bloch and Parry (1982), Moore (1978).

63 See Alexander (1989) on the importance of the sociological classics and the limits to historicism.

64 Scott (1988a) has made this argument most convincingly for the discipline of history.

65 The question of the epistemological place of categories in the context of an overall relational and narrative approach is a major theme of Harrison White (1992b). Calhoun (1991a) discusses categories and relationships by bringing White's "structural equivalence" and "indirect relationships" to the study of nationalism and identity.

66 And see Harrison White's (1992a) response to this criticism of what Brint sees as an overly relational approach to sociology.

REFERENCES

Abbott, Andrew 1983: "Sequences of Social Events," *Historical Methods* 16(4): 129.

Abbott, Andrew 1984: "Event Sequence and Event Duration," *Historical Methods* 17(4): 192.

Abbott, Andrew 1988a: *The System of Professions: An Essay on the Division of Expert Labor*. Chicago: University of Chicago Press.

Abbott, Andrew 1988b: "Transcending General Linear Reality," *Sociological Theory* 6: 169–86.

Abbott, Andrew 1990: "Conceptions of Time and Events in Social Science Methods: Causal and Narrative Approaches," *Historical Methods* 23(4): 140–50.

Abbott, Andrew 1992: "From Causes to Events: Notes on Narrative Positivism," *Sociological Methods and Research*. 20(4): 428–55.

Abell, Peter 1984: "Comparative Narratives," *Journal for the Theory of Social Behavior* 14: 309–31.

Abell, Peter 1987: *The Syntax of Social Life*. Oxford: Oxford University Press.

Abrams, Philip 1980: "History, Sociology, Historical Sociology," *Past and Present* 87: 7.

Abrams, Philip 1982: *Historical Sociology*. Ithaca, NY: Cornell University Press.

Alexander, Jeffrey C. 1982: *Positivism, Presuppositions, and Current Controversies*, vol. 1 of *Theoretical Logic in Sociology*. Berkeley and Los Angeles: University of California Press.

Alexander, Jeffrey C. 1983: *The Classical Attempt at Theoretical Synthesis: Max Weber*, vol. 3 of *Theoretical Logic in Sociology*. Berkeley and Los Angeles: University of California Press.

Alexander, Jeffrey C. 1988a: *Action and Its Environment: Towards a New Synthesis*. New York: Columbia University Press.

Alexander, Jeffrey C. 1988b: *Durkheimian Sociology: Cultural Studies*. Cambridge: Cambridge University Press.

Alexander, Jeffrey C. 1989: *Structure and Meaning: Rethinking Classical Sociology*. New York: Columbia University Press.

Alexander, Jeffrey C. 1991: "Sociological Theory and the Claim to Reason: Why the End is Not in Sight," *Sociological Theory* 9(2): 147–53.

Aminzade, Ron. 1992: "Historical Sociology and Time," *Sociological Methods and Research* 20(4): 456–80.

Aronowitz, Stanley 1992: *The Politics of Identity: Class, Culture, Social Move-*

ments. New York: Routledge, Chapman and Hall, Inc.

Asante, Molefi Kete 1987: *The Afrocentric Idea*. Philadelphia: Temple University Press.

Atkinson, R. F. 1978: *Knowledge and Explanation in History: An Introduction to the Philosophy of History*. Ithaca, NY: Cornell University Press.

Barthes, Roland 1974 (1966): "Introduction to the Structural Analysis of the Narrative," Occasional Paper, Centre for Contemporary Cultural Studies, University of Birmingham, tr. Richard Miller. New York: Hill and Wang.

Bearman, Peter 1991: "The Social Structure of Suicide," *Sociological Forum* 5 (September).

Bearman, Peter 1993: *Relations into Rhetorics*. New Brunswick, NJ: Rutgers University Press.

Beidelman, T. O. 1980: "The Moral Imagination of the Kaguru: Some Thoughts on Tricksters, Translation, and Comparative Analysis," *American Ethnologist* 7(1): 27–42.

Belenky, Mary F., Blythe M. Clinchy, Nancy R. Goldberger, and Jill M. Tarule 1986: *Women's Ways of Knowing: The Development of Self, Voice, and Mind*. New York: Basic Books.

Bell, Daniel 1976: "The Disjuncture of Realms: A Statement of Themes," in *The Cultural Contradictions of Capitalism*. New York: Basic Books.

Bell, Daniel 1980: "The Return of the Scared?," *The Winding Passage*. New York: Basic Books.

Bell, Susan Groag and Marilyn Yalom, eds 1990: *Revealing Lives: Autobiography, Biography, and Gender*. Albany: State University of New York Press.

Benhabib, Seyla 1981: "Rationality and Social Action: Critical Reflections on Weber's Methodological Writings," *The Philosophical Forum* 12(4): 356–74.

Berg, Maxine 1987: "Women's Work, Mechanisation and the Early Phases of Industrialisation in England," in *The Historical Meanings of Work*, ed. Patrick Joyce. Cambridge: Cambridge University Press, pp. 64–98.

Bernstein, Basil 1971: *Class, Codes, and Control*. New York: Schocken.

Bertaux, Daniel 1981: *Biography and Society*. Beverly Hills: Sage.

Bertaux, Daniel and Martin Kohli 1984: "The Life Story Approach: A Continental View," *Annual Review of Sociology* 10: 215–37.

Bloch, Maurice and Jonathon Parry, eds 1982: *Death and the Regeneration of Life*. Cambridge: Cambridge University Press.

Block, Fred and Margaret Somers 1984: "Beyond the Economistic Fallacy: The Holistic Social Science of Karl Polanyi," in *Vision and Method in Historical Sociology*, ed. Theda Skocpol. New York: Cambridge University Press, pp. 47–84.

Bossy, John 1982: "Some Elementary Forms of Durkheim," *Past and Present* 95.

Bourdieu, Pierre 1977: *An Outline of a Theory of Practice*, tr. Richard Nice. New York: Cambridge University Press.

Bourdieu, Pierre 1984a: *Distinction*. Cambridge, MA: Harvard University Press.

Bourdieu, Pierre 1984b: "The Habitus and the Space of Life-Styles," in *Distinction*.

Bourdieu, Pierre 1985: "Social Space and the Genesis of Groups," *Theory and Society* 14: 723–44.

Bourdieu, Pierre 1990: *The Logic of Practice*. Stanford: Stanford University Press.

Brint, Steven 1992: "Hidden Meanings: Cultural Content and Context in Harrison White's Structural Sociology," *Sociological Theory* 10(2): 194–207.

Brooks, Peter 1984: *Reading for the Plot: Design and Intention in Narrative*. New York: Alfred A. Knopf.

Brown, Richard Harvey 1987: "Positivism, Relativism, and Narrative in the Logic of the Historical Sciences," *American Historical Review* 92(4): 908–20.

Brown, Richard Harvey 1990: "Rhetoric, Textuality, and the Postmodern Turn in Sociological Theory," *Sociological Theory* 8(2): 188–97.

Bruner, Jerome 1986: *Actual Minds, Possible Worlds*. Cambridge, MA: Harvard University Press.

Bruner, Jerome 1987: "Life as Narrative," *Social Research* 54(1): 11–32.

Burguiere, Andre 1982: "The Fate of the History of Mentalities in the *Annales*," *Comparative Studies in Society and History* 24(3): 424–37.

Calhoun, Craig J. 1980: "Community: Toward a Variable Conceptualization for Comparative Research," *Social History* 5: 105–29.

Calhoun, Craig J. 1991a: "Imagined Communities and Indirect Relationships: Large-Scale Social Integration and the Transformation of Everyday Life," in *Social Theory for a Changing Society*, ed. Pierre Bourdieu and James S. Coleman. Boulder, CO: Westview Press, and New York: Russell Sage Foundation, pp. 95–120.

Calhoun, Craig J. 1991b: "Morality, Identity, and Historical Explanation: Charles Taylor on the Sources of the Self," *Sociological Theory* 9(2): 232–63.

Calhoun, Craig J. 1991c: "The Problem of Identity in Collective Action," in *Macro–Micro Linkages in Sociology*. Beverly Hills, CA: Sage, pp. 51–75.

Canning, Kathleen (forthcoming): "Contesting the Power of Categories: Discourse, Experience, and Feminist Resistance," *Signs*.

Carr, David 1985: "Life and the Narrator's Art," in *Hermeneutics and Deconstruction*, ed. Hugh J. Silverman and Don Idhe. Albany: State University of New York Press, pp. 108–21.

Carr, David 1986: "Narrative and the Real World," *History and Theory* 25(2): 117–31.

Carrithers, Michael, Steven Collins, and Steven Lukes, eds 1985: *The Category of the Person: Anthropology, Philosophy, History*. Cambridge: Cambridge University Press.

Cartwright, Nancy 1983: *How the Laws of Physics Lie*. Oxford: Clarendon Press.

Chartier, Roger 1988: *Cultural History: Between Practices and Representations*, tr. Lydia G. Chochrane. Princeton, NJ: Princeton University Press.

Chodorow, Nancy 1978: *The Reproduction of Mothering*. Berkeley: University of California Press.

Cohen, Jean L. 1985: "Strategy or Identity: New Theoretical Paradigms and Contemporary Social Movements," *Social Research* 52: 663–716.

Cohen, Jean L. and Andrew Arato 1992: *Civil Society and Political Theory*. Cambridge, MA: MIT Press.

Coleman, James 1990: *Foundations of Social Theory*. Cambridge, MA: Harvard University Press.

Collingwood, Robin G. 1970 (1939): *An Autobiography*. Oxford: Oxford University Press.

Collini, Stefan, Donald Winch, and J. W. Burrow, eds 1983: *That Noble Science of Politics: A Study in Nineteenth Century Intellectual History*. Cambridge: Cambridge University Press.

Collins, Patricia Hill 1990: *Black Feminist Thought: Knowledge, Consciousness, and the Politics of Empowerment*. Boston: Unwin Hyman.

Collins, Patricia Hill 1992: "Transforming the Inner Circle: Dorothy Smith's Challenge to Sociological Theory," *Sociological Theory*: 73–80.

Connolly, William E. 1992a: *Identity/Difference: Democratic Negotiations of Political Paradox*. Ithaca, NY: Cornell University Press.

Connolly, William E. 1992b: "The Irony of Interpretation," in *The Politics of Irony*, ed. D. Conway and John Seery. New York: St Martin's Press, pp. 119–50.

Crites, Stephen 1986: "Storytime: Recollecting the Past and Projecting the Future," in *Narrative Psychology: The Storied Nature of Human Conduct*, ed. Theodore R. Sarbin. New York: Praeger, pp. 152–73.

Daniel, E. Valentine 1984: *Fluid Signs: Being a Person the Tamil Way*. Berkeley: University of California Press.

Danto, Arthur C. 1985: *Narration and Knowledge: Including the Integral Text of Analytical Philosophy of History*. New York: Columbia University Press.

Davis, F. James 1991: *Who is Black? One Nation's Definition*. Philadelphia: Pennsylvania State University.

Di Stefano, Christine 1990: "Dilemmas of Difference: Feminism, Modernity, and Postmodernism," in *Feminism/Postmodernism*, ed. Linda J. Nicholson. New York and London: Routledge, pp. 63–82.

Didion, Joan 1992: *After Henry*. New York: Simon & Schuster.

DiMaggio, Paul 1988: "Interest and Agency in Institutional Theory," in *Institutional Patterns and Organization: Culture and Environment*, ed. Lynn G. Zucker. Cambridge, MA: Ballinger, pp. 3–22.

Dray, William H. 1957: *Laws and Explanations in History*. London: Oxford University Press.

Dumont, Louis 1977: *From Mandeville to Marx*. Chicago: University of Chicago Press.

Dumont, Louis 1982: *Essays on Individualism*. Chicago: University of Chicago Press.

Dworkin, Ronald 1982: *The Politics of Interpretation*. Chicago. University of Chicago Press.

Eley, Geoff (forthcoming): "Is All the World a Text? From Sociological History to the History of Society Two Decades Later," in *The Historic Turn in the Human Sciences*, ed. Terrence J. McDonald. Ann Arbor: University of Michigan Press.

Elshtain, Jean 1981: *Public Man, Private Woman: Women in Social and Political Thought*. Princeton: Princeton University Press.

Fantasia, Rick 1988: *Cultures of Solidarity*. Berkeley and Los Angeles: University of California Press.

Ferccero, John 1986: "Autobiography and Narrative," in *Reconstructing Individualism: Autonomy, Individuality, and the Self in Western Thought*, ed. Thomas C. Heller, Morton Sosna, and David E. Wellbery. Stanford, CA: Stanford University Press, pp. 16–29.

Flax, Jane 1990a: "Postmodernism and Gender Relations in Feminist Theory," in *Feminism/Postmodernism*, ed. Linda Nicholson. New York and London: Routledge, pp. 39–62.

Flax, Jane 1990b: *Thinking Fragments: Psychoanalysis, Feminism, and Postmodernism in the Contemporary West*. Berkeley and Los Angeles: University of California Press.

Foucault, Michel 1972: *An Archaeology of Knowledge*, tr. Alan Sheridan. New York: Pantheon.

Foucault, Michel 1973 (1970): *The Order of Things: An Archaeology of the Human Sciences*. New York: Vintage.

Fraser, Nancy 1989: *Unruly Practices: Power, Discourse, and Gender in Contemporary Social Theory*. Minneapolis: University of Minnesota Press.

Fraser, Nancy and Linda Gordon 1992: "Contract versus Charity, Participation and Provision: A Reconsideration of Social Citizenship," paper presented at the University of Michigan.

Fraser, Nancy and Linda J. Nicholson 1990: "Social Criticism without Philosophy: An Encounter between Feminism and Postmodernism," in *Feminism/Postmodernism*, ed. Linda J. Nicholson. New York and London: Routledge, pp. 19–38.

Freeman, Mark 1984: "History, Narrative, and Life-Span Developmental Knowledge," *Human Development* 27: 1–19.

Friedland, Roger and Robert R. Alford 1991: "Bringing Society Back In: Symbols, Practices, and Institutional Contradictions," in *The New Institutionalism in Organizational Analysis*, ed. Walter W. Powell and Paul J. DiMaggio. Chicago: University of Chicago Press, pp. 232–63.

Gadamer, Hans George 1989: *Truth and Method*. New York: Continuum.

Gagnier, Regenia 1991: *Subjectivities: A History of Self-Representation in Britain, 1832–1920*. New York: Oxford University Press.

Gallie, W. B. 1968: *Philosophy and the Historical Understanding*. New York: Schocken Books.

Gardiner, Patrick 1952: *The Nature of Historical Explanation*. Oxford: Clarendon Press.

Geertz, Clifford 1983: "Local Knowledge: Fact and Law in Comparative Perspective," in Clifford Geertz, *Local Knowledge*. New York: Basic Books.

Genette, Gerard 1980: *Narrative Discourse: An Essay in Method*, tr. Jane E. Lewin. Ithaca, NY: Cornell University Press.

Gergen, Kenneth J. 1973: "Social Psychology as History," *Journal of Personality and Social Psychology* 26: 309–20.

Gergen, Kenneth J. 1977: "Stability, Change, and Chance in Understanding Human Development," in *Life-Span Development Psychology: Dialectical Perspectives in Experimental Research*, ed. Nancy Datan and Wayne W. Reese. New York: Academic Press.

Gergen, Kenneth J. 1985: "The Social Constructionist Movement in Modern Psychology," *American Psychologist* 40: 266–75.

Gergen, Kenneth J. and Mary M. Gergen 1986: "Narrative Form and the Construction of Psychological Science," in *Narrative Psychology: The Storied Nature of Human Conduct*, ed. Theodore R. Sarbin. New York: Praeger, pp. 22–44.

Giddens, Anthony 1977: "The 'Individual' in Writings of Emile Durkheim," in *Studies in Social and Political Theory*. New York: Basic Books.

Giddens, Anthony 1985: *The Constitution of Society: Outline of the Theory of Structuration*. Cambridge: Polity Press; Berkeley: University of California Press.

Gilligan, Carol 1982: *In a Different Voice: Psychological Theory and Women's Development*. Cambridge, MA: Harvard University Press.

Gordon, Linda 1986: "What's New in Women's History," in *Feminist Studies/Critical Studies*, ed. Teresa de Lauretis. Bloomington: Indiana University Press.

Gould, Roger V. 1991: "Multiple Networks and Mobilization in the Paris Commune, 1871," *American Sociological Review* 56(6): 716–28.

Gould, Stephen Jay 1988: "Mighty Manchester," *New York Review of Books*, October 27.

Gould, Stephen Jay 1989: *Wonderful Life: The Burgess Shale and the Nature of History*. New York and London: W. W. Norton.

Graham, Elspeth, Hilary Hinds, Elaine Hobby, and Helen Wilcox, eds 1989: *Her Own Life: Autobiographical Writings by Seventeenth-Century Englishwomen*. London: Routledge.

Griffin, Larry J. 1991: "Narrative, Event Structure Analysis, and Causal Interpretation in Historical Sociology," paper presented at the Social Science History Association meeting, New Orleans, November.

Habermas, Jürgen 1979: *Communications and the Evolution of Society*. Boston: Beacon Press.

Habermas, Jürgen 1984: *Theory of Communicative Action*, vol. I of *Reason and the Rationalization of Society*, tr. Thomas McCarthy. Boston: Beacon Press.

Hacking, Ian 1984: "Five Parables," in *Philosophy in History*, ed. Richard Rorty, J. B. Schneewind, and Quentin Skinner. Cambridge: Cambridge University Press, pp. 103–24.

Hacking, Ian 1990a: *The Taming of Chance*. Cambridge: Cambridge University Press.

Hacking, Ian 1990b: "Two Kinds of 'New Historicism' for Philosophers," *New Literary History*, 21: 343–64.

Halbwachs, Maurice 1980 (1950): *The Collective Memory*. New York: Harper & Row.

Hales, Susan 1985: "The Inadvertent Rediscovery of Self in Social Psychology," *Journal for the Theory of Social Behavior* 15 (October): 237–82.

Haraway, Donna 1991: *Simians, Cyborgs, and Women: The Reinvention of Nature*. New York and London: Routledge.

Hart, Janet 1992: "Cracking the Code: Allegory and Political Mobilization in the Greek Resistance," *Social Science History* 16(4).

Hawthorne, Geoffrey 1976: *Enlightenment and Despair*. London: Cambridge University Press.

Hempel, Carl. G. 1959 (1942): "The Function of General Laws in History," reprinted in *Theories of History*, ed. Patrick Gardiner. New York: Free Press.

Hempel, Carl. G. 1965: "Aspects of Scientific Explanation," in *Aspects of Scientific Explanation*. New York: Free Press.

Hobbes, Thomas 1962: "Philosophical Rudiments Concerning Government and Society," in *The English Works of Thomas Hobbes*, vol. II, ed. Sir William Molesworth. London and Aalen: Scientia Verlag.

Hoggart, Richard 1959: *The Uses of Literacy*. Harmondsworth: Penguin.

hooks, bell 1984: *From Margin to Center*. Boston: South End Press.

Isaac, Larry W. and Larry J. Griffin 1989: "Ahistoricism in Time-Series Analyses of Historical Processes," *American Sociological Review* 54: 873–90.

Jameson, Fredric 1981: *The Political Unconscious: Narrative as a Socially Symbolic Act*. Ithaca, NY: Cornell University Press.

Jordan, June 1981: *Civil Wars*. Boston: Beacon.

Joyce, Patrick, ed. 1987: *The Historical Meanings of Work*. Cambridge: Cambridge University Press.

Joyce, Patrick 1991: *Visions of the People: Industrial England and the Question of Class, 1848–1941*. Cambridge: Cambridge University Press.

Kemper, Susan 1984: "The Development of Narrative Skills: Explanations and Entertainments," in *Discourse Development: Progress in Cognitive Development Research*, ed. Stan A. Kuczaj II. New York: Springer-Verlag, pp. 99–124.

Kermode, Frank 1984: "Secrets and Narrative Sequence," in *On Narrative*, ed. W. J. T. Mitchell. Chicago: University of Chicago Press.

Kiser, Edgar and Michael Hechter 1991: "The Role of General Theory in Comparative-Historical Sociology," *American Journal of Sociology* 97: 1–30.

Kleinman, Arthur 1988: *The Illness Narratives*. New York: Basic Books.

Lamont, Michele 1992: *Money, Morals, and Manners: The Culture of the French and American Upper-Middle Class*. Chicago: University of Chicago Press.

Laqueur, Thomas 1981: "Bodies, Death, and Pauper Funerals," *Representations* 1(1): 109–31.

Laqueur, Thomas 1990: *Making Sex: Body and Gender from the Greeks to Freud*. Cambridge, MA: Harvard University Press.

Larson, Magali Sarfatti 1977: *The Rise of Professionalism: A Socioligical Analysis*. Berkeley: University of California Press.

Laslett, Barbara 1992: "Thinking about the Subject," Newsletter of the Comparative and Historical Sociology Section of the American Sociological Association, vol. 5.

Lawrence, Charles R., III 1992: "The Word and the River: Pedagogy as Scholarship as Struggle," *Southern California Law Review*. 65(5): 2231–98.

Lemert, Charles 1992: "Subjectivity's Limit: The Unsolved Riddle of the Standpoint," *Sociological Theory*: 63–72.

Lieberson, Stanley 1992: "Einstein, Renoir, and Greeley. Some Thoughts about Evidence in Sociology," *American Sociological Review* 57(1): 1–15.

Linde, Charlotte 1986: "Private Stories in Public Discourse: Narrative Analysis in the Social Sciences," *Poetics* 15: 183–202.

Lloyd, Christopher 1986: *Explanation in Social History*. New York: Basil Blackwell.

Longino, Helen 1990: *Science as Social Knowledge*. Princeton, NJ: Princeton University Press.

Lorde, Audre 1984: *Sister Outsider*. Trumansberg, NY: The Crossing Press.

Lyotard, J. F. 1984: *The Post-Modern Condition: A Report on Knowledge*. Minneapolis: University of Minnesota Press.

MacIntyre, Alasdair 1973: "The Essential Contestability of Some Social Concepts," *Ethics* 1.

MacIntyre, Alasdair 1980: "Epistemological Crises, Dramatic Narrative, and the Philosophy of Science," in *Paradigms and Revolutions*, ed. Gary Gutting. Notre Dame: University of Notre Dame Press, pp. 54–74.

MacIntyre, Alasdair 1981: *After Virtue: A Study in Moral Theory*. Notre Dame: University of Notre Dame Press.

MacKinnon, Catharine 1989: *Toward a Feminist Theory of State*. Cambridge, MA: Harvard University Press.

McNall, Scott, Rhonda Levine, and Rick Fantasia, eds 1991: *Bringing Class Back In: Contemporary and Historical Perspectives*. Boulder, CO: Westview Press.

Mann, Michael 1986: "The Origins of Social Power," in *A History of Power From the Beginning to A.D. 1760*, vol. I. Cambridge: Cambridge University Press.

March, G. James and Johan P. Olsen 1984: "The New Institutionalism: Organizational Factors in Political Life," *American Political Science Review* 78(3): 734–49.

Marshall, T. H. 1964 (1949): "Citizenship and Social Class," in *Class, Citizenship, and Social Development: Essays by T. H. Marshall*. New York: Doubleday, pp. 65–123.

Martin, Joanne, Martha S. Feldman, Mary Jo Hatch, and Sim B. Sim 1983: "The Uniqueness Paradox in Organizational Stories," *Administrative Science Quarterly* 38: 438–53.

Marx, Karl 1978 (1852): "The Eighteenth Brumaire of Louis Bonaparte," in *The Marx-Engels Reader*, 2nd edn, ed. Robert C. Tucker. New York: W. W. Norton.

Mauss, Marcel 1985: "A Category of the Human Mind: The Notion of Person; the Notion of Self," in *The Category of the Person*, ed. Michael Carrithers, Steven Collins, and Steven Lukes, tr. W. D. Halls. Cambridge: Cambridge University Press, pp. 1–25.

Maynes, Mary Jo 1989: "Gender and Narrative Form in French and German Working-Class Autobiographies," in *Interpreting Women's Lives: Feminist Theory and Personal Narratives*, ed. Personal Narratives Group. Bloomington: University of Indiana Press, pp. 103–17.

Megill, Allan 1989: "Recounting the Past: 'Description,' Explanation, and Narrative in Historiography," *American Historical Review* 94(3): 627–53.

Megill, Allan 1991: "Fragmentation and the Future of Historiography," *American Historical Review* 96 (June).

Melucci, Alberto 1989: *Nomads of the Present: Social Movements and Individual Needs in Contemporary Society*. Philadelphia: Temple University Press.

Meyer, John W. and Brian Rowan 1977: "Institutionalized Organizations: Formal Structure as Myth and Ceremony," *American Journal of Sociology* 83: 340–63.

Meyer, John W. and John Scott 1983: *Organizational Environments: Ritual and Rationality*. Beverly Hills, CA: Sage.

Miller, Nancy K. 1991: *Getting Personal: Feminist Occasions and Other Autobiographical Acts*. New York: Routledge.

Mink, Louis O. 1966: "The Autonomy of Historical Understanding," in *Philosophical Analysis and History*, ed. William H. Dray. New York: Harper & Row, pp. 160–92.

Mink, Louis O. 1978: "Narrative Form as a Cognitive Instrument," in *New Directions in Literary History*, ed. Ralph Cohen. Baltimore: Johns Hopkins University Press, pp. 107–24.

Minow, Martha 1987: "Foreword: Justice Engendered," 101 *Harvard Law Review* 10.

Minow, Martha 1990: *Making All the Difference: Inclusion, Exclusion, and American Law*. Ithaca, NY: Cornell University Press.

Mitchell, W. J. T., ed. 1981: *Recent Theories of Narrative*. Chicago: Chicago University Press.

Mitroff, Ian and R. H. Killman 1975: "Stories Managers Tell: A New Tool for Organizational Problem Solving," *Management Review* 64: 18–28.

Moore, Barrington, Jr 1978: *Injustice: The Sources of Obedience and Revolt*. Cambridge, MA: Harvard University Press.

Needham, Rodney 1978: *Primordial Characters*. Charlottesville: University of Virginia Press.

Nehamas, Alexander 1985: *Nietzsche: Life as Literature*. Cambridge, MA: Harvard University Press.

Nicholson, Linda, ed. 1990: *Feminism/Postmodernism*. New York: Routledge.

Novick, Peter 1988: *That Noble Dream: The "Objectivity Question" and the*

American Historical Profession. Cambridge: Cambridge University Press.

Novick, Peter 1991: "My Correct Views on Everything," *American Historical Review* 96.

Ortner, Sherry 1991: "Narrativity in History, Culture, and Lives." CSST Working Paper no. 66, University of Michigan.

Parkin, Frank 1979: *Marxism and Class Theory: A Bourgeois Critique*. New York: Columbia University Press.

Personal Narratives Group, ed. 1989: *Interpreting Women's Lives: Feminist Theory and Personal Narratives*. Bloomington: University of Indiana Press.

Pizzorno, Alessandro 1978: "Political Exchange and Collective Identity in Industrial Conflict," in *The Resurgence of Class Conflict in Western Europe Since 1968*, ed. C. Crouch and A. Pizzorno. London: Macmillan, pp. 277–98.

Pizzorno, Alessandro 1985: "On the Rationality of Democratic Choice," *Telos* 63: 41–69.

Polanyi, Karl 1944: *The Great Transformation*. New York: Rinehart & Co.

Polanyi, Karl 1977: *The Livelihood of Man*, ed. Harry W. Pearson. New York: Academic Press.

Polanyi, Livia 1985: *Telling the American Story*. Norwood, NJ: Ablex Publishing.

Polkinghorne, Donald 1988: *Narrative Knowing and the Human Sciences*. Albany: State University of New York Press.

Poovey, Mary 1988: *Uneven Developments*. Chicago: University of Chicago Press.

Powell, Walter W. and Paul J. DiMaggio, eds 1991: *The New Institutionalism in Organizational Analysis*. Chicago: University of Chicago Press.

Putnam, Hilary 1975: "The Meaning of Meaning," in *Mind, Language and Reality: Philosophical Papers*, vol. 2. Cambridge: Cambridge University Press.

Quadagno, Jill and Stan J. Knapp 1992: "Have Historical Sociologists Forsaken Theory? Thoughts on the History/Theory Relationship," *Sociological Methods and Research* 20(4): 481–507.

Reddy, William M. 1987: *Money and Liberty in Modern Europe: A Critique of Historical Understanding*. Cambridge: Cambridge University Press.

Reed, John Shelton 1989: "On Narrative and Sociology," *Social Forces* 68(1): 1–14.

Reichenbach, Hans 1947: *Elements of Symbolic Logic*. New York: Macmillan.

Reid, Alistair 1978: "Politics and Economics in the Formation of the British Working Class: A Response to H. F. Moorhouse," *Social History* 3(3): 347–61.

Ricoeur, Paul 1979: "The Human Experience of Time and Narrative," *Research in Phenomenology* 9: 25.

Ricoeur, Paul 1981: "Narrative Time," in *On Narrative*, ed. W. J. T. Mitchell. Chicago: University of Chicago Press, pp. 165–86.

Ricoeur, Paul 1984–6: *Time and Narrative*, 2 vols, tr. Kathleen McLaughlin and David Pellauer. Chicago: University of Chicago Press.

Ross, Dorothy 1991: *The Origin of American Social Science*. New York: Cambridge University Press.

Ruddick, Sara 1989: *Maternal Thinking: Toward a Politics of Peace*. New York: Ballantine Books.

Sahlins, Marshall 1976: *Culture and Practical Reason*. Chicago: University of Chicago Press.

Sandel, Michael 1982: *Liberalism and the Limits to Justice*. Cambridge: Cambridge University Press.

Sarbin, Theodore R., ed. 1986: *Narrative Psychology: The Storied Nature of Human Conduct*. New York: Praeger.

Schafer, Roy 1981: "Narration in the Psychoanalytical Dialogue," in *On Narrative*, ed. W. J. T. Mitchell. Chicago: University of Chicago Press, pp. 25–49.

Schafer, Roy 1983: *The Analytic Attitude*. New York: Basic Books.

Scholes, Robert and Robert Kellogg 1966: *The Nature of Narrative*. London: Oxford University Press.

Scott, Joan Wallach 1988a: *Gender and the Politics of History*. New York: Columbia University Press.

Scott, Joan Wallach 1988b: "On Language, Gender, and Working-Class History," in *Gender and the Politics of History*, pp. 53–67.

Scott, Joan Wallach 1991: "The Evidence of Experience," *Critical Inquiry* 17(3): 770.

Seabrook, Jeremy 1982: *Working Class Childhood*. London: Gollancz.

Seidman, Steven 1991: "The End of Sociological Theory: The Postmodern Hope," *Sociological Theory* 9(2): 131–46.

Sewell, William H. Jr 1986: "Theory of Action, Dialectics and History: Comment on Coleman," *American Journal of Sociology* 43: 166–72.

Sewell, William H. Jr 1992: "Introduction: Narratives and Social Identities," *Social Science History* 16(3): 479–88.

Sewell, William H., Jr forthcoming: "Three Temporalities: Toward a Sociology of the Event," in *The Historic Turn in the Human Sciences*, ed. Terrence J. McDonald. Ann Arbor: University of Michigan Press.

Shively, JoEllen 1992: "Perceptions of Western Films among American Indians and Anglos," *American Sociological Review* 57(6): 725–34.

Smelser, Neil. 1959: *Social Change in the Industrial Revolution*. Chicago: University of Chicago Press.

Smircich, Linda 1983: "Concepts of Culture and Organizational Analysis," *Administrative Science Quarterly* 28: 339–58.

Smith, Dorothy E. 1987: *The Everyday World as Problematic: A Feminist Sociology*. Boston: Northeastern University Press.

Smith, Dorothy E. 1990a: *Texts, Facts, and Femininity: Exploring the Relations of Ruling*. London and New York: Routledge.

Smith, Dorothy E. 1990b: *The Conceptual Practices of Power: A Feminist Sociology of Knowledge*. Boston: Northeastern University Press.

Somers, Margaret R. 1986: *The People and the Law: Narrative Identity and the Place of the Public Sphere in the Formation of English Working Class Politics, 1300–1850: A Comparative Analysis*. Ph.D. Dissertation, Harvard University.

Somers, Margaret R. 1992: "Narrativity, Narrative Identity, and Social Action: Rethinking English Working-Class Formation," *Social Science History* 16(4).

Somers, Margaret R. 1993: "Citizenship and the Place of the Public Sphere: Law, Community, and Political Culture in the Transition to Democracy," *American Sociological Review* 58(5): 587–620.

Somers, Margaret R. 1994a: "Where is Sociology after the Historic Turn? Knowledge Cultures and Historical Epistemologies," in *The Historic Turn in the Human Sciences*, ed. Terrence J. McDonald. Ann Arbor: University of Michigan Press.

Somers, Margaret R. 1994b: "Property, Law, and the Public Sphere in the Formation of Modern Citizenship Rights," in *Early Modern Conceptions of Property*, ed. John Brewer. London and New York: Routledge.

Sonenscher, Michael 1987: "Mythical Work: Workshop Production and the *Compagnonnages* of Eighteenth-Century France," in *The Historical Meanings of Work*, ed. Patrick Joyce. Cambridge: Cambridge University Press, pp. 31–63.

Spence, Donald P. 1982: *Narrative Truth and Historical Truth: Meaning and Interpretation in Psychoanalysis*. New York: W. W. Norton.

Stack, Carol B. 1974: *All Our Kin*. New York: Harper and Row.

Steedman, Carolyn 1987: *Landscape for a Good Woman: A Story of Two Lives*. New Brunswick, NJ: Rutgers University Press.

Steedman, Carolyn 1988: *The Radical Soldier's Tale: John Pearman, 1819–1908*. London and New York: Routledge.

Steedman, Carolyn 1990: *Childhood, Culture, and Class in Britain: Margaret McMillan, 1860–1931*. New Brunswick, NJ: Rutgers University Press.

Steedman, Carolyn 1992: *Past Tenses: Essays on Writing. Autobiography and History*. London: Rivers Oram Press.

Steinmetz, George 1992: "Reflections on the Role of Social Narratives in Working-Class Formation: Narrative Theory in the Social Sciences," *Social Science History* 16(3): 489–516.

Stone, Lawrence 1979a: "Death," in *The Past and the Present*. Boston and London: Routledge & Kegan Paul, pp. 242–59.

Stone, Lawrence 1979b: "The Revival of Narrative: Reflections on an Old New History," *Past and Present* 85: 3–25.

Swift, Graham 1983: *Waterland*. New York: Washington Square Press.

Tavris, Carol 1992: *The Mismeasure of Woman*. New York: Simon & Schuster.

Taylor, Charles 1989: *Sources of the Self*. Cambridge, MA: Harvard University Press.

Taylor, Charles 1991: "Overcoming Epistemology," in *After Philosophy: End or Transformation?* ed. Kenneth Baynes, James Bohman, and Thomas McCarthy. Cambridge, MA: MIT Press, pp. 464–88.

Thompson, E. P. 1971: "The Moral Economy of the English Crowd," *Past and Present* 50: 77–136.

Thompson, F. M. L. 1981: "Social Control in Victorian Britain," *Economic History Review*, 2nd series, 34(2): 189–208.

Tilly, Charles 1984: *Big Structures, Large Processes, Huge Comparisons.* New York: Russell Sage Foundation.

Tilly, Louise, J. W. Scott, and M. Cohen 1976: "Women's Work and European Fertility Patterns," *Journal of Interdisciplinary History* 6: 447–76.

Touraine, Alain 1985: "An Introduction to the Study of Social Movements," *Social Research* 52(4): 749–87.

Towes, John E. 1987: "Intellectual History after the Linguistic Turn: The Autonomy of Meaning and the Irreducibility of Experience," *American Historical Review.* 92(4): 879–907.

Townsend, William 1979 (1786): *Dissertation on the Poor Laws 1786 by a Well-Wisher of Mankind.* Berkeley and Los Angeles: University of California Press.

Turner, Victor W. and Edward M. Bruner, eds 1986: *The Anthropology of Experience.* Urbana: University of Illinois Press.

Veyne, Paul 1984 (1971): *Writing History: Essay of Epistemology,* tr. Mina Moore-Rinvolucri. Middletown, CT: Wesleyan University Press.

Vincent, David 1981: *Bread, Knowledge and Freedom: A Study of Nineteenth-Century Working Class Autobiography.* London: Europa Publications.

Violi, Patrizia 1992: "Gender, Subjectivity and Language," in *Beyond Equality and Difference: Citizenship, Feminist Politics and Female Subjectivity,* ed. Gisela Bock and Susan James. New York and London: Routledge, pp. 164–76.

Walzer, Michael 1982: *Spheres of Justice.* New York: Basic Books.

Wellman, Barry and S. D. Berkowitz 1988: *Social Structures: A Network Approach.* Cambridge: Cambridge University Press.

White, Harrison C. 1992a: "A Social Grammar for Culture: Reply to Steven Brint," *Sociological Theory* 10(2): 209–13.

White, Harrison C. 1992b: *Identity and Control: A Structural Theory of Social Action.* Princeton, NJ: Princeton University Press.

White, Harrison C., Scott A. Boorman, and Ronald L. Breiger 1976: "Social Structure from Multiple Networks, I. Blockmodels of Roles and Positions," *American Journal of Sociology* 81(4): 730–80.

White, Hayden 1981: "The Value of Narrativity in the Representation of Reality," in *On Narrative,* ed. W. J. T. Mitchell. Chicago: University of Chicago Press, pp. 1–23.

White, Hayden 1984: "The Question of Narrative in Contemporary Historical Theory," *History and Theory* 23: 1–33.

White, Hayden 1987: *The Content of the Form.* Baltimore: Johns Hopkins University Press.

White, James Boyd 1984: *When Words Lose Their Meaning: Constitutions and Reconstitutions of Language, Character, and Community.* Chicago: University of Chicago Press.

Williams, Gareth 1984: "The Genesis of Chronic Illness: Narrative Reconstruction," *Sociology of Health and Illness* 6: 175–200.

Williams, Patricia J. 1988: "On Being the Object of Property," *Signs* 14(5).

Williams, Patricia J. 1991: *The Alchemy of Race and Rights*. Cambridge, MA: Harvard University Press.

Williams, Raymond 1976: *Keywords: A Vocabulary of Culture and Society*. London: Oxford University Press.

Witherell, Carol and Nel Noddings, eds 1991: *Stories Lives Tell: Narrative and Dialogue in Education*. New York: Teachers College Press.

Wright, Erik Olin 1985: *Classes*. London: Verso.

Yeatman, Anna 1990: "A Feminist Theory of Social Differentiation," in *Feminism/Postmodernism*, ed. Linda J. Nicholson. New York and London: Routledge, pp. 281–99.

Zald, Mayer 1991: "Sociology as a Discipline: Quasi-Science and Quasi-Humanities," *The American Sociologist* 22(3–4): 165–87.

Zerilli, Linda M. G. 1991: "Rememoration or War? French Feminist Narrative and the Politics of Self-Representation," *Differences* 3(1): 1–19.

Zucker, Lynne G. 1991: "The Role of Institutionalization in Cultural Persistence," in *The New Institutionalism in Organizational Analysis*, ed. Walter W. Powell and Paul J. DiMaggio. Chicago: University of Chicago Press, pp. 83–107.

3

Dark Thoughts about the Self

Charles Lemert

Increasingly, the Self is subjected to dark thoughts by writers belonging to two different groups.

The first is a group of individuals who believe in the Self. For the most part, they consider themselves to be like all other persons in having one. Just the same, members of this group tend to brood. Their broodings are either historical or philosophical in nature comprising a growing list of works attempting to explain the history or source of the Self. By and large, they consider the Self a moral or natural thing, out there in real history, thus susceptible to analysis.

A classic sample of writing and thinking under the influence of this group's culture is William James's disquisition on the "me" as one of four parts of the Self. Today, James's way of talking would be cause for embarrassment. In 1890, when James wrote *Principles of Psychology*, it was perfectly normal:

> The Empirical Self of each of us is all that he is tempted to call by the name of *me*. But it is clear that between what a man calls *me* and what he simply calls *mine* the line is difficult to draw. We feel and act about certain things that are ours very much as we feel and act about ourselves. Our fame, our children, the work of our hands, may be as dear to us as our bodies are, and arouse the same feelings and the same acts of reprisal if attacked.   *(James 1981 [1890]: 279)*

The cultural assumptions behind the statement are evident. "Each of us" possesses a Self which is "what a man calls *me*." Moreover, he (James's man, that is) is evidently a hard-working gentleman of note in his community. He is a man prepared to defend his personal as well as capital property – his "me," his children, and presumably his woman, as well as his body. Subsequent writers in this tradition are disposed to the cultural habits of the gentleman patriarch, but they continue to write and speak from the point of view of a universal human nature in which the "me" who has a Self may well be, if not "a man," some wispy likeness to the figure James had in the back of his mind. [1]

Current representatives of this first group, being sensitive to changing times, avoid James's naive attachments to bourgeois European culture. Just the same, they retain many of his assumptions. Prominent current examples taken from the great number of those who might be located in the James group are Charles Taylor (1989), Craig Calhoun (1991), Anthony Giddens (1991), and Norbert Wiley (1994). Contrary to snide castigations of them by their cultural opponents, those in this group should not be assumed to be arrogant purveyors of a morally fixed position. William James, for example, in *The Varieties of Religious Experience*, wrote with fine sensitivity to the inner struggles of the human Self. In his chapter on the "Divided Self," he referred to man's interior life as "a battle-ground for what he feels to be two deadly hostile selves, one actual, the other ideal" (James (1960 [1902]: 176). [2] What is common to those in this group is *not* (necessarily) an absence of human feeling or moral subtlety but a set of assumptions about that "ideal" which strains harshly against actual life. This is what distinguishes them from others, as I will attempt to show.

The second group comprises individuals who write and talk about an aspect of human experience that *appears* to be closely related to the Self, the subject of the first group's preoccupations. Yet, when using the term "Self," if at all, those in this second group use it without heavy brooding. Instead they use "Self" much as others use the phrase "former Soviet Union" to refer to a once evident thing that has lost empirical salience. Members of this second group tend to write in one of several styles that serve, among other effects, to put the first group's broodings into stark relief. They frequently write in verse or other strange but sometimes amusing styles. Very often they tell personal stories. This does not mean, as some suppose, that they are light-hearted, or frivolous.

An example of the second group's thinking could be the following passage from Gloria Anzaldúa's *Borderlands/La Frontera*:

> The world is not a safe place to live in. We shiver in separate cells in enclosed cities, shoulders hunched, barely keeping the panic below the surface of the skin, daily drinking shock along with our morning

coffee, fearing the torches being set to our buildings, the attacks in
the street. Shutting down. Woman does not feel safe when her own
culture, and white culture, are critical to her; when the males of all
races hunt her as prey.

Alienated from her mother culture, "alien" in the dominant culture, the woman of color does not feel safe within the inner life of
her Self. Petrified, she can't respond, her face caught between *los
intersticios*, the spaces between the different worlds she inhabits.

(Anzaldúa (1988: 20)

Anzaldúa is writing about herself as a Chicana, *tejana*, lesbian
native to the dangerous economic and territorial borderlands between
Mexico and the US Southwest. She writes of herself, an historically
concrete experience, not of *the* Self.[3] Just as often, those in this
group use the word "identity" where the others use "Self." Though
they differ among themselves in many ways, none speaks of Self
as a universal property of human nature, or anything of this sort.
Others included in this group are: Patricia Hill Collins (1990), Donna
Haraway (1991), Trinh T. Minh-ha (1989), Judith Butler (1990),
Jeffrey Weeks (1991), Gayatri Chakravorty Spivak (1988), among many
others (see, for example, Seidman 1992).

Very often, though not always, those in the second group are
individuals whose ancestors were not European or, if they were,
only by descent through extraordinarily complicated bloodlines; and
they are less inclined to present themselves as sexually straight. It
may be said, however awkwardly, that they tend to have had life
experiences that are dark, in the several senses of the word –
including the racial. Notice of these sometimes occurring attributes
in the second group puts the first group into even deeper relief.
Those in the first group who brood over the Self tend, by and large,
to be white, male, and of apparently less complicated blood histories
and superficially more familiar sexual orientations. Thus the irony that
members of the first group, being usually light in their experience,
are dark in their broodings over the fate the Self; while members
of the second group, being dark in their experience, treat the Self
lightly because they consider Self unsafe or uncertain (or both),
somehow.[4] Why any or all of these differences might exist is the
subject I venture cautiously to discuss.

SELF AND IDENTITY

In particular, I want to consider a single proposition that is far
more historical than philosophical, namely: *That the concepts "Self"*

and "identity" have less in common than is normally assumed because they belong to two different series of historical events. There are at least three reasons why the proposition must be treated with caution. (1) The historical evidence for it is drawn from a near present – beginning most notably in the early to mid-1950s. [5] All claims argued on the basis of evidence from a near history are, necessarily, controversial. (2) The tradition wherein conceptual terms referring to *apparently* similar entities are used in theoretical discussions as virtual *identicals* is old, noble, and deep within its culture. In other words, when identity theory is turned reflexively on "the Self," identity theory *itself* is part of the problem. (3) Those who are identified with identity theories separable-in-principle from Self-theories often use concrete attributions, like "dark" or "colored," in reference to themselves but in ways that discourage use of these attributions by others not considered identical to them. In other words, identity theories that reject sweeping, sometimes universal, principles of identification limit the discussion, both philosophically and politically.

These three are only the most obvious reasons for caution in considering the statement that "Self" and "identity" may refer to different, rather than identical, events. Overall, the proposition, if it is a proposition, is fraught with theoretical and political trouble. This, almost certainly, is why willingness to consider it in the first place is still another point of demarcation between the two groups. The first group tends to assume "Self" and "identity" are at least good enough identicals that their differences, if any, may be ignored. The second group tends to allow (and sometimes insist on) the difference but without making philosophical noise over it. This may be why the second group writes, and speaks, outside official philosophical and theoretical language. Having refused to identify "identity" with "Self," they recognize that the identification *itself* was founded on a principle of language and thought so essential that making too much fuss over it would render incoherent anything said.

In order to consider the proposition that "Self" and "identity" refer to two different series of historical events it is important not to ascribe the two groups with dark thoughts about the Self to one or the other term. Further discussion should discover more historically sensitive names for the two groups. Since, therefore, members of both theoretical and moral groups identify themselves with one or more definite reference groups, both, thereby, can be assumed to believe in a "we," however much they differ in their use of this pronoun.

Members of the first group frequently use "we" as William James did in the passage quoted at the beginning. When William James says, "We feel and act about certain things that are ours very much as we feel and act about ourselves ..." he uses the pronoun heavily (one might say darkly). James's "we" is the rhetorical "we" of a man who trusts that his intuitions are reliably in tune with certain universal human essences. The usage clearly exaggerates the importance of what we now recognize to be a very narrow zone of social viability (the culture of James's Harvard and of late nineteenth-century liberal culture, generally). Just the same, James does not hesitate to identify his local experience, unreflexively, with the universal human condition. Today, those in the first group are more reflexive with respect to inferences from their experiences. Still they use some version of James's intuitively universal human "we." By contrast, when Anzaldúa uses "we" it is concrete, without the least intent to universalize beyond the experiences to which it refers, as in: "We shiver in separate cells in enclosed cities, shoulders hunched, barely keeping the panic below the surface of the skin ..." The "we" of this second group is concrete. It refers to occasional, but deeply understood, groupings of individuals sharing similar or same historical experiences, usually below, or marginally outside, the world to which the first group's "we" refers.

Thus, for simplicity's sake, it is possible to label the first, the *strong-we group*; the second, the *weak-we group*. The difference between the *strong-* and *weak-we* positions is not, however, one of degree.[6] The strong-we is strong because it enforces the illusion that humanity itself constitutes the final and sufficient identifying group. Conversely, the weak-we position locates practically meaningful sense of oneself in concrete historical relations with local groups. The wisdom of these categorically soft labels lies in the way they offer around overly abstracted complaints and countercomplaints.

The temptation is great to deride the strong-we position as "essentialist," the weak-we as "tribalist" – terms which miss what is principally at issue. Though it is indeed true that there are adherents of the strong-we position who believe most sincerely that true knowledge and political freedom require allegiance to universal essences, few of those seriously defending the Self hold so uncomplicated a position. This is most evidently so among those strong-we theorists to whom I have referred, each of whom struggles seriously – not with essential Truth, but with moral dilemmas. Taylor, for instance, concludes his spirited defense of the Self with the dilemma "that the highest spiritual ideals and aspirations also threaten to lay the most crushing burdens on humankind" (1989: 519). The conclusion follows necessarily from the assumption with which he began: "Selfhood and the good, or in another way selfhood and morality, turn out to be inextricably intertwined themes" (1989: 3). While it would be difficult indeed to say that the complicated and subtle argument that links this assumption to its concluding dilemma is essentialist, in the usual sense of the term, it is perfectly apt to diagnose it as strong-we. Taylor (1989: part II) clearly sets himself at odds with the Cartesian self which is the original archetype of the essential Self. What he does not do is what he does not want to do: Give up the deep cultural assumptions that permit him to use the word "humankind" and to believe in the definite article in the phrase "*the* highest spiritual ideals and aspirations." Taylor plainly does not allow for the possibility that many, upon reading the phrase, would rightly and naturally ask: "Whose, exactly?" These are not, however, matters merely of rhetorical taste. What characterizes even the very best of the strong-we thinkers is that the Self is among those substantial moral entities that entail a final moral dilemma. The only way around it, from within the strong-we culture, is the crude assertion of the abstract Truth of the Human. In other words, as an alternative to essentialism, Taylor and other left-liberal strong-we thinkers are left with a dilemma for which the only answer is liberal hope: "The dilemma of mutilation is in a sense our greatest spiritual challenge, not an iron fate" (Taylor 1989: 521) – an equivocation requiring at least a strong (if implicit) faith in universal progress. [7]

By contrast, those who identify themselves with a weak-we culture are very much less inclined to view mutilation and destruction as a moral "dilemma." They, usually, have an explicit, if not always universally persuasive, theory of the moral and political origins of the mutilations they experience, which theories, in turn, are very often the historical bases upon which they define their weak-we culture. As a result, they often explain the destruction of their local cultures with reference to the strong-we culture's confusion of its "ought" with the "is" of humanity. In other words, those in a weak-we culture would be inclined to argue that Taylor was wrong from the start. Selfhood and the good – that is, the strong Self and *the* good – are not for them "inextricably intertwined," as Taylor supposes. They appear that way only from within strong-we cultures. Thus, among the weak-we writers, there is either no explicit theory of the Self, or a theory stated in terms that retain but the thinnest of rhetorical associations with the strong-we Self, such as:

By insisting on self-definition, Black women question not only what has been said about African-American women but the credibility and the intentions of those possessing the power to define. When Black

women define ourselves, we clearly reject the assumption that those
in positions granting them the authority to interpret our reality are
entitled to do so.   (*Collins 1990; 106–7*)

The differences between strong- and weak-we ways of speaking
about the Self (when such talk exists in the first place) bespeaks
differences in culture, rooted in different histories.

If there could be but one question at issue between the two groups
it might be: Can individual human persons identify with Humanity
itself without a too severe loss of historical coherence? A strong-we
thinks, yes; a weak-we, no. Whichever choice is made, an entirely
different history is told – one with a Self; one without.

THE INHERENT WEAKNESS OF THE STRONG-WE POSITION

The strong moral claims made from the strong-we position require
delicate social historical conditions. In particular, they cannot be
strongly asserted outside an enduring culture in which rival moral
claims are incapable of compelling adherents of the strong-we
position to doubt the universality of their convictions. The inherent
weakness of the strong-we position is that the likelihood that such
conditions could pertain *in fact* are slim. Though some relatively small
local cultures may approximate this condition, it has never existed
with impressive force in the historical region to which the strong-we
position is native, that is: the Euro-American sphere of moral influence between, roughly, 1750, or earlier, and 1968. [8] While there
are historical instances in which proponents of the strong-we position
have enjoyed a virtual hegemony over legitimate moral claims in
the realm, there are few instances where that hegemony was ever
thorough enough to eliminate active, if ineffective, counter-claims.

The very existence of a potential counter-claim necessarily weakens
the inherent logic of the strong-we position. Consider just one,
salient illustration, the United States of America. Few national
cultures have made a stronger strong-we claim; in its case, that the
local revolutionary principles of the late-eighteenth century American
colonies were self-evidently identical with the universal needs, rights,
and aspirations of all human beings. Yet, from its first formal declaration in 1776, this colonial claim was frustrated by direct experience. Buried in (and eventually deleted from) Thomas Jefferson's
1776 draft of what became the Declaration of Independence is the
following complaint against the British throne: "He has waged cruel
war against human nature itself, violating its most sacred rights of

life and liberty in the persons of a distant people, who never offended him, captivating and carrying them into slavery in another hemisphere, or to incur miserable death in their transportation hither." The colonial congress abruptly removed this passage in order to satisfy the demands of Georgia and South Carolina. Jefferson must have anticipated their objections for the language of his deleted paragraph is notably vague. The violation of human nature in the mistreatment of "a distant people, who never offended" is described with an indefiniteness that leaves open, at least rhetorically, his precise reference. Does Jefferson refer in this passage (as throughout the Declaration) to violations against the humanity of the Euro-American colonists? Or to the African-American indentured slaves? Neither in the Declaration of Independence nor in the 1787 Constitution nor in the 1791 Bill of Rights is the slavery of African-Americans explicitly addressed, even though the slave system was one of the most distinctive features of the colonial economic system. [9] In other words, the American colonists' revolutionary insistence that their regional rights to independence were founded on the universal principles of human nature were self-evidently contradictory. They won just the same. But the inherent weakness of the American revolutionary claim to a strong-we position endured as the most unrelenting moral contradiction in the United States. Race is no less an "obsession" today than it was in the 1940s when Myrdal wrote *An American Dilemma*, or at the turn of the century when Du Bois declared the color line the problem of the 20th century, or in 1835 when Tocqueville (1969 [1835]: 340) declared race "America's most formidable evil threatening its future." [10]

The inability of the white, Euro-American colonists to square their strong-we position with the actual history of their relations to African- and Native-American people is an evil that threatens, among much else, the strong-we position itself (Tocqueville 1969 [1835]: 316–63). This is self-evident. As a result, in the United States the strong-we claim to universality rested on the weak foundational necessity that the "other slaves," the darker ones, not ever be able to assert their own "we" position. Given the moral logic of the Enlightenment principles in the American Declaration and Constitution this could only be prevented by the overt or covert acceptance of a principle obnoxious to the evidence of daily life, namely: that only the Euro-Americans are truly human. Liberal European societies faced a similar, if less proximate, moral dilemma in the facts of their colonial empires.

Just the same, for the better part of two centuries in the West, the strong-we position has enjoyed extraordinarily good historical luck. Though its claim of proper identification with the "human nature" itself was manifestly incoherent, the claims of those in what would become the weak-we position were unable to effect significant instability in the Euro-American spheres of cultural influence. Not, that is, until the late 1950s and 1960s when European and American states made similar mistakes that eventually proved fatal to their strong-we positions. By formally allowing the civil rights of African-Americans (and other groups), the Americans gave all weak-we groups in the US their moral independence. This had the same effect as the simultaneous "mistake" of the European powers in allowing their African and Asian colonies to rebel. Thereafter, their respective strong-we positions were crippled. Having granted civil or state status to others, strong-we cultures legitimized weak-we identities. To the extent that these groups achieved civil or political, if not economic, legitimacy, the moral claim of the strong-we position (that its truths were universal) became self-evidently contradicted. Jefferson's vague statement in 1776 was finally completed with the logical effect he must have anticipated. There is no self-evident human nature!

This, of course, is an historically arguable interpretation based on a history of the quite near present.[11] Yet, the existence of the argument is *not* arguable, which fact is enough to limit the force of any strong-we position. And this could be said to be the historical basis for considering the proposition that "Self" and "identity" belong to two different series of historical events. If the moral ideal of the Self requires historical conditions supportive of its corresponding strong-we claim, then the Self, as a universal attribute of human moral consciousness, is deeply qualified. This obtains when *either* the conditions themselves change (as some argue they have) *or* there is enough doubt about the historical conditions to generate debate entailing uncertainty about strong-we claims. That at least the latter is taking place is evident, if not self-evident.

WEAK-WE IDENTITIES AND A STRONG SELF: SOME EMPIRICAL CASES

Without asking any more than open consideration of the above description of the present situation, it is possible to examine cases illustrating the differences between the weak- and strong-we identities (accordingly the differences between identity theories and Self-theories). The cases I draw from interviews taken as part of an ongoing team research project comparing five major identity groupings in American society.[12]

David [13]

The first illustration is a seemingly pure-type strong-we. In many superficial respects it is the near-perfect case of that historical individual who could be said to have a Self. Appearances notwithstanding, what strikes one in analyzing the case is that appearances do not stand up, suggesting that if this individual was not proof of the strong-we position, then perhaps that proof would be hard to come by. The suspicion was reinforced by evidence that David's identity situation must be relatively common even though there are few comparable accounts in recent literature (e.g., Raines: 1992). At the time of interview, David was 49 years of age, white, male, professional (a physician in family practice), financially comfortable though not wealthy, divorced with children. He had grown up in the 1950s in a small city in Kentucky. David's father had been a modestly successful all-purpose attorney in his smallish, barely Southern city. His mother's adult life was spent mostly, as it was then put, "at home" — as mother, wife, PTA member. For whatever reason, David's younger brother and sister did not figure in David's story. All in all, the family culture was socially and politically conservative, but unremarkably so. David's childhood was, thus, like millions of white, middle-class childhoods in the late 1940s and 1950s.

So was his adult life. In the 1960s, David became a student activist. He was inspired by the civil rights movement to work for fair housing and other liberal causes. In 1968 he campaigned for Robert Kennedy, then Eugene McCarthy. He was a liberal. He did not go to Chicago. In the 1970s, David graduated medical school, served an undistinguished residency, began his career in a small group practice in the East. He married. His children were born. In the 1980s, David's marriage broke up. He involved himself as best he could in the lives of his children, struggled with the divorce, learned to cook and keep a house, dated somewhat obsessively, felt miserable, and entered therapy. In the third year of his treatment, David began to remember some things about his childhood.

David reports discovering feelings for his parents that were mixed. He talked about his father as a depressive. He remembered his mother in more contradictory ways — a victim of her marriage who acted out her frustrations; a caring but uncertain mother. He could never remember being held physically by either of them, though he believes he was. About this time, he reports the sudden discovery of other feelings for a sixth member of his childhood household.

She, it turns out, was a person with whom he had remained in contact through Christmas cards, regular visits, phone calls. But not until a certain moment in his coming to his emotional self did this person appear for what she seems to have been. "Annie" had been seventeen when David was born. She was hired to care for him, later for his brother and sister. She was not well educated, not middle class, not white. With the support of his therapist, David began to spend more time with Annie, thus to learn more about his childhood. What he had begun to suspect about his biological parents was confirmed. Many of the stories Annie recounted took the same form. For instance, in one reported instance Annie was so fearful of the parents' inability to control their anger that she telephoned David's grandmother. The father's parents came immediately. They sat David's parents down in private and, according to the report, the grandmother – in the presence of Annie – instructed their son and daughter-in-law to change their ways, curse less, and above all to obey Annie. Thereafter, whenever David's father began to lose control, Annie told him to leave the children to her. According to David's report, the father never disobeyed.

Even allowing for distorted memory, David came to realize that, if he had an emotionally satisfying relation with any adult in his family of origin, it had been with Annie. For example, from the transcript:

> Come to think of it, the best moments when I was a small kid were Tuesday afternoons after school when Annie did the ironing. I'd go downstairs to the basement and sit on a carton or something and listen. Annie talked to me. I can't remember my father ever talking like that. When he did tell stories, it was usually to an audience at a holiday meal, usually after a few drinks. Annie talked though, and she sang. I can't really remember [what] songs she sang. I remember only that these moments made me feel good. [Later,] Annie said she remembered those times too. She told me also about her coming to get me on the bus on Sundays which [was her] day off to take me to church. I don't remember that too well either, but it sounds right.

Annie was, in effect, David's mother. David is white. Annie is black.

If Annie was David's mother, in whatever sense, in what sense is David white? This is a question about which our culture does not permit us to talk. For David to consider that in *some* sense he might think of himself as something other than white, perhaps even black, is a thought that contradicts strong-we claims at their foundation. This threat (to use Tocqueville's word) may explain the two most striking features of this narrative report of David's discovery of his relation to a black person: first, memory of the relation was deeply repressed; second, it may have been repressed because feelings in the relationship were forbidden. If the repression was a psychological effect, the effect of the taboo was political. In this conjunction of the psychological and political in David's account is another demarcation between Self-theories and identity theories. The weak-we position is of necessity overtly political in that, as in David's case, its experience is that of having been formed in a series of prohibitions, punishments, taboos, and penalties. By contrast, Self-theory insists that the strong-we is a moral fact that presents itself as though it were beyond politics. In the case of David, the Self is presumed to be a moral zero-signifier (Doar and Lemert 1991; Levin, 1993; Lemert 1993) – that one type of individual who is least consciously responsible for his identity because he, in and of himself, is considered, though without notice, to be the model for essential humanity. Zero-signifiers cannot be openly political. They must, therefore, forget who they are.

Thus, the silence with respect to narratives like David's is a politically enforced imperative of the culture. When David's identity as a white, middle-class male is considered in itself, it possesses very little *specific* content. To this day there is, to my knowledge, only one compelling description of this identity type in the sociological literature – Erving Goffman's description of the pure normal individual:

> Even where widely attained norms are involved, their multiplicity has the effect of disqualifying many persons. For example, in an important sense there is only one complete unblushing male in America: a young, married, white, urban, northern, heterosexual Protestant father of college education, fully employed, of good complexion, weight and height, and a recent record in sports. Every American male tends to look out upon the world from this perspective, constituting one sense in which one can speak of a common value system in America.   (Goffman 1963: 128)

Goffman here describes the pure identity without particular content, [14] the identity whose only reference is Civilization itself, the identity whose only specification is still some such generality as The American Way. Historically, he is what is meant by the Self. The degree to which, appearances notwithstanding, it is an historically unstable type is doubly indicated: by Goffman's hint as to just how narrowly distributed it might be; by the suggestion of David's narrative that in many cases the strong-we Self is a deception lost to memory.

In the course of the project that produced the David narrative, other personal narratives were taken and analyzed. The project-team organized its interviewing into five identity categories, includ-ing: African-American, Latino, Gay–Lesbian–Bisexual, and "Asian-American." [15] Reports of individuals who identify themselves with one of these identities differed markedly from reports of individuals in the fifth group which we came to label "white-guys." With rare exception, all those but the white-guys reported specific, sometimes excruciatingly detailed, determinations of their identities.

Naranja [16]

By contrast to David, consider the following identity report:

> Naranja is a nineteen year old Dominican woman. She comes from a working class family and is currently enrolled in college. Although Naranja does identify as Latina, her identity is centered upon her Dominican heritage. Her Dominican and Latino identity seem to be driven by the rejection she experiences in American society ... [She reports having] had to struggle with her racial identity in the past. She says she could never deny she was Black because she clearly is Black. Prior to college she would say "I look Black" and now she says "I know that I am Black." She understands race now as a phenotypical characteristic and not only as the Black culture of the US. Naranja is also very aware of the difference between Latino cultures. She is very careful to speak from her own experience and not to generalize.   (Mendéz 1992: 55)

Other reports are similar to this one on Naranja: a great many identity choices – in her case: Latina, Black, Dominican; as well as the unvoiced: feminist, and African-American – are held as possibilities, made as actual choices, and negotiated with consider-able equanimity by the tactic of speaking carefully from "her own experience."

As the research progressed, it was learned that from group to group the particulars of identifications varied. Just the same, others gave identity reports similar to Naranja's – that is, personal identity choices determined by political realities which varied, as one would expect. For examples: Latinos all tended to present some variant of the early school experience of having been taken as Black or choosing to accept this identification for what amounted to the political reality of school life. Asian-Americans were more concerned with being taken by whites as members of a single group, while each was made aware at home of his or her specific ethnic culture – Korean, Japanese, Vietnamese. Bisexuals reported a dual struggle: on the one hand, with closet choices; on the other, with experiences of suspicion, sometimes hostility, from the wise on either side, straight or gay.

Sato [17]

With no exception, individuals identifying with any of the groups other than "white-guy" reported experiences of struggles with decisions to identify with one or more of several options. For example, the following is the verbatim report of Sato (a fictitious name) – a college-age, male, bisexual who also identifies as Japanese-American:

> At some point in the third grade I decided to rebel against my Japanese culture because its seemed like such a pain in the butt. And I was also getting a lot of shit because, like, [in the seventh grade] I ... still very much like[d] my last Asian hero ... this Samurai Warrior, Miomoto Musashi ... What happened was in the second grade for Halloween everyone came dressed up and I came dressed up as a samurai warrior because I was very into that at the time. I had all these fake swords I had [bought] when I was in Japan, and I went and everyone kinda looked at me, gave me these stares and stuff and made me feel very self-conscious and made fun of and so next year it was even worse because I went as Robin Hood – you know a real WASPy role model – and I got stares and so it made me think to myself: God, I can't win at this in any way so I said fuck it, and started blowing off Japanese school way too much.

Then, later in the same report, Sato continues:

> I've walked in gay marches and stuff but I don't feel very empowered by it all. Like I feel very much that up until now I was very apolitical but like I was being very political in a very personal sense ... and number two I'm starting to now feel more of a sense of a drive to be more political being Asian American in terms of being bi[sexual] ... I am, like, there are so few Asian American bi people here or Asian American queer people in general so it is good for someone to actually speak out, to say HEY we are here and we do have a voice.

Sato's still young-adult politics were, clearly, shaped by the child-hood experience of having no certain identity. His emerging adult identification is defined by circumstances in which he can "be" someone giving public voice to his several identities, each inflecting the other: male, Asian-American, Japanese-American, bisexual, queer.

Theodore [18]

By contrast, the white males interviewed were unable to produce similarly specific, confident, or inflected statements about them-selves. One is particularly striking in comparison to Sato. Theodore was white, male, 20 years old, middle class, from Boston, *and* gay. Although he considered himself "definitely" gay and was out as such, sexual orientation did not form as significant a role in Theodore's identification as it did for Sato. When asked if he identified with any particular social group, Theodore said:

> ... Yeah, I guess ... no I don't think I really mean, I guess I do in some ways, but I don't think I really feel, like, allegiance to one particular group, like, I don't really identify with the white male group very much because ... I think of the white, male stereotype as very negative ... I get a lot of advantages from that, I mean, like all that crap, but I don't think I really am proud of being a white male, um, I much more strongly identify with, um, being a gay man, it's just something I feel a lot stronger about.

This report cannot be interpreted to mean that white, gay men do not identify more strongly than this with their sexual orientation. But what is distinctive about Theodore's report is how, in this one case, the white-male identification is an insufficient support. By contrast, the voice Sato gave was one in which his bisexual identity gained political and personal meaning *in relation to* his Japanese/Asian-American identification. The purer white guy, Theodore, had no such inflectional base with which to support his out-gay self-understanding. Such was the silencing effect apparent in other interviews of persons, straight or gay, in the white-male identity circumstance. Silenced, where others are voiced.

One could say, therefore, that still another difference between strong- and weak-we positions is derived from answers to the ques-tions: "Who, here, is silent about what, and why? Who has a voice, about what, and why?" In the reports, these are the questions that lead to coherent interpretation of the differences between white-guys, like David, and others, like Naranja and Sato (with Theodore being a white-guy exception who proved the rule).

The strong-we position, its inherent instability notwithstanding, is founded on a code of silence about the impossibility that any one Self could be universal. The code entails a double prohibition: first, against recognition of one's own complexity and, second, against the public legitimacy of any weak-we identity. Thus, David lived most of his life in silent ignorance of a complex identity. That silence extended from an early childhood prohibition on feelings for Annie to adult prohibitions against white-to-black cross-racial identifications. At both moments in this white man's biography, the cultural code of silence prohibited him from talking about feelings for and identifications with those in certain racial, gender, sexual relations. The prohibition on such talk owes to liberalism's understanding of its liberalism in these matters as blindness – blindness to color, blindness to differences (see Morrison 1992, Gates 1992; compare Scott 1991). The blind eye/the silent voice, both, serve to establish our authority as the voices of liberal truth. These are liberalism's best intentions. The white-guy is the particular embodiment of liberal culture's identifications with humanity. This is a culture of which the foundation is the Self – the moral subject which, as many have observed, is the modern equivalent to the soul. The moral Self, like the soul, can have only one identification: with Humanity, if not God.

Against the strong-we Self, are those who do not respect these prohibitions; those who, in fact, never respected them, even when they obey (Scott 1991). Both Naranja and Sato – and others in their identity circumstances – speak freely, but they speak in a relation to a world different from David's. They are individuals who remember much more, perhaps everything (or everything necessary) about their pasts. Among them are those who, in the past generation, seem able miraculously to remember back through their own individual experiences into the history of their several collective pasts. Sato affirms, thus recollects, his Japanese-American identity in articulate relation to his queer identity. His voice – uttered in reports, conversations, political marches – has the effect of creating, if only for a while, a tactical identity of many parts. The important thing is that Sato could not say what he is, were he to respect the liberal prohibition. Concretely, he cannot "be" within the strong-we position. Sato and Naranja are able to "be" only by identification with concrete features of their histories, but at a cost. If David, the white-guy, pays the price of forgetting his personal past in order to become a certified member of liberal culture, then individuals like Sato and Naranja pay the price of self-exclusion from that culture (that is, from official humanity) in order to become a speaking, vocal member of their cultures. Each makes a political choice: David, in order to have a Self; Sato and Naranja, in order to be in relation to others. One desires to be, as the saying goes, fully human, that is: officially human. The others desire to be who they were before official Humanity destroyed, or tried to destroy, their archives.

DARK THOUGHTS AMONG THE STRONG-WE

To return from these few empirical cases to the established literatures of the two groups, their complicated differences are plain to see. Those in the strong-we group are in the untenable position of having to keep what Goffman (1959: 141–2) called a dark secret – a secret so deep that to confess it would destroy the presentation. Like Jefferson's moral and logical dilemma with respect to African slaves, no proponent of the strong-we position can admit the legitimate claims of those in the weak-we position, whatever he may see or believe. Such an admission destroys the moral claims whereby a local culture presents itself as though it were universal. Dark secrets, whether in culture or individual character, must be kept in silence. It is possible, therefore, to consider the official literature in the strong-we tradition with respect to its moral obligation to keep the dark secret of western culture.

In *Sources of the Self*, Charles Taylor provides a careful, thoughtful, and sensitive reconstruction of the history and prospects of the Self. I cite one passage near the beginning of this long book:

> I want to defend the strong thesis that doing without frameworks is utterly impossible for us; otherwise put, that the horizons within which we live our lives and which make sense of them have to include these strong qualitative discriminations. Moreover, this is not meant just as a contingently true psychological fact about human beings which could perhaps turn out one day not to hold for some exceptional individual or new type, some superman of disengaged objectifcation. Rather, the claim is that living within such strongly qualified horizons is constitutive of human agency, that stepping outside these limits would be tantamount to stepping outside what we would recognize as integral, that is, undamaged human personhood.
>
> (Taylor 1989: 27)

This, obviously, is a strong-we position, as one sees immediately in the pronouns "us," "our," and "we" — as in "the horizons within which we live our lives." But, it is not a naive strong-we. Taylor's "undamaged human personhood" is lodged not in universal properties of human cognition, being, or practice. Rather, the Self is defined in relation to moral orientations which, in turn, are unavoidably social:

> My self-definition is understood as an answer to the question who I am. And this question finds it original sense in the interchange of speakers. I define who I am by defining where I speak from, in the family tree, in social space, in the geography of social statuses and functions, in my intimate relations to the ones I love, and also crucially in the space of moral and spiritual orientation within which my most important defining relations are lived out. *(Taylor 1989: 35)*

Self-definition, thus, is the narrative product of a "quest" within moral frameworks for a sense of the good in relation to others. Using the strong-we, Taylor says (1989: 51–2): "because we cannot but orient ourselves to the good, and thus determine our place relative to it and hence determine the direction of our lives, we must inescapably understand our lives in narrative form, as a 'quest.'"

If the openness of "quest" seems to soften the strong-we language, then the surprisingly declarative language ("we cannot but," "we must inescapably") reminds that "we" are still within strong-we culture. Quite apart from the way style reveals conviction, the strong-we claim is apparent when one applies the silence test suggested in the previous section. About what is Taylor silent, and why? The simplest answer is: concrete human differences. While Taylor's orienting framework is vastly more reflexive and contemporary than William James's, he still assumes a social world of coherent and available speakers and listeners, of traceable and presumably definite family trees, of competent and faithful intimates, to say nothing of "moral and spiritual" spaces in relation to which the quest for goods of an "undamaged human personhood" may be well lived out.

To begin to stipulate the numbers and names of human individuals for which *none* of these conditions are normally available would be to begin a list that seems never to cease to end — South Bronx and Ethiopia yesterday, Somalia and the Cabrini Green housing projects today, and tomorrow ... (See, *inter alios*, Kotlowitz 1991; Garbarino et al. 1992.) It is enough to refer to Gloria Anzaldúa's description of the borderlands to suggest the extent to which Taylor's moral spaces, like his strong-we, are less universally available than he supposes. In other words, Taylor's silence on the possibility of real, verified, and concrete differences in the human condition weakens the very intent of his moral theory of the Self. He had intended, evidently, to generate a theory in which *oughts* derive from the *is* of daily lives. Having said nothing on the real *is* of daily lives different from those organized by his own moral framework, he provides an *ought* of the good Self from which many millions of people could at best judge the miserableness of their *is*. Many, perhaps most, human persons have reason to consider Taylor's "undamaged human personhood" neither an "is" nor an "ought." This does not make Taylor's argument worthless, not by any means. It does, however, suggest the extent to which, behind its moral delicacy, it remains a strong-we claim.

Again, the decisive question with respect to the history of Self is history itself. Most strong-we theorists of the Self would agree. Most have at least an implicit theory of history in respect to which they take some stand on the crucial question of modernity. Modernity, thereby, might be provisionally defined as that historical period in which "human personhood" (or Self) enjoys the normal expectation that it will remain "undamaged."[19] Taylor argues that the modern theory of the Self came into its own first with theories of "inwardness," beginning with Descartes and Locke, in which the Self is, on the one hand, freed from classical identifications with God, being, or nature while, on the other hand, put at risk of being the "unsituated, even punctual self" (p. 514). Yet, though the book is, as the subtitle states, a history of the making of modern identity, Taylor takes his stand so deep within the moral framework of modernity that he is silent with respect to views that go beyond interpreting that culture as one with a "multiplicity of goods" giving rise to "conflicts and dilemmas" (p. 514). Leaving aside considerations of postmodernity, one might reasonably expect a more direct consideration of the dilemmas of the modern Self created by world and social conditions radically changed since mid-twentieth century.

One of Taylor's most robust advocates, Craig Calhoun entertains his most serious reservations on just this point: "The relationship of social change to change in persons and moral frameworks remains largely an enigma" (Calhoun 1991: 260). Calhoun then enumerates some of the changes in world order Taylor fails to address directly:

the introduction of democratic politics, the rise of state bureaucracies, the shrinking size of the family, the transformation in numbers
of people working away from their homes and/or among relative
strangers, the growth of cities, the increased ease of travel, the conquest and loss of empires, the globalization of the economy, the
change in living standards, the increase in capacity to kill in war,
and so on.[20]   *(Calhoun 1991: 260)*

Had Taylor not intended to lodge the modern Self with moral
orientations in a concrete social life, then he might not be held
accountable to real social history. That he did, makes him responsible. Given that Taylor is unarguably sensitive to the issue
and more than competent to the task, one can only conclude that
he did not because he could not. In effect, Taylor set out to define
and defend the[21] ideal of the moral Self. He, thus, assumes Self as
his subject and, therefore, cannot question its own history.

The effect of this incapacity is most evident in strong-we theorists
like Calhoun who recognize this limitation of Taylor's framework
yet still defend its value to the revitalization of contemporary social
theory. The defense, unfortunately, is itself limited. Calhoun himself
admits: "Taylor says relatively little about how our understandings
of the larger social world impinge on our sense of who we can be"
(Calhoun 1991: 261). But, of course, Taylor *does* say quite a bit
about that larger social world. This is precisely his point. Self as
product of moral orientation to and with others is what the modern
Self is. What he does *not* do is what he cannot: consider "the
larger social world" in the concrete sense of a world with so great a
"multiplicity of goods" as to possess no universal necessities in
any other than the theoretical sense. What Taylor's position cannot
admit is what no strong-we position admits: that there are weak-we
positions from which the claims of universal humanity pale relative
to their more local histories. As a result, Taylor (and Calhoun)
use the terms "personhood," "human agency," "Self," and "identity"
as though they are interchangeable, thus virtual identicals (e.g.,
Taylor 1989: 3).[22] This is possible only from within the moral
framework in which, however lightly, one believes it possible and
good to identify oneself with Humanity itself. Those who do, leave
local identities in the dark under the cover of Self.

Were we to use Taylor's position as a standard to classify current
strong-we theories of the Self, it might be said that Taylor's view
is *neo-modernist*. If so, then other variants of the strong-we might
be *classically modernist* (Mead 1934: Wiley 1994), *radical modernist*
(Giddens 1991), and *pseudo-postmodern* (Gergen 1991). George Herbert

Mead, it hardly need be said, represents the refinement of James's classic theory of the social Self in which its constitutive elements are posited as invariant properties. The position is so strong-we that even current attempts to revise it end up in the same place, as in Norbert Wiley's view (1994: 144) that "All selves at all times ... have an I—me—you, present—past—future structure." At the other extreme of the strong-we is Giddens's radicalized modernist theory of the Self. Giddens takes the promising step of beginning with an attempt to define self-reflexivity as a distinctive aspect of modernity itself (1991: 34) and, thus, as an historical process:

> Self-identity is not a distinctive trait, or even a collection of traits, possessed by the individual. It is *the self as reflexively understood by the person in terms of her or his biography.* Identity here still presumes continuity across time and space; but self-identity is such continuity as interpreted reflexively by the agent. This includes the cognitive component of personhood.   *(Giddens 1991: 53)*

Presumably, the view is "radicalized" (Giddens's own term) because Giddens is attempting to define, in general terms, the moral space of Self in real, late-modern societies.

Like Taylor's, Giddens's modern Self is constituted in narrative (Giddens 1991: 54). Unlike Taylor, Giddens attempts to measure the theoretical incongruities between Self-theories and identity theories by the remarkable method of identifying them. The reflexive modern Self is, thus, one who is capable of "self-identity." In his attempt to get beyond classic Self-theory, Giddens ends up perilously close. The theoretical warrant for using "Self" and "identity" as though they were identicals is the classic modern theory that the Self is, in Mead's words, that human capacity to be an "object to itself" (1934: 136). As Calhoun points out (1991: 233), Mead's view is cognitive, while Taylor's is existential, hence moral. One might add, then, that Giddens's is historicist in an abstract sense. But the same result is gained. If Self is the capacity (cognitive, moral, or practical) to identify oneself as an object, and identity is the cognitive, moral, or historical recognition of that self-same Self as object over time, then, according to any of these views, modern identity must rely largely, if not entirely, on a shared (even if tacit) ideal of the universal moral Self. Otherwise, it is impossible to avoid the disengaged punctual Self (to which Taylor objects) or the disembedded individual (the absence of which, according to Giddens, defines late-modernity),[23] to say nothing of the worst-case alternative, the abstract quasi-ontological structures of Wiley's I—me—you.[24]

There is no theoretical way around it. Unless one begins on a much more concrete historical plane than do Giddens and Calhoun (not to mention Taylor), discussions of the Self can only move deeper and deeper into the dark cultural reserves of the strong-we position. The alternative course is to consider the weak-we position as the historically, if not morally or theoretically, necessary way out. But this would entail a decision about the actual historical conditions under which people have lived since, say, 1968 or so – conditions which have brought about dark thoughts within the culture of the strong-we position.

The weak-we position is not universally available. Were the position a matter of definition, one might say this is so by definition. Still, however much a native strong-we might wish to identify with a weak-we position, he would find himself not only out of Taylor's moral limits of undamaged human personhood, but quite literally in the dark.

Weak-we identities exist in actual, if excluded, histories, and this subverts all the usual categories, moral and intellectual. Patricia Hill Collins (1990), for example, describes a theory of black feminist identity that both is and is not related to a Self. Collins says, beginning with a quotation from Nikki Giovanni:

> Giovanni suggests: "We Black women are the single group in the West intact. And anybody can see we're pretty shaky. We are ... the only group that derives its identity from itself. I think it's been rather unconscious but we measure ourselves by ourselves, and Black women's survival is at stake, and creating self-definitions reflecting an independent Afrocentric feminist consciousness is an essential part of that survival.   *(Collins 1990: 104)*

All the terms are there, just as in the strong-we position: "We," "the single group in the West," "the only group," "essential." But they are differently inflected. The "we" and all that follows makes no claims for all humanity. Whatever one's own we, one is either in and of it, or not. There is a forbidden territory between any particular weak-we and the strong-we.

Strong-wes find this objectionable. This explains their broodings. But the question, when put as the weak-wes do, is not philosophical. It is a matter of fact in which the facts of the matter are entirely up to those taking the objectionable position. There is no other way. To the strong-we this is the darkest possible circumstance.

NOTES

1 The term "man," here, suffers from its historical ambiguities. On the one hand, it is not necessarily the case that the cultural attitude referred to is held only and always by a person of the male gender. On the other, insofar as the attitude toward Man is evidently rooted in the most revered elements of modern western humanism, it has functioned over several centuries to define the universal moral standard of all persons adhering, or subject, to that culture, regardless of their gender – or, for that matter, their race, class, world position, or sexual orientation.

2 I thank Karl Scheibe for help in understanding James, and Craig Calhoun for help throughout.

3 Though, in the quoted text, someone (a copy editor, a page proofer, an editor – if not Anzaldúa) capitalized "Self," those in this group, when they use the term, use it without the grand metaphysical sense implied by the upper case. This because, as Anzaldúa puts it, they usually do not "feel safe within the inner life" of the Self.

4 The differences between the two groups are not sufficiently explained by references to the presence or absence of any philosophical conviction, such as essentialism. The power of the second group arises less from the cogency of its attack on principles than from the authority of its complexly fractured historical experiences which, by little more than being described seriously, pose questions the first group's culture cannot answer from within. Rorty (1989), among others, discusses this point (see also Lemert 1992a). It would seem, therefore, about time to move beyond the debate over essentialism which is not able to account for real differences among real people with respect to a subject like the Self. For example, where does one locate a feminist theorist like Dorothy Smith (1987)? On the one hand, she could be said to be an "essentialist" by virtue of her commitments to "the standpoint of women" as the seemingly universal basis for a revolutionary sociology. On the other hand, however, throughout her writings, there is a dark brooding over the experiences of women. Yet, she broods not over the Self, but the subject – a related but different matter (Lemert 1992b). Whether or not Smith is said to be an essentialist does not begin to account for the absence of a well-articulated theory of the Self in her writings. Much the same kind of comment could be made with reference to Afrocentric social theorists such as Molefi Asante (1987). Like Smith's feminist standpoint, Asante's Afrocentrism is essentialist without a theory of the Self. To compound the analysis, Asante's position might be called (in the term I describe below) "strong-we," except for the fact that it refers to the fractured historical experiences of people of African descent throughout the world. Neither Afrocentrisms nor feminist standpoint theories make universal claims as to the essence of Man. Again, the philosophical categories cannot do the work recent history demands.

5 The most decisive and self-conscious first break with Self-theory was, probably, Erving Goffman's *Presentation of Self in Everyday Life* in which he said that the Self "is a *product* of a scene that comes off, and is not a *cause* of it" (Goffman 1959: 252). Though *Presentation* was published in 1959 [1956], its ideas were in his 1953 doctoral dissertation and early essays, in particular "On Face-Work" (Goffman 1955). By 1963, in *Stigma*, Goffman had explicitly distinguished social and personal "identities" from each other and both from the classic notion of the Self understood as the "core" of one's being (1963: 56). (Also, it is possible that Goffman [1963: 123–6] was among the first to use the now popular phrase "politics of identity.") In these early works, Goffman clearly acknowledged associations between his identity theories and the other important identity theorists of the early 1950s, Erik Erikson and David Riesman. Who influenced whom is a separate story. Another not-so-separate connection is that between these events in social theory (the separation of Self-theories and identity-theories) and events in the political world (the beginnings of the civil rights movement in the US in Montgomery in 1955 and the growing revolution of colonial subjects in Asia and Africa throughout the 1950s). That the two series of events occurred simultaneously is hardly a coincidence – especially since the social theories dealt more or less directly with issues of world change: Riesman with loss of First World character (in *The Lonely Crowd*, 1950), Erikson with rebellion in the character of young people (in *Childhood and Society*, 1950), and Goffman (1959, 1963) with normal deviance.

6 Nor is it simply a difference of kind. Since the weak-we always refers its immediate (if long neglected) identity reference to the historic power of the strong-we culture, the two reference groups are historically linked in a way that confounds differences of degree and kind.

7 The equivocation is explicit, if displaced, in other left-liberal strong-we thinkers. James, it is well known, equivocated by deferring all of the problems associated with his strong theory of the "me" into the analytically distinct (and theoretically unresolved) "social self" in which, in that famous phrase that has since shaped Self-theory, "a man has as many social selves as there are individuals who recognize him" (James 1981[1890]: 281). James, thus, passed the confusion on to subsequent generations. In a somewhat parallel move, Wiley formalizes and historicizes the Jamesian equivocation in recommending that the Self is a pure universal structure, while "identities," though they are "housed in selves," are the home of differences and particularities (Wiley 1994; 144). Calhoun's solution has the advantage of being historical in intent, though theoretically homologous to Wiley's. In his argument for a strong theory of the Self he responds to the differences described by some postmodernists: "Decentering is not the alternative to inwardness; it is its complement" (Calhoun 1991: 259). Finally, Giddens's doctrine of a "radicalized modernity" is a nearly pure type of theoretical equivocation, as in his definition of Self-identity as "the self as reflexively understood

by the person in terms of her or his biography" (Giddens 1991: 53).
To which even a postmodernist might reply: Go figure! There is,
however, nothing, in principle, wrong with equivocations of this sort
except that they do not allow a clear enough analysis of the historical
questions: Are "Self" and "identity" referents to the same, or different,
historic events? Is the historical world that supported the moral assumptions of the Self still the unequivocally dominant, or even real, world;
or not?

8 Some would argue an earlier date than the Enlightenment. Taylor (1989),
for example, believes modern culture began in the seventeenth century
with Descartes, whose notion of interiority was, in turn, Augustinian.

9 The controversy over the effect of the deletion on Jefferson is enough
evidence that the passage was trouble for everyone. Later, Jefferson ad-
mitted the obvious fact that the North American slave trade was as
much the responsibility of the colonies as of the British throne, and
that he was attempting to get the abolitionist text by South Carolina
and Georgia (see Wills 1978: 66–8). In fact, as Wills points out (p. 67),
Jefferson himself delayed publication of "Notes of the State of Virginia"
in recognition that his position on slavery would be trouble for his
fellow Virginians. That Jefferson not only recognized the difference between
white and black slavery, and its effects, is evident from the long section
in "Notes" (1943 [1781], 659–66) where he systematically compares
African slaves in North America to white slaves in the Roman Empire.
Though he here calls for the abolition of slavery, Jefferson nonetheless
provides detailed observations on the cultural inferiority of the African
slaves, for example: "But never could I find that a black had uttered
a thought above the level of plain narration ..." (p. 663) In the same
place he refers to the poetry of "Phyllis Whately" – by whom he meant
Phillis Wheately, the African slave whose written poetry was of such
astonishing excellence as to have required the attestation of a jury of
learned gentlemen in Boston in 1772. Currently, Henry Louis Gates
makes the Wheately incident the sign of the extent to which Euro-
American culture rested on the assumption of the impossibility of black
literacy (e.g., Gates 1992: ch. 3). The point is that the slavery of Africans
was an unresolvable moral dilemma for Jefferson, for the colonial congress, for the Americans generally. From the beginning, Americans have
been forced into the moral and intellectual dilemma of denying one or
another undeniable: either the universality of human nature, or the
inferiority of some humans.

10 Hacker (1992) uses the term "obsession" in relation to the long tradition
of American inability to deal with race. Compare Myrdal's (1944)
"dilemma," Du Bois's (1989 [1903]: 10) "the problem of the twentieth
century is the problem of the color line," and Tocqueville's (1969 [1835])
"formidable evil." All four agree that, throughout American history,
white relations with blacks are not a problem but the problem that most
deeply threatens American strong-we claims.

11 Of the many arguments against this historical privileging of the 1960s, Schlesinger's (1991) is the most cogent.

12 Interviews reported here were taken and transcribed between September, 1991 and March, 1993 by members of a research group at Wesleyan University: Chris Krauss, Peter Levin, Lucinda Mendéz, Joy Rhoden, and John Yoo working with the author. Their contributions are used with permission and thanks.

Group members chose to name the project the "Fractured Identities Project," after Haraway (1991). Haraway credits Chela Sandoval, among others, with the term "fractured identities." The modern history of the idea under different names can be traced at least to bell hooks (1981), Audre Lorde (1984), and various writings in Moraga and Anzaldúa (1981). The classic source is Anna Julia Cooper's (1892) *A Voice From the South*. The phrase "Ain't I a Woman," used by hooks and others, was originally Sojourner Truth's in 1851. It could be argued, as Collins (1990) does by implication, that the black feminist standpoint position is, by its historical nature, anti-essentialist, thus "fractured."

References to material from the interviews are coded "FI" for "fractured identities." Reports used here are preliminary, thus illustrative.

13 All names used are fictions. Other details are fictionalized in order to protect the identities of subjects. The David interview is coded FI9/21/91LC.

14 As Goffman extends the list to an ever more fractured limit, ending with the joke ("a recent record in sports"), he creates, technically speaking, a type without tokens. Even in the 1950s the number of individuals who might have possessed all of the attributions (including the good complexion) was necessarily small relative to the cultural power of the type to represent "a common value system in America." The theoretical function of zero-signifiers is to define the system of types central to a culture and to define them in the absence of particular cultural contents (see Lemert 1993). Zero-signifiers also define negatively as when "race" functions as a trope to define the culture by stipulating its others without precise or accurate reference to their actual racial identities; or, even, in the absence of any such thing as race (Gates 1992: ch. 3).

15 "Asian-American" comprises no particularly coherent group except to census takers, demographers, and those who rely on their products. One of the striking historic facts is that, from an official point of view, "Latino" (or, to use the official term, "Hispanic") comprises ethnic groups in America at least as varied as those grouped under "Asian-Americans." Yet, Latino culture in the United States considers itself a cultural unity to a degree that "Asian-Americans" do not.

16 FI5/21/92MC.

17 FI5/1/92YJ.

18 FI15/11/91LP.

19 Conversely, the crisis of modernity could be defined as the growing

awareness that the Self is damaged by fragmentation wrought of dis-engaged instrumentalism (compare Taylor 1989: ch. 25).

20 Even Calhoun's list could be revised to include: those permanently excluded from access to politics or bureaucracies; those for whom family, work, travel do not exist; and so on.

21 The "the" is a virtual "the." Though Taylor clearly acknowledges the authority of competing moral claims (this is one of the ways he defines modern culture), his strong-we position requires a prior, deeper belief in the "*the* good"; hence, since the good and selfhood are intertwined, of a general, if not universal, ideal moral Self.

22 Though strong-we Self-theories avoid classically essentialist commitments, their views of the Self as the moral agent of *the* good entail a prior belief in a common Humanity. One may admit, as Taylor does, a multiplicity of goods but only as historical circumstances (ultimately, threats) to personhood or the Self. This follows necessarily from his beginning assumption that the good and the Self are inextricably inter-twined. While it might be said that "inextricably intertwined" is a gentle version of "logically required," the two expressions have the same effect. It is often said that the Self is the modern counterpart to the Soul; by extension, Humanity is such to Being. Though the prior terms are homologues (not analogues) to the latter, the theoretical, and moral, consequence is the same. Everything depends on whether or not local, weak-we cultures aspire to goods that are sufficient to be *the* good, for them. Once it is granted that any weak-we culture possesses a good sufficient unto it, the ideal of universal Humanity (however tacitly held) collapses. Strong-we culture depends, therefore, on keeping the secret that it is, in fact, a powerful weak-we.

Attempts to keep the secret normally rely on one of two strategies: (1) Taylor's, that is: refer the moral dilemma of modernity to hope which (as I have argued above) is nothing more than a referral to a general theory of universal progress; or (2) a more or less overt equi-vocation, of which Wiley's (1994: 146) is the most patent: "This theory of the self ... is only a theory of the democratic agent. Nevertheless, it is a powerful picture of how the human mind works ..."! To which, the weak-we skeptic replies: "*Only* a theory of the democratic agent? of the human mind?" (compare n. 7 above).

23 Though Giddens describes the disembedding of the Self as an existential circumstance in modernity, he also argues that modernity re-embeds the individual in a more global social environment (Giddens 1990). The late-modern Self's embeddedness in global social space seems to be one of Giddens's most important empirical references for the reflexive Self (1990: 149).

24 It is just as important to call attention to the other extreme, the pseudo-postmodern self, of which Gergen (1991) is one example. Though Gergen presents his "saturated self" as postmodern, it remains a strong-we posi-tion in that the conditions of the postmodern life are seen as saturating,

populating, besieging, and troubling the Self. His position, thus, is no different from that of Giddens, who rejects the idea of the postmodern in which, says Giddens (1990: 149), the Self is "dissolved and dismembered by the fragmenting of experience."

REFERENCES

Anzaldúa, Gloria 1988: *Borderlands/La Frontera: The New Mestiza*. San Francisco: Spinsters/Aunt Lutte Press.

Asante, Molefi 1987: *The Afrocentric Ideal*. Philadelphia: Temple University Press.

Butler, Judith 1990: *Gender Trouble: Feminism and the Subversion of Identity*. New York and London: Routledge.

Calhoun, Craig 1991: "Morality, Identity, and Historical Explanation: Charles Taylor on the Sources of the Self," *Sociological Theory*, 10 (2).

Collins, Patricia Hill 1990: *Black Feminist Thought: Knowledge, Consciousness, and the Politics of Empowerment*. Boston: Unwin Hyman.

Cooper, Anna Julia 1988 [1892]: *A Voice From the South*. Oxford and New York: Oxford University Press.

Doar, Julie and Charles Lemert 1991: "Women of Color and White Guys." American Sociological Association, unpublished.

Du Bois, W. E. B. 1989 [1903]: *Souls of Black Folk*. New York: Bantam.

Erikson, Erik 1950: *Childhood and Society*. New York: W. W. Norton & Co.

Garbarino, James, Nancy Dubrow, Kathleen Kostelny, and Carole Pardo 1992: *Children in Danger: Coping With the Consequences of Community Violence*. San Francisco: Jossey-Bass.

Gates, Henry Louis, Jr 1992: *Loose Canons*. Oxford and New York: Oxford University Press.

Gergen, Kenneth 1991: *The Saturated Self: Dilemmas of Identity in Contemporary Life*. New York: Basic Books.

Giddens, Anthony 1990: *The Consequences of Modernity*. Stanford CA: Stanford University Press.

Giddens, Anthony 1991: *Modernity and Identity: Self and Society in the Late Modern Age*. Stanford CA: Stanford University Press.

Goffman, Erving 1955: "On Face-work: An Analysis of Ritual Elements in Social Interaction," *Psychiatry: Journal for the Study of Interpersonal Process* 18(3): 213–31.

Goffman, Erving 1959: *Presentation of Self in Everyday Life*. New York: Anchor/Doubleday.

Goffman, Erving 1963: *Stigma: Notes On the Management of Spoiled Identity*. New York: Simon and Schuster.

Hacker, Andrew 1992: *Two Nations: Black and White, Separate, Hostile, Unequal*. New York: Scribner's.

Haraway, Donna 1991 [1985]: "Manifesto for Cyborgs," in *Simians, Cyborgs, and Woman*. Routledge.

hooks, bell 1981: *Ain't I A Woman?* Boston: South End Press.

James, William 1960 [1902]: *The Varieties of Religious Experience*. London and New York: Collins/Fontana.

James, William 1981 [1890]: *Principles of Psychology*, vol. I. Cambridge, MA: Harvard University Press.

Jefferson, Thomas 1943 [1781]: "Notes on the State of Virginia," in Saul Padover, ed., *The Complete Jefferson*. Duell, Sloan & Pearce.

Kotlowitz, Alex 1991: *There Are No Children Here*. New York: Doubleday.

Lemert, Charles 1992a: "General Social Theory, Irony, Postmodernism," in Steven Seidman and David Wagner, eds, *Postmodernism and Social Theory: The Debate over General Theory*. Oxford, UK and Cambridge, MA: Basil Blackwell, pp. 17–46.

Lemert, Charles 1992b: "Subjectivity's Limit: The Unsolved Riddle of the Standpoint," *Sociological Theory* 10: 63–73.

Lemert, Charles 1993: "Politic Semiotics and the Zero-Signifier in Semiotics," in Pertti Ahonen, ed., *Semiotics and Politics*. Berlin: Walter de Gruyer, & Co.

Levin, Peter 1993: The White-Guy Identity. Wesleyan University thesis, unpublished.

Lorde, Audre 1984: *Sister Outsider*. Trumansburg, NY: Crossing Press.

Mead, George Herbert 1934: *Mind, Self and Society*. Chicago: University of Chicago Press.

Mendéz, Lucinda Margarita 1992: "Latino Identity: Barriers and Prospects." Wesleyan University thesis, unpublished.

Moraga, Cherríe and Gloria Anzaldúa, eds 1981: *This Bridge Called My Back*. New York: Kitchen Table/Women of Color Press.

Morrison, Toni 1992: *Playing in the Dark*. Cambridge, MA: Harvard University Press.

Myrdal, Gunnar 1944: *An American Dilemma*. New York: Harper and Brothers.

Raines, Howell 1992: "Grady's Gift," *New York Times Magazine* (December 1).

Riesman, David with Nathan Glazer and Reuel Denney 1950: *The Lonely Crowd: A Study of the Changing American Character*. New Haven: Yale University Press.

Rorty, Richard 1989: *Contingency, Irony, and Solidarity*. Cambridge, UK and New York: Cambridge University Press.

Schlesinger, Arthur 1991: *The Disuniting of America: Reflections on a Multi-cultural Society*. Knoxville, TN: Whittle Books.

Scott, James 1991: *Domination and the Arts of Resistance*. New Haven: Yale University Press.

Seidman, Steve 1992: "Race, Sexuality and the Politics of Difference." Unpublished.

Smith, Dorothy 1987: *The Everyday World as Problematic: A Feminist Sociology*. Boston: Northeastern University Press.

Spivak, Gayatri Chakrovorty 1988: "Can the Subaltern Speak?" in Cary Nelson and Lawrence Grossberg, eds, *Marxism and the Interpretation of Culture*. Urbana: University of Illinois Press.

Taylor, Charles 1989: *Sources of the Self*. Cambridge, MA: Harvard University Press.

Tocqueville, Alexis de 1969 [1835]: *Democracy in America*. New York: Anchor/Doubleday.

Trinh T. Minh-Ha 1989: *Woman, Native, Other*. Bloomington: Indiana University Press.

Weeks, Jeffrey 1991: *Against Nature: Essays on History, Sexuality, and Identity*. London: Rivers Oram Press.

Wiley, Norbert 1994: "The Politics of Identity in American History" (ch. 4, this volume); originally American Sociological Association, 1992.

Wills, Gary 1978: *Inventing America: Jefferson's Declaration of Independence*. New York: Doubleday.

4

The Politics of Identity in American History

Norbert Wiley

I take the position that there is a universal human nature, characterizing all human beings in the same generic way, at all times and places. Human nature has the distinguishing feature of being rational, symbolic, abstract, semiotic, linguistic, and so on, a point I will clarify as this chapter proceeds. This feature evolved in our line of primates in a way that is not currently understood (Bickerton 1990 has what may be the boldest current hypothesis), although phylogenetic evolution is not a major concern of this chapter. I will refer to this uniquely human trait as the reflexive self, the semiotic self, or simply as the self.

The notion of identity, etymologically a "sameness," which could refer to generic human nature, is normally used in a more specific way (Gleason 1992 [1983]). It usually refers to some long-term, abiding qualities which, despite their importance, are not features of human nature as such. Identities individuate and allow us to recognize individuals, categories, groups, and types of individuals. They can be imposed from without, by social processes, or from within, in which case they are often called self-concepts. They may also imply habit in various senses, including Pierre Bourdieu's "habitus." Identities, then, are nested within and express the qualities of selves and collections of selves.

The line between (particular) identities and (generic) selves is not easy to draw. History is notorious with peoples who thought their

For comments on earlier drafts thanks are due to Randall Collins, Vincent Colapietro, Fred Matthews, H. S. Thayer, and David Westby. These ideas are treated at greater length in Wiley (forthcoming).

historically specific identities were universal, and who therefore used the name of their tribe as the name of their species. Despite the difficulty of applying this distinction, I will use the terms "self" and "identity" in the way indicated, as distinguished by degree of generality.

Institutions frequently endow individuals with identities, with historically specific traits, that are claimed to be those of universal human nature. This is done not only by states and governments but also by religions, economies and legal systems.

The recent discussion of the "death of man" and the decentering of the self or subject in continental social theory is largely the analysis of historically specific identities, including the kind imposed by institutions. The people who had (or "housed") these identities may have looked upon them as humanity itself, and it is a profound contribution for scholars like Foucault and Derrida to have shown how long-term identities can come and go. Nevertheless to call these goings the "death of man" or the "effacement of the subject" is a category error, not unlike the one the primitives themselves made, for it equates (particular) identities with the (generic) self.

Given these definitions, the politics of identity is the struggle over the qualities attributed, socially and institutionally, to individuals and groupings of individuals. Some may argue that these qualities are the essence of human nature, at least for the groupings to whom they are assigned, and an exhaustive description of the selves in question. In rebuttal others may argue that there are no such things as selves and that the assigned qualities, including the semiotic structures within which they reside, are nothing more than talk or discourse. In my view these claims, both of which erroneously equate identities and selves, are the rhetoric of politics. It is a mistake to say that identities are trans-historical and universal, but it is also a mistake to say that personhood and selves are not. The selves are generic human structures, and the identities, any one of which may or may not be present, are distinct from and inhere in these structures.

The politics of identity in American history is largely a struggle over the definition of politically sensitive categories of people, especially minority groups. This struggle concerns the qualities that will be socially and institutionally applied to these groups, which will define their rights and duties, and which will affect the quality of their lives. American history, characterized by continuous flows of immigration, has had a constant debate over the politics of identity (Curti 1980). Ethnicity, race, religion, and social class have been staple issues in this debate. In recent years gender and sexual orientation have been added as well, with still other issues possibly in the wings.

In the American past there have been two major theories for explaining the self and its identities: the faculty psychology (Howe 1987) of the founding fathers and the semiotic theory (Thayer 1981; Colapietro 1989) of the classical pragmatists. Neither theory is current and usable for today's politics of identity. The course of theology, philosophy and science in the nineteenth century eroded the founding fathers' approach, and the twentieth century has had a somewhat similar effect on pragmatism. Today's discussion is largely between positions that define the self as a pseudo-problem: biological and cybernetic arguments that reduce the self to a lower, ontological level and cultural-linguistic positions, such as those of the post-structuralists, that reduce (or "sublate") the self to a higher level. Both of these positions eliminate selves and their identities, and, because of this displacement, neither comes to grips with the politics of identity. By arguing that selves do not exist these positions are really saying that theory cannot contribute to this question. When theory evades or ducks a question, it still gets confronted, but in other media, such as politics, law, mass media, religion, and informal social channels. My position in the current discussion of identity is that the pragmatic solution was discarded too soon, that the elements of a usable neo-pragmatism are available, and that this approach can be made superior to the two reductions.

This chapter has four parts. It begins with a brief sketch of the founding fathers' faculty psychology; second it reviews classical pragmatism; third it turns to the contemporary politics of identity; and finally it shows how a revised pragmatism might be used for the current situation.

The Founding Fathers and Faculty Psychology

There is a significant literature on the psychological and social philosophies of the founding fathers (e.g., Wills 1978, 1981; White 1978, 1987; Diggins 1984; Boorstin 1948; Howe 1987; Matthews 1990) but not much comparing these views to those of the pragmatists (Diggins 1979; Lavine 1984). Some scholars discuss both the founding fathers and the pragmatists in detail but do not systematically compare the two (Wolfe 1970; Flower and Murphey 1977; Curti 1980). My purpose is merely to indicate how faculty psychology, or rather "psychologies," explained the politics of identity in the revolutionary and constitution-building period, and to show why this explanation was no longer usable when the "new immigrants," primarily Catholics and Jews, appeared in the populist-progressive era.

The politics of identity in the revolutionary period centered on the human variations that were problematic at the time, primarily "race" (blacks, Indians, and Europeans), gender and social class. Religious conflict, which had been a serious colonial problem, was mitigated by the separation of church and state. It did not again become a major problem until late in the nineteenth century, and homosexuality, of course, did not get politicized until late in the twentieth.

The theorists of the revolutionary period, especially Thomas Jefferson, Alexander Hamilton, and James Madison, were practical intellectuals using ideas to build institutions. They were not pure theorists, and their writings are not replete with footnotes and bibliographies. The Declaration of Independence and the Constitution in particular are free-standing documents, the theoretical origins of which must be inferred, and sometimes guessed at, indirectly.

The founders drew eclectically on the English-speaking philosophers of their times: the empiricists Thomas Hobbes, John Locke, and David Hume, and the Scottish moralists Francis Hutcheson, Adam Smith, Adam Ferguson, and Thomas Reid, among others. These philosophers differed from each other, the moralists, for example, being closer to everyday beliefs and common sense. There is also scholarly dispute over which philosophers had the most influence over the Declaration of Independence, the Constitution, and the beliefs of individual founding fathers (Howe 1982).

Nevertheless the founders shared a broad perspective on human nature. In their view human beings were essentially characterized by a set of relatively static and private capacities and powers, some of which distinguished them from the other animals. These were not the innate ideas that the empiricists so opposed, but innate properties or possibilities. The actual list of faculties was not the same for all these thinkers, but it centered on the triad of passions, interests, and reason (Howe 1987; Hirschman 1977). In the hierarchy of moral dignity reason was the highest faculty, then the (still rational but self-serving) interests, and finally the highly emotional passions. The problem of human nature, however, was that the strength or power of the faculties reversed the moral hierarchy, with passions strongest, then interests, and finally reason.

In the Constitution the state was viewed as though it were human nature writ large, i.e., as though it too contained faculties of differing dignity and strength. The system of checks and balances was intended to get the best results from the political "faculties" with the least risks.

But the politics of identity, which was another offshoot of the founders' faculty psychology, was not worked out with much precision, nor did it continue to be usable as the nineteenth century progressed.

The founders' interpretations of their own minorities – blacks, Indians, women, and the poor – though not uniform or very explicit, were related to the faculty profiles attributed to these groupings. In contrast to the propertied white males, in whom reason was thought to be relatively strong, the minorities were viewed as having weaker reason and stronger passions. This might be called the theory of unequal or skewed faculties, although it was not applied in the same way to all minorities. Nevertheless Indians and blacks were not offered citizenship, women were not allowed to vote or hold office, and property regulations, albeit minor ones, restricted the political rights of white males.

The underlying reasons for or causes of these inferior faculty mixtures were even more obscure in the founders. They did not have the twentieth-century distinction between heredity and environment, or biology and culture. These categories did not appear until after Darwin expanded the domain of the biological and the pragmatists and early anthropologists counter-expanded the domain of the cultural. These are now taken-for-granted categories, but the founders had to work with blunter tools.

Jefferson was notoriously ambiguous about the blacks and the Indians, mixing hereditarian and environmental ideas in ways that are both unattractive and make little sense today (Boorstin 1948: 81–98). Of course the founders were power-brokering a compromise between slave and free states, giving them a self-interest in not looking too closely at racism. They were also following the egalitarian Declaration of Independence with the much less egalitarian Constitution, giving them reason to ignore this inconsistency as well. They not only lacked the concepts, but also the good faith to use them unblinkingly.

The founders were also cryptic about social classes. Locke had said classes originate in the state of nature, unequal land ownership having resulted from the invention of money. He thought the poor had less time and energy to develop their rational powers, thereby making them more prone to passions and less fit for democracy (Macpherson 1962: 221–38). In the famous "Federalist 10," Madison is reminiscent of Locke when he refers to the "diversity in the faculties of men, from which the rights of property originate" and the "different and unequal faculties of acquiring property" (Madison 1961: 130–1; Epstein 1984). Locke, however, was talking primarily about how unequal faculties are the effect of inequality, and Madison was making them the cause. Why do Madison's humans (actually, white males) have unequal faculties in the first place? Were they born this way (heredity)? Taught this way (culture)? Or was Madison tacitly drawing on the Calvinist notion of the elect, a concept that would again entail superior faculties in some, but would not fit into the heredity–environment scheme.

Underneath the notion of unequal faculties, then, the fathers had several obscure, now out-of-date explanations. They were not like the racist, social Darwinists of the late nineteenth and early twentieth centuries. Nor were they like the more culturological pragmatists and early anthropologists of that same time period. They had a third position, which straddled the distinction between biology and culture, using concepts and categories that are now obsolete.

Still, the founders' politics of identity, despite its philosophical roughness, was a "workable" scheme for the times. Of course it was backed up by a great deal of brute force, especially against the blacks and the Indians, and this limited its durability. What made it obsolete as the nineteenth century proceeded, however, is difficult to say, both because of the complexity of the question and the paucity of relevant scholarship.

Most American historians think the central event of that century was the Civil War, although there is little agreement on either its causes or effects. The war in general and the Gettysburg Address in particular certainly deepened the American commitment to equality, but this was not anchored in a new theory of human nature, and it seems an exaggeration to call it a "refounding" (Wills 1992: 40). Nor did this commitment deliver equality for American blacks. The Civil War weakened the founders' theory of human nature, but it did not replace it.

Perhaps a stronger, if less bloody, cultural force was the Darwinian revolution. This paradigm elevated the power of the biological, particularly the randomly biological. The extra-biological overtones of faculty psychology, along with its teleological or goal-directed system of faculties, made it incongruent with Darwinism.

By the end of the century, when Jim Crow laws had moved race relations back toward slavery and the new immigrants seemed not quite human, the founders' theory of human nature was completely inadequate. The industrialization of the United States and the ethnic-religious peculiarities of the new immigrants completely overloaded the old democratic paradigm. Out of this confusion and political ferment came America's second great theory of democracy, that of classical pragmatism.

THE POPULIST-PROGRESSIVE PERIOD AND CLASSICAL PRAGMATISM

The three major pragmatists were Charles Sanders Peirce, William James, and John Dewey, George Herbert Mead being the lesser-known fourth. In addition there were many other contributing scholars, both within and tangential to the movement (Thayer 1981). The specific contribution of pragmatism, or we might say its unity, is unclear, both because of the looseness of the movement and because scholars have not done enough work on it (Hollinger 1980). Pragmatism's unity is usually thought to be in its logic, method, or the corresponding epistemology. This not only makes the unity mushy, but also politically rudderless. Pragmatism, as some kind of vague social engineering, can be, and often has been, right-wing and centrist as well as moderately leftist.

I am more interested in pragmatism's self theory, the family resemblance of which can be drawn from Peirce, Dewey, James, and Mead. This theory, though incomplete, is not mushy at all. The idea of the semiotic self is a technically sophisticated construction, giving anchorage to pragmatism's much looser theories of logic and epistemology. It also gives applied pragmatism a distinctly democratic rudder, orienting it to a populist blend of equality and freedom. In addition the theory of the semiotic self is useful in framing and conceptualizing today's politics of identity.

But the pragmatist theory of self and identity did not directly replace that of the founding fathers. By the middle of the nineteenth century, well before the appearance of pragmatism, the American transcendentalists were already moving from faculty psychology to a literary form of German idealism (Flower and Murphey 1977: vol. 1, pp. 397–435). Then Darwinism finished the job. It displaced faculty psychology and created a vacuum in the theory of the self, much like the one that exists today.

Evolution implied a biological reduction of the self, suggesting that variations in human identity were the expression of physical variation in human bodies. In the wide variety of social Darwinist, eugenic, and racist positions in the populist-progressive period, the politics of identity was a kind of zoology, and the political implications, particularly for minorities, were decidedly undemocratic.

In the United States the initial response to Darwinism's reductionism was neo-Hegelianism, which went beyond transcendentalism's literary idealism. This was a move to the opposite kind of self reductionism, to the other side of the boat. The British neo-Hegelian, Edward Caird, referred to these two reductions as "levelling down" and "levelling up," his own position implying the latter. As he put it, "We must 'level up' and not 'level down'; we must not only deny that matter can explain spirit, but we must say that even matter itself cannot be fully understood except as an element in the spiritual world" (Caird, 1968 [1889]: 35, quoted approvingly by the early Dewey 1969 [1890]: 183).

The pragmatists, particularly the Dewey–Mead Chicago wing, began with a religious reliance on neo-Hegelianism (see Murphey 1968 for the Harvard wing's religious reliance on Kant). By the turn of the century, both Dewey and Mead had moved into their less dialectical and more secular versions of pragmatism. Eventually, in a reminiscence on this period, Mead took the position that neo-Hegelianism, like social Darwinism, was itself incompatible with democracy (Mead 1964 [1929]).

The interesting thing about this roughly 1870–90 period is the parallel with today's politics of identity. The conflict between the down-levelling social Darwinists and the up-levelling neo-Hegelians was approximately the same as that between the two current reductions I mentioned earlier.

When Dewey and Mead emerged from neo-Hegelianism they developed a position that opposed both reductionisms, i.e. the classical pragmatist theory of the semiotic self. This position was close to that of Peirce and compatible with that of William James. For the politics of identity it offered a second American theory of human variation, more persuasive than what was left of faculty psychology, and, as it turned out, strong enough to explain and soften the identity stresses of the populist-progressive period.

The pragmatist theory of the self was located in an evolutionary framework, i.e. it was intended to explain, or at least begin to explain, how humans evolved, phylogenetically, from the lower primates. In addition it applied an evolutionary analogy to social change. Although pragmatism was compatible with Darwinism, this being part of its superiority to faculty psychology, it was not biologically reductionist as the various social Darwinisms were. Instead the pragmatists interpreted evolutionary theory in such a way that it explained the emergence of human uniqueness and symbolic power, including the capacities for democratic government.

The pragmatist theory of the self never jelled into some specific, definitive statement or set of ideas. Still less did it ever become enunciated by the United States government as its official social psychology. Just as with the founding period, the shift to a new theory of the self, with implications for the politics of identity, must be inferred indirectly (see Hamilton and Sutton 1989 for an analysis of how pragmatist theory entered the legal process).

To appreciate the impact of pragmatism it should be seen in a systematic triad of philosophy, sociology, and anthropology. While the pragmatists were arguing that human nature is essentially symbolic and semiotic, the early sociologists were showing that social life is based on symbolic interaction, and the anthropologists were showing that this interaction produces culture. Internal semiotic, interpersonal interaction and the cultural product were intrinsically connected ideas, each being more powerful because of the relations among the three. Of course the concept of culture also sharpened the distinction between heredity and environment, permitting a reasoned argument that human variation was not caused biologically but environmentally, this environment being conceived primarily as semiotic, interactional, and cultural.

The battle between pragmatism and social Darwinism was fought for a long time, at many levels and on many fronts. It not only went on in the three disciplines I mentioned – philosophy, sociology, and anthropology – it also proceeded in popular magazines, the politics of private organizations, and public affairs generally. By the time W. I. Thomas and Florian Znaniecki wrote *The Polish Peasant in Europe and America* (1918–20), in opposition to social Darwinism's "ordering and forbidding" (vol. 1, p. 3) political implications, the theoretical triad was completely in place. Biological reductionism as a politics of identity was in retreat, and it would fade out by the end of the 1920s (Wiley 1986).

In its fight with social Darwinism the pragmatist coalition had an important ally in psychological behaviorism, the position of John Watson. In a way behaviorism was also biologically reductionist, for the difference between humans and the other animals was erased. But it did not explain human variation by innate biological mechanisms, the traits, genes, and instincts of social Darwinism. Instead human variation was a product of learning, a process highly influenced by the environment. Pragmatism's compatability with behaviorism was quite limited, surrounded by important incompatibilities, and the alliance was at best unstable. Nevertheless behaviorism's rise in psychology was an important factor in social Darwinism's decline.

Behaviorism as such never became influential as a model for the democratic actor, i.e. for the politics of identity. Pragmatism and the disciplinary triad took that role. But behaviorism did become quite influential as a model for the economic actor. In other words the "economic man" of classical economics was transformed from utilitarianism to behaviorism. Behaviorism's victory in the economy limited the institutional impact of pragmatism, although the latter did gain hegemony in political life.

In the fourth section, on neo-pragmatism, I will discuss the pragmatist theory of the self in more detail. For now, let me just sketch the differences between pragmatism and faculty psychology, indicating how these differences strengthened pragmatism's role in the turn-of-the century politics of identity crisis.

1   *Dialogical*. The self of pragmatism was dialogical, both interpersonally and internally (Taylor 1991: 31–41). The self was initially formed in dialogue with caretakers, and this dialogue was constitutive of whatever identities the self would take on. Moreover the inner life of the self, both in content and form, was a continuation of interpersonal dialogue. In contrast, the self of faculty psychology was unitary and monological. When it entered into dialogue with others, it did so from a fully formed psychological base. Later I will show that the dialogical self is also trialogical (and semiotic). This is because all dialogue, both inter- and intrapersonal, entails a self–other–self reflexive loop. I will refer to this three-place loop as the "structure," in contrast to the "content," of the semiotic self.

2   *Social*. From dialogicality comes sociality. The pragmatists' self was inherently social and therefore public and political. For faculty psychology the individual and society were at a distance, requiring social contracts in politics and markets in economics to unite them. For the pragmatists the individual and the social were interpenetrating. This is because all conscious processes were based on an outside or social perspective. Markets and social contracts merely refined an already existing social solidarity.

3   *Horizontal*. For faculty psychology human nature was a vertical structure, consisting in a hierarchy of faculties. For pragmatism it was a horizontal structure, consisting of temporal phases of the self. For Peirce these phases were called the "I" and the "you." For Mead they were the "I" and the "me." I will look at these temporal phases in more detail later, but for now I want to point out that pragmatism's horizontality suggested a generic uniformity in everyone's rational processes. To describe this uniformity, pragmatism demoted the passions of faculty psychology into the less influential category of impulses. In turn, interests and reason were merged in the horizontal semiotic process.

4 *Egalitarian.* The pragmatist theory of the self was distinctly egalitarian. All humans had the same psychological equipment in
the same way. Human variation into identity groupings and unique
individualities was a matter of differing symbols and their interpretations. The social Darwinists were explaining human identities, particularly ethnicity, biologically, by what they were calling
"instincts." The pragmatists explained the same differences non-
biologically and semiotically, as a matter of signs, communication,
and interpretation. The pragmatists' self was extremely plastic,
communication could produce all manner of variations, and the
perplexing variations in the new immigrants could be fully explained semiotically, interactionally, and culturally.

5 *Voluntarist.* Concerning the psychological freedom of the person
or citizen, the founding fathers were somewhere between Calvinist
determinism and Locke–Hume compatibilism, i.e., between hard
and soft determinism. The pragmatists, instead, attributed a capacity for self-determination or psychological freedom to the individual, i.e., they believed people could have chosen otherwise.
In contrast to the semi-determinism of the founding fathers, this
freedom had more deeply libertarian implications for law, civil
liberties, and democratic self-government.

6 *Cultural.* Finally the pragmatists' self was part of the great cultural turn of the late nineteenth and early twentieth centuries.
The anthropologists, particularly Franz Boas and his students,
discovered culture macroscopically and from above. The pragmatists discovered it microscopically and from below. The human
semiotic/symbolic capacity is the motor of culture. Once humans
were theorized as semiotic, the psychological preconditions of culture had been found and the cultural level itself could be discovered. Neither British empiricism nor Scottish moralism had
the idea of culture, although the latter's "common sense" was
a move in that direction. The concept of culture was useful if
not indispensable for democracy, for it explained variation in
identities in a way that was compatible with an egalitarian form
of government.

The founding fathers, to their great credit, created a sturdy if quite
imperfect democracy. Unfortunately, like that of the Athenians,
their democracy was symbiotic with slavery. Similarly the founders'
theory of the self was theoretically undisciplined and allowed of a
slave psychology. The pragmatists' self, more so than that of the
fathers, had an elective affinity with democratic institutions. In addition the pragmatists got rid of slave psychology once and for all,

showing how blacks and non-blacks alike have the standard, generic psychological equipment.

These six traits made pragmatism a better democratic instrument than faculty psychology had been. Neither social Darwinism nor neo-Hegelianism could have been a democratic replacement for faculty psychology, the former reducing the self to the body and the latter, to the community. In contrast, pragmatism was a workable way of viewing human nature, despite the new stresses of industrialization, immigration and urbanization, and if there was a "second founding," this was it.

THE POLITICS OF IDENTITY TODAY

The pragmatist coalition, in my opinion, saved American democracy in the early twentieth century. At the very least, it looks as though citizenship rights and civil liberties would have diminished if social Darwinism had not been checked by pragmatism. But the politics-of-identity crisis of the turn of the century declined as the immigrants gradually became assimilated, and, perhaps more than coincidentally, pragmatism declined with it. James (1910), Peirce (1914), and then Mead (1931) died, leaving no great disciples. Dewey at Columbia lived until 1952, but turned his interest more specifically to education. Except for the logical line of C. I. Lewis, W. V. Quine, and Nelson Goodman, pragmatism trickled off in the 1930s, to be replaced by logical positivism. In the decades since pragmatism's decline there have always been disciples of Peirce, Dewey, and Mead, but not many important new developments or ideas. At the present time there are some influential calls for a neo-pragmatism in several disciplines, but not much new theory. The basic ideas of the pragmatist coalition, particularly those of equality and freedom, are still influential in the democratic institutions, but they are "living off their capital."

In the meantime, America's politics-of-identity situation has become more critical. The Catholics and Jews, who were central to the turn-of-the-century crisis, have been politically incorporated, but the other minorities are now in pronounced dissent. As of recent decades, blacks, Hispanics, and woman are demanding a fuller participation in democratic life In addition Asian-Americans, new and old, are forming into a powerful minority group. Beyond this there is now a completely new identity problem coming from dissatisfied homosexual Americans, who are also asking for full citizenship.

Exacerbating this crisis is the fact that capitalism's living standards, especially in the United States, have plateaued for about twenty years. During the prosperous post-Second World War years – until approximately the 1973 oil shock – a workable way of placating minorities was built into the expanding economy, for the growing pie automatically increased everyone's share. Now there is both stalled growth and upward income redistribution, i.e., a static pie of increasingly unequal slices. These economic stresses are worsening the identity tensions.

As I mentioned earlier, the two American theories of the democratic personality – faculty psychology and pragmatism – are not in a position to meet the current challenge. Instead the levelling down and levelling up strategies of biological (Deglar 1991) and cultural (Rosenau 1992) reduction are the focus of discussion. But reductionist theories were not useful for the politics of identity in the late nineteenth century, nor are they any more so today.

In this theoretical vacuum the possibility of a revitalized neo-pragmatism offers an intriguing prospect. I see this as the challenge of completing the pragmatic synthesis in a way that the classical pragmatists never quite did, and of incorporating ideas from other developments in philosophy. In the next section I turn to these possibilities.

NEO-PRAGMATISM AND THE CONTEMPORARY POLITICS OF IDENTITY

The key insight of the pragmatists, for the politics of identity, was in seeing human variation as the result of a highly plastic, semiotic process. This process explained identity variation in a way that was compatible with democracy. These theorists sketched the semiotic nature of the self in broad outlines, but they did not work it out in detail. The two who contributed the most were Peirce and Mead – James and Dewey having worked primarily in other areas of pragmatism. Neither Mead nor especially Peirce ever completed their theories of the self. In addition, each worked with somewhat different terms and concepts, making it difficult to combine the two sets of insights.

Recently Peirce's theory of the semiotic self, which he never integrated, was systematized by the Peircean scholar, Vincent Colapietro (1989). Colapietro did not actually complete Peirce's theory of the self, but he went a long way toward making it more coherent (Wiley 1992). His interest was primarily in Peirce, and he did not attempt to combine Peirce and Mead (but see Rochberg-Halton 1986: 24–40 for some probes in that direction). In a private communication to me, however, Colapietro suggested a tentative way of linking the two theories. This has to do with visualizing the self as a present–past–future, I–me–you semiotic triad.

The major difference between Peirce and Mead, for present purposes, is in the temporal direction of the internal dialogue. Mead has this conversation going temporally backwards, from present to past, or I to me. Peirce has it going forward, from present to future, or I to "you" (i.e., one's own self in the immediate future). Both versions produce a highly plastic, semiotic self, but at present they are side by side and have never been combined. Moreover, they are obviously not both right. If the self is a dialogue between present and future, then it is not a dialogue between present and past, and vice versa.

Colapietro suggests a way of combining the two dialogical theories. He dovetails them by linking them both to the sign–object–interpretant structure of the semiotic triad. The details of this synthesis are somewhat technical, but I will gradually work my way back to the ordinary language of the politics of identity.

Peirce's great semiotic insight was in seeing that thought is not in the dyadic form of representation–object but in the triadic form of sign–object–interpretant. One should keep in mind that Peirce, confusingly, used the word "sign" in two senses: for the overall semiotic triad and, in addition, for one of its three elements. In the triadic scheme the "sign" (second sense of word) can be a mere physical vehicle or designator of a concept, e.g. the marks on a page or the sound of a voice, but it is also, more commonly, itself a concept. When the latter, the triad becomes one of (1) thought, (2) object, and (3) interpretation of thought. Peirce's semiotic triad is dynamic and in potentially perpetual motion, involving an indefinite amount of interpretation and reinterpretation. To stretch a metaphor, it is more a (triadic) moving picture than a (dyadic) snapshot.

The sign and the interpretant are in a dialogical relationship, discussing the object so to speak. In addition the interpretant of one moment often becomes the sign of the next. Peirce anchored his semiotic triad in his metaphysical categories – firstness, secondness, and thirdness – thereby locating semiotics in his overall philosophy, although that is outside the scope of this chapter.

Colapietro's suggestion is that the semiotic process entails both Peirce's I–you and Mead's I–me dialogues. To do this he draws on Peirce's idea that the "self is a sign" (first sense of word), although Peirce never indicated which part of the self is sign (second sense of word), which part object, and which part interpretant. Colapietro's suggestion synthesizes three triads: present–past–future, I–me–you and sign–object–interpretant.

The self on this view is a constant process of self-interpretation, as the present self interprets the past self to the future self. In dialogical terms, the I and the you interpret the me in order to give direction to the you. Semiotically the I-present functions as a sign, the me-past as the object, and the you-future as the interpretant. As the self moves down the time line its semiotic process is constantly transformed, with a past interpretant becoming a present sign and then a future object. The content, i.e., the specific topic of the internal conversation, may be anything, including the stories and narratives with which people interpret themselves, but its semiotic form or structure is one which integrates the three triads mentioned above.

In terms of the politics of identity, to get back to the theme, the I–me–you triad is the overall structure of the self. All selves at all times – subsequent to our evolution from the primates – have an I–me–you, present–past–future structure. And they all think in the grooves of the corresponding semiotic triad. Exactly what they think, their specific semiotic contents, is a matter of "identities" and other semiotic meanings. Similarly the power of the self versus that of the community, a historical variable, is also a matter of identities, ranging from the communality of traditional societies to the heightened individuality of contemporary ones.

Although identities are more general than individual signs, they are less general than the semiotic structure. They are historically specific and "housed" in these structures. Thus I am distinguishing three semiotic levels within the self: (1) individual signs, e.g., thoughts, (2) systematic complexes of signs, e.g., the ethnic, class, gender, and sexual orientation identities and self-concepts of this paper, and (3) the generic capacity for semiosis, anchored in the I–you–me structure.

The strength of Colapietro's suggestion is that it offers a way of visualizing a truly pragmatic theory of the self, i.e., one that unites the disparate strands of the movement and provides a new solution to the problem of pragmatism's unity. More specifically, it unites Peircean and Meadean self theory at the core, the semiotic (or "selfing") process. Mead's I–me reflexivity and Peirce's I–you interpretive process each become part of a more inclusive semiotic process, the I–me–you triadic conversation. This triad is the structure of the self, the universal generic human nature with which I began this paper and which the reductions are unable to explain.

Viewed in this way, the voluntarist and egalitarian qualities of the self are both more solidly anchored. Voluntarism or freedom is built into the semiotic process, which in turn emerges over time. The agent or I of the present interprets the history or me of the past to and with the you of the future. This interpretation does not mirror, nor is it caused by, the past. It creates, and it does so by a kind of cognitive reality construction. It defines and redefines the situation in a somewhat undetermined manner. The action itself, which may flow from the interpretation, can be viewed as determined (e.g., by the greater good) or "compatible" with determinism. But the freedom is still there, back a step, in the creative act of interpretation. This is not "free will" in the narrow and traditional sense but "semiotic freedom," which amounts to or, better said, results in the same thing. The clarification of the roles of the I, me, and you – present, past, and future – in the semiotic process thus explains pragmatism's theory of voluntarism or freedom.

The notion of the self having an overall semiotic structure, within which it engages in concrete interpretations, is also helpful in grounding pragmatism's egalitarianism. All humans have and are this structure. This is where rationality, and consequently dignity, lie. In addition, moral power, e.g., Kant's self-inviolability and Durkheim's self-sacredness, is inherent in this structure.

In contrast, identities are more superficial. For example, both men and women have the same semiotic structure, the universal human attribute. Then at a more specific, identity level, they have biological differences, along with cultural interpretations of these differences. Then, getting still more specific, there are, within genders, a variety of sexual identities that people can adopt, the various gay orientations being one cluster of them. The same structure–identity distinction can also be applied, with the same egalitarian implications, to ethnic groups, religious groups, social classes etc.

It is true that theories of the self have often carried political agendas. If structure and identity are not kept separate, it is easy enough to smuggle traits of the dominating elites into the (alleged) nature of the self. It is understandable that intellectuals who represent minority groups are suspicious of the "self" and drawn to decenterring positions. Foucault was a homosexual and Derrida is, by origin, a colonial Jew, for example. These minority connections may well have made the decentering, culturally reductionist position especially attractive to these thinkers (Johnson 1993).

Nevertheless pragmatism's theory of the self as the foundation and location of human rights does the same job, and, in my opinion, with fewer political risks. In particular, the theory of democracy and legal equality, especially for minorities, becomes less solidly grounded once the level of the self is theoretically annihilated. In other words, the politics of identity, at the present time, can best be adjudicated with a democratic theory of human nature, such as that offered by neo-pragmatism.

CONCLUSION.

This paper began with definitions and abstractions, then turned, more concretely, to American political history, and ended with an attempt to apply still more abstractions to contemporary politics. Theory has many offices, but using abstractions to throw light on concrete social problems is one of its most important.

I attempted to contextualize the current politics-of-identity whirl-wind, showing how comparisons, precedents, and parallels from the past can help interpret the present. The theoretical models of the self which I distinguished, those of faculty psychology and classical pragmatism, were not written into law or any other government documents. They were implicit, in the air, and part of the common sense of the times.

The same is true for self theories today. For example, the two reductions that I distinguished (along with their nineteenth-century parallels) are sets of philosophical premises that operate like leaven in public life, even though intellectuals, in their own media, might be quite explicit about them.

The neo-pragmatist contender too, along with the semiotic suggestions I made, is a set of background assumptions, which may or may not influence formal politics. One of its strengths, however, is that, since the progressive period, it has been part of the common sense of American public life. The notions that the individual interprets, symbolically communicates, and lives in a culture now have an implicit "category" status in American ordinary language. The calls for neo-pragmatism are therefore calls for a clarification and development of twentieth-century American tradition.

In the formal battle of ideas, however, as opposed to the inertia of tradition, neo-pragmatism is not presently a well-developed position, even though a good deal of promising scholarship is going on. There are new pragmatisms in philosophy (Malachowski 1990; West 1989), literary criticism (Gunn 1992; Mitchell 1985) and law (Brint and Weaver 1991), as well as in other disciplines. So far, however, these neo-pragmatisms are relatively confined to method and correspondingly limited to the "mushiness" of that approach.

The fourth section of this chapter, in which I de-emphasized evolution and theorized the semiotic self, is an attempt to contribute something substantive to neo-pragmatism. This theory of the self is not offered as a solution to the politics-of-identity crisis. It is not a method or program for public life, but only a theory of the democratic agent. Nevertheless, it is a powerful picture of how the human mind works, and its voluntarist and egalitarian implications may be useful in the current politics of identity.

Let me recapitulate the argument of this paper. American democracy has worked with two theories of human nature, the faculty psychology of the founding fathers and the semiotic self of the pragmatists. Although the pragmatists themselves never quite completed their theory of the self, this is where the movement's unity lies and this is what gave the United States a "second founding." For the current political challenge, both in the United States and other countries, neo-pragmatism offers a powerful theory of the irreducible democratic agent. In particular the semiotic concept of identity refutes both reductions, for upward reduction mistakes identities for the body and downward reduction mistakes them for the self. Finally the semiotic self explains both freedom and equality, giving democracy the foundation it needs in human nature.

References

Bickerton, Derek 1990: *Language and Species.* Chicago: University of Chicago Press.

Boorstin, Daniel J. 1948: *The Lost World of Thomas Jefferson* New York: Henry Holt and Co.

Brint Michael and William Weaver, eds 1991: *Pragmatism in Law and Society.* Boulder: Westview Press.

Caird, Edward 1968 (1889): *The Critical Philosophy of Immanuel Kant,* vol. 1. New York: Kraus Reprint Co.

Colapietro, Vincent M. 1989: *Peirce's Approach to the Self.* Albany: State University of New York Press.

Curti, Merle 1980: *Human Nature in American Thought.* Madison: University of Wisconsin Press.

Deglar, Carl N. 1991: *In Search of Human Nature.* New York: Oxford University Press.

Dewey, John 1969 (1890): *John Dewey: The Early Works,* vol. 3. Carbondale: Southern Illinois University Press.

Diggins, John P. 1979: "The Socialization of Authority and the Dilemmas of American Liberalism," *Social Research* 46: 454–86.

Diggins, John P. 1984: *The Lost Soul of American Politics.* New York: Basic Books Inc.

Epstein, David F. 1984: "A Study of Federalist 10," in David F. Epstein, *The Political Theory of the Federalist.* Chicago: University of Chicago Press, pp. 59–110.

Flower, Elizabeth and Murray G. Murphey 1977: *A History of Philosophy in America,* 2 vols. New York: G. P. Putnam's Sons.

Gleason, Phillip 1992 (1983): "Identifying Identity: A Semantic History," in his *Speaking of Diversity.* Baltimore: Johns Hopkins University Press, pp. 123–49.

Gunn, Giles 1992: *Thinking Across the American Grain: Ideology, Intellect and the New Pragmatism.* Chicago: University of Chicago Press.

Hamilton, Gary G. and John R. Sutton 1989: "The Problem of Control in the Weak State," *Theory and Society* 18: 1–46.

Hirschman, Albert O. 1977: *The Passions and the Interests.* Princeton: Princeton University Press.

Hollinger, David A. 1980: "The Problem of Pragmatism in American History," *The Journal of American History* 67: 88–107.

Howe, Daniel Walker 1982: "European Sources of Political Ideas in Jeffersonian America," *Reviews in American History* 10: 28–44.

Howe, Daniel Walker 1987: "The Political Psychology of *The Federalist*," *William and Mary Quarterly* 46: 485–509.

Johnson, Barbara 1993: Introduction, to Barbara Johnson, ed., *Freedom and Interpretation: The Oxford Amnesty Lectures.* New York: Basic Books, pp. 1–16.

Lavine, Thelma Z. 1984: "Pragmatism and the Constitution in the Culture of Modernism," *Transactions of the Charles S. Peirce Society* 20: 1–10.

Macpherson, C. B. 1962: *The Political Theory of Possessive Individualism: Hobbes to Locke.* Oxford: Clarendon Press.

Madison, James: 1961 (1787): "Federalist 10," in Alexander Hamilton, James Madison, and John Jay, *The Federalist.* Cambridge: Harvard University Press, pp. 129–36.

Malachowski, Alan, ed. 1990: *Reading Rorty.* Cambridge, MA: Basil Blackwell Inc.

Matthews, Fred 1990: "The Attack on 'Historicism': Allan Bloom's Indictment of Contemporary American Historical Scholarship," *American Historical Review* 95: 429–47.

Mead, George Herbert 1964 (1929): "The Philosophies of Royce, James and Dewey in their American Setting," in *Mead: Selected Writings.* Indianapolis: Bobbs Merrill, pp. 371–91.

Mitchell, W. J. T. ed. 1985: *Against Theory: Literary Studies and the New Pragmatism.* Chicago: University of Chicago Press.

Murphey, Murray G. 1968: "Kant's Children: The Cambridge Pragmatists," *Transactions of the Charles S. Peirce Society* 4: 3–33.

Rochberg-Halton, Eugene 1986: *Meaning and Modernity.* Chicago: University of Chicago Press.

Rosenau, Pauline Marie 1992: *Post-Modernism and the Social Sciences.* Princeton: Princeton University press.

Taylor, Charles 1991: *The Malaise of Modernity.* Concord, Ontario: House of Anansi Press Ltd.

Thayer, H. S. 1981: *Meaning and Action: A Critical History of Pragmatism,* 2nd edn. Indianapolis: Hackett Publishing Co.

Thomas, William I. and Florian Znaniecki 1918–20: *The Polish Peasant in Europe and America.* Boston: Richard G. Badger.

West, Cornel 1989: *The American Evasion of Philosophy.* Madison: University of Wisconsin Press.

White, Morton 1978: *The Philosophy of the American Revolution.* New York: Oxford University Press.

White, Morton 1987: *Philosophy, The Federalist and the Constitution*. New York: Oxford University Press.

Wiley, Norbert 1986: "Early American Sociology and the *Polish Peasant*," *Sociological Theory* 4: 21–40.

Wiley, Norbert 1992: Review of Vincent M. Colapietro's *Peirce's Approach to the Self, Symbolic Interaction* 15: 383–7.

Wiley, Norbert forthcoming: *The Semiotic Self*. Cambridge: Polity Press.

Wills, Gary 1978: *Inventing America*. Garden City: Doubleday & Co.

Wills, Gary 1981: *Explaining America*. Garden City: Doubleday & Co.

Wills, Gary 1992: *Lincoln at Gettysburg: The Words that Remade America*. New York: Simon & Schuster.

Wolfe, Don M. 1970: *The Image of Man in America*, 2nd edn. New York: Thomas Y. Crowell Co.

5

From Universality to Difference: Notes on the Fragmentation of the Idea of the Left

Todd Gitlin

The contentious "political correctness" dispute in the academy is only the ruffled surface of a profound shift in ideas and feelings. Its background is the defeat of the Left as a live political and intellectual force I want, in this chapter, to weigh and account for the rise of specialized identities as foundations for knowledge and politics in the universities. At one level, the proliferation of specialized angles of vision can be understood as the consequence of two decades of the movement of new populations into the university. But it is also the latest phase in a longer-running process: the weakening, even breakdown, of ideals that were traditionally the preserve of the Left, specifically Marxism and the liberalism of individual rights. That is why it will not do simply to call for the restoration of the grand old academy. Conservatives and reformers of every description are going to have to navigate in more turbulent waters.

MEDIA PANICS AND DEEP CURRENTS

Media panics come and go, but deep currents abide. The immediate PC panic seems to have peaked as a subject of fascination in the

I am grateful to Ruth Rosen, Marshall Berman, Tom Engelhardt, Mary Felstiner, Richard Flacks, Tom Hayden, Gerda Lerner, and Robert Jay Lifton for discussions and arguments with and against me, though I alone bear responsibility. This chapter was previously published in *Contention*, vol. 2, no. 2 (Winter 1993).

media. The pinnacle of alarm was probably reached in the *annus demonicus* 1990–1 when, after a showy release of trial balloons from Lynne Cheney, William Bennett, George Will, and other archdeacons of the Right, alarms rippled across the covers of *Newsweek* ("New McCarthyism," "Thought Police"), *New York*, and *The Atlantic*. Dinesh D'Souza's *Illiberal Education* commanded tremendous attention, much of it, if not favorable, at least serious – including an unreflective endorsement by C. Vann Woodward in *The New York Review of Books*, taking the most dubious of D'Souza's lurid anecdotes at face value. None other than President George Herbert Walker Bush took the occasion of Ann Arbor's spring 1991 commencement to trash "political correctness," a phrase which, shorn of its original ironic intent, began to appear routinely in the press to designate left-of-center opinions of many sorts.

One year on, the media's fitful spotlights have wheeled away from PC and on toward other fronts in the ongoing cultural war. Republicans have moved on as well, at least for the moment, parading "family values" against marauders from the margins of perversity. Many of Dinesh D'Souza's horror stories have been called into serious question, even discredited.[1] The PC-correcting National Association of Scholars has been countered by two incipient groups, Teachers for a Democratic Culture and the Union of Democratic Intellectuals.

The terms of the culture war, and the exact makeup of the contending teams, have not stood still either. The running battle between preservationists and reformers – these labels only a first approximation, leaving aside (for the moment) that preservationists aim to preserve a university that constantly changes and reformers don't agree on their reforms – is not a war between two fixed camps waving two unvarying banners. While the same anecdotes continue to be recycled and the same anathemas cast, one senses a shift in the texture of the dispute. The polarizing rhetoric of the preservationists has had the effect of bringing to the surface something of a malaise, perhaps a reappraisal, throughout the Academic Left and the uncommitted as well. Also, I sense that some of the PC-Correctors have developed a softer edge. The hard reconstructionists – reckless canon-smashers, speech muzzlers, and kneejerk reverse racialists in the ranks of the PC – were always far fewer in number than claimed by the PC-Correctors; but while some of the hard reconstructionists have further hardened their views, their numbers, I suspect, have dwindled. Although the momentum of extravagant movements is hard to gauge, I do not get the sense that the ranks of Afrocentrists, Goddess-worshippers, and canon-trashers are growing, or that Alice Walker, the Right's *bête noire*, has succeeded in bumping Shakespeare, as charged. [2]

Not that exponents of curricular cleansing should be expected to cease collecting horror stories – if for no other reason than that stories continue unfolding. They *deserve* collection. Some stories are true and important, even if Dinesh D'Souza tells them. But much of the Right stops at the point of denunciation – just when the conversation might get interesting. The PC atmosphere is as thick as it is not because of the stupidity or malevolence of the partisans, as right-wing publicists assume. Rather, the contests in question, the significant and the absurd, flourish because the various forms of blindness and insight have their uses, their soil, their roots.

THE THICKENING OF IDENTITY POLITICS

Plainly, *one* immediate cause of the anti-PC groundswell is the rise of identity politics – the convergence of a cultural style, a form of logic, a badge of belonging, and a claim to insurgency. As critics observe, identity politics shapes not only the content but also the rhetoric and structure of truth-claims. What began as a claim to dignity, a recovery from exclusion and denigration, and a demand for representation, has also developed a hardening of the boundaries. The long-overdue opening of political initiative to minorities, women, gays, and others of the traditionally voiceless developed its own methods of silencing. Some energy once liberated has been recaptured. At the extreme, tracing the "genealogy" of ideas, or demonstrating their constructedness replaces an assessment of their validity, utility, virtue, or vice. Standards and traditions now appear as nothing other than the camouflage of interests. All claims to knowledge are presumed to be addressed from and to "subject positions" which, like the claims themselves, have been "constructed" or "invented" collectively by self-designated groups. Sooner or later, all disputes issue in propositions of the following sort: The central subject for understanding is the difference between X (e.g., women, people of color) and Y (e.g., white males). P is the case because my people, X, see it that way; if you don't agree with P, it is (or more mildly, is probably) because you are a member of Y. And further: since X has been oppressed, or silenced, by Y – typically, white heterosexual males – justice requires that members of X, preferably (though not necessarily) adherents of P, be hired and promoted; and in the student body, in the curriculum, on the reading list, and at the conference, distinctly represented.

This logic is more than a way of thought. Identity politics is a form of self-understanding, an orientation toward the world, and a structure of feeling which is characteristic of developed industrial societies [3] (For purposes of this discussion I beg the juicy question of whether it is characteristic of human societies altogether.) Identity politics presents itself as – and many students and other young people experience it as – the most compelling remedy for anonymity in an otherwise impersonal world. This cluster of recognitions, this system of feelings, seems to answer the questions: Who am I? Who is like me? Whom can I trust? Where do I belong? But identity politics is more than a mind-set and a sensibility felt and lived by individuals. It is a pattern of belonging, a search for comfort, an approach to community. The sense of membership is both a defense and an offense. It seems to overcome exclusion and silencing. Moreover, in a world where other people seem to have chosen up sides, and worse, where they approach you – even disrespect or menace you – as a type, it seems necessary to choose, or find, or invent, one's strength among one's own people. From popular culture to government policy, society has evidently assigned you a membership. Identity politics turns necessity to virtue.

For all the talk about the social construction of knowledge, identity politics de facto seems to slide toward the premise that social groups have essential identities. At the outer limit, those who set out to explode a fixed definition of humanity end by fixing their definitions of blacks or women. In the dark of separatist theory, they must be, and have always been, essentially the same. Anatomy once again becomes destiny. The revolt against silencing now threatens to drown out individual difference, complication, self-contradiction. But even short of this definitional absolutism, the ensemble of dispositions which make up identity politics is lived and embodied with an intensity and a consistency that mark it as a way of being, a deep aesthetic, a mode of consciousness, a relation to the world, and a set of relations all at once. This identity politics is, indeed, already a tradition in its second generation, transmitted and retransmitted, modified and transmitted again, institutionalized in jargons, mentors, gurus, conferences, associations, journals, departments, publishing subfields, bookstore sections, jokes, and reinforced through affirmative action and the growing numbers of faculty and students identified and identifying themselves as being "of color."

In this setting, identity politics promises a certain comfort. But what was once an enclave where the silenced could find their voices in order to widen the general conversation often freezes now into a self-enclosed world. In the academy, the pioneering work in the

early 1970s toward making women's studies legitimate, bolstering
labor studies, rethinking the damage done by slavery and the
slaughter of the Indians in the course of Manifest Destiny, opening
up the canon to hitherto silenced traditions – all this work was
done by scholars who had one foot in the civil rights and antiwar
movements, scholars who came to their specialties already bearing
something of a universalist or cosmopolitan bent. But much of the
succeeding work tended to harden and narrow in the course of
being institutionalized. Identity politics in the strict sense became
an organizing principle among the academic cohorts who had no
political experience before the late sixties. Politics for them had
always been the politics of interest groups – laced as it was with
revolutionary rhetoric. After the late 1960s, as race, gender, and
sometimes class became the organizing categories by which critical
temperaments have addressed the world in the humanities and social
sciences, faculty working this territory came to display the confidence
of an ascending class speaking predictably of "disruption," "subversion," "rupture," "contestation," and the "struggle for meaning." The
more their political life is confined to the library, the more aggressive
their language. They radiate *savoir faire* and an aura of solidarity, a
heady mixture that graduate students in search of a cloistered style
of intellectual companionship and collective identity can identify with
– *especially during the barren Republican years.*

But identity politics is not simply a product of the academic
hothouse. It also thrives in the society at large – in the media of
the mass and the media of the margins alike, in schools and in street
lore. Some students carry the rhetoric of their particular group to
campus with them. Alert to slights – and God knows there are
plenty of real offenses – they cultivate a cultural marginality which
is both defensive and aggressive. Fights over appropriate language,
over symbolic representation (whether in the form of syllabus or
curriculum or faculty or in cuisine), over affirmative action and
musical styles and shares of the public space *are, to them, the core of
"politics." Just as these cohorts have their clothes and their music, they
have "their politics" – the principal, even the only form of "politics" they
know.*

The boundaries of the group sometimes soften and sometimes
harden, but the hardening is more wounding, more dramatic, more
memorable – and for media purposes, more narratable. And so, there
is reason to expect more horror stories. Many on the Left squirm
at acknowledging that horror stories do not have to be concocted.
To cite only cases that I have witnessed myself, or heard described
from colleagues on the Left at major universities in the past year,

cases which are not the fevered products of right-wing hysteria: There are the Women's Studies students who walk out of a course because there are "not enough readings by women of color," even though one-third of the assignments have been written, in fact, by women of color. There is the Native American graduate student in History who complains that the books about female industrial workers in a women's history course fail to describe Native Americans. There are the graduate students in English who refuse to read Flannery O'Connor because she wrote a story called "The Artificial Nigger"; ditto for Wallace Stevens because he wrote "In a Nigger Cemetery." There are the graduate students in Sociology who boycott classes when their faculty, racially the most integrated on campus, proposes to hire an extravagantly qualified white male (whose main subject is the social world of an African-American boxing gym) to teach race relations — this protest becoming the main activity of the activist Left at the precise time when, outside the campus, the State is savaging the budget for all levels of education, which will have the effect of making it harder for most students of color to attend college. There is the leading student of color who proclaims that "objectivity is only another word for white male subjectivity." There circulates among *enragé* students an absurd reductionism which treats literature as nothing more than a manifesto reflecting race, class, and gender positions, or history as if it were nothing other than the two-toned struggle of victims against white male victimizers. Often enough, these currents operate in silent partnership with administrators who lack a coherent academic philosophy and whose main objectives are to cool out insurgencies before they develop into controversies and at the same time to keep their schedules free to arrange the corporate-sponsored streamlining of their campuses.

The specialists in difference may do their best to deny the fact that, for a quarter of a century, they have been fighting over the English department while the Right has held the White House as its private fiefdom. But academic currents are not so insulated from the larger social world as parochial theory may presume. The legitimacy of racial animus on the national scale — the boldness of right-wing politicians, the profusion of straightforward race prejudice among students — have all made the Academic Left edgier and more offensive. Affirmative action has been successful enough to create a critical mass of African-Americans who feel simultaneously heartened, challenged, and marooned. The symbolic burden they bear is enormous. Absent plausible prospects for fighting the impoverishment of the cities, unemployment, police brutality, crime, or any of the economic dimensions of the current immiseration, it is more convenient

– certainly less risky – to accuse a professor of racism. Identity politics is intensified when antagonistic identities are fighting for their places amid shrinking or zero-sum resources. For many reasons, then, the proliferation of identity politics leads to a turning inward, a grim and hermetic bravado which takes the ideological form of paranoid, jargon-clotted, postmodernist groupthink, cult celebrations of victimization, and stylized marginality.

Identity politics is not free-standing; it is also reactive, a relation of one identity to another. The hostility to diversification of the curriculum cannot be reduced to white defensiveness, but is hardly free of it either. The situation of white males of the Left is delicate. White males, like anyone else, feel ambivalent about being leapfrogged by upstarts who in the process (they feel) end up devaluing their own achievement. Supply and demand being what they are, a distinctly higher-paying market in qualified scholars of underrepresented identities heightens white resentment. Whites, especially males, are thrown into conflict. They, we, find ourselves outsiders. If it falls to us to defend ideals of commonality, when we downgrade difference in behalf of a search for a universally applicable humanism, we look, from the outside, like conservateurs circling the wagons against heathen assaults.

The United States and the United Class

I have been speaking about social wellsprings of the recent emergence of identity politics. I want to turn now to the unfolding logic, the *longue durée* of the big ideas at stake. For today's intellectual anxiety is more than the product of specific demographic changes, momentous as these are. The changing color of the campuses has been superimposed on major fault-lines in the history of ideas. Our time scale must stretch. We must also speak about the fate of two centuries in the history of everyday thinking, the "common sense" zone where ideas form and crystallize, fight and combine and break up in relation to other ideas.

For the thickening of identity politics is relative: we have to ask, thickening compared to what? Compared to "universalism," "common culture," "the human condition," "liberality," "the Enlightenment project" – the contrary position wears different labels. I shall group them all under the heading of commonality politics – a frame of inquiry, understanding, and action which understands "difference" against the background of what is *not* different, what is shared among persons and groups. This distinction is one of shadings, not absolutes, for differences are always thought and felt against a background of what does not differ, and commonalities are always thought and felt in relation to differences. Still, the shadings are deeply felt, whence the intellectual polarization that shows up in debates about the complex of problems including the curriculum, diversity, and so on. The point I wish to defend here is that the thickening of identity politics is inseparable from the fragmentation of commonality politics. In large measure, things fell apart *because* the center could not hold. For chronologically, the breakup of commonality politics predates the thickening of identity politics. The weaker the commonality politics, the greater the opportunity for a growth of identity politics, which in turn, at least up to a point (there are, after all, self-limiting reversals), helps weaken the prospects of a vital commonality politics – which are the politics of the Left if the term is to have any meaning.

The social history and the *Geistesgeschichte* must be grasped together. The multicultural or centrifugal surge, on the campuses and off, is the product of *two* intersecting histories. There is, obviously, the last quarter-century of America's social and demographic upheavals. But these, in turn, have taken place within the history that snakes forward throughout the West since the revolutions of 1776, 1789, and 1848. Throughout this period and beyond, believers in a common humanity clustered around the two great progressive ideals: the liberal ideal enshrined in the Declaration of Independence and, later, in the Declaration of the Rights of Man and Citizen; and the radical and socialist ideal which crystallized as Marxism. Even the political metaphor of Left and Right, which has survived for two centuries, is rooted in the assumption that history is a single story proceeding along a single time-line. The idea of *a* Left derives, strictly speaking, from the seating arrangements of the French National Assembly,[4] but two-sided political symmetry has another intuitive appeal. Like the Christian division of history into before and after, the language of Left and Right stems from the idea of a universal history. Revolution, like the story of Christ, splits history down the middle. The essential categories are the past and the future. There are old regimes and new regimes, those which want to conserve and those which want to change. The Left has always liked this melodrama, casting itself as action thrusting into the Future while the Right represents reaction, the dead hand of the Past.

The idea of the Left relies on the Enlightenment – the belief in the universal human capacity, and need, for reason. The counterpart of a single God would be a single humanity. Such legitimacy as the Left enjoyed in the West rested on its claim to a place in the grand story of universal human emancipation. Two hundred years of revolutionary tradition, whether liberal or radical, from the American through the Russian, the Chinese, and the Cuban, along with their western echoes, were predicated on the ideal of a universal humanity. The Left addressed itself not to particular men and women but to all, in the name of their common standing. If the population at large was incapable, by itself, of seeing the world whole and acting in the general interest, some enlightened group took it upon itself to be the collective conscience, the founding fathers, the vanguard party. As we shall see, even Marx, lyricist of the proletariat, ingeniously claimed that his favored class was destined to stand for, or become, all humanity. Even nationalist revolutions – from 1848 to the present – were to be understood as tributaries to a common torrent, the grand surge of self-determination justified by the equivalent worth of all national expressions. Whether liberals or socialists, reformers or revolutionaries, the men and women of the Left aimed to persuade their listeners to see their common interest as citizens of the largest world imaginable. *All* men were supposed to have been created equal, workingmen of *all* countries were supposed to unite. Historians of women are right to point out that the various founding fathers were not thinking of half the species; yet potentially inclusive language was in place.

The American founders made no bones about it: Dissolving the bands that tied them to the British Empire, they felt impelled to justify themselves to the entire world not only by itemizing their specific grievances against King George III but by stating first their conviction that "all men are created equal and that they are endowed by their Creator with certain inalienable rights." Not "all colonists" or "all whites" or even "all Americans" but "all men" – although it was to take decades of suffering and political clamor to pry open the definition of "men" and include enslaved African-Americans and women. Thirteen years later, with the help of the Marquis de Lafayette and his American-inspired rhetoric, the French revolutionaries produced a "Declaration of the Rights of Man and Citizen" – not a "Declaration of the Rights of Frenchmen" – declaring men equal "in respect of their rights" (though again, crucially, failing to take women into account).[5] The membership that counted for political rights was membership in the human race. The member, in the liberal ideal, was the irreducible individual, equal before the law.

The United States, in theory, was the homeland of this idea. Was this not the place where the Enlightenment first came down to earth? America, said the founding documents, was the living incarnation of the search for a common humanity. It was to be more than a new nation – it was, in principle, the embrace of a shared aspiration and therefore the idea that what the world has in common was precisely that aspiration. America declared itself *as* a dream, a dream of the living future of humanity; a decisive episode in the unfolding of the world's entire potential; a chapter in the revelation of humanity to itself. From this there flowed the idea of America as a refuge, America as the home of the New Adam, the land of the free. By this reckoning, America was embryonic humanity itself. It was inclusive: the alloy of worthy, rational individuals. From this sense of America as the microcosm or prefiguration of humanity, there also flowed the idea that those designated as civilly and legally free were entitled not only to their privileges but to the manifold brutalities of Manifest Destiny – by erasing "lesser" cultures who did not fit, they made the world safe for a fit humanity. In the American idea, when humans reasoned together, what they produced was America – and those who objected, or were judged incapable, had forfeited their rights. It wasn't just by force of arms that the Americans conquered a continent – it was also by force of the idea that there were no geographical bounds to Americanness; that America was entitled to flow as far as it could.

From a Theory to End All Classes to a Theology without God

The power of the discourse of political rights was such that it could be generalized by extrapolation. Thus, within 50 years, women grossly subordinated in the anti-slavery movement were working up a politics based on their constituting half of a human race that was supposed to share equal rights. The story of this movement and its implications for a commonality politics belongs in another place. Here I wish to focus on the tradition of unbounded commonality politics that, for the rest of the nineteenth century and much of the twentieth, promised to overcome difference: Marxism, that ingenious embodiment of Enlightenment rationality, drawing plausibility from the growth of industrial capitalism in Europe. Marxism linked the *is* and the *ought* so compellingly that it gathered a world-making momentum for more than a century. Marxism, in all its colorations, became the core of what may be called the idea of the Left – the struggle to usher in, to speak in the name of, and to represent common humanity.

In the world of ideas and motivations, Marxism's importance was as a philosophy of history, not as an economic theory; and so

I am interested here in its framing of the meaning of history
and the universal destiny of humankind, not in such matters as
the labor theory of value, the falling rate of profit, and so on. The
ambition of Marxism was a precondition for its significance. True,
Marx's universalism was a glory not yet capable of realization. Like
Christianity, it was predicated on a faith. It was meant as a universalism with a difference – a faith to unmask bad faiths. In
many a tract and letter, Marx dripped scorn for contemporary ideas
about the common good. [6] These were nothing more than masks for
particular interests – ideologies as opposed to the Truths they pur-
ported to be. Even in the *Communist Manifesto*, he resorted to the
scathing tone he reserved for the naive and the disingenuous, sneer-
ing, for example, at Germany's "True" Socialists for claiming to
represent "not the interests of the proletariat, but the interests of
Human Nature, of Man in general ..."[7] Generations of Marxists
went on to insist that tender-mindedness about universal humanity is
premature, obscurantist, and in sum – curse of curses! – "idealist."

Marx's genius was to argue that the imagined future was already
in the making, that all humanity was already present, represented
only in a class destined to overcome all differences by ending all
classes. The Left was to be a marriage of body and soul, muscularity
and brains – proletariat and party – prefiguring a world in which
the limits imposed by the division of labor have broken down.
There exists, Marx asserts in his early writings, a universal identity:
the human being as maker, realizing his "species being" in the course
of transforming nature. [8] With the audacity of a German idealist
primed to think in first principles, Marx adapts from Hegel the idea
that a "universal class" will give meaning to history. Beginning with
people uprooted from the land, his universal class is bound for
classlessness. Its universality prefigures the final universality. As
inexorable capitalism simplifies the class structure, the proletariat
has the potential to become a majority. As the world market spreads
and "entire sections of the ruling classes are, by the advance of
industry, precipitated into the proletariat," many an astute bourgeois
changes sides and "the other classes decay and finally disappear,"
so only a shrinking minority of exploiters will remain to be expro-
priated. [9] The proletariat is not only right, it is – it is destined
to be – the embodiment of might. No utopian wish, no moralist
prayer, it is a near-universal destiny. Like electricity, it is driven
by potential. Pure dynamo, it is more than its present mean condition: it points to, intimates, is becoming or rather (and here Marx's
grammatical flourish invokes the future as if it were already taking
place in the present) it *is* the future in embryo.

In keeping with Marx's sense of the future already unfolding, he argues that the universal class destined to redeem history will follow in the footsteps of the universal class that has already appropriated and transformed history: the "constantly revolutionizing" bourgeoisie, whose "need of a constantly expanding market for its products chases [it] over the whole surface of the globe ... nestl[ing] everywhere, settl[ing] everywhere, establish[ing] connections everywhere, ... giv[ing] a cosmopolitan character to production and consumption in every country," destroying "all old-established national industries," generating "universal interdependence of nations," making "national one-sidedness and narrow-mindedness ... more and more impossible," in sum, "creat[ing] a world after its own image." [10] The universality of capital is the crucible for the universality of labor. In Engels's words, "the exploited and oppressed class (the proletariat) can no longer emancipate itself from the class which exploits and oppresses it (the bourgeoisie) without at the same time forever freeing the whole of society from exploitation, oppression and class struggles ..." [11]

But not without help. To accomplish its glorious mission, this class to end all classes requires a universal midwife: the revolutionary communist. No matter where the communist originates, this agent of universal history overcomes his (Marx's revolutionary is, by implication, male) particular class and particular place. Taking a cue from the international bourgeoisie, the revolutionary communist prefigured the working men of the future, who "have no country." [12] To every particular circumstance and cause, the universal priesthood of communists is charged with bringing the glad tidings that History is the unfolding of Reason. The communist party, like God, has its center everywhere and nowhere, and like the church of Jesus is charged with distilling ultimate meaning from the material life. The proletariat is his nation. Like the émigré Marx, he is at home nowhere and everywhere, this denationalized [13] world citizen, prefigured by Lafayette and Tom Paine, free to teach people of all nations that their destinies are intertwined; for all the world is becoming one, "national differences and antagonisms between peoples are daily more and more vanishing," [14] and the proletariat must be taught that not a historical event or a struggle against oppression rises or falls which does not have its part to play in the great international transfiguration.

Thanks to "logic" and "insight," [15] Marx's emissary discerns the truth that the overwhelming majority of human beings are united in and by a single category — labor. Once the gap between use-value and exchange-value is overcome, all class division and hence

all socially-created difference shall be overcome. So the task of communists is, in the midst of national and particular struggles, to
"point out and bring to the front the common interests of the
entire proletariat, independently of all nationality." They "always and
everywhere represent the interests of the movement as a whole." [16]
The universalities ring out: *common ... entire ... always ... everywhere
... the movement as a whole.* However rebuked by local interests,
the communist universalist belongs to *the* Left, the one true international church, where the Englishman and the German, the Indian
and the Chinese, meet to prefigure the borderless world to come.

Such is the lyric of Marxism, the rhetoric that imparted to revolutionaries a sense of common cause for a century after the death
of the founding father. And therefore Marxism-Leninism, the universalist technology of revolution and rule later codified by Stalinists,
is, if not the unshakable shadow of Enlightenment Marxism, at least
its scion. Lenin's Bolshevik Party thrives on and requires this lineage, even if Lenin and Marx are not identical. The leap to the
voluntarism of Lenin's Bolsheviks was not inevitable, but Marxism
under wartime conditions made it possible. Provisionally or permanently, Lenin's centralized, dictatorial Party arrogates to itself the
privileges that by rights belong to the Revolution.

The Party, the International, this directive force that sees all and
knows all and acts in the ostensibly general interest, becomes the
incarnation of the Enlightenment's faith in the knowability of the
human situation. Lenin brought into the twentieth century a fusion
of thought and action which brilliantly, and dangerously, updated
Marx. In Lenin's thinking, the will of the Bolshevik Party rescues
the working class from its parochialism – that is, its attachment
to particular proletarians. Without the Party's high-minded theorizing
and planning, Lenin argues, the working class would be capable of
nothing more than "trade-union consciousness" – the defense of its
own identity. Farther down a road already surveyed by Marx, Lenin
makes intellectuals essential to the revolution, thereby securing the
dominion of universal ideals.

What Lenin develops in theory, the October Revolution of 1917
accomplishes in action. When the Russian detonator fails to set off
the larger European bomb, Lenin devises a theory for bridging
from *a* to *the* universal Revolution. Just as imperialism is "the highest
stage of capitalism," so anti-imperialism will be the highest form of
anti-capitalism, the passion that unites the world proletariat. On
a world scale, Lenin argues, imperialism now constitutes "radical
chains" [17] – the form of oppression which will unite the oppressed to
bring down the global system. The road to Paris, Lenin says, will

lead through Beijing. Later, after Stalin's detour through "socialism in one country," the globalist passion of Leninism will be resurrected in the idea of the Third World Revolution.

Marxism, then, had the grandeur of a universalist dynamic, which Leninism did nothing to weaken. What a distance to the broken and desiccated "Marxism" of the contemporary Cultural Studies curriculum, as described in this recent passage from Michael Bérubé:

> The current Marxism of cultural studies, it turns out, is a Marxism that stopped believing in historical inevitability long before the Wall came down; it is a Marxism that denies the primacy or unity of "class" (and emphasizes the relevance of race, gender, sexuality, subjectivity), no longer believes in an intellectual vanguard, no longer believes in the centrality of Europe, no longer believes that the base "determines" the superstructure, that the ruling class owns the ruling ideas, that class struggle is inevitable, or that ideology is just "false consciousness."[18]

The shapeless *mélange* that results remains Marxist only in a nostalgic sense. Instead of a brief for unification, it has become a list of subcultures.

In short, Marxism without a revolutionary proletariat is a theology without God. Failing to take its poetry from the future, as Marx recommended, this gestural Marxism dresses up in a wardrobe from the past. From a history which is either failed or catastrophic, it salvages icons. Perhaps the good father is to be protected from the depredations of bad brothers and bad sons — the real (or early) Marx unblemished by Engels, or the one read by Luxemburg, not Lenin, or by Lenin and Trotsky, not Stalin. Perhaps there is, after all, a global working class in embryo, but it has been unfortunately misled, or its hour has not yet come round — give it time! This shapeless "Marxism" lacking a labor theory of value, lacking the transcendent homogenization of a universal class, lacking a universalizing agency, shrinks into normal sociology, a set of analytic tools with which to grasp the globalization of capital — valuable tools for analysis, indeed, but hardly a mission, let alone the invocation of a universal spirit.

THE NEW LEFT AND THE FUTILE SEARCH FOR SUBSTITUTE UNIVERSALS

For generations after the Russian Revolution, Marxism persisted. Nothing secures a faith better than institutionalization, even a bad institutionalization. As a faith, Marxism held onto not only its universalizing spirit, not only its moral authority as a critique of capitalism, but also the peculiar prestige that accrues to historical materiality. It was a religion that borrowed authority from the fact that the Church, when all was said and done, for all its corruption and barbarism, *existed*. Efface Stalinism at a theoretical level, so partisans could argue, and a purified Marxism – at least a purified Marxist *identity* – would remain. From 1935 to 1939 and again after the Nazi invasion of the USSR, the Popular Front could even conjure a new commonality – a cobbled-together anti-Fascist fusion. In the end, Marxists could always ask rhetorically, what was the alternative that promised a universal transformation, universal justice, a single humanity? And so, partly by default, from one revision to the next, Marxism remained the pedigreed theoretical ensemble hovering over all left-wing thought.

And yet, once the anti-Fascist alliance was broken, the universalist promise of Marxism proceeded with its fated unraveling. It wasn't simply the Cold War and McCarthyism that wrecked the Marxist prospect in America. It was the failure of Marxism to live up to its universalist – that is to say, its internationalist – prospects. The Czech putsch of 1948 and, even more, the crushing of the Hungarian Revolution of 1956, should have made obvious that Soviet Marxism was mainly *raison d'état*. (The collapse of European communism in 1989–90 was to eliminate the *état* altogether, to leave Marxist socialists standing in pure air.)

From this point of view, the intellectual radicalism of the early sixties can be seen as a search for a substitute universalism. Having dismissed Marxism for what C. Wright Mills called its "labor metaphysic," the New Left tried to compose a surrogate universal. Its "agencies of change" were meant to proceed in a common direction. "The issues are interrelated" was the New Left's approach to a federation of single-issue groups – so that, for example, the peace, civil rights, and civil liberties movements needed to recognize that they had a common enemy, the Southern Democrats, "Dixiecrats," who choked off any liberal extension of the New Deal. More grandly, in a revival of Enlightenment universalism, Students for a Democratic Society (SDS)'s Port Huron Statement spoke self-consciously in the name of all humanity: "[H]uman brotherhood [*sic*] must be willed

... as the most appropriate form of social relations." The universal solvent for particular differences would be the principle that "decision-making of basic social consequence be carried on by public groupings": i.e., participatory democracy. In theory, participatory democracy was recommended and available to all. In practice, it was tailored to students (elite students at that, "housed now in universities")1[9] – people collected in "knowledge factories" as the industrial proletariat had been collected in mills and mines; young people who were skilled in conversation, had time on their hands, and, uprooted from the diversities of their respective upbringings, were being encouraged to think of themselves as practitioners of reason. When the early New Left set out to find common ground with a like-minded constituency, it reached out to the impoverished – the Student Nonviolent Coordinating Committee (SNCC) to sharecroppers and SDS to the urban poor, who, by virtue of their marginality, might be imagined as forerunners of a universal democracy. If students and the poor were not saddled with "radical chains" in the system of production, at least they could be imagined with radical *needs* for political participation.

Around this time, the student movement was not alone in searching for a transcendent collective identity. Social theorists were also straining to produce new universal identities. If humans were not essentially labor, perhaps they were essentially language. There developed, then, the post-historical structuralism of Claude Lévi-Strauss – universalities through binary oppositions and the denial of history. In America, there were Paul Goodman's collective assortment of the alienated, and Herbert Marcuse's free-floating, totalizing refugees from one-dimensional society. In an attempt at a synthesis of Marxism and language theory, we got Jürgen Habermas's objective of undistorted communication. There were various attempts to preserve Marxism as a totality by multiplying epicycles, *à la* medieval Ptolemaics, in futile attempts to patch the theory.

But the student movement's attempts at universalism broke down – both practically and intellectually. In fact, the ideal of participatory democracy was only secondary for the New Left. The passion that drove students – including Berkeley's Free Speech Movement – was the desire to support civil rights as part of a movement with a universalist design. The New Left was a movement-for-others searching for an ideology to transform it into a movement-for-itself, but participatory democracy was too ethereal an objective with which to bind an entire movement, let alone an entire society. Freedom as an endless meeting was alluring only to those who had the taste to go to meetings endlessly. The universalist impulse regressed. Enter, then, the varieties of Marxism by which universalist students could imagine either that they were entitled to lead a hypothetical proletariat (Progressive Labor's Stalinism and subsequent functional equivalents) or that they themselves already prefigured a "new working class" (as in the anti-Progressive Labor French "new working class" theory imported to SDS around 1966–7).

But these attempts at recomposing a sense of a unified revolutionary bloc were weak in comparison with centrifugal pressures. Such unity as had been felt by the civil rights movement began to dissolve as soon as legal segregation had been defeated. Blacks began to insist on black leadership, even exclusively black membership. When feminist stirrings were greeted with scorn by unreconstructed men, the principle proliferated. If white supremacy was unacceptable, neither could male supremacy be abided. One group after another demanded the recognition of difference and the protection of separate spheres for distinct groupings. This was more than an *idea* because it was more than strictly intellectual; it was more of a structure of feeling, a whole way of experiencing the world. Difference was now lived and felt more acutely than unity.

The crack-up of the universalist New Left was muted for a while by the exigencies of the Vietnam war and the commonalities of youth culture. If there seemed in the late 1960s to be one big movement, it was largely because there was one big war. But the divisions of race and then gender and sexual orientation proved far too deep to be overcome by any rhetoric of unification. The initiative and energy went into proliferation – feminist, gay, ethnic, environmentalist. The very language of collectivity came to be perceived by the new movements as a colonialist smothering – an ideology to rationalize white male domination. Thus, by the early 1970s, the goals of the student movement and the various left-wing insurgencies were increasingly subsumed under the categories of identity politics. Separatism became automatic. Left-wing politics became "racialized."[20] Now one did not imagine oneself belonging to a common enterprise; one belonged to a caucus.

This is what Allan Bloom and Roger Kimball miss: *The late New Left politics of dispersion and separateness, not the early New Left politics of universalist aspiration, were the seed-ground of the young faculty who were to carry radical politics into the academy in the 1980s.* The founders of women's and black studies in the 1970s had a universalist base in either the old or the New Left. But their recruits, born in the early or later 1950s did not. By the time they arrived on campuses in the early seventies, identity politics was the norm. They had no direct memory of either a unified Left or a successful left-of-center Democratic Party. In general, their experience of active politics was segmented, not unified. The general Left was defeated, and that defeat was a huge background presence so obvious it was taken for granted. For these post-1960s activists, universalist traditions were empty, mass movements were sectoral movements-for-themselves. But this condition was not resented, not experienced as a loss — rather, it was felt as a marker of generational solidarity and a motor of exhilarating opportunities.

This profusion of social agents took place throughout the society, but nowhere more vigorously than in the academy, where resistance to fragmentation was weakest. Here, in black and ethnic studies, women's studies, gay and lesbian groupings, and so on, each movement could feel the exhilaration of group-based identity. Each felt it had a distinct world to win — first, by establishing that their group had been suppressed and silenced; then, by exhuming buried work and exploring forms of resistance; and finally, by trying to rethink society, literature, and history from the respective vantages of the silenced, asking what the group and, indeed, the entire world would look like if those hitherto excluded were now included, or brought to the fore. And since the demands of identity politics were far more winnable in the university than elsewhere in the society, the struggles of minorities multiplied. When academic conservatives resisted, even mocked these angles of vision, they only confirmed the convictions of the marginal — that their embattled or not-yet-developing perspectives needed to be separately institutionalized. In the developing logic of identity-based movements, the world was all periphery and no center, or, if there was a center, it was their own. The mission of insurgents was to promote their own interests; for if they would not, who would?

From these endeavors flowed extraordinary achievements in the study of history and literature. Spurious wholes were decomposed, exposed as partisan and partial. Whole new areas of inquiry were opened up. Histories of the world and of America, of science and literature, are still reverberating from what can legitimately be called a revolution in knowledge. But as hitherto excluded territories were institutionalized, the lingering aspiration for the universal subject was ceded. A good deal of the Cultural Left felt its way, even if half-jokingly, toward a spurious unity based not so much on a universalist premise or ideal but rather on a common enemy — that notorious, Platonically ideal type of the While Male. Beneath this they had become, willy-nilly, pluralists, although this fact was at first frequently disguised by the rhetoric of general revolution hanging over from the late sixties. The idea of a unitary Left with an emphasis on what unifies the whole looked, to the insurgents, pale by comparison.

Soon, difference was being practiced, not just thought, at a deeper level than commonality. It was more salient, more vital, more present – all the more so in the 1980s, as practical struggles for university facilities, requirements, and so forth culminated in fights over increasingly scarcer resources. For the participants in these late-sixties and post-sixties movements, the benefits of this pursuit were manifold – a sense of community, an experience of solidarity, a ready-made reservoir of recruits. Seen from outside as fragments in search of a whole, the zones of identity politics are experienced from within as worlds unto themselves. The political-intellectual experience of younger academics could be mapped onto other centrifugal dispositions in post-Vietnam America. Group self-definitions embedded in political experience merged with other historicist and centrifugal currents, and lingering efforts to fathom the unity of the human project came to appear nostalgic.

These days, it sometimes seems that the *Zeitgeist* is blowing nothing but fragments. Not only is the idea of the Left fragmented, so is the idea of a single America. For in fact, the icon of America as a unity – "one nation under God" – has also been growing fragile. The apparently unified popular culture of the fifties, predicated on the "typical American" who resonates to Dean Martin and Perry Como, *I Love Lucy* and *Father Knows Best*, began to break apart and could never be reassembled again into a false whole. Immigration, the various challenges to racial segregation, white flights to the suburbs, and fractional "life-style" marketing shattered false unities that had been taken for granted. After the fifties, in fact, the idea of America the indivisible was unraveling. America as a whole was increasingly a negation – a culture that recognized itself as a whole insofar as it was not communist. America came to recognize itself as half of a binary opposition; anti-communism required communism. The binary oppositions lined up: tyrannical communism, American freedom; atheist communism, American godliness; backward communism, American prosperity; communist rationing, America's consumer splendor.

But the Vietnam war gashed a fatal hole in American anti-communism, and damaged its capacity to unify the national mystique, for anti-communism proved capable of its own conspicuous crimes. With the support of social movements and a centrifugal youth culture, segments of the population broke away from the liberal consensus. "The market" proved to be centrifugal as well – a plural, not a singular. Beyond the loyalties that had once been possible to what

David Riesman called "the standard package of consumer goods," product styles and labels were proliferating their own versions of difference. Consumer society was developing into a scatter of life-style islands.

Against all the centrifugal tendencies, it was the achievement of conservatives to reassemble an anti-communist revival in 1980, with enough magnetic pull to hold together Ronald Reagan's otherwise unwieldy Republican coalition throughout the 1980s. But when communism and the Cold War collapsed, so did the conservatives' basis for unity and much of the self-confidence of their image of an America at one with itself. At the same time, the Cultural Right, along with its donors, felt frustrated that, for all its political victories in recent years, it had still failed to conquer the commanding heights of "adversary culture": universities and the media.[21] At the same time, the declining estate of the university made it an inviting target. All this amid the overall crisis in national identity, the problem of what is to unify the nation given non-European immigration and given the end of the Cold War, which for forty-plus years had bid to solve the perennial American identity crisis on the cheap. There emerged – there continues – an enemy crisis. Conservative thought went into convulsions. Absent the Soviet Union, purveyors of unity could only try out one surrogate unifying enemy after another: drugs; terrorists; Japan; Mexican immigrants; General Noriega; political correctness; Saddam Hussein; spreaders of AIDS. Each had a certain vogue, each could generate a spike in public opinion polls, but none has the capacity, in truth, to cement a centrifugal America. All are holding actions. The idea of the common America and the idea of the unitary Left, these two great legacies of the Enlightenment, have hollowed out together.

AN INCLUSIVE COMMONALITY?

In short, there has been a curious reversal since the nineteenth century. Then, there were aristocracies who unabashedly stood for the privileges of the few. Today, the aspiring aristocrats of the Academic Right tend to speak the language of universals – canon, merit, reason, individual rights, transpolitical virtue. By the same token, they hold the Left guilty of special pleading – a degradation of standards, affirmative action (which it considers racial preference), diehard relativism. Seized by the psycho- and sociologic of polarization, committed to pleasing its disparate constituencies, an Academic Left obsessed with differences fails to reckon with commonalities.

Rather the Left fractures. One segment, the Party of Nietzsche, hermetically sealed in the academy, cheerfully pleads guilty, turns the tables, and indicts the indicters, proclaiming that all general knowledge is special pleading anyway, that standards are threadbare, and that common conversation is a euphemism for cacophony. The other, the Loose Canonists, responds that a common conversation requires general agreement on speech rules, that such is requisite for a decent society. But, it goes on, the intellectual commons is not simply a "heritage." It is incomplete; it cannot be "handed down"; it has, in fact, to be brought into being by admitting voices previously slighted and suppressed; a universal history, a universal philosophy, a universal literature cannot be found but must be made. The preservationist Right is opposed to both but has no interest in clarifying the difference between the two.

I hope to have shown that there is plenty of inflammable history piled like brush within burning distance of the current fires. The symbolic stakes are long in the making; on the foreshortened scale of academic disputes, the territorial stakes are not inconsiderable either. The bitterness of the academic disputes is infused with the bitterness of federal funding fights in the arts and humanities, which in turn are infused by the acrimony of the long-running culture war that threatens modernity. (Or better, perhaps modernity would not be able to recognize itself were it not perennially at war with – and thus yoked to – anti-modernity. This subject awaits another occasion.) Polarizers on every side have a stake in their polarization, and to this extent the outlook for solution is not auspicious.

Overpolarization is always, in part, a misrepresentation of motives. The Right tends to see in the Left nothing but *la trahison des clercs*. The Left tends to see in the Right nothing but the protective tropism of white males whose ill-gotten privileges are coming under long overdue attack. The Right, if it wishes to be intellectually serious, needs to understand that hardly any of the Left is Afrocentric; needs to acknowledge that affirmative action has arguments (and didn't become a political issue as long as it was the children of alumni who were the beneficiaries of admission preferences); needs to acknowledge that the PC orthodoxy in the *economics* department is neoclassical, as Robert Kuttner has pointed out, not neo-Marxist. The Left needs to face some of the ugly outcomes of centrifugal motion – race hatred, political impotence, the declining utility of the narcissism of small differences. Intolerance is no one's monopoly, and *tu quoque* is by itself a rhetorical device of limited truth-value.

And, further, the Left needs to understand that the universalism of the Academic Right, whether in the natural law theories of Leo

Strauss's students or the rights-based pluralism of Arthur M. Schlesinger, Jr, is no strictly cynical political ploy cooked up disingenuously for the consternation of democrats or the greater glory of Manifest Destiny. Like all moral panics, the anti-PC crusade did not concoct the conditions in which it has stirred. Rather, Messrs. Bennett, Cheney, Bloom, and D'Souza have addressed a widely felt longing. *They know that, along with our local, multiple, situated, historically specific selves, we harbor an unassuaged longing for a sense of human community.* Those who think the unity of the world is guaranteed by a single market should be challenged by those whose idea of a single planet requires a single standard of human rights in a single greenhouse. The Left is right to ask insinuatingly: *Whose human community? Who is inside, who outside?* But once the question is asked, that is not the end of the conversation. If there is to be a Left in more than a sentimental sense, its position ought to be: *This desire for human unity is indispensable. The ways, means, basis, and costs are a subject for disciplined conversation. If among human differences in a broken world, no principle of unity is − yet − self-evident, then how might it be formed? Let's get on with it.*

Perhaps, then, there is a synthesis in the making: Neither camp holds the undisputed initiative. Many sensitive, sensible scholars have been seeking out, and often enough finding, a central ground where the distinctly "multicultural" reality of American life, indeed the "multicultural" nature of western and other cultures themselves, can be taken seriously but not all-importantly. There has been much virtue in an attunement to the historical and particularist limits of knowledge. Now, alongside the indisputable premise that knowledge of many kinds is specific to time, place, and interpretive community, thoughtful critics are placing the equally important premise that there are unities in the human condition and that, indeed, the existence of common understandings is the basis of all communication (= making common) across boundaries of language and history and experience. Today, some of the most exciting scholarship entails efforts to incorporate new and old knowledge together in unified narratives. Otherwise there is no escape from solipsism, whose political expression cannot be the base of liberalism or radicalism or, for that matter, cultural conservatism.

From many quarters there is a growing distaste for group solipsism. Historians and sociologists normally pegged as conservative − Nathan Glazer and Diane Ravitch, for example − have declared themselves multiculturalist. [22] No less a canon-conserving academic of the Cultural (not Political) Right than John Searle has helped puncture the Bennett−D'Souza *canards* about Stanford's Cultural,

Ideas, Values Program.[23] Among others, Leo Marx has tellingly argued that "the canon" is always revisionist, and reminded us that his cohort of graduate students in the 1940s had to fight to include good grey, gay Walt Whitman in the American literary canon at the cost of losing John Greenleaf Whittier and James Russell Lowell.[24] Such literary canon-openers as Edward Said and Henry Louis Gates, Jr, have argued forcefully against the wrong-headed, ham-handed, reductionist, and – if this were not bad enough – banal premise that all propositions only mask the interests of the proposers.[25] Reed Way Dasenbrock has exploded the terms of the dispute by arguing that "the West" is essentially "multicultural."[26] The intellectual historian David Hollinger[27] and others have been battering at the Berlin Wall erected between the camps; with the result that something of a third position is actively being sought and is already looming in outline.[28] There is a widespread conviction that the terms of the debate need to be – are being – transfigured. Indeed, now, Gerald Graff has made a strong case for normalizing the canon dispute, incorporating it into the academy's foreground by "teaching the conflict."[28]

Just as all the sound has not been noise, perhaps not all the fury has been wasted.

NOTES

1 See Todd Gitlin, "An Intolerance of the New Intolerance," *Los Angeles Times Book Review*, April 14, 1991, pp. 2, 9; the exchange of letters among John Hope Franklin, George H. Fredrickson, Jon Wiener, Gene H. Bell-Villada, and C. Vann Woodward, *The New York Review of Books*, September 26, 1991, pp. 74–6; Jon Wiener, "What Happened at Harvard," *The Nation*, September 30, 1991, pp. 384–8; "Illiberal Education Fact Sheet," distributed at "The P.C. Frame-Up: What's Behind the Attack," conference at the University of Michigan, November 17, 1991; Gerald Graff, *Beyond the Culture Wars: How Teaching the Conflicts Can Revitalize American Education* (New York: Norton, 1992), ch. 2.
2 Graff, *Beyond the Culture Wars*, ch. 2.
3 Josh Gamson, "Silence, Death, and the Invisible Enemy: AIDS Activism and Social Movement 'Newness,'" *Social Problems*, vol. 36, no. 4 (October 1989), pp. 353–4, 357–8.
4 James H. Billington, *Fire in the Minds of Men: Origins of the Revolutionary Faith* (New York: Basic Books, 1980), p. 27.
5 Billington, *Fire*, p. 21, citing J. Thompson, *The French Revolution* (New York: Oxford University Press, 1966), pp. 41–2.
6 For this point I am indebted to Marshall Berman.
7 Karl Marx and Friedrich Engels, "The Communist Manifesto," in Robert C. Tucker, ed., *The Marx–Engels Reader* (New York: Norton, 1972), p. 356.

8 Karl Marx, "Economic-Philosophical Manuscripts of 1844: Selections," in Tucker, ed., Marx–Engels Reader, pp. 52–103.
9 Marx and Engels, "The Communist Manifesto," in Tucker, ed., Marx–Engels Reader, pp. 343–4.
10 Ibid., pp. 338–9.
11 Friedrich Engels, "Preface to the German Edition [of the Communist Manifesto] of 1883," in Tucker, ed., Marx–Engels Reader, p. 334.
12 Marx and Engels, "Communist Manifesto," in Tucker, ed., Marx–Engels Reader, p. 350.
13 James H. Billington's term. Fire, p. 275.
14 Marx and Engels, "Communist Manifesto," in Tucker, ed., Marx–Engels Reader, p. 350.
15 Marx, "Contribution to the Critique of Hegel's Philosophy of Right: Introduction," in Tucker, ed., Marx–Engels Reader, p. 21.
16 Marx and Engels, "Communist Manifesto," in Tucker, ed., Marx–Engels Reader, p. 346.
17 Marx, "Critique of Hegel's Philosophy of Right: Introduction," in Tucker, ed., Marx–Engels Reader, p. 22.
18 Michael Bérubé, "Pop Goes the Academy," Village Voice Literary Supplement (April 1992), p. 11.
19 Students for a Democratic Society, The Port Huron Statement (New York: Students for a Democratic Society, 1962), p. 1.
20 Michael Omi and Howard Winant, Racial Formation in the United States: From the 1960s to the 1980s (London and New York: Routledge, 1986), p. 64.
21 On big business's interest in the 1970s in shifting the campuses' ideological center of gravity rightward, see Leonard Silk and David Vogel, Ethics and Profits (New York: Simon and Schuster, 1976).
22 Nathan Glazer, "In Defense of Multiculturalism," The New Republic, September 2, 1991, pp. 18–22; Diane Ravitch, "In the Multicultural Trenches," Contention, vol. 1, no. 3 (Spring 1992), pp. 29–36.
23 John Searle, "The Storm over the University," in Paul Berman, ed., Debating P.C. (New York: Dell, 1992), pp. 106–8 (originally published in The New York Review of Books, December 6, 1990.)
24 In a talk to the American Studies Association, New Orleans, November 1, 1990.
25 Edward W. Said, "The Politics of Knowledge," in Berman, ed., Debating P.C., pp. 172–89. (Originally published in Raritan, Summer 1991); Henry Louis Gates, Jr, "Whose Canon Is It, Anyway?" in Berman, ed., Debating P.C., pp. 190–200 (originally published in The New York Times Book Review, 1989); and "Pluralism and Its Discontents," Contention, vol. 2, no. 1 (Fall 1992), pp. 69–78.
26 Reed Way Dasenbrock, "The Multicultural West," Dissent (Fall 1991), pp. 550–5.
27 David A. Hollinger, "Postethnic America," Contention, vol. 2, no. I (Fall 1992), pp. 79–96.

28 Graff, *Beyond the Culture Wars*. It may be objected that "teaching the conflicts" places the critical cart before the literary horse, since untutored, unlettered students are not in a position to grasp what is at stake in the canon wars until they have first been immersed in great works of literature whose pre-eminence reformers seek to undermine. On the other hand, "teaching the conflicts" might generate some enthusiasm, sorely needed, for reading elemental books in the first place. This is an empirical, not a principled question.

6

The Formation of We-Images: A Process Theory

Stephen Mennell

The problem of identity formation in sociology is a paradigmatic example of what Craig Calhoun (1991) has called the "entirely abstract macro–micro divide." I agree that the divide is, in a sense, entirely abstract; but so long as sociologists use concepts which make it seem real, it is real in its consequences for the discipline. The fact is that there *is* a division between two bodies of theory about identity formation.

On the one hand, we have a familiar set of ideas about how the self is constructed. Self-identity is seen as a universal human property, and its acquisition a social process through which all normal human beings must pass. The writings of George Herbert Mead, as transmitted and developed through the work of symbolic inter-actionist sociologists and the psychoanalytic theory of identification,[1] are central here. Common to this body of thought is the assumption that every person in his or her lifetime passes through a sequential process in which various stages of development can be picked out in the ongoing flow.

On the other hand, we have a diverse body of ideas about how various categories of people – communities, classes, elites, ethnicities, genders – come to share a sense of collective identity and, through perceptions of interests common to individual members of their

This chapter was written while I was head of the Department of Anthropology and Sociology, Monash University, Australia. I should like to acknowledge the support of the Research Committee of the Faculty of Arts there, who contributed towards the cost of my attending the ASA Pittsburgh conference.

category, begin to tackle problems of collective action. This problematic runs from the Enlightenment period through Marx and the other principal occupants of the sociological pantheon to contemporary feminism; and from Marx via economics and economists like Kenneth Arrow to present-day rational choice theory. Although particular theories – again, most obviously Marxism – embody predictions of the development of particular kinds of collective consciousness, there is less consensus among sociologists about any overall model of the sequential development of we-identities in the course of the growth of human society: such models smack of ideas of "progress," and "progress" is (rightly) suspect. One thing that most of these diverse sociological notions about collective identity do have in common, however, stems perhaps from the division between these theories and those others dealing with self-identity. That is, they tend implicitly to picture the construction of we-identities as taking place through some sort of psychological or conceptual coming together of individuals, each of whom is pre-equipped with a personal self-identity. In other words, there is often an implicit social contract – or even Robinson Crusoe – element in the theories. [2] We all know how misleading that is. Human beings have never, even before the emergence of the species in its present form, been solitary animals: their self-images and we-images have always – since the acquisition of the uniquely human capacity for self-reflection – been formed over time within groups of interdependent people, groups that have on the whole steadily increased in size.

THE FILO PASTRY OF IDENTITY

Many years ago (before sexist phraseology was frowned upon), Kluckhohn and Murray (1948: 35) wrote that:

Every man is in certain respects
  (a) like all other men
  (b) like some other men
  (c) like no other man

This neat dictum is useful in thinking about social habitus and identity. It recognizes (level (a)) that there are many characteristics that human beings share in common with all other members of the species, and (level (c)) that there are also ways in which every individual human personality is unique – if only because, as Alfred

Schutz was to contend, each of us has a unique biographical situation and a unique permutation of experience sedimented into a unique stock of knowledge. But more important, Kluckhohn and Murray's level (b) draws attention to the characteristics which all human beings share in common with *certain* other human beings in the particular groups to which they belong. In recent years, Pierre Bourdieu (1984) has popularized the term "habitus" for dealing with this level.[3]

Habitus is a useful word in referring to the modes of conduct, taste, and feeling which predominate among members of particular groups. It can refer to shared traits of which the people who share them may be largely unconscious; for the meaning of the technical term "habitus" is, as Norbert Elias used to remark, captured exactly in the everyday English expression *second nature* – an expression defined by the *Oxford English Dictionary* as "an acquired tendency that has become instinctive." The very *taken-for-granted* quality of habitus in this sense makes it particularly potent in conflicts between groups, for the components of the habitus of one's own group seem to be inherent, innate, "natural," and their absence or difference in the habitus of other groups seems correspondingly "unnatural" and reprehensible.

Habitus is closely related to the notion of *identity*. The difference is perhaps that "identity" implies a higher level of conscious awareness by members of a group, some degree of reflection and articulation, some positive or negative emotional feelings towards the characteristics which members of a group perceive themselves as sharing and in which they perceive themselves as differing from other groups. But there is no great value in drawing fine distinctions here. The more important, and immediately obvious, point is that habitus and identification, being related to group membership, are always – in the modern world where people belong to groups within groups within groups – multi-layered. It is possible that in the very early stages of human social development, when all people lived in very small and isolated hunter-gatherer bands, social habitus and identification had only a single layer: when people said "we," it always referred to the same specific group of people (Elias 1991: 182–3, 202). In more complex societies there are always many layers, according to the number of interlocking layers in a society that are woven into a person's habitus: one is a Yorkshire-born English European who is also entwined in a worldwide network of academics.

One does not have to be an uncritical believer in "progress" to recognize that the very long-term trend-line in the development of human society has been towards larger and larger networks of interdependent people organized in more and more interlocking layers. Already in the eighteenth century, when a sense of membership of a nation-state was not yet strongly established in the habitus of a large proportion of Europeans, intellectuals like Kant (1970 [1784]: 521–53) were already perceiving humanity as a whole as an all-embracing unity. Now, through world systems theory and the globalization debate, sociologists have begun to recognize that all human beings in the world are interdependent with each other to an extent that, until quite recently, they were not. Perhaps for many people – especially intellectuals – the sense of identification with common humanity is growing, but it would be unrealistic to say that that was the most important, the most affectively charged, component of habitus and identity helping to steer the conduct of the overwhelming majority of the world's population.

In this light, it can be seen that various layers of habitus simultaneously present in people today may be of many different vintages. Strong identification with kinship groups and local communities historically preceded that with state-societies, while at the present day for most people the sense of national or ethnic identity is much stronger (emotionally and in its consequences for actual conduct) than any that they feel for supranational groupings, as Europeans for example or simply as citizens of the world. Earlier and later layers of identity may conflict with one another:

> The change in we-identity that takes place in the course of the transition from one stage of development to another can be elucidated in terms of a conflict of loyalties. The traditional conscience-formation, the traditional ethos of attachment to the old survival unit of family or clan – in short, the narrower or broader kin-group – dictates that a more well-off member should not deny even distant relations a degree of help if they ask for it. High officials in a newly independent state thus find it difficult to refuse their kinsmen their support if they try to obtain one of the coveted state posts, even a lowly one. Considered in terms of the ethos and conscience of more developed states, the preferment of relations in filling state posts is a form of corruption. In terms of the pre-state conscience it is a duty and, as long as everyone does it in the traditional tribal struggle for power and status, a necessity. In the transition to a new level of integration therefore, there are conflicts of loyalty and conscience which are at the same time conflicts of personal identity.
>
> (Elias 1991: 178–9)

That there was a sequentially ordered process of development through history does not mean, of course, that the same sequence

is replicated in each individual's lifetime development, though it
is worth recalling that sociologists have studied the sequence of
identity acquisition in the course of the political socialization of
children (Greenstein 1965). Nor, even more emphatically, does a
long-term trend-line mean that there is always and inevitably a
progressive shift in the direction of more inclusive layers of identity.
Events in the former Yugoslavia can serve to remind us that less
inclusive layers of identity – especially "ethnic" ones – can be
socially constructed and become affectively more charged than formerly were identifications with a nation-state. The matter can perhaps
be best conceptualized in terms of changing balances between different layers of habitus and identity, tilting first one way and then
the other in the context of historical events, even if over the longer
term – in the *histoire des conjonctures* or still more the *longue durée*
– the trend has been towards the formation of more inclusive layers
of identity.

This multi-layered conception of habitus and identity may convey
an image of some sort of egocentric planetary system, with the individual self-conception at the centre, various levels of group identity
in orbits ranging outwards to the distant Pluto of humanity as a
whole. But when we remember how James, Cooley, Mead, and the
whole symbolic interactionist tradition have stressed the way in
which each person's self is formed by a reflexive process, in which
our perception of how others see us plays a paramount part, it is
easy to see that individual self-images and group we-images are not
separate things. Elias uses a different (mixed, but vivid) metaphor which
makes that clear:

> the social habitus of individuals forms, as it were, the soil from which
> grow the personal characteristics through which an individual differs
> from other members of his society. In this way something grows out
> of the common language which the individual shares with others
> and which is certainly a component of the social habitus – a more
> or less individual style, what might be called an unmistakable indi-
> vidual handwriting that grows out of the social script ... the indi-
> vidual bears in himself or herself the habitus of the group, and ... it
> is this habitus that he or she individualises to a greater or lesser
> extent.   (Elias 1991: 182–3)

One reason why the gap between micro-level and macro-level theories
of identity has persisted is, I believe, that symbolic interactionist
and similar traditions have continued to work with egocentric models
of the "individual" and "society," and "society" beyond the face-

to-face group or community has remained undifferentiated. These implicit assumptions can be seen in such key notions as "taking the role of *the* other" and "*the* generalized other" (both in the singular). "The other" is little more than Alter in Parsons's and Shils's (1951) famous dyadic model. On the other hand, macro-level theories have generally taken no cognizance of the fact that every process of socialization is also a process of individualization, and have thus veered towards excessive determinisms. What are needed, given the multi-layered character of habitus in complex societies, are propositions about *general processes*, about the dynamics of we-images and their connection with personal self-images in unequal and fluctuating power balances between groups of many kinds: men and women, rich and poor, blacks and whites, gays and straights, colonized and colonizers, First and Third World countries. Elias's model of established–outsiders relations is a promising start in this direction.

Established–Outsiders Relations

The mutual conditioning of processes of meaning and power was central to Elias's thinking. In inventing the concept of established–outsiders relations, he was seeking categories which, though simpler in themselves than the familiar terms of Marxist and Weberian debates, would yet enable him to grapple better with the complexities of identity and inequality actually observed within the flux of social interdependencies.

The concept was first developed in the limited context of a fairly conventional study of a small community in the English Midlands (Elias and Scotson 1965), focusing especially on relations between two neighborhoods, both occupied mainly by outwardly similar working-class families. But in later work by Elias and others, the ideas have been extended in their application to class relations in cities, to "race" and "ethnic" relations, to the power balances between men and women, heterosexuals and homosexuals, and many other contexts (Elias 1976; Mennell 1989: 115–39).

Looked at singly, the people of the two different neighborhoods in the community Elias studied differed very little from each other: they had similar occupations, similar houses, and most lived similarly respectable lives. The principal difference between them as groups was that the houses in one neighborhood (the "Village") were several decades older that those in the other (the "Estate") and a number of key families in the former were long established and formed a closely-knit network. They monopolized the key positions in local churches, associations, and other focuses of community life, in which the residents of the Estate played little part. This had happened in an unplanned way over the years. But the established group developed an ideology which represented the outsiders as rough, uncouth, dirty, and delinquent — although in fact only a very small minority of the Estate families were other than thoroughly respectable! In this process, gossip played a vital part. Gossip is highly selective and distorting. Through it people compete in demonstrating their fervent adherence to their own group norms by expressing their shock and horror at the behavior of those who do not conform. Only the items of news least flattering to the outsider group ("blame gossip") were relayed — the perfectly acceptable behavior of the great majority was not news. Blame gossip conveyed a highly simplified presentation of social realities, based on a *"minority of the worst."* The established group also gossiped about themselves, which in itself was a powerful source of social control restraining potential infringements of their own norms of respectability. But, in this gossip about themselves, selectivity tended to operate in the opposite direction: it tended to be "praise gossip," based on a *"minority of the best."* [4]

A general conclusion from this case study, of wider relevance to theories of identity, is that,

> By and large ... the more secure the members of a group feel in their own superiority and their pride, the less great is the distortion, the gap between image and reality, likely to be; and the more threatened and insecure they feel, the more likely is it that internal pressure, and as part of it, internal competition, will drive common beliefs towards extremes of illusion and rigidity.
>
> (*Elias and Scotson 1965: 95*)

Why the people of the Estate did not retaliate is also of general relevance. They did not retaliate, in brief, because they did not have the power, being excluded from key positions in community associations and being members of only a much looser-knit and less effective communications network. In addition, there was a personal or psychological component,

> because, to some extent, their own conscience was on the side of the detractors. They themselves agreed with the "village" people that it was bad not to be able to control one's children or to get drunk and noisy and violent. Even if none of these reproaches could be applied to themselves personally, they knew only too well that they

did apply to some of their neighbours. They could be shamed by
allusion to this bad behaviour of their neighbours because by living
in the same neighbourhood the blame, the bad name attached to it,
according to the rules of affective thinking, was automatically applied
to them too.   (1965: 101–2)

To put it another way, an unfavorable collective "we-image" was
incorporated into the individual self-image of the people living on
the Estate. In describing the social process by which that we-image
was created – along with the correspondingly favorable we-image
and we-ideal enjoyed by the "villagers" – Elias also used the twin
terms *group charisma* and *group disgrace*: the creation of group charisma
by and for a more powerful, established group is inseparable from
the imposition on and internalization of group disgrace by members
of an outsider group.[5] Note, however, that Elias specifically argues
against the idea that status hierarchies are based on consensus:
he points out that there are always tensions and conflicts and feelings
of resentment between established and outsiders.

How this ambivalence and resentment finds expression, however,
varies according to circumstances. In the case of the Estate, it was
most obviously seen in the behavior of a minority of children, whose
rowdyism and petty delinquency was only encouraged by the dis-
approval of the "villagers." Again, Elias's thinking went beyond a
small case study to some general propositions about the connection
between the formation of group identities and the predominant power
balances between groups.

When the power ratios between established and outsiders is very
unequal, the oppressed and exploited cannot escape from their
position. This is one of the conditions which makes it most likely
that they will take into their own we-image what the established say
about them. This process of stigmatization is a very common element
in domination within such highly unequal power balances, and it
is remarkable how across many varied cases the content of the
stigmatization remains the same. The outsiders are always dirty,
morally unreliable, and lazy, among other things. That was how in
the nineteenth-century industrial workers were frequently seen: they
were often spoken of as the "Great Unwashed." That was how
whites often perceived blacks. In an extreme case, such as the
Burakumin in Japan, the opprobrium heaped on them by the established may enter deep into the consciousness of members of the
outcaste.

Unchanging power ratios, however, are very much the exception.
It often happens that the tensions created when groups are forced

together into interdependence result in a shift – either slow and oscillating or sudden and dramatic – toward a more even power ratio. When power ratios become less uneven, the imposed sense of inferiority is weakened. Inequalities previously taken for granted are challenged. The problem of inequalities between social groups has occupied the mind and conscience in the twentieth century perhaps more than ever before. It has seen an astonishing sequence of emancipation struggles: of workers, of colonial peoples, of blacks, of women, of homosexuals. In each case, the tension-balance of power between these outsider groups and their established counterparts has changed, not to equality certainly, but toward a somewhat less uneven balance. Even the balance of power between children and adults has become noticeably less unequal.[6] Why have these changes come about?

In part it is the continuing process of what Elias called *functional democratization*. Longer and more differentiated chains of interdependence mean that power differentials diminish within and among groups because incumbents of specialized roles are more interdependent and can thus exert reciprocal control over each other. The power chances of specialized groups are further increased if they manage to organize themselves in a cohesive way, since they are then able to act collectively to disrupt the wider mesh of interdependencies – in effect withholding things that the other groups need. In ways such as these, the increasing division of social functions and lengthening chains of interdependence lead to greater reciprocal dependency and thus to patterns of more multi-polar control within and among groups. Yet that is only one side of the story. These same processes of differentiation create problems of coordination and are thus accompanied – with leads and lags – by processes of integration. That is to say, larger-scale organization in state and economy forces groups of people together in closer interdependencies than formerly; and these new patterns create new concentrations of power resources, new inequalities. For all the diminution of inequalities, for instance between employers and employees, or between men and women, new inequalities constantly emerge. For example, large organizations present a paradox. On the one hand, rectilinear chains of command are no longer adequate, and management style shifts to one of negotiation and "team-work." At the same time, the number of tiers in organizational hierarchies increases and creates the possibility of new monopolizations of power. In consequence informalization of relations with immediate superiors can go hand in hand with increasing alienation from remote authorities. Moreover, in the twentieth century, cheap transport and increased mobility

over long distances have made it still more common throughout
the world for displaced groups to impinge on older-established groups.
Wars, too, have played their part on an increasing scale. Groups
of people whose skins are of different colors or who have been
brought up in different ways of life are increasingly thrust together,
and established–outsiders patterns are a characteristic result.

One example from the field of race relations will have to suffice
as an illustration of how shifts in the power ratio at the center of
an established–outsiders relationship is characteristically reflected
in the construction of identity or we-images. In the ante-bellum
South, the "Negro" was represented as lazy, feckless, lacking any
foresight, and having a happy-go-lucky, child-like, and essentially
inept nature. This image of "Black Sambo" was used in resisting
the case for emancipation. Yet it probably appeared to have some
basis in fact too, for extremely unequal power ratios have profound
psychological effects on the outsiders:

> some blacks may have deliberately played the "Sambo" role because
> they perceived it as what their masters wanted and because it en-
> abled them, on the one hand, to gain limited privileges and, on the
> other, to avoid punishment. But probably as important was the fact
> that slaves had few opportunities to develop modes of behaviour
> thought appropriate by adult whites. Like children, they had only
> limited possibilities for initiating independent action. However, unlike
> children that dependence was permanent and maintained by powerful
> sanctions.
>
> (Dunning 1986: 113, cf. Elkins 1959 and Abrams 1982: 241–50)

The abolition of slavery changed little immediately in this nexus
of power and identity. Only with the movement of blacks to the
northern cities of the USA on a large scale from the 1920s did the
power ratio between American blacks and whites slowly begin to
shift. In the towns it was possible to organize and for social cohesion
to develop. Particularly important has been the growth of a black
bourgeoisie: the differentiation within the black population of a
stratum rising in status and in economic power has constituted a
strand of functional democratization, and helped to blur the formerly
rigid and caste-like boundary between black and white. As is usually
the case when highly unequal power differentials begin to shift in
favor of outsiders, in the 1960s and 1970s the inherent group
tensions – hitherto quiescent or evident only sporadically –
exploded openly. These were also the years of the "black power"
movements promoting black pride ("black is beautiful") and even,

for a time, separatism to repair the we-image damaged by decades of oppression. These are typical manifestations when differentials between established and outsiders are diminishing. Despite the Los Angeles riots in 1992, a time of very bad economic conditions, tensions appeared to have become manifested less dramatically in recent years. This characteristic trajectory of the power–identity nexus seems also to have been followed over the last couple of decades by the women's movement. [7]

INCREASING MUTUAL IDENTIFICATION?

Does the process of functional democratization therefore also involve a long-term trend towards increasing mutual identification? The answer seems to be yes, *ceteris paribus* – that is, subject to the reservations already mentioned, including the creation of new inequalities of power by the same process of the division of social functions which is at the same time diminishing earlier inequalities, and subject to some other reservations that we have yet to discuss.

Alexis de Tocqueville (1961 [1840]: vol. II, pp. 195–200; cf. Stone and Mennell 1980: 1–46) pointed out "that manners are softened as social conditions become more equal," citing the attitude of Mme de Sévigné in the late seventeenth century towards the executions of peasants after a local rising, an attitude which from a later standpoint seems strikingly callous. In more equal societies, he suggests, people more readily identify with the sufferings of others. Much more recently, of course, Foucault (1977) pointed to a similar change in attitudes towards suffering, though without offering as much in the way of sociological explanation as did Tocqueville. Elias, on the other hand, offers an account that links micro- and macro-level theorizing about identification processes, and relates them to historical evidence.

The division of social functions under the pressure of competition means, *ceteris paribus*, that individuals have constantly to attune their actions to those of more and more others. The habit of foresight over longer chains grows. In Goudsblom's neat phrase, 'more people are forced more often to pay more attention to more other people' (1989: 722). With this comes a change in the way of considering others. The individual's image of other people becomes "psychologized": it becomes more permeated by observation and experience. Perception of others becomes richer in nuances, and freer from the instant response of spontaneous emotions (Elias 1978–82: vol. II, pp. 272–4).

What this means is seen more clearly in relation to historical evidence. In a society with a lower division of social functions, where chains of interdependence were short and life was more insecure and unpredictable, other people were perceived in a simpler way. Elias argued that in warrior societies other people and their actions were perceived in more unqualified terms as friend or foe, good or bad; and the responses were correspondingly unrestrained and undifferentiated. With the greater complexity of society which gradually develops, however, people become accustomed to looking further down a human chain and reacting more dispassionately.

> Only then is the veil which the passions draw in front of their eyes slowly lifted, and a new world comes into view – a world whose course is friendly or hostile to the individual person without being *intended* to be so, a chain of events that need to be contemplated dispassionately over long stretches if their connections are to be uncovered.   (Elias 1978–82: vol. II, p. 273)

The greater permeation of conduct by observation is seen clearly in the transition of manners in sixteenth-century Europe. In the manners books of Erasmus and Della Casa, Elias argued, psychological insights and personal observation play a larger part than in their medieval precursors, and the reader is urged to take more conscious account of how his or her own behavior will be interpreted by others. This he interpreted as one effect of the emergence then in process of a new courtly upper class drawn from fragments both of the old warrior class and the mercantile class, within a relatively open but highly competitive society, in which the various strata were generally becoming more closely integrated. Later, when court society reached its zenith, the art of human observation was refined still further. As Elias demonstrated at length especially in *The Court Society* (1983), preservation of one's social position under severe competitive pressure necessitated a more "psychological" view of people, involving precise observation of oneself and others in terms of longer series of motives and causal connections. Yet this was not quite the same as what is today called psychology. In a sense, the courtly art of observation remained far closer to reality: it was never concerned with the individual in isolation, but always with individual people in relation to others in a social context. Only later – under the influence of the solipsistic strain in western philosophy increasingly prominent from the Renaissance onwards, and also colored by the still greater constraints and inhibitions of classic bourgeois society – did "psychology" take on its more modern guise.

One of the principal faults of that, maintains Elias, is that too often it implicitly assumes that the essential determinants of a person's behavior come from "inside," independent of his or her relation to others, and are related to others almost as an afterthought. What Elias provided here was in effect an historicization of Goffman *avant la lettre*. Goffman, of course, stressed the effect of social settings on self-identity: total institutions were natural experiments on what could be done to the self (Goffman 1968). On the other hand, Elias more than Goffman shows how "the presentation of self in everyday life" (Goffman 1971) is itself shaped and changed through historical process. [8]

The social process of "psychologization," linked to the division of labor and functional democratization at the "macro-" or structural level, is a process of transition in mutual identification. Taking more conscious account of how one's behavior will be interpreted by others can also be described as a higher level of identification with others. Of course in the court society described by Elias, the boundaries within which identification was felt were quite narrow. That is the significance of Mme de Sévigné's jocular attitude to the punishment of peasants, or of Voltaire's being horsewhipped by an aristocrat's servants. There remained great scope for expansion of identification in subsequent stages of social development. The growing sense of identification with the nation-state, quite recent for most people in most countries, is the aspect of this expansion which has attracted most attention. Eugen Weber, in his classic *Peasants into Frenchmen* (1976), shows how late was any marked sense of Frenchness in the minds of people in the remoter areas of the territory long within the boundaries of the French state. He shows how, partly through the intentional use of the expanding educational system but mainly through the unplanned consequences of processes like improved communications, urbanization, industrialization, migration and military conscription, the peasantry was integrated into the French state and simultaneously civilized in manners, customs, and beliefs. Weber's emphasis on denser networks and improved communications in the growth of national identity parallels that of Benedict Anderson in *Imagined Communities* (1983), who especially uses the notion of "print capitalism" in his account of the origin and spread of nationalism. Both books, concerned with developments on broader canvases, seem to bear out the value of Elias's stress on social networks and gossip in we-image formation in the microcosm of a local community.

The other side of the coin from nationalism is the issue of the development of "citizenship" (Marshall 1950; Bendix 1969; Turner

1986) and welfare state institutions in capitalist countries. A particularly interesting contribution in this area is Abram de Swaan's
In Care of the State (1988), which employs an unusual mixture of
rational choice theory and Eliasian historical sociology in accounting
for similarities and differences in the rise of social welfare, public
health, and educational provision in the USA, Britain, France,
Germany, and the Netherlands. De Swaan provides an antidote to
any suspicion that the rise of the welfare state involves a spontaneous
movement of the *Zeitgeist* or an instant outbreak of enlightened
altruism. He stresses rather how functional democratization works:
only when dependency relations are more stable and symmetrical
does a mutual sense of identification develop. And collective action
usually proceeded through the conflict of groups pursuing their own
interests but adapting slowly to the recognition that, willy-nilly,
they were reciprocally dependent on each other.

This emphasis on integration processes and the formation of more
inclusive we-images within a spreading web of interdependence may
seem at odds with interpretations of nationalism which stress its
emergence in the context of *breaking* structures and disintegration (see
for instance Hobsbawm 1990, 1992). The Austro-Hungarian empire
and its various successor nation-states is the classic case; and, topically
and traumatically, in the former Yugoslavia, we are currently witnessing the further disintegration of one of those successor states. Are
the two interpretations incompatible? Possibly not, if Norbert Elias
was right in his hypothesis that people generally feel the greatest
emotional identification, have the most emotionally charged we-
images, in relation to their *survival units*. This is the intentionally quite
general term that Elias uses to designate the level of social organization which for the time being meets the most significant proportion of its members' needs for survival – food, shelter, clothing,
protection, and meaning among them. In the industrial world, though
not everywhere or for everyone, nor for as long as people sometimes
imagine, the survival unit has typically been the nation-state, which
for a long time sociologists unthinkingly made synonymous with a
"society." For a relatively short time the nation-state constituted
"a territorially-bounded 'national economy' which formed a building
block in the larger 'world economy,' at least in the developed regions
of the globe" (Hobsbawm 1990: 173–4). At least as important, it
was a unit often in competition with others not just economically
but politically and militarily; where competition with outsiders is
enough to pose a threat to the security of people's way of life,
emotional identification with one's own unit is likely to be strong.
But in earlier times and in other contexts the survival unit was the

tribe, the lineage, or the local community. And today we are seeing signs of the nation-state being superseded as the effective survival unit by supra-state levels of organization. By the 1990s, "all small and practically all medium-sized states ... had plainly ceased to be autonomous, in so far as they had once been so" (Hobsbawm 1990: 175), and even the USA's economic autonomy was greatly diminished. The development of political institutions typically lags behind the unplanned process of economic integration. The United Nations is not very far down the track of representing global society as a survival unit, but in western Europe the EC is acquiring real functions that affect member individuals in their everyday lives. This is emotionally very difficult for many Europeans, who feel powerful identification with their own nations: for them, the most inclusive "we" refers to fellow citizens of their own country, and the citizens of other member countries of the EC still remain, to varying degrees, "they."[9] Elias (1991: 211) speaks of this as a "drag effect," but expects the sense of European identity gradually to increase (and indeed there is empirical survey evidence of this beginning to happen).

None of this involves dewy-eyed optimism or faith in the inevitability of "progress." Stinchcombe has observed that "It is the great tragedy of social life that every extension of solidarity, from family to village, village to nation, presents also the opportunity of organising hatred on a larger scale" (1975: 601).[10] This is very much in the spirit of Elias, who always stressed that however much the civilizing process might be associated with the internal pacification of territory within the process of state-formation, it did not affect the use of violence in war between states; and in his later years he was centrally concerned with the threat of mass destruction (see Haferkamp 1987; Mennell 1987). (Who, after the euphoria of 1989–91 has dissipated, is yet to say his fears were misplaced?)[11]

Obviously it is all a good deal more complicated than a steady climb up a ladder toward more all-embracing we-identities. Three specific examples will serve to illustrate this. First, within the EC there is the interesting case of the Scottish National Party, which, in the 1992 UK election, campaigned (with quite indifferent popular success, as it happened) not for Scottish independence from Britain *tout court*, but for a "Scotland within Europe." That is, the party simultaneously sought to appeal to the emotionally charged we-image of Scots as Scots and, recognizing that the old-fashioned view of the sovereignty of a Scottish nation is nowadays much compromised by the chains of interdependence which bind Scots to the UK and to the EC, also to promote a positive we-image with the wider European grouping. [12]

The second examplar is the recent history of Australia. From the first European settlement in the continent in 1788 and through to the Second World War, the effective survival unit for Australians was in a real sense the British Empire. Not only was Australian trade overwhelmingly with Britain, but the military defense of the empire was a collective enterprise to which Australia contributed but on which it was also clearly dependent. The defense and foreign policy link began to be reoriented toward the USA in the exigencies of the Second World War, and trade began to shift toward Asia in the 1950s and decisively in the 1970s, following Britain's entry into the EC. Here too, however, there was a drag effect, with a large proportion of Australians continuing into the 1950s and 1960s to think of themselves as British-overseas. Since the 1970s that has markedly declined, but Australia, as a small nation (in terms of population) closely entangled in a world economy and global society, is still looking for a wider we-identity. Politically (or economically) motivated exhortations to Australians to identify with Asia seem as yet unconvincing, given that the cultural and institutional roots of Australia are still preponderantly European (see Mennell 1992).

Third, Yugoslavia. It is easy to think, in light of recent events, that emotional identification with the Yugoslavian state as a survival unit was never strong or widespread, that people did not feel strongly about themselves as "we Yugoslavs." "In melancholy retrospect," writes Hobsbawm (1990: 173), "... the Yugoslav revolution succeeded in preventing the nationalists within its state frontiers from massacring each other almost certainly for longer than ever before in their history." Under Tito, Yugoslavia seemed stable, therefore it may be inferred that there was a strong sense of national identity; since the advent of Milosevic, the country has disintegrated, therefore it is tempting to conclude that people's identity as Serbs, Croats, Slovenes, and Bosnians was always stronger than their identity as Yugoslavs. And indeed in discussions of identity there is always a risk of *post hoc, ergo propter hoc*. Unless we have reliable empirical evidence of how people felt before as well as after, there is a risk of circularity. As Hobsbawm points out (in criticism of Gellner 1983), the necessary "view from below, i.e the nation as seen not by governments and the spokesmen and activists of nationalist (or non-nationalist) movements, but by the ordinary persons who are objects of their action and propaganda, is exceedingly difficult to discover" (Hobsbawm 1990: 10–11). Furthermore, the "view from below" and the "view from above" interact with each other. Abram de Swaan has commented:

> What explains the resurgence of nationalist identifications in formerly communist countries is not their inherent unavoidability but the disintegration of the communist state apparatus and the resulting chaos, which prompts people to find new forms of organisation to help them compete for the open positions of power and profit. Thus, activists seek in a process of trial and error to kindle those identifications that will evoke the greatest response, i.e the strongest popular support. Such experiments in finding the most effective common denominator will occur most intensively during times of transition and upheaval, when struggles for position are intensified and the lines of competition are being redrawn.   (de Swaan 1992: 12)

Thus, a couple of points need to be made before we abandon too easily the idea that there is, *ceteris paribus*, a long-term trend from less inclusive to more inclusive we-images, and that that is associated with a broad trend towards larger-scale survival groups. To begin with, it has to be remembered that it needs only a small minority who think of themselves more strongly as Serbs or Croats than as Yugoslavians to set in train the mayhem we are witnessing. And, more important, that mayhem has in effect suddenly reduced the scale of the survival units actually functioning within the former territory of Yugoslavia; that fact, plus the impact of the mayhem itself, would surely be enough to precipitate an emotional reordering of we-images. We-images are formed in *histoire événementielle* as well as in the *longue durée*; local and short-term reversals are certainly to be expected in response to events such as we have witnessed. Wider levels of identification often remain very tenuous and tentative: "they may be undone by more pressing concerns manifesting themselves in the inner circles of identification" (de Swaan 1992: 18–19).

Perhaps the greatest lacuna in theories of identity is in the area of our understanding of the emotional dynamics of we-images among large and complex groups of interdependent people, and particularly the connection between long-term processes of state formation on the one hand and the constructed memory of specific events on the other. But even here, the gap between theories of identity formation in individuals and in groups may not be as wide as it sometimes seems. Freud noted a parallel:

> ... in the so-called earliest childhood memories we possess not the genuine memory-trace but a later revision of it, a revision which may have been subjected to the influences of a variety of later psychological

forces. Thus the "childhood memories" of individuals come in general
to acquire the significance of "screen memories" and in doing so offer
a remarkable analogy with the childhood memories that a nation
preserves in its store of legends and myths.   *(1975 [1901]: 88)*

Elias picks up the point in his *Studien über die Deutschen* (1989),
which is concerned with how events, power struggles, national
achievements and national failures have become sedimented in the
collective makeup of a whole nation.

> Sociologists face a task here which distantly recalls the task that
> Freud began. He sought to show the connection between the outcome
> of the conflictual channeling of drives in a person's development and
> their resulting personality habitus. But there are also analogous con-
> nections between a people's long-term fortunes and experience and
> their social habitus at any time in the future. At this stratum of
> personality structure too – let us provisionally call it the "we-stratum"
> – there are often complex symptoms of disturbance at work, which
> are scarcely less than the individual neuroses in strength and in capacity
> to cause suffering.   *(1989: 27, my translation)*

In talking about the national habitus of the Germans, Elias
acknowledged that he was transgressing onto what was, in the Federal
Republic of Germany, an area of taboo (1989: 7–8). After all, any
idea of "national character" is unfortunately – if unnecessarily –
redolent of the Nazis' racial stereotypes. Of course, what Elias is
concerned with has nothing whatsoever to do with notions of
biological "Aryans." The "Aryan" physical types favoured by the
National Socialist regime can plainly be found in Denmark, the
Netherlands and elsewhere, but the Danes and the Dutch are vastly
different in national habitus from the Germans. To hammer the
obvious point home, Elias discusses at some length (1989: 17–20)
how Dutch history – the experiences of an erstwhile maritime power
long dominated more by a class of rich merchants than by its traditional nobility – is reflected today in Dutch outlook and ways of
behaving. He further extends the three-way comparison between
Germany, England, and France that he had begun in *The Civilising
Process*. Compared with England and – in spite of the Revolution
– even with France, German social development was marked by
very great discontinuities. Unlike the French, today Germans do
not carry in their habitus very many marks of the ways of courtiers.
Among the few, Elias remarks in passing, are the typical German
customs surrounding beer drinking (often to inebriation, yet within
the framework of a certain habituated discipline even in drunkenness?,

which he traces back to the economically and culturally impoverished German courts after the disaster of the Thirty Years War (1989: 12–13, 131–2). The taming of warriors took a different course in Prussia: they were turned less into courtiers on the French model than bureaucratized as administrators and professional soldiers. That helps explain the military inheritance in the national habitus: Elias writes at length (1989: 61–158) about the long persistence in Germany of the practice of dueling, the great social importance attached to it, and its spread from the officer corps to the middle classes in the universities. The definition of "good society" in terms of the idea of social worthiness to give satisfaction in a duel imparted a very different character from that prevalent by the late nineteenth century in Parisian or London society. Later, moreover, "If one asks how Hitler was possible, then with the benefit of hindsight the spread of these socially sanctioned models of violent action and of social inequality belong among the prerequisites" (1989: 27, my translation).

The contradictory traits of diverse origins and the tensions between them, which Elias depicts in his collection of essays on the Germans, can serve to remind us of the contradictory trends evident in western Europe more generally at the present day. Although it is by no means yet as strong for most people as the we-image associated with the nation-state, the sense of identity as "we Europeans" is growing. Yet that is happening at the same time as a resurgence of neo-Nazism and hostility of many Europeans toward new waves of outsider migrants. This hostility may now be less often expressed in the vocabulary of biological racism, and more frequently as a feared threat to the *cultural* heritage of established residents. That at least has the merit of making more manifest and less latent the connection of these fears with questions of habitus and identity.

CONCLUSION: CHANGES IN THE WE–I BALANCE

The argument of this chapter tends to lend support to Craig Calhoun's assertion that the macro–micro divide is entirely abstract. The gap between bodies of theory dealing with identity formation in individuals and groups may be more apparent than real, an artifact of our customary modes of concept formation. The argument has drawn principally on the writings of Norbert Elias, who campaigned for a "process sociology" that did not treat "individual" and "society" as separate entities. His ideas seem, however, to be compatible with those of the many writers who have more recently contributed to the debate about nationalism. Elias stressed the need, when looking at processes of habitus- and identity-formation over long periods, to think in terms of "changes in the We–I balance" (1991: 155–237). He contended, on the one hand, that long-term increases in the scale and complexity of social interdependence produced more and more complex layers of we-image in people's habitus and sense of identity. On the other hand, he argued that the individual person's mode of self-experience had itself changed in the course of social development, and that the preoccupation of much of modern western philosophy and sociology with the experience of the single isolated adult individual is itself the product of the European civilizing process from the Renaissance onwards. Resisting this image of the human being as *homo clausus* and attempting to think in terms of pluralities of *homines aperti* is one way of improving our grasp of processes of identity formation.

NOTES

1 See de Swaan (1992) for a discussion of the Freudian theory of identification from a viewpoint similar to my own. Abram de Swaan and I are old friends, and on arrival in Pittsburgh discovered we had both written from an Eliasian perspective on the topic of identification.

2 This is evident in the (rather catchy) title of the Pittsburgh miniconference: "From Persons to Nations."

3 This was also the word that Elias used in German when his study of civilizing processes was published in 1939, though the English translation (1978–82) usually renders this as "personality makeup." In his later works, Elias began to use "habitus" in English too.

4 Note that these ideas could equally be expressed in the fashionable jargon of "discourse" and "narrative"; but I am allergic to fashions in jargon, and prefer not to do so.

5 Elias first used these terms in an unpublished paper presented at the Max Weber Centenary Conference in Heidelberg, 1964. Some sociologists have found it hard to accept the group reference of the term "charisma," in contrast to its individual reference in Weber's usage. Note the connection, not spelled out very much by Elias, between this discussion and that concerning the advance of thresholds of shame and embarrassment, and of standards of self-constraint, in *The Civilising Process*.

6 On changes in the power ratio between children or young people and their elders, see Elias (1989: 37ff) and Kapteyn (1985). This issue is bound up with the question of the trend towards "informalization" in contemporary societies, or more exactly a diminution in the formality/informality span or gradient; again, see Elias (1989: 33–60).

7 Two or more outsider identities can of course intersect. Patricia Hill Collins's study of *Black Feminist Thought* (1990) is a useful example. She shows, among other things, how American black women's typical his-

torical experience of being "outsiders within" white homes as domestic servants was distinct from that of male blacks, and how "Mammy" and "Jezebel" stereotypes played a part in their oppression analogous to, but different from, that of "Black Sambo."

8 For a comparison of Elias and Goffman, see Kuzmics (1986). Interestingly, Goffman cited the original 1939 German edition of *The Civilising Process*; Leonard Broom tells me that Goffman would have known of Elias's work through Edward Shils in a seminar at Chicago in the late 1940s.

9 The principle of 'subsidiarity', now much bandied about within the EC, is a response in part to these feelings. The notion embodies a recognition that, on the one hand, the interdependence of the EC member countries is now so great that there are decisions which unavoidably have to be taken at the level of Brussels, and on the other hand that other decisions (such as famously the contents of the British sausage) ought to be taken at the lowest possible level, close to the smaller categories of people they actually affect.

10 I am grateful to Arthur Stinchcombe, who was present when the original version of this chapter was presented in Pittsburgh, for drawing my attention to his essay "that bears on many of the same topics from a different point of view, which is I think compatible" (personal communication).

11 This ambivalence about the process of "civilization" was not peculiar to Elias's late works, but was present from the beginning. English-speaking readers have always failed to perceive, and German-speaking readers have failed to draw attention to, the ambiguity in the very title of Elias's 1939 *magnum opus*, *Über den Prozess der Zivilisation*: the word *Prozess* in German means both "process" and "*trial*" (in the legal sense of trial).

12 For an earlier Scottish nationalist view by a distinguished Marxist, see Tom Nairn, *The Break-up of Britain* (1977).

References

Abrams, Philip 1982: *Historical Sociology*. Shepton Mallet: Open Books.

Anderson, Benedict 1983: *Imagined Communities: Reflections on the Origins and Spread of Nationalism*. London: Verso.

Bendix, Reinhard 1969: *Nation-Building and Citizenship*. Garden City, NY: Doubleday.

Bourdieu, Pierre 1984: *Distinction: A Social Critique of the Judgment of Taste*. London, Routledge.

Calhoun, Craig 1991: "Chair's Message," *Perspectives: The Theory Section Newsletter* (American Sociological Association), 14(4): 1–2.

Collins, Patricia Hill 1990: *Black Feminist Thought*. New York: Unwin Hyman.

Dunning, Eric 1986: "Race relations," in G. Hurd, ed., *Human Societies*, 2nd ed. London: Routledge and Kegan Paul, pp. 110–33.

Elias, Norbert 1976: "Een theoretisch essay over gevestigden en buitenstaanders," Introduction to *De Gevestigden en de Buitenstaanders*. Utrecht: Het Spectrum (Dutch translation of *The Established and the Outsiders*), pp. 7–46.

Elias, Norbert 1978–82 (1939): *The Civilising Process*, vol. I: *The History of Manners*. New York: Urizen, 1978; vol. II: *Power and Civility* (title of British edition is *State-Formation and Civilisation*). New York: Pantheon, 1982.

Elias, Norbert 1983 (1969): *The Court Society*. Oxford: Basil Blackwell.

Elias, Norbert 1989: *Studien über die Deutschen: Machtkämpfe und Habitusentwicklung im 19. und 20. Jahrhundert*. Frankfurt: Suhrkamp (English translation, *The Germans: Essays on Power Struggles and the Development of Habitus in the Nineteenth and Twentieth Centuries*, forthcoming. Oxford: Polity Press).

Elias, Norbert 1991: *The Society of Individuals*. Oxford: Basil Blackwell.

Elias, N. and Scotson, J. L. 1965: *The Established and the Outsiders: A Sociological Enquiry into Community Problems*. London: Frank Cass.

Elkins, Stanley 1959: *Slavery*. Chicago: University of Chicago Press.

Foucault, Michel 1977: *Discipline and Punish: The Birth of the Prison*. New York: Pantheon.

Freud, Sigmund 1975 (1901): *The Psychopathology of Everyday Life*. Pelican Freud Library, vol. 5. Harmondsworth: Penguin.

Gellner, Ernest, 1983: *Nations and Nationalism*. Oxford: Basil Blackwell.

Goffman, Erving 1968 (1961): *Asylums*. Harmondsworth: Penguin.

Goffman, Erving 1971 (1959): *The Presentation of Self in Everyday Life*. Harmondsworth: Penguin.

Goudsblom, Johan 1989: "Stijlen en beschavingen," *De Gids* 152: 720–2.

Greenstein, F. 1965: *Children and Politics*. New Haven: Yale University Press.

Haferkamp, Hans 1987 : "From the Intra-state to the Inter-state Civilising Process," *Theory, Culture and Society* 4(2–3): 545–57.

Hobsbawm, E. J. 1990: *Nations and Nationalism since 1780*. Cambridge: Cambridge University Press.

Hobsbawm, E. J. 1992: "Ethnicity and Nationalism in Europe Today," *Anthropology Today* 8(1): 3–8.

Kant, Immanuel 1970 (1784): "Idea of a Universal History from the Point of View of a Citizen of the World," in *Kant's Political Writings*. Cambridge: Cambridge University Press.

Kapteyn, Paul 1985: "Even a Good Education Gives rise to Problems: The Changes in Authority between Parents and Children," *Concilium* 5: 19–33.

Kluckhohn, Clyde and Henry A. Murray, eds 1948: *Personality in Nature, Society and Culture*. New York: Knopf.

Kuzmics, Helmut 1986: "Verlegenheit und Zivilisation: Zu einigen Gemeinsamkeiten und Unterschieden in Werk von E. Goffman und N. Elias," *Soziale Welt* 37(4): 467–86.

Marshall, T. H. 1950: *Citizenship and Social Class and Other Essays*. Cambridge: Cambridge University Press.

Mennell, Stephen 1987: "Comment on Haferkamp," *Theory, Culture and Society* 4(2–3): 559–61.

Mennell, Stephen 1989: *Norbert Elias: Civilisation and the Human Self-Image.* Oxford: Blackwell (revised paperback edn entitled *Norbert Elias: An Introduction,* 1992).

Mennell, Stephen 1992: "The Crisis of Europeanness Overseas: A View from Australasia," paper presented at UNESCO/Council of Europe conference on "Europe into the Third Millennium," University of Exeter, UK, April 9–12, 1992 (forthcoming).

Nairn, Tom 1977: *The Break-up of Britain.* London: New Left Books.

Parsons, Talcott and Edward Shils 1951: "Values, Motives and Systems of Action," in Parsons and Shils, eds, *Toward a General Theory of Action.* Cambridge MA: Harvard University Press, pp. 45–275.

Stinchcombe, Arthur L. 1975: "Social Structure and Politics," in Nelson W. Polsby and Fred Greenstein, eds, *Handbook of Political Science,* vol. 3. Reading, MA: Addison-Wesley, pp. 557–622.

Stone, John and Stephen Mennell, eds 1980: *Alexis de Tocqueville on Democracy, Revolution and Society.* Chicago: University of Chicago Press.

Swaan, Abram de 1992: "Widening Circles of Identification: Emotional Concerns in Sociogenetic Perspective," paper presented at *Theory, Culture and Society,* Tenth Anniversary Conference, Seven Springs, Pennsylvania, August 16–19, 1992.

Tocqueville, Alexis de 1961 (1840): *Democracy in America,* 2 vols. New York: Schocken.

Turner, Bryan S. 1986: *Citizenship and Capitalism: The Debate over Reformism.* London: Allen & Unwin.

Weber, Eugen 1976: *Peasants into Frenchmen: The Modernisation of Rural France, 1870–1914.* Stanford, CA: Stanford University Press.

7

Identity Theory, Identity Politics: Psychoanalysis, Marxism, Post-Structuralism

Eli Zaretsky

Beginning in the late 1960s a new form of political life emerged, especially in the US, which more recently has been termed "identity politics." It had two main characteristics: first, an emphasis on difference rather than commonality; second, the local or particular community of identity – such as lesbianism or the African-American community – was intended as the central point of identification for the self.

While the term "identity politics" is new, the concern with "identity," of course, is quite old. We note it in the shift from tribal societies to empires in the ancient world, in the "imagined communities" of early modern nationalism, and in the many movements of our time, ranging from Marcus Garvey to Zionism, that rejected the universalizing ideals of liberalism and Marxism.

The identity politics that emerged in the early 1970s, therefore, must be situated historically. In the immediate sense, I will argue, it emerged out of the breakdown or transformation of the "New Left" – it is a post-1968 phenomenon – and in a larger sense it was part of a global shift in the character of capitalism, one which contained as one of its fundamental components, a realignment or reorganization of the division between the public and the private.

In questioning this phenomenon, the most important question we want to raise is how to distinguish progressive and reactionary forms of identity politics. The assertion made in 1969 and 1970 that new political tendencies such as radical feminism or gay liberation would go beyond and supplant Marxism received compelling support with the collapse of all western communist regimes except Cuba twenty years later. However, this collapse was accompanied by the emergence of new and intense forms of nationalism linked to new forms of domination. In the United States, the emphasis on particularist identities has been accompanied by the decline, if not loss, of a sense of a common left, while the new forms of identity, such as "woman," have themselves come under attack for a false inclusiveness under the general rubric "essentialism." The Republican Convention of 1992 was as much "identity politics" as is a women's center or a special program for Hispanic-Americans. We need a way to distinguish not only among different tendencies but to distinguish desirable and undesirable tendencies within them.

To that end I want to introduce two distinctions. The first is between movements that situate themselves within a universalistic polity but insist upon forms of cultural separation or "multiculturalism" – in other words, movements that presuppose a distinction between culture and polity – and movements that seek full self-determination in the form of separate states. In this chapter, I am only concerned with the former, which describes most forms of identity politics. One consequence of this distinction is in calling attention to the fact that identity politics, in general, presupposes universalism.

The second distinction is between the identity politics of racial and ethnic groups such as African-Americans, Hispanics, Native Americans, and that of gays, lesbians, and women. Both groups share a central concern for identity. For both a synechdocal identity – white, male, western, heterosexual, ethno- and andro-centric – functions as part of a hegemonic logic of domination. Both have sought to reclaim a stigmatized identity, to revalue the devalued pole of a dichotomized hierarchy such as white/black, male/female or heterosexual/gay. However, the second group – women, gays – in addition has a special relation to what had previously been considered the private sphere of the family and personal life. The sphere of personal life had played a fundamental part in the politics of the 1960s even before the emergence of identity politics, as is suggested by such phenomena as the counterculture or the changes in sexuality of that time. In one sense, 1968 represented the triumph of the private sphere – it ushered in an apolitical age of narcissism. But 1968 also ushered in a period in which the women's liberation movement, based as it was on the politicization of the private sphere, was the one radical movement to survive and, indeed, flourish.

Now, it is generally believed today that the use of the term identity is drawn from post-structuralist philosophy. Identity in philosophy refers to at least two separable questions – first, what gives a thing or person its essential nature, i.e., its *eidos* or form, and thus its continuity through time, and second, what makes two things or two persons the same. The notion of identity involves negation or difference – something *is* something, *not* something else. Post-structuralists, such as Derrida, problematized identity, for example by arguing that identity presupposes differences, that it involves the suppression of difference, or that it entailed on endless process of deferral of meaning. Post-structuralism, therefore, contributed to the complication of identity politics by introducing what is sometimes termed a politics of difference, a politics aimed less at establishing a viable identity for its constituency than at destabilizing identities, a politics that eschews such terms as groups, rights, value, and society in favor of such terms as places, spaces, alterity, and subject positions, a politics that aims to decenter or subvert, rather than to conquer or assert. Before the question of identity evolved into the question of difference, however, there was a prior history.

It is a commonplace of both the politics of identity and of difference that they repudiate and supersede both psychoanalysis and Marxism. In this chapter I will argue that identity politics is better understood not as a repudiation of Marxism and psychoanalysis but as having emerged in a discrete space created by what might be considered a tacit division of responsibility between them and specifically on the basis of a distinct tradition based on psychoanalysis.

In both the United States and France (the two countries in which 1968 was most profound) the turn toward identity politics made psychoanalysis its target perhaps equally with Marxism, and in the United States more so.[1] There gay activists identified psychiatry as the "enemy incarnate" and Kate Millett called Freud "the strongest individual counterrevolutionary force in the ideology of sexual politics."[2] Without being aware of its origins within psychoanalysis, and specifically in psychoanalysis as the "other" of Marxism, the critical or progressive aspects of identity politics cannot be distinguished from the reactionary.

To understand those origins we must begin with the Enlightenment idea that in understanding society we can separate, in theory, a grid of abstractly equal individuals from their concrete determinations, such as (over time) race, nationality, gender, or religion. Insofar as we can distinguish a moment of birth for modern "identity politics" it lies in the Romantic movement's protest against this "abstract grid" of the Enlightenment, especially the protest on behalf of small, neglected, and oppressed nations.[3] While Romanticism criticized the Enlightenment on the basis of particularity, however, the

Marxist critique of the Enlightenment posited a genuinely alternative universalism. Marx rejected the Enlightenment view that freedom in the public shpere – the freedom of abstractly equal citizens or of exchanging individuals in the marketplace – could coexist with class relations in the sphere of production. Not until exchange and production were reunited, *bourgeois* and *citoyen* made one, could selves be free and whole. The Marxist emphasis on the healing and reuniting of society through the triumph of the concrete over the abstract, of use over exchange, claimed to subsume and surpass the Romantic critique of the Enlightenment and anticipates the twentieth-century phenomenon of identity.

Marxism, however, constituted its critique of the Enlightenment on the basis of what we can now see was a specific phase in the history of capitalism, namely industrialization, a phase characterized by the removal of socially organized production from the home and the consequent apparent division between a "public sphere" which Marxists equated with industry and the state and the private sphere of the family, and it was on the basis of this division that psychoanalysis emerged.[4] In one sense this was an advance. Reflecting the "separation" of the individual from his or her societal determinants – the individual's place in the social division of labor, which before the rise of modern capitalism could not have been "separated" – psychoanalysis developed a method for considering the individual in abstraction from his or her social relations, e.g. race, gender, class, etc. This method presumed that although we are different in different contexts there is an underlying person – an identity – that runs through all of them, and that this can be analyzed. This belief that personal or subjective identity can be separated, at least temporarily, from societal determination linked psychoanalysis to the whole project of freedom and autonomy that came down from the Enlightenment.

At the same time, the division between the public and the private occluded their unity in two ways that shaped the history of the question of identity in the twentieth century.

First, the separation of personal life from capitalist production gave rise to the characteristically modernist and quintessentially psychoanalytic idea that the basis of life was to be found in the private sphere – and that the "social" was secondary, derived, and often false.

In addition, the separation between the public and the private occluded the perpetuation of relations of domination – those beyond legitimate authority – into modern society. It did this politically by rendering those relations "private." Perhaps the most important forms of domination thereby occluded were those that occurred within the family, especially those of men – as husbands and fathers – over women.

In both cases – i.e., identity and authority – the asymmetric division between the private and the public anchored the tendency toward psychologization, toward an illusory sense of personal responsibility, and toward guilt as an affective interpersonal steering mechanism that is built into the structure of capitalist society and that was reinforced by the structure of industrialism. Psychoanalysis came to occupy it for a while overwhelming cultural position because it reflected the illusory or imaginary way in which modern personal life is lived, namely as something separate, individual, without connection to sociey. Because of this illusory basis, personal life is lived, to a great extent, in what Lacan called the imaginary register – the register of narcissism – which analysis took as its province.

Psychoanalysis, therefore, supplied an unacknowledged theory of the "whole" or to-be-reunited individual for much of the twentieth century. Whereas the social and behavioral sciences used such concepts as "social role," only pyschoanalysis along with literature spoke to the idea of a deep self, the idea that we are in some sense "whole." This history, repudiated in the 1970s, nonetheless continues to shape our thinking. In this chapter I trace four stages in the evolution of our contemporary conception of identity: (1) classical psychoanalysis, coinciding with the initial separation of the family from the economy as a general feature of the culture; (2) the hegemony of psychoanalysis in the forties and fifties and the Frankfurt School attempt to transform psychoanalysis into a discourse on domination, especially during the 1960s; (3) the emergence of identity politics and the rejection of the earlier model of the public/private split; and (4) Foucault's critique of identity as the most sophisticated attempt to reformulate the question of identity in the light of the changes in contemporary capitalism.

Classical Psychoanalysis and the Public/Private Split

Psychoanalysis emerged at the moment when the psychological, internal, subjective, and personal separated off from the social, the rational, the instrumental; its content, Freud wrote, was "what is most intimate in mental life, everything that a socially independent person must conceal."[5]

Freud dealt with the questions of identity and difference that I have alluded to above by introducing – in chapter 7 of *The Inter-*

pretation of Dreams – two separate but inextricable conceptions of the subject or psyche, to use his word. One was the classical Enlightenment conception of a self-enclosed subject who inwardly represents to him- or herself a world to which he or she is only externally related. The other was the processes he there calls the "dream work" – i.e., condensation, displacement, considerations of representability as these work over or play upon "transcriptions" or memories of perceptions through which the world is known. The latter model was the historically new one, of course. By showing how representations of the world were continually dissolved and remade within the individual it allowed Freud to cut through the previous hereditarian or environmentalist models of the mind without wholly rejecting them. Along with his imaginatively extended conception of sexuality and the equation of sexuality with infancy, it led to a formulation of "identity" as "within" the individual and, in a sense, prior to society. But by retaining two models of the mind in such forms as primary and secondary process, or unconscious and conscious, Freud problematized the Enlightenment conception of the subject but retained his connections with it.

Freud, in fact, did not use the term "identity" except in an incidental way. Rather his term was "identification." He began to use this term, along with the term "narcissism," in his response to the holistic or humanistic notions of identity that Adler and Jung had posed against psychoanalysis. In his mature theory, identification is the basic mechanism by which the self develops. According to his 1914 essay, "On Narcissism," through identification with the parents, we constitute an "ego-ideal" which establishes the "self-respect" from which repression proceeds. The ego-ideal also "has a social side; it is ... the common ideal of a family, a class or a nation." "That which he [*sic*] projects ahead of him as his ideal is merely his substitute for ... the time when he was his own ideal." [6] In 1915 Freud explained self-criticism – later the supergo – through identification: "the shadow of the object fell upon the ego, so that the latter would henceforth be criticized by a special mental faculty like an object." [7] In 1923. Freud explained separation from the mother in similar terms, calling identification a transformation of "object-libido into narcissistic libido," involving "an abandonment of sexual aims, a desexualization."

In *Group Psychology and the Analysis of the Ego* Freud argued that groups too could in part be understood through the private worlds of their members. Freud defined a group as "a number of individuals who have put one and the same object in the place of their ego ideal and have consequently identified themselves with one another."[8] The fact that each member of the group substituted an idealized image for their own defective ego-ideal sustained them in a common ideology of "self-mastery." "Each individual ... feels within himself the strength of the whole group."[9] *Civilization and Its Discontents* (1930) expands on this theme. The fact that aggression is restricted or forbidden within such groups as nations, religions, or political movements raises the self-esteem of their members. It is always possible to bind together "people in love," Freud wrote, "so long as there are other people left over to receive the manifestations of their aggressiveness."[10]

THE ATTEMPTS TO REWORK PSYCHOANALYSIS

It is obvious that Freud's approach to the identity of both individuals and groups was critical and destabilizing. This was not the case with the psychoanalytic movement that supplanted him.

It was Erik Erikson several decades after Freud, who formulated the analytic concept of identity as distinct from identification. Erikson defined identity as "the ability to maintain inner sameness and continuity," and explained it as the outcome of "the selective repudiation and mutual assimilation of childhood identifications, and their absorption in a new configuration." Erikson's aim was to "add" a social dimension to psychoanalysis. Thus he defined identity as the product of an interaction between self and society. Rather than societal norms being grafted upon the individual, as a vulgar Marxist or "social control" perspective might suggest, Erikson argued that the society into which the individual is born makes him or her its member by influencing epigenetically the manner in which he or she solves the tasks of development.[11] He claimed that the problem of identity was as strategic to his time – the 1940s and 1950s – as sexuality was to Freud's. He situated the problem in relation to a particular social group – youth – and he saw it as a special problem in America because of its disparate class and racial composition, its immigrants and Native Americans. Thus he wrote of the difficulty in sustaining "ego ideals" in a land "characterised by expanding identifications and by great fears of losing hard-won identities."[12]

But Erikson worked with a holistic, integrative, and ultimately oppressive conception of culture which foretold the later decline of psychoanalysis. By the mid-fifties, as the growth of mass consumption and the beginnings of the "baby boom" intensified the concern with primary institutions such as the family, schools, and health care, psychoanalysis became the institutional core of a vast network of satellite organizations and activities including counseling, testing, welfare, education, personnel, law (especially new branches such as juvenile and domestic relations), religion, and literature, but this "success" was inseparably linked, from its contribution, to the attempt to maintain the hegemony of the "American way of life" in areas that reached from bars to high schools, from suburban families to the new "women's films", and that extended to the influence of psychiatry abroad. [13] The "psychoanalytic tradition of moral safe-guarding" argued that "every homosexual is a latent heterosexual," that "the anatomical equipment of the female child puts her at a disadvantage in relations to the possessor of the phallus," and that Kinsey's "erroneous conclusion in regard to homosexuality" will be "used against the United States aboad, stimatizing the nation as a whole in a whisper campaign." [14] As for politics, according to Norman Podhoretz: Freud supplied "the most persuasive and author-itative theoretical foundation for believing that human possibilities were strictly and insurmountably limited. Human nature was fixed and given and not, as the 'liberal imagination' would have it, in-finitely malleable ... Evil was not imposed from without by institu-tions or caused by unnecessary restraints: it came from within." [15]

The Frankfurt School writings on psychoanalysis in the 1950s and 1960s were an attempt to restore its critical dimension. Two points are especially important. The first is Herbert Marcuse's argument in his 1955 *Eros and Civilization* that psychoanalysis was "already social." The second was the use of psychoanalysis read in this way against classical Marxism. In recognition of what Norman O. Brown called "the superannuation of the political categories" of the 1930s many radical intellectuals now began to argue that issues of identity were more important to modernity than issues of economics. [16] After Erikson, American psychoanalysis dropped the term "identity" for the more intrapsychic term "self," but, by the 1960s, Freud more than Marx increasingly became the warrant for the argument – one of the key ideas of the New Left – that a society of "abundance" can be based on the suppression or distortion of personal identity.

Until the 1960s Wilhelm Reich had been nearly alone in using psychoanalysis as the basis for a critical theory, but Reich based his criticism of capitalism on its repression of sexuality – especially genital sexuality – reflecting the public/private distinction. Marcuse, by contrast, criticized Reich for viewing sexuality as a "panacea" and turned instead to the concepts of identification and narcissism. [17]

The Frankfurt School tradition had always criticized what Hork-heimer and Adorno called Marxism's assumption of a "nature-dominating, rational ego." Horkheimer called the Marxist elevation of labor into "a transcendent category of human activity" an "ascetic ideology" which, insofar as socialists shared it, made them "into carriers of capitalist propaganda." [18] Now Marcuse interpreted Freud to be arguing that the view of the ego as involved in a project of mastery was a later, defensive construction, "antagonistic to those faculties and attitudes which are receptive rather than productive, which tend toward gratification rather than transcendence." The foundation of the self, Marcuse argued, was an originary identification or primary narcissism which survives as "the oceanic feeling." Although this is often misunderstood as egotistic withdrawal from reality, Marcuse maintained, in fact it constitutes "a fundamental relatedness to reality, [a] libidinal cathexis of the objective world."

Whether or not Marcuse's reading of Freud was accurate is not so important as the fact that by 1955 a conception of human nature had begun to develop within the Freudo-Marxist tradition that shared important ideas with subsequent feminist, gay liberation, and ecology movements: a critique of instrumental rationality, a desire for a new connectedness with nature, a redefinition of sexuality beyond its genital, heterosexual limits, and a search for new agents of critique. But this conception was never able to break with the male-centered assumptions built into both psychoanalysis and Marxism. By the mid-1960s, then, in the work of such authors as Adorno, Marcuse, and Lasch, narcissism had come to mean something quite different – the collapse of identities, the borderline personality, the "me"-generation.

IDENTITY POLITICS AND THE RENEGOTIATION OF THE PUBLIC/PRIVATE SPLIT

Although the phenomenon of identity politics in the United States was anticipated during the 1950s and 1960s by the "black power" movement, the most important force in redefining the question of identity was, without question, the emergence of the women's liberation movement. While in one sense the women's movement that emerged in the late 1960s was part of a continuing struggle for women's equality, in another sense its unique and world historical achievement – making it much more than a form of identity politics – rested in its laying bare the social nature of the family, the "public" nature of the "private," the internal connections that exist between the family and the economy. This redefinition coincided with major structural changes, especially the large-scale entry of women into a "post-industrial," service-based, and increasingly international-ized economy, which threw into question earlier forms of politics based upon the public/private split – in particular, much of social democratic politics, e.g., the trade union movement, the "family wage," the welfare state as traditionally conceived.

The convergence of the concern for identity on the part of the African-American and other racial and ethnic movements during the 1970s, along with the redefinition of the relations between the public and the private on the part of the women's movement, gave rise to the defining ideas of identity politics – those of iden-tity and difference. Until those ideas developed, society was still conceptualized in the manner of psychoanalysis – as a grid of abstractly equal individuals whose major differences were personal. What I wish to stress here, however, is that in the transition to the focus on *group* identity, psychoanalysis continued to play a central role.

While psychoanalysis did not have a theory of difference it did have, and had always had, a theory of domination: this was the concept of transference. In the 1950s and 1960s mostly around the issue of race in France – where the main issue for the Left was decolonization – several theorists, especially Fanon, combined existentialism, with its agonistic conception of the relation of self and other, and psychoanalysis to conceptualize the colonist/colonial relation.

For example, according to Octave Mannoni's 1964 *Prospero and Caliban*, the issues raised by colonialism were not merely those of economic inequality but rather of understanding how economic in-equality was "embodied in struggles for prestige, in alienation, in bargaining positions and debt of gratitude, and in the invention of new myths and the creation of new personality types." The inability of the French communists to think at this level, Mannoni argued, meant they played little role in French decolonization.[19] Fanon, Mannoni's critic, stressed the ways in which recognition could not be "given," but had to be taken, violently, as the prelude to genuine democratization.

In the United States in the early 1970s the founding works of identity politics also drew upon psychoanalysis. *Eros and Civilization* was crucial to Dennis Altman's early writing on gay identity which argued that "procreative sexuality" buttressed what Marcuse had called the "performance principle" and that the "perversions" were actually incipient rebellions. Altman also captured the main thrust of the new politics by describing the shift in "homosexual" from an adjective – implying there was a "neutral" "person" who had a particular sexual orientation – to a noun, implying that being gay was constitutive of identity.

Nancy Chodorow's 1978 *The Reproduction of Mothering* also combines a theory of domination (male supremacy) with a theory of the centrality of prestige or recognition. Chodorow took her key term, "gender identity," from Robert Stoller's 1968 *Sex and Gender*, where it refers to an unalterable cognitive sense of femaleness or maleness, but she expanded Stoller's usage in order to characterize men and women in terms of different psychic structure, values and orientations to the world. According to Chodorow, girls achieve "an unambiguous and unquestioned gender identity" by identifying with the mother's maternal attributes, whereas, the boy's gender identity is based on his *difference* from the mother. [20]

The Reproduction of Mothering was a restatement of psychoanalysis as a story of women's identity, one which threw into relief the ways in which Freud's original story had been centered on men. Throughout the book psychology is restated in gynocentric and matricentric terms aimed at raising women's self-esteem as the analytic discourse had lowered it. Girls achieve "an unambiguous and unquestioned gender identity," their basic "sense of self is connected to the world," their "endopsychic object-world" more complex than men's. The psychology of men is radically othered, as the psychology of women had been within classical psychoanalysis. Nonetheless, Chodorow's work, reflecting its descent from classical psychoanalysis, was entirely situated within the family – the system of production is separated off from what is termed the "sex-gender" system – and the family has become the mother/child bond.

Formulations such as Fanon's, Altman's, or Chodorow's remain intermediate between psychoanalysis and identity politics. A more drastic break toward the construction of politicized group identities around formerly "private" characteristics was taken by other such as Adrienne Rich and other advocates of radical lesbianism. Whereas Chodorow defined women in relation to men who oppress them, and in that sense as part of a totality, radical lesbianism was characterized by the assertion of women's "identity" without regard to men, as suggested by the phrase "the woman-identified-woman." Perhaps the key text in developing a radical lesbian perspective, Adrienne Rich's "Compulsory Heterosexuality," was written *against* works such as Chodorow's that linked women's identity to heterosexual marriage and childrearing. While "freedom" or "tolerance" for lesbians had been an important feminist demand, "Compulsory Heterosexuality" argued that support for lesbianism as a "sexual preference" was merely liberal, a matter of individual rights. Lesbianism,

Rich argued, is not a matter of sexual preference any more than race is a matter of skin color. In both cases what is at stake is *identity*. In contrast to the analytic emphasis on sexuality, which reflected its heavy freighting of the private sphere, Rich and others saw lesbianism as membership in a community based on shared experiences, i.e., on identification. Thus for Blanche Cook, lesbians are "women who love women, who choose women to nurture ... Lesbians cannot be defined simply as women who practice certain physical rites together."[21]

The identity formulations of the 1970s such as Rich's have proven impossible to maintain. Under the rubric of "anti-essentialism," a series of theorists have argued that no one is simply a lesbian, or a woman, or a black person – rather we all combine many types and levels of social and cultural determination.[22] The ultimate logic of this view is that each of us is unique and weaves together the sociocultural dimensions of our identity in a unique way. But that logic was staunchly resisted by identity theorists. Thus, although the breakup of identity communities such as that of "women" in the 1970s often took place in the name of opposing identity formulations such as "lesbian" or "women of color," at another level those communities and those of their critics divided because they tended toward forms of prescriptive authoritarianism sometimes as confining as traditional gender roles.

It was at this juncture – the 1970s – that "the linguistic turn" – the development of cultural and sociocultural theories based on the model of language – offered a new way of formulating identity, one that bypassed many of the problems in which psychoanalysis had long been mired. In particular, the famous distinction between *langue* and *parole* suggested a fruitful way of conceptualizing the relation between the individual and society, according to which each individual carries the society (*langue*) around in his or her head, but also that each time we speak we do so on the basis of codes that have dissolved and been remade within us (*parole*). On this basis, gender, race and other societal factors could be understood as "codes" possessing a grammar and semantics of their own, while these codes – i.e., "culture" – are continually remade in different discourses and so can interpellate different subjectivities. This approach seemed to offer a pathway through the false dichotomy between social and psychological approaches that had been built into the discussion of personal life from its early twentieth-century beginnings.

Lacan's contribution was to bring Freud into relation with this development and it was through Lacan that Freud entered into the post-structuralist dialogue concerning the nature of the "subject," as identity came to be called. As Lacan plausibly argued, the contents of the Freudian unconscious were word and thing presentations, not "instincts," and the laws that governed their combinatorial possibilities were the laws that explained puns and jokes, not those that explained disease.

But taken by itself, and Lacan did take it by itself, this insight was a one-sided reading of Freud emphasizing the psyhe as language but not as representation, unbound but not bound processes, ambiguity but not identity, id but not ego. This one-sidedness runs through all of Lacan's readings of Freud. For example, in the *Séminaire* he equates the ego with narcissism whereas what is profound in Freud's account is the interplay of narcissism and mastery. Further, *every* important post-structuralist writer on psychoanalysis – Derrida, Deleuze, Irigaray, Kristeva – though differing with Lacan in many ways, followed him in one variation of another of his initial mistake.

MICHEL FOUCAULT AND THE POST-STRUCTURALIST THEORY OF THE SUBJECT

The key figure in developing a post-structuralist theory of the subject was Foucault. While he is the only post-structuralist who has not devoted a major work to psychoanalysis, he once termed his entire *oeuvre* "an archaeology of psychoanalysis." What makes Foucault's approach to identity particularly interesting, in my view, is that he grasped the need to argue not just against Freud but against Freud as he had been combined with Marx.

Foucault rejected the distinctions between inside and outside, intra-psychic and social, and the concept of "internalization" on which, as we have seen, classical psychoanalysis, with its subterranean relationship to Marxism, rested. He rejected the idea of a state that holds power apart from its subjects, an idea that underlies the concepts of alienation and repression, and substituted the study of what he called "subjectification," the "modes of inquiry," and "dividing practices" by which "human beings are made into subjects." In various studies he tried to show how we are made into subjects from "above," e.g., in prisons, schools, and hospitals, but also from "below," e.g., through confessional or communicative practices such as psychoanalysis.

The result was a new conception of the subject, one which rejected any conception of "instincts," drives, "inner world," "psychic reality," or the like. According to this conception, discipline "works not from the outside but from within, not at the level of the entire society but at the level of detail, and not by constraining individuals and their actions but by producing them ... a negative, exterior power gives way to an internal, productive power." In *Discipline and Punish* Foucault used the panopticon, Bentham's nineteenth-century model of universal surveillance, in a prison setting to describe the process by which modern human beings turn themselves into self-observing subjects. He wrote: "he who is subjected to a field of visibility, and who knows it ... inscribes in himself the power relation in which he simultaneously plays both roles." [23] This conception was intended to replace the "repression hypothesis," shared by the Frankfurt School and by Lacan. In his *History of Sexuality* Foucault contested the antinomy law/sex. [24] For him law (power) and sex are mutually constitutive; there is a secret collaboration between the public and the private. Sex is not relegated to a shadow existence. It is exploited as *the* secret by talking about it endlessly. [25] Marxism and psycho-analysis "share the same 'representation of power.'" They are both "haunted by the monarchical model of a unique centralized power." [26] By contrast society should be conceptualized as separated into a plurality of power strategies, discourses, and practices, all of which intersect, succeed one another, and are distinguished by the type of discourse formation to which they pertain and by their degree of intensity, but not by their relation to any totality. [27] Thus, if we "overthrow" structures, discourse, and power strategies according to Foucault, there is no "true" or essential identity waiting to be liberated. For Foucault, identity is not something whose assertion leads to liberation but rather something we need to be liberated from. Thus, he wrote, the purpose of studying genealogy was "not to discover the roots of our identity but to commit [ourselves] to its dissipation." [28]

Insofar as he adopted this idea, Foucault can be described as a post-structuralist thinker, i.e., a theorist of non-identity. In contrast to the totalizing Marxisms of the 1960s, for which the crucial task was mediation, the theorists of "non-identity" of the 1970s and 1980s sought to describe "fragments that are related to one another only in that each of them is different, without having recourse to any sort of original or subsequent totality." Thus, what the Frankfurt School took to be signs of decay – the loss of fixed identities, con-fusion over fundamental principles of order, decline of legitimate authority – was taken by some as the harbinger of some new form of society. The term "subject" emerged to replace "individual," "ego" or "self," but "subject" is a word that takes from discourse theory the idea that culture is composed of subject positions, not individuals.

For Derrida, for example, "the subject becomes a signifying ... subject only by inscribing itself [sic] in [a] system of differences." Luce Irigaray's early work is an example of how this approach helps separate questions of difference in regard to sex and gender from questions of priority, anteriority, originality, and superiority.

Let me summarize. With Freud a new conception of the individual entered western thought: an individual largely shaped by and pre-occupied with the private, the internal, the subjective. The traditional Enlightenment conception of "man" as public, active, rational was not rejected but was situated and problematized. In the history of psychoanalysis before 1968 great efforts were made to combine this conception with the major social theories of our time: empirical social science, especially its concept of culture, and Marxism. These made important advances but ultimately failed, especially because of their inability to conceptualize difference. After 1968, it was as if the private became public. The issues that Freud had described as intra-psychic and familial were acted out on a social scale and on a political stage. The actors, however, were no longer individuals but sharply defined *identities* whose relations to one another became increasingly problematic. Finally, with Foucault, we have our most important effort to recast this history into a new and coherent social theory.

Hence, the identity impulse that emerged in the 1960s and 1970s – rather than being understood solely as a drastic break or a new beginning – is better understood as part of a long and complex development. In the course of the past century a new terrain of modern society – that of personal life and personal identity – received its initial theorization. Before the politics of identity and difference that characterize our day can be evaluated, therefore, they need to be situated within the general framework of a critical theory of society, a framework that is itself constantly changing.

When the question of identity is situated in that framework, three points emerge as crucial. First, we must understand the Enlightenment not as a monolith but as a conflicted phenomenon whose meaning remains to be determined. In particular we must grasp the significance of that moment in the Enlightenment at which individual identity was separated from any sociocultural determination. Freud's emphasis on the non-identity of the individual and the social serves as a signifier for that moment and a reminder of the fact that individual rights are prior to any politics but that they "always already" depend on politics.

Second, questions of identity cannot be separated from questions of domination and therefore from institutional critique. It is not only interpersonal forms of domination that are important but systemic, structural ones for which the term mediation may still be useful. Thus, to say, as I have, that the history of the question of identity has been profoundly shaped by the shifting dynamics of the public/private split is to say that it has been shaped by the history of twentieth-century capitalism.

Both of these points may be subsumed under my third, the need to take an historical viewpoint. Just as Marxism lost touch with its own roots in the Enlightenment, so the identity theorists from the 1970s on have little comprehension of *their* history, especially the history of the sixties and seventies. The emergence in the last few years of clearly reactionary forms of identity politics based on racial and national exclusion shows how relevant the need to situate the problem of identity historically still is.

NOTES

1 In France I have in mind the repudiation of Lacan by such figures as Deleuze, Foucault, Roustang, Irigaray, and Derrida. Czechoslovakia should be considered the third country in which 1968 was most profound.

2 Ronald Bayer, *Homosexuality and American Psychiatry: The Politics of Diagnosis* (New York: Basic Books, 1981), p. 105; Kate Millett, *Sexual Politics* (Garden City, NY: Doubleday, 1969).

3 Thus Walter Scott whose "Minstrelsy of the Scottish Border" hoped "to contribute somewhat to the history of my native country ... whose manners and character are daily dissolving into that of her sister and ally." Walter Scott, *Minstrelsy of the Scottish Border* (London, 1883) quoted by Anthony Appiah, *Critical Inquiry* (Winter 1991), p. 349.

4 Eli Zaretsky, *Capitalism, the Family and Personal Life* (New York: Harper and Row, 1976).

5 Sigmund Freud, *Complete Introductory Lectures* (New York: Norton, 1966), p. 18.

6 Standard Edition, ed. James Strachey, vol. XIV, pp. xiv, 88, 91, 95–7.

7 "Mourning and Melancholia" was written in 1915 though not published until 1917.

8 Standard Edition, pp. 18, 116.

9 Karl Abraham, "Psychoanalytic Notes on Coué's System of Self-Mastery," *International Journal of Psychoanalysis*, VII (1926).

10 Standard Edition, pp, 21, 114–16 Freud's understanding of the way in which identification and aggression are linked and interdependent processes was further developed by Melanie Klein, especially in her concept of projective identification (i.e. identification through projection) which Klein called the "prototype of an aggressive object relation," and which she argued is the major form of communication between the infant and the mother.

11 Erik Erikson, "The Problem of Ego Identity," *Journal of the American Psychoanalytic Association*, vol. 4 (January 1956) (italics added).

12 Erik Erikson, "A Memorandum on Identity and Negro Youth" (1964), in Stephen Schlein, *A Way of Looking at Things: Selected Papers 1930–1980* (New York: Routledge, 1987), p. 647; *Childhood and Society* (New York: Norton, 1950), pp. 282–83, 412–13. "We live in a country," he wrote, "which attempts to make a superidentity out of all the identities imported by its constituent immigrants."

13 Peter Berger, "Towards a Sociological Understanding of Psychoanalysis," *Social Research* 32 (1965): 27–8.

14 Kenneth Lewes, *The Psychoanalytic Theory of Male Homosexuality* (New York: Simon and Schuster, 1988), p. 137; Sandor Rado, "A Critical Examination of the Concept of Bisexuality," *Psychosomatic Medicine*, vol II, no. 4 (October 1940); Bayer, *Homosexuality*, pp. 28, 30; Elizabeth Young-Bruehl, *Anna Freud: A Biography* (New York: Summit Books, 1988), pp. 428–9; E Bergler, "Homosexuality and the Kinsey Report," in A Krich, ed, *The Homosexuals as Seen by Themselves and 30 Authorities* (New York: Citadel Press, 1954).

15 Norman Podhoretz, *Breaking Ranks: A Political Memoir* (New York: Harper and Row, 1979), p. 48. As Arthur Miller later recalled his psychoanalysis during the 1950s: "My difficulties were surely personal, but I could not help suspecting that psychoanalysis was a form of alienation that was being used as a substitute not only for Marxism but for social activism of any kind. New York ... was swollen with rivulets of dispossessed liberals and leftists in chaotic flight from the bombarded old castle of self-denial, with its infinite confidence in social progress and its authentication-through-political-correctness of their positions at the leading edge of history. As always, the American self ... needed a scheme of morals to administer ... this time the challenge handed lost ones like me was not to join a picket line or a Spanish brigade but to confess to having been a selfish bastard who had never known how to love." Arthur Miler, *Timebends: A Life* (New York: Grove Press, 1987), pp. 320–1.

16 Norman O. Brown, *Life Against Death* (Middletown, CT: Wesleyan University Press, 1959), p. ix.

17 Herbert Marcuse, *Eros and Civilization* (Boston: Beacon Press, 1955), p. 218.

18 Martin Jay, *The Dialectical Imagination: A History of the Frankfurt School and the Institute of Social Research, 1923–1950* (Boston: Little, Brown, 1973), pp. 57, 129.

19 Octave Mannoni, *Prospero and Caliban* (Ann Arbor: University of Michigan Press, 1990), pp. 8, 46–7, 63.

20 Nancy Chodorow, *The Reproduction of Mothering* (Berkeley: University of California Press, 1978), pp. 142, 158, 63, 166–70, 214; Robert Stoller, *Sex and Gender: On the Development of Masculinity and Femininity* (New York: Science House, 1968).

21 Shane Phelan, *Identity Politics: Lesbian Feminism and the Limits of Community* (Philadelphia: Temple University Press, 1989), pp. 73–4.
22 For example, Elisabeth Spelman, *Inessential Woman* (Boston: Beacon Press, 1989).
23 Michael Foucault, *Discipline and Punish: The Birth of the Prison* (New York: Pantheon Books, 1977), p. 203.
24 "The law is what constitutes desire and the lack instituting desire" is how Foucault formulated what everyone would have recognized as Lacan's theory.
25 Judith Butler, *Gender Trouble: Feminism and the Subversion of Identity* (New York: Routledge, 1990), p. 29.
26 Didier Eribon, *Michel Foucault* (Cambridge, MA: Harvard University Press, 1991), p. 272.
27 Jürgen Habermas, *Philosophical Discourse on Modernity* (Cambridge: Polity Press, 1987), p. 127.
28 Michel Foucault, *Language, Counter-Memory, Practice* (Ithaca, NY: Cornell University Press, 1977), p. 162.

8

Malcolm X and the Black Public Sphere: Conversionists v. Culturalists

Manthia Diawara

In this chapter, I shall discuss black conversionist and culturalist discourses and their relation to the lifeworld, politics, and economics in *The Autobiography of Malcolm X* by Alex Haley and Malcolm X. The contrast between calls for blacks to convert away from a putatively pathological black culture and calls for affirmation of black culture is an old but still powerful theme. It structures much discourse in the contemporary black public sphere.

My analysis focuses on the battle for custody between the conversionists and culturalists over the first part of the *The Autobiography*, which includes such pivotal chapters as "Homeboy," "Harlemite," "Detroit Red," and "Hustler." I shall argue that, in spite of the conversionist discourse of the second half of the book, which warns the reader against embracing the early chapters, they constitute the appeal of the book today, giving significance to the inner-city youth's identification with Malcolm X as a homeboy, and making Detroit Red the archetype of Rap songs and new black male films in the 1980s and 1990s. A culturalist reading, which resists the definition by the second part of the book of the first part of the book as black pathology, is better able to account for the popularity of Malcolm X among the youth who see a mirror image of their own lives in the experience of Detroit Red.

What fascinates the reader in *The Autobiography* is the detailed description of black life in Harlem, particularly the night life. Malcolm X presents Harlem in the 1940s in a cultural, political, and economic setting. Harlem's night life attracts blacks as well as soldiers recruited to fight in the Second World War, whites from midtown, and tourists. The constitution of audiences around the black good-life institutions (clubs, bars, theaters, dance halls) and entertainers in Harlem causes concern for black and white relations during a climate of war. Harlem's culture in the text defies the ban on interracial relations and subverts the code of morality imposed on black and white soldiers during the Second World War.

Crucially, Detroit Red's relation to, and fascination with, this black culture in Harlem, the way in which he looks and takes pleasure in the institutions and entertainers, are grounds for identification with him and the text which are not convincingly deconstructed in the last part of The Autobiography.

THE CONVERSIONISTS

> How ridiculous I was! Stupid enough to stand there simply lost in admiration of my hair now looking "white," reflected in the mirror in Shorty's room.
>
> The Autobiography of Malcolm X

Conversionist discourses deploy narratives about the worst sinners to justify the need for transformation. In The Autobiography, Malcolm X confesses at the end of the chapter entitled "Caught" that "I have never previously told anyone my sordid past in detail. I haven't done it now to sound as though I might be proud of how bad, how evil, I was."[1] Malcolm X tells the story of his perdition which leads to his discovery of Allah and the religion of Islam as proof that he has been there, so to speak, down with the rest of the people, and that they, too, can join him on the other side. He states that once motivated, "no one can change more completely than the man who has been at the bottom. I call myself the best example of that" (p. 261). The difficulty of conversion is not emphasized here; Malcolm X only stresses the superiority of his new world over the old one. Conversionist discourses, whether they are motivated by religion, science, or politics, always underestimate culture or liken it to pathology. Conversionists, whether they are politicians or religious leaders, build their audiences by blaming the culture of the people they are trying to convert. They always expect people to come to a revolutionary consciousness, or a spiritual awakening, and walk out of their culture, shedding it like a shell or a cracked skin, in order to change the world.

The rhetoric of the second half of The Autobiography seems to move too rapidly to its conclusion, condemning black culture with the demise of Detroit Red. In The Autobiography, Malcolm X uses alienation as an analytic tool for degrading the Harlem culture which he describes so well in part I of the book. He assigns Detroit Red's passage from observer of culture to participant, underlining black people's consumption and their relation to style as major manifestations of estrangement. Malcolm X's critique of the "conked" hair style as an unnatural desire for black people to look "white" (p. 54) is consistent with the position of other conversionists on black hair, and it informs the decision by many black youths to abandon the conked hair styles for so-called "natural" styles such as the "Afro."[2]

Malcolm X also detects symptoms of alienation in the manner in which black people buy products:

> I was really a clown, but my ignorance made me think I was "sharp." My knob-toed, orange-colored 'kick-up' shoes were nothing but Florsheims, the ghetto's Cadillac of shoes in those days. (Some shoe companies made these ridiculous styles for sale only in the black ghettoes where ignorant Negroes like me would pay the big-name price for something that we associated with being rich).   (p. 78)

The metamorphosis from Detroit Red to Malcolm X requires the protagonist of The Autobiography to deny one part of himself for every piece of knowledge gained from the Nation of Islam: "'You don't even know who you are,' Reginald said. 'You don't even know, the white devil has hidden it from you, that you are of a race of people of ancient civilizations, and riches in gold and kings. You don't even know your true family name, you wouldn't recognize your true language if you heard it'" (p. 160). Conversionists of the religious or political kind are, particularly, prone to self-denial. Once in Ghana, at a party given for his birthday, Malcolm X says: "'You wonder why I don't dance? Because I want you to remember twenty-two million Afro-Americans in the U.S.!'" And, as an afterthought, he adds, "But I sure felt like dancing! The Ghanaians performed the high-life as if possessed. One pretty African girl sang 'Blue Moon' like Sarah Vaughan. Sometimes the band sounded like Milt Jackson, sometimes like Charlie Parker" (p. 358).

Through conversion, Malcolm X not only attempts to abandon expressive styles in language, dress, and hair associated with the way of life of some black ghetto people, he also speaks of Detroit Red as if he were a different person: "I still marvel at how swiftly my previous life's thinking pattern slid away from me, like snow off a roof. It is as though someone else I knew of had lived by hustling and crime. I would be startled to catch myself thinking in a remote way of my earlier self as another person" (p. 170). Malcolm X associates Detroit Red with death and a menace to society: "Awareness came surging up in me – how deeply the religion of Islam had reached down into the mud to lift me up, to save me from being what I inevitably would have been: a dead criminal in a grave, or, if still alive, a flint-hard, bitter, thirty-seven-year-old convict in some penitentiary, or insane asylum" (p. 287).

The first part of *The Autobiography* is carefully crafted to lead up to Detroit Red's transition from unemployed hick to hustler to hardened criminal and drug addict. Even the linear disposition of the chapters – "Detroit Red," "Hustler," "Trapped," and "Caught" – presupposes an inevitable descent that, for Malcolm X, can be reversed only through conversion:

> Today, when everything that I do has an urgency, I would not spend one hour in the preparation of a book which had the ambition to perhaps titillate some readers. But I am spending many hours because the full story is the best way that I know to have it seen, and understood, that I had sunk to the very bottom of the American white man's society when – soon now, in prison – I found Allah and the religion of Islam and it completely transformed my life. *(p. 150)*

Malcolm X attempts to account for the rough edges in the text, such as the places where the reader identifies with Detroit Red's love for black culture, by assimilating them to a state of alienation. He asserts against Detroit Red that "what makes the ghetto hustler yet more dangerous is his 'glamor' image to the school-dropout youth in the ghetto" (p. 311).

Toward the end of the first part of *The Autobiography*, Detroit Red sinks to the bottom, and the narrator with him, as if black culture has died with them. The black cultural figure most present in the chapter entitled "Trapped" is Billie Holiday, whose end as a drug addict bears a strong resemblance to Detroit Red's last days in Harlem. It is interesting from a stylistic standpoint that Malcolm X and Alex Haley put Billie Holiday and other tragic figures at the end of the first part of the book. It helps the conversionists' case that culture is a dead end. Malcolm X traps Detroit Red in a hole and leaves him only the choice to convert, inducing the reader, too, to identify with the sermon of change. Crucially, when Detroit Red returns to Harlem as Malcolm X, he wants to change it completely.

Malcolm X makes an important contribution to the art of the autobiography through his recourse to alienation which enables him to distance himself from Detroit Red. As I have shown, Malcolm X often refers to Detroit Red as another person in the text; this stylistic device generates an autobiographical text in the form of a sermon. Malcolm X and Alex Haley have shaped *The Autobiography* as a preacher would a sermon: they do not intend the reader to be entertained by Detroit Red's story; they want him/her to understand the symbolism behind it and let it serve as a lesson. With Malcolm X and Alex Haley, the autobiographical intent changes from an intimate and personal story to a public and conversionist essay.

The recourse to change in conversionist discourse coincides with the modernist impulse toward the constant renewal of things. Every conversionist discourse addresses an epistemological crisis which requires the author's contemplation for a solution. Malcolm's autobiography includes moving scenes where he cogitates about situations of crisis and imagines how to get out of them. His reflections on these moments always mark him as an outsider to culture, a philosopher charged with the desire to change things, and a utopian reconstructionist.

The most quoted lines from *The Autobiography* dealing with an epistemological crisis come from the passage in which Malcolm's English teacher, Mr Ostrowski, tells him: "A lawyer – that's no realistic goal for a nigger. You need to think about something you can be. You're good with your hands – making things. Everybody admires your carpentry shop work. Why don't you plan on carpentry?" (p. 36). In this passage, the young Malcolm is asked to accept a stereotype of himself and his people as a reality. Malcolm's reaction to it embodies the reasons why young blacks put the fairness of the system into question, and identify with a lawbreaker ideology through which they feel that they can overcome the obstacles placed in front of them by the likes of Mr Ostrowski.

But for me, Malcolm X describes his dissatisfaction with epistemological crises more effectively when he delineates them as a coming into consciousness from a state of innocence, as new knowledge displaces business as usual and enables movement forward. These are the moments of discovery in *The Autobiography*, moments when Malcolm X is with the group but feels the most lonely, lost in contemplation of a better future for black people. For instance, there is a lovely reflexive passage in the opening chapter of the book, where Malcolm X tells about the satisfaction he derives from working in the family garden: he says,

> I loved especially to grow peas. I was proud when we had them on
> our table. I would pull out the grass in my garden by hand when

the first little blades came up. I would patrol the rows on my hands and knees for any worms and bugs and I would kill and bury them. And sometimes when I had everything straight and clean for my things to grow, I would lie down on my back between two rows, and I would gaze up in the blue sky at the clouds moving and think all kinds of things.   (p. 8)

The clouds moving in the horizon are leitmotifs for change in *The Autobiography*. For instance, years later, during his trip to Mecca, Malcolm pictures his new predicament, after the break with Elijah Muhammad, through the sky as a tableau: "I remember one night at Muzadalifa with nothing but the sky overhead I lay awake amid sleeping Muslim brothers and I learned that pilgrims from every land – every color, and class, and rank; high officials and the beggar alike – all snored in the same language" (p. 344). The leitmotif occurs for the third time when Malcolm X returned to the States:

I remember there in the holy world how I used to lie on the top of Hector's Hill, and look up at the sky, at the clouds moving over me, and daydream, all kinds of things. And then, in a funny contrast of recollection, I remember how years later, when I was in prison, I used to lie on my cell bunk – this would be especially when I was in solitary: what we convicts called 'The Hole' – and I would picture myself talking to large crowds.   (p. 365)

We are in 1965, when Malcolm X makes this last allusion to the sky and the clouds. The epistemological crisis in question concerns how to build a black nationalist organization that inter- pellates Christians, Jews, Buddhists, Hindus, agnostics, and atheists. As Malcolm X puts it, at that time, "I have friends who are called capitalists, Socialists, and Communists! Some of my friends are moderates, conservatives, extremists – some are even Uncle Toms! My friends today are black, brown, red, yellow and white!" (p. 375). Malcolm X was a complex man who constantly revised his thinking. As the recurrence of the tableau of clouds in the sky shows, he was very American in his dreams, in the sense that he was impatient with the obstacles placed in front of black people. Like the founding fathers, he was prepared by all means necessary to remove these obstacles in order to move into progress, into better and better societies. Malcolm X was also a modernist through the reflexive way in which he looked into the clouds, and kept revising his style in order to build larger audiences for his ideas.

Other conversionists, since Malcolm X, have resorted to Marxism, Afrocentrism, Liberation Theology, and Black Nationalism as public-sphere building themes among black people. In fact, Malcolm X's *The Autobiography* stands out as an inspiration for these conversionist schools, with its detailed discussions of identity politics, class struggle, black self-determination, and religion. Conversionists continue to ring the wake-up bell for black people, and, much in the manner of Malcolm X, treat black culture as pathology (pp. 312–14).

Yet, there is much evidence that Malcolm the modernist is conflicted about his thoroughgoing embrace of a conversionist stance. Malcolm X emphasizes in *The Autobiography* that his success as a public speaker depends on the fact that he is a "homeboy" who "never left the ghetto in spirit ... could speak and understand the ghetto's language" (p. 310), and has been schooled as a hustler like most ghetto kids (p. 296). But it is possible to argue that Malcolm X's purist philosophy is too demanding in the sense that it incorporates only black people who have left their culture behind. To use a statement from the Black Arts Movement, Malcolm X's philosophy in the second part of *The Autobiography* does not address itself to the mythology and life style of black people. Malcolm X, himself, ponders several times over the shortcoming of his purist philosophy through statements such as "my old so-called 'Black Muslim' image, kept blocking me" (p. 375), and "Numerous people said that the Nation of Islam's stringent moral restrictions had repelled them – and they wanted to join me" (p. 316). Nonetheless, Malcolm X remains a conversionist who believes that "it was a big order – the organization I was creating in my mind, one which would help to challenge the American black man to gain his human rights, and to cure his mental, spiritual, economic, and political sicknesses" (p. 315).

CULTURALISTS

> Then, suddenly, we were in the Roseland's jostling lobby. And I was getting waves and smiles and greetings. They shouted "My man!" and "Hey, Red!" and I answered "Daddy-O."
>
> *The Autobiography*

There is another way to look at the epistemological crisis Malcolm shared with other black people without reverting to a view of black culture as pathology. This demands a partisan identification with culture, a belief that *culture* knows, and that it can be channeled to create and capitalize on epistemological breaks. My culturalist approach stipulates that — contrary to the conversionists's view of "authentic black culture" as either an emanation of the Church, or of a true revolutionary consciousness, or of a separatist gesture toward Africa — religion, revolutionary theories, and the political economy are all specifications of black culture. [3]

The view that conversionist discourses are but enunciations of particular theories of black culture enables us, first of all, to distinguish culture from its particular manifestations in the Church, in arts, or politics. I shall define culture here as a way of life aimed at reproducing the black good life. [4] A major part of black culture in America is created through attempts to liberate the lifeworld from colonizing systems. Blacks often derive the good life from institutions built against them through a system of reversibility of the signification of those institutions. They test the limits of modern institutions for inclusion and emancipation of multicultural lifeworlds. Hence, black culture is the last frontier of American modernism.

Secondly, a view of culture as that which encompasses the Church, the black nationalist tradition, and other ideological movements not only liberates us from the monopoly that these institutions place on black culture but also legitimizes other specifications of culture such as economic narratives, art in the context of international politics, as well as other cultural forms engendered through black peoples's relation to more and more complex systems. In other words, we can no longer afford to locate and fix black culture in a specific ideological institution, lest we run the risk of overlooking newer manifestations of culture which are more effective in the production of a black good-life society and ethics in relation to the political economy in the so-called global village.

Malcolm's popularity today resides as much in the specification of black culture through his personal transformation and his description of the economics of Harlem high life in the 1940s as in his conversionist discourse in favor of black self-determination.

HOMEBOY

> I still was country, I know now, but it all felt so great because I was accepted.
>
> *The Autobiography of Malcolm X*

But people would watch for clues from Bird and Dizzy, and if they smiled when you finished playing, then that meant that your playing was good. They smiled when I finished playing that first time and

from then on I was on the inside of what was happening in New York's
music scene.

>   Miles Davis, *Miles: The Autobiography*

The young Malcolm's flight from Lansing, Michigan, to Boston,
and later to Harlem, points toward a rift between the country and
the city, which Malcolm X himself characterizes as a protest against
white racism and black petit-bourgeois ideals of order and respectability. Malcolm Little makes his break with the country after the
crisis that ensues from an encounter with Mr Ostrowski, his school-
teacher. He says,

> If I had stayed on in Michigan, I would probably have married one
> of those Negro girls I knew and liked in Lansing. I might have
> become one of those state capitol building shoeshine boys, or a Lansing
> Country Club waiter, or gotten one of the other menial jobs which,
> in those days, among Lansing Negroes, would have been considered
> "successful."   (p. 38)

By 1940, when Malcolm Little leaves Lansing to go to Boston,
his image of cities has come from his half-sister, Ella, and from black
music. Ella's visit to Lansing helps shape the phantasmagoria of
city life for the young Malcolm because she instills in him a sense
of pride, freedom, and mobility:

> A commanding woman, maybe even bigger than Mrs. Swerlin, Ella
> wasn't just black, but like my father, she was jet black. The way she
> sat, moved, talked, did everything, bespoke somebody who did and
> got exactly what she wanted. This was the woman my father had
> boasted of so often for having brought so many of their family out of
> Georgia to Boston. She owned some property, he would say, and she
> was in "society."   (p. 32)

Jazz music and musicians are the other forces beckoning Malcolm
Little to the city. In the 1940s, as James Naremore puts it, some
people associated jazz "with flappers, skyscrapers, and the entire
panoply of the twentieth century modernity."[5] Malcolm Little, too,
used music to contemplate the city, and to detach himself from the
country: "Sometimes, big bands from New York, out touring the
one-night stands in the sticks, would play for big dances in Lansing.
Everybody with legs would come out to see any performer who
bore the magic name 'New York.' Which is how I first heard Lucky
Thompson and Milt Jackson, both of whom I later got to know well
in Harlem" (p. 28).

By the time he leaves Michigan, Malcolm Little has already developed a resentment toward the Jim Crow system that places obstacles in the way of black people's movements into modernity, secularism, and progress. It is rewarding to compare Malcolm's arrival in the city to Walter Benjamin's description of the *Bohème* in his classic book, *Charles Baudelaire: A Lyric Poet in the Era of High Capitalism*. Benjamin states: "The brutal, starved, envious, wild Cain … has gone to the cities to consume the sediment of rancour which has accumulated in them and participate in the false ideas which experience their triumph there. This characterization expresses exactly what gave Baudelaire solidarity with Dupont. Like Cain, Dupont had 'gone to the cities' and turned away from the idyllic."[6]

We can say that Malcolm Little, too, has gone to the cities to get even with the modernists. The chapter dealing with Malcolm's arrival in Boston is appropriately entitled "Homeboy," and it opens with the following remarks: "I looked like Li'l Abner. Mason, Michigan was written all over me. My kinky, reddish, hair was cut hick style, and I didn't even use grease in it" (p. 39). At one level in *The Autobiography of Malcolm X*, a homeboy is understood as someone, usually from the country, who has come to the city through a network of migration, in search of the American dream, among other migrants from the same region. A new form of kinship develops between the homeboys which leads the members of the group to empathize with one another, to help each other in finding work, and to prepare one another for life in the city. To put it in the words of Malcolm's homeboy, Shorty, "Man, this is a swinging town if you dig it … You're my homeboy – I'm going to school you to the happenings" (p. 44).

Malcolm Little, as a homeboy, brings together the characteristics of a hustler and a cosmopolitan artist. A homeboy is a bohemian who is angry at the world for not getting his fair share. Malcolm Little joins other similarly positioned homeboys to take revenge on the system for standing between them and the American dream. The homeboys, as today's Rap music and the resurgence of *film noir* made by black directors reveal to us, form a group of professional conspirators who believe that the most important thing in life is to be paid in full. Today's homeboys, like Malcolm Little, are impatient with the system, and more prone to take power than receive it from a public sphere that they perceive as erected against them. They believe, as one homeboy tells Malcolm Little in *The Autobiography*, that "The main thing you got to remember is that everything in the world is a hustle" (p. 48).

To empathize with homeboys who are hustlers is a kind of speci-fication of black cultural criticism of the colonization of the black lifeworld by modern systems. There are several places in *The Auto-biography of Malcolm X* where he identifies with lawbreakers on the ground that the homeboys are not allowed, because of racism, to develop their skills in such productive areas as the sciences, linguis-tics, and the arts. About an old pickpocket in Small's Paradise, he says: "to wolves who still were able to to catch some rabbits, it had meaning that an old wolf who had lost his fangs was still eating" (p. 90).

But identification with lawbreakers is not the only way black structures of feeling are expressed in *The Autobiography*. Malcolm's cosmopolitan artistic sensibility is another way black culture is felt in the book. Malcolm Little is a *flâneur* looking for modernism in the ballrooms, the bars, and the streets frequented by the world's greatest and hippest musicians. Malcolm's search for musical speci-fications of black culture in the 1940s can be compared to the quest of Miles Davis during the same time. In his autobiography, Davis states that he enrolled in the Julliard School of Music in order to be in New York, near Charlie Parker. Later, Davis travels from New York to Los Angeles, and back to New York, looking for "Bird." He considers these years as studying for the "master's degrees and the Ph.D.'s from Minton's University of Bebop under the tutelage of professors Bird and Diz. Man, they was playing so much incredible shit" (p. 61).

Malcolm Little spends a good deal of his time looking at and soaking up the styles and world views of great musicians like Duke Ellington, Count Basie and Lionel Hampton: "They'd be up there in my chair, and my shine rag was popping to the beat of all their records, spinning in my head. Musicians never have had, anywhere, a greater shoeshine-boy fan than I was" (p. 50).

It is easy to see why the young Malcolm admires these musicians. They appear to be free, to be in control of their lives at a time when the only life styles available to black people are those imposed on them. The musicians, with their zoot suits, conked hairs, and music that fascinate both blacks and whites, seem to have more power than people in other spheres; most of all, they appear to be like a commodity, desired by everyone, which therefore enjoys an enviable position in the marketplace. You guess right: Malcolm X, the conversionist, criticizes this situation in the second half of the book as alienation from the spiritual, economic, and political true course.

Detroit Red, on the other hand, wants to lose himself in the musicians' specification of black culture. "Sometimes I would be down there standing inside the door jumping up and down in my gray jacket with the whiskbroom in the pocket, and the manager would have to come and shout at me that I had customers upstairs" (p. 51). In his secular imagination, Detroit Red considers musicians such as Duke Ellington, Lionel Hampton, and Billie Holiday as leading black people toward spiritual, economic, and political fulfillment. If it was true that the revolution presupposed by Malcolm X, in which black people will chill away from identifying with commodification and take control over the modes of production, was out of the reach of the musicians, for Detroit Red, music nonetheless helped people to pass the time. As Detroit Red's reading of a song by Lionel Hampton reveals, the musicians provided the public sphere with philosophical narratives which defined the culture and the reality of the time:

> The people kept shouting for Hamp's "Flyin' Home," and finally he did it. (I could believe the story I'd heard in Boston about this number – that once in the Apollo, Hamp's "Flyin' Home" had made some reefer-smoking Negro in the second balcony believe he could fly, so he tried-and jumped-and broke his leg, an event later immortalized in song when Earl Hines wrote a hit tune called "Second Balcony Jump." *(p. 74)*

Detroit Red is a homeboy who wanted to be intoxicated by the city, and the night life was where he found black cosmopolitan culture. Unlike the 1920s when black writers specified the best of culture, in the 1940s, the energy lay in the music scene. Detroit Red became a *flâneur* and soaked up the Harlem night life like a sponge. When he was completely modernized, he posed the way "hipsters" wearing their zoots "cool it," and took a picture to send home, with "hat dangled, knees drawn close together, feet wide apart, both index fingers jabbed toward the floor. The long coat and swing chain and the Punjab pants were more dramatic if you stood that way" (p. 52).

THE PERIODIZATION OF 1940S HARLEM

Malcolm's story operates on several levels. It is also the story of the development of the black public sphere and the creation of audiences for black culture in Harlem in the 1940s. In addition to being a personal account of his own growth and decline, Malcolm's account is an economic narrative that reveals how black art was channeled toward greater economic well-being for blacks and how that channeling came to an end.

In *The Autobiography*, Malcolm X portrays the 1940s as a period when new doors opened for black people in America: "Old Man Roundtree, an elderly Pullman porter and a friend of Ella's, had recommended the railroad job for me. He had told her the war was snatching away railroad men so fast that if I could pass for twenty-one, he could get me on" (p. 70). The war years saw night life flourish in Harlem when good-time-loving servicemen crowded the streets and the bars. "Up and down along and between Lenox and Seventh Avenues, Harlem was like some technicolor bazaar. Hundreds of Negro soldiers and sailors, gawking and young like me, passed by" (p. 74).

It is important to distinguish this attempted resurgence of a black entertainment industry in Harlem during the war from the Harlem Renaissance and its night life, which came to an end in 1929, after the stock market crash. There were still some of the same clubs and ballrooms like the Savoy, Small's Paradise, Minton's, and the same theaters like the Apollo. But the most obvious difference between the 1920s and the 1940s involves the decreased influence of writers and political figures such as W. E. B. Du Bois, Langston Hughes, Marcus Garvey, and Alan Locke, and the increased popularity of entertainers such as Duke Ellington, Dizzy Gillespie, Billy Eckstine, Billie Holiday, Ella Fitzgerald, and Diana Washington in the black public sphere.

As *The Autobiography* indicates, Detroit Red derives his cultural and political formation from the bars and streets of Harlem, or, to paraphrase Miles Davis, from the universities of Small's Paradise and the Bradock Hotel, where the bars were jam-packed with famous black entertainers. Today our own situation bears similarities with the 1940s, with our reliance on Rap music, the films of Spike Lee, and such popular novelists as Terry McMillan, for dominant definitions of black culture.

Finally, like Detroit Red, I too am fascinated by 1940s Harlem, when arts and entertainment were hitched to economic activity in the community. It is still not clear to me why the jazz clubs moved to midtown around 1945, leaving many Harlemites without jobs in the formal and informal sectors. Maybe the imminent end of the war and the desire to return to the status quo had something to do with it. Maybe it was racism, as Miles Davis states in his autobiography: "If it's one thing white people are united on it is that they all hate to see black people making the money they think belongs to them. They were beginning to think that they owned these black musicians because they was making money for them" (p. 73).

According to Malcolm X, hustlers like Detroit Red may have turned to armed robbery after the 1943 Harlem riot, and the change of music scene from uptown to 52nd Street. "Things had grown so tight in Harlem that some hustlers had been forced to go to work. Even some prostitutes had gotten jobs as domestics, and cleaning office buildings at night. The pimping was so poor, Sammy had gone on the job with me" (pp. 114–15). Malcolm's deteriorating economic status coincides with a decline in the audience for black culture and a decline in the solidity of the black economic public sphere in Harlem.

If my point, in comparing culturalist discourse with conversionist discourse, is not clear by now, let me summarize the argument by way of conclusion. First of all, my reversal of the relations between culture and materialist and ideological systems such as economics, religion, and politics has as its purpose the removal of culture from the pathological spaces that these systems reserve for it. By turning these systems upside down as parts of black cultural specifications, it is easy to see that conversionists themselves enunciate culture even as they call it something else, and embrace it even as they denigrate it.

My aim in this chapter is to open the door to criticism, not to start a grand theory. A more inclusive view of culture empowers us to criticize the black Church's monopoly on ethics, while at the same time we recognize its historical importance to black people. It seems to me that the definition of ethics should be tied to culture, and to the creation of audiences. Malcolm's embrace of the Nation of Islam and then Islam itself constituted a move beyond Christian morality, toward a secularization of the just and the true; beyond "black culture is bad," toward a more inclusive ethics. In other words, black people do not divorce ethics from the material conditions that reproduce the black good life. We should be unafraid to embrace a multiplicity of cultural expressions as we pursue the good life for ourselves and each other.

NOTES

1 *The Autobiography of Malcolm X* by Alex Haley and Malcolm X (New York: Ballantine Books, 1992), p. 150.
2 Robin D. G. Kelley, "The Riddle of the Zoot: Malcolm Little and Black

Cultural Politics during World War II," in *Malcolm X in Our Own Words*, ed. Joe Wood (New York: St Martin's Press, 1992), p. 155. See also Kobena Mercer, "Black Hair/Style Politics," *New Formations* 3 (Winter 1987), p. 49.

3 The reversal I have in mind bears resemblance to post-structuralists' reversal of the relation between linguistics and semiotics. For Roland Barthes, who turns Ferdinand de Saussure upside down, semiotics can no longer be considered as an extension of linguistics, it becomes the definition of linguistics. The inversion of Saussure's theory opened up limitless possibilities for Barthes and other post-structuralists. To paraphrase Barthes himself, if literature is now seen as a language, its meaning no longer resides in religion, sociology, or identity politics, but in the relation of the parts to the whole. *Essais critiques* (Paris: Seuil, 1964), p. 257.

4 For concise definitions of culture see Raymond Williams, "The Analysis of Culture," in *Culture, Ideology and Social Process*, ed. Tony Bennett, Graham Martin, Colin Mercer and Janet Woollacott (London: Batsford Academic and Educational Ltd, 1981), p. 43; and Stuart Hall, "Cultural Studies: Two Paradigms," in *Culture, Ideology and Social Process*, p. 21. I take the concepts of lifeworld and public spheres from Jürgen Habermas' *The theory of Communicative Action*, I. *Reason and the Rationalization of Society* (Boston: Beacon Press, 1984).

5 James Naremore, *The Films of Vincente Minnelli* (Cambridge: Cambridge University Press, 1993), p. 52.

6 Walter Benjamin, *Charles Baudelaire: A Lyric Poet In the Era of High Capitalism* (London: Verso Press, 1983) p. 25.

9

The New Urban Color Line:
The State and Fate of the Ghetto
in PostFordist America

Loïc J. D. Wacquant

Tryin' to survive, tryin' to stay alive
The ghetto, talkin' 'bout the ghetto
Even though the streets are bumpy, lights burnt out
Dope fiends die with a pipe in their mouth
Old school buddies not doin' it right
Every day it's the same and it's the same every night
I wouldn't shoot you bro' but I'd shoot that fool
If he played me close and tried to test my cool
Every day I wonder just how I'll die
The only thing I know is how to survive.
                    Too Short, "The Ghetto."[1]

FROM RACE RIOTS TO SILENT RIOTS: CHANGING VISIONS
OF THE GHETTO

Twenty years after the uprisings that lighted fires of frustration and rage in the black slums of the American metropolis, the ghetto has returned to the frontline of national issues. Only, this time, the open racial uprisings that tore through the Afro-American communities of northern cities in defiant revolt against white authority

This chapter is a revised and expanded version of "Redrawing the Urban Color Line: The State of the Ghetto in the 1980s," originally published in Craig Calhoun and George Ritzer, eds, *Social Problems* (New York: McGraw-Hill, 1992).

have given way to the "slow rioting" (Curtis 1985) of black-on-black crime, mass school rejection, drug trafficking and internal social decay.[2] On the nightly news, scenes of white policemen unleashing state violence on peaceful black demonstrators demanding mere recognition of their elemental constitutional rights have been replaced by reports on drive-by shootings, homelessness, and teenage pregnancy. Black ministers, local politicians, and concerned mothers still agitate and demonstrate, but their pleas and marches are less often directed at the government than at the drug dealers and gangs who have turned so many inner-city neighborhoods into theaters of dread and death. The vision of "Negro" looters and black power activists reclaiming forceful control over their community's fate (Boskin 1970) and riding the crest of a wave of racial pride and self-assertion has given way to the loathsome imagery of the "underclass," a term that purports to denote a new segment of the minority poor allegedly characterized by behavioral deficiency and cultural deviance (Auletta 1982; Sawhill 1989), a menacing urban hydra personified by the defiant and aggressive gang member and the dissolute if passive teenage "welfare mother," twin emblematic figures whose (self-)destructive behavior is said to represent the one a physical threat and the other a moral attack on the integrity of American values and national life.

The wave of social movements that energized the black community and helped lift collective hopes through the 1960s (Morris 1984; McAdam 1981) has subsided and, with it, the country's commitment to combating racial inequality. This is well reflected in the changing idiom of public debate on the ghetto. As the "War on Poverty" of Lyndon B. Johnson was replaced by the "War on Welfare" of Ronald Reagan (Katz 1989), the issue of the societal connection between race, class, and poverty was reformulated in terms of the personal motivations, family norms, and group values of the residents of the inner city, with welfare playing the part of the villain. The goals of government policy, too, were downgraded accordingly: rather than pursue the eradication of poverty – the optimistic target that the Great Society program was set to reach by 1976 as a tribute to the nation's bicentennial – and the diminution of racial disparities, the state is now content to oversee the containment of the first in crumbling minority enclaves (and in the jails that have been built at an astounding pace in the past decade to absorb the most disruptive of their occupants) and "benign neglect" of the second. Accordingly, the focus of social research has shifted from the urban color line to the individual defects of the black poor, from the ghetto as a mechanism of racial domination and economic oppression (Clark

1965; Liebow 1967; Rainwater 1970), and the structural political
and economic impediments that block the full participation of poor
urban blacks to the national collectivity, to the "pathologies" of the
so-called underclass said to inhabit it and to the punitive measures
that may be employed to minimize their claim upon collective resources and to force them into the peripheral segments of an expanding low-wage labor market (e.g., Ricketts and Sawhill 1988,
Mead 1989).[3]

These shifts in the symbolic representation and political treatment
of the ghetto, however, can hardly efface the fact that the ominous
forewarning of the 1968 National Advisory Commission on Civil
Disorders (Kerner Commission 1989: 396, 389) has come true: "The
country [has moved] toward two societies, separate and unequal"
as a consequence of "the accelerating segregation of low-income,
disadvantaged Negroes within the ghettos of the largest American
cities." While the black middle class has experienced real, if tenuous,
progress and expansion thanks largely to governmental efforts and
(secondarily) to increased legal pressure upon corporate employers
(Collins 1983; Landry 1987; Son et al. 1989), urban black poverty
is more intense, more tenacious, and more concentrated today than
it was in the 1960s (Wilson 1987). And the economic, social, and
cultural distance between inner-city minorities and the rest of society
has reached levels that are unprecedented in modern American
history as well as unknown in other advanced societies.

Not the Same Old Ghetto

Is this to say, borrowing the words of historian Gilbert Osofsky
(1971: 189), that there is an "unending and tragic sameness about
black life in the metropolis," that of the "enduring ghetto," which
perpetuates itself through time unaffected by societal trends and
political forces as momentous as the onset of a postindustrial economy, the enactment of broad civil rights and affirmative action
legislation, and the reorganization of urban space under the twin
pressures of suburban deconcentration and central-city gentrification?
Quite the contrary. For underneath the persistence of economic
subordination and racial entrapment, the ghetto of the 1980s is quite
different from that of the 1950s. The communal ghetto of the
immediate post-war era, compact, sharply bounded, and comprising
a full complement of black classes bound together by a unified
collective consciousness, a near-complete social division of labor, and
broad-based communitarian agencies of mobilization and representation, has been replaced by what we may call the hyperghetto of

the 1980s and 1990s (Wacquant 1989, 1991), whose spatial configuration, institutional and demographic makeup, structural position and function in urban society are quite novel. Furthermore, the separation of the ghetto from the rest of American society is only apparent: it is one of "lifeworld," not "system," to use a conceptual distinction elaborated by Habermas (1984). It refers to the concrete experiences and relations of its occupants, not to the underlying ties that firmly anchor them in the metropolitan ensemble – if in exclusionary fashion. For, as I shall argue in this chapter, there are deep-seated causal and functional linkages between the transformation of the ghetto and changes in the structure of the US economy, society, and polity over the past three decades.

Analysis of the economic and political factors that have combined to turn them into veritable domestic "Bantustans" reveals that ghettos are not autonomous social entities that contain within themselves the principle of their own reproduction and change. It demonstrates also that the parlous state of America's historic "Black Belts" is not the simple mechanical result of deindustrialization, demographic movements, or of a skills or spatial "mismatch" rooted in ecological processes, and still much less the product of the rise of a "new" underclass, *in statu nascendi* or already "crystallized" into a "permanent" fixture of the American urban landscape (Loewenstein 1985; *Chicago Tribune* 1986; Nathan 1987), whether defined by its behavior, income, culture, or isolation. It is the product, rather, of a transformation of the *political* articulation of race, class, and urban space in both discourse and objective reality.

The ghetto is still with us but it is a different "kind" of ghetto: its internal makeup has changed along with its environment and with the institutional processes that simultaneously chain it to the rest of American society and ensure its dependent and marginal location within it. To understand these differences, what the ghetto is and means to both insiders and outsiders, one must sweep aside the discourse of the "underclass" that has crowded the stage of the resurging debate on race and poverty in the city (Fainstein 1993) and reconstruct instead the linked relations between the transformation of everyday life and social relations inside the urban core, on the one hand, and the restructuring of the system of forces, economic, racial, and political, that account for the particular configuration of caste and class it materializes. Accordingly, the main focus of this analysis will on the *external* factors that have reshaped the social and symbolic territory within which ghetto residents (re)define themselves and the collectivity they form, and it addresses the *internal* production of its specific social order and consciousness only indirectly. This emphasis is not born of the belief that structural determination constitutes the *alpha* and *omega* of identity formation, far from it. It rests, rather, on two premises, one theoretical and the other empirical.

The first premise is that elucidation of the objective conditions under which identity comes to be constructed, asserted, and disputed in the inner city constitutes a sociological prerequisite to the analysis of the experiential *Lebenswelt* of the ghetto and its embedded forms of practice and signification. It is in this objective space of material and symbolic positions and resources that are rooted the strategies deployed by ghetto residents to figure out who they are and who they can be. While I have no doubt that such an analysis remains unfinished absent the complement of an "indigenous perspective" (*à la* Aldon Morris) throwing light on the complexities of identity formation "from below" (or, to be more precise, from within), I also believe that populist celebration of "the value of blackness" and of the richness of "oppositional black culture" (hooks 1992: 17) offers neither a substitute, nor an adequate starting point for a rigorous assessment of the state and fate of the ghetto at the close of the Fordist era.

The second premise of this inquiry is that the reality of the ghetto as a physical, social, and symbolic place in American society is, whether one likes it or not, largely being decided – indeed imposed – from outside, as its residents are increasingly dispossessed of the means to produce their own collective and individual identities. A brief contrast of the opposed provenance, uses, and semantic charge of the vocabularies of "soul" and "underclass" is instructive in this respect. The notion of soul, which gained wide appeal during the racial turmoil of the 1960s, was a "folk conception of the lower-class urban Negro's own 'national character'" (Hannerz 1968: 54). Produced from within for in-group consumption, it served as a symbol of solidarity and a badge of personal and group pride. By contrast, "underclass status" is established wholly from the outside (and from above) and forced upon its putative "members" by specialists in symbolic production – journalists, politicians, academics, and governmental experts – for purposes of control and disciplining (in Foucault's sense of the term) and without the slightest concern for the self-understanding of those who are arbitrarily lumped into this analytical fiction. Whereas the folk concept of soul, as part of an "internal ghetto dialogue" toward an indigenous reassessment of black identity (Keil 1966), was appraisive, the idiom of underclass is a derogatory label, an identity that nobody claims except to pin it on an Other. That even "insurgent" black intellectuals such as

Cornel West should embrace the idiom of underclass is revealing of the degree to which the ghetto has become an *alien object* on the landscape of American society.

Three Preliminary Caveats

Three caveats are in order before drawing a portrait of social conditions and living in the contemporary inner city, using Chicago as an illustrative case. First, it must be emphasized that the ghetto is not simply a topographic entity or an aggregation of poor families and individuals but an *institutional form*, that is, a particular, spatially based, concatenation of mechanisms of *ethnoracial closure and control*. Briefly put, a ghetto may be ideal-typically characterized as a bounded, racially and/or culturally uniform sociospatial formation based on the forcible relegation of a negatively typed population – such as Jews in medieval Europe and African-Americans in the modern United States – to a reserved territory in which this population develops a set of specific institutions that operate both as a functional substitute for, and as a protective buffer from, the dominant institutions of the encompassing society (Wacquant 1991). The fact that most ghettos have *historically* been places of widespread and sometimes acute material misery does not mean that a ghetto necessarily has to be poor – certainly, the "Bronzeville" of the 1940s was more prosperous than most Southern black communities – nor that it has to be uniformly deprived.[4] This implies that the ghetto is not a social monolith. Notwithstanding their extreme dilapidation, many inner-city neighborhoods still contain a modicum of occupational, cultural, and family variety. Neither is the ghetto entirely barren: amidst its desolation, scattered islets of (relative) economic and social stability persist, which offer fragile but crucial launching pads for the strategies of coping and escape of its residents, and new forms of sociability continually develop in the cracks of the crumbling system.

Second, one must resist the tendency to treat the ghetto as an alien space, to see only what is different in it, in short to *exoticize it*, as proponents of the scholarly myth of the "underclass" have been wont to do in their grisly tales of "antisocial" behavior that resonate so well with journalistic reports (from which they are often drawn in the first place) and with common class and racial prejudice against the black poor. Indeed, a cursory sociology of sociology would show that most descriptions of the "underclass" reveal more about the *relation* of the analyst to the object, and about his or her racial and class preconceptions, fears, and fantasies, than they do about their putative object; and that representations of "underclass areas" bear the distinctive mark of the ostensibly "neutral" (that is, dominant) gaze set upon them from a distance by analysts who, all too often, have rarely set foot in one.[5] Ghetto dwellers are not a distinctive breed of men and women in need of a special denomination; they are ordinary people trying to make a living and to improve their lot as best they can under the unusually oppressive and depressed circumstances imposed upon them. Though their cultural codes and patterns of conduct may, from the standpoint of a secure outside observer, appear peculiar, quixotic or even "aberrant" (a word so often reiterated when talking about the ghetto that it has become virtually oxymoronic with it), on closer examination, they turn out to obey a social rationality that takes stock of past experiences and is well suited to their immediate socioeconomic context and possibilities (Wacquant 1992a).

The third caveat stresses, against the central premise of American poverty research, that the ghetto does not suffer from "social disorganization" – another moralizing concept that had by now best be banned from the social sciences. Rather, it is *organized differently* in response to the relentless press of economic necessity, social insecurity, racial enmity, and political stigmatization. The ghetto comprises a particular type of social order, premised on the racial marking and dualization of space, "organized around an intense competition for, and conflict over, the scarce resources" that suffuses an environment replete with "social predators" (Sanchez-Jankowski 1991: 22, 183–92) and politically constituted as inferior. Finally and relatedly, one must keep in mind that ghetto dwellers are not part of a separate group somehow severed from the rest of society, as many advocates of the "underclass" thesis would have us believe. They belong, rather, to unskilled and socially disqualified fractions of the black working class, if only by virtue of the multifarious kinship and marital links, social ties, cultural connections, and institutional processes that cut across the alleged divide between them and rest of the Afro-American community (Aschenbrenner 1975; Collins 1983: 370; Pétonnet 1985).[6]

FROM THE "COMMUNAL" GHETTO OF THE 1950S TO THE "HYPERGHETTO" OF THE 1980S

The process of black ghettoization – from initial piling up and expansion to sudden white flight and disinvestment, followed by abrupt increases in joblessness, crime, educational retardation, and other social dislocations – is old and well known: it goes back to the initial formation of the ghetto as an institution of *racial exclusion* in the early decades of the century.[7] It must be emphasized at the outset that blacks are the only group to have experienced ghettoization in American society. White immigrants of various peripheral provenance (Italians, Irish, Polish, Jews, etc.) initially lived in heterogeneous *ethnic neighborhoods* which, though they may have been slums, were temporary and, for the most part, voluntary way-stations on the road to integration in a composite white society; they were not, *pace* Wirth (1927), ghettos in any sense other than an impressionistic, journalistic one. Segregation in them was only partial, and based on a mixture of class, nationality, and citizenship. The residential confinement of blacks, on the other hand, was (and still is) unique in that only Afro-Americans have had to live in areas where "segregation was practically total, essentially unvoluntary, and also perpetual" (Philpott 1978: xvi).[8] Moreover, the forced separation of blacks went beyond housing to encompass other basic institutional arenas, from schooling and employment to public services and political representation, leading to the development of a parallel social structure without counterpart among whites.

What is distinctive about black ghettoization today is, first, that it has become spatially as well as institutionally differentiated and *decentered*, split, as it were, between a decaying, if expanding, urban core on the one hand, and satellite working-class and middle-class neighborhoods located on the periphery of cities and, increasingly, in segregated suburbs often adjacent to the historic Black Belt. The second novel feature of black ghettoization in postFordist America is its sheer scale and "the intensity of the collapse at the center of the ghetto," as well as the fact that "the cycle still operates two decades after fair housing laws have been in effect" (Orfield 1985: 163). Indeed, in that very period when legal changes were presumed to bring about its amelioration, the inner city has been plagued by accelerating physical degradation, rampant insecurity and violence, and degrees of economic exclusion and social hardship comparable only to those of the worst years of the Great Depression.

Physical Decay and Danger in the Urban Core

Walk along 63rd Street on the South Side of Chicago, within a stone's throw of the University of Chicago campus, along what used to be one of the city's most vibrant commercial strips, and you will witness a grim spectacle repeated over and over across the black ghettos of America – in Harlem or in the Brownsville district of Brooklyn in New York City, in Camden, New Jersey, on the East Side of Cleveland, or in Boston's Roxbury.[9] Abandoned buildings, vacant lots strewn with debris and garbage, broken sidewalks, boarded-up store-front churches, and the charred remains of shops line up miles and miles of decaying neighborhoods left to rot since the 1960s.

Forty years ago, 63rd Street was called the "Miracle Mile" by local merchants vying for space and a piece of the pie. There were nearly 800 businesses, and not a single vacant lot in an eighteen-by-four block area. The neighborhood was lively as people streamed in from other parts of town, joining in crowds so dense at rush hour that one was literally swept off one's feet upon getting out of the elevated train station. Large restaurants were open around the clock; no fewer than five banks and six hotels were present; and movie houses, taverns, and ballrooms never seemed to empty. Here is the description of the street by the only white shopkeeper left from that era:

It looks like Berlin after the war and that's sad. The street is bombed out, decaying. Seventy-five per cent of it is vacant. It's very unfortunate but it seems that all that really grows here is liquor stores. And they're not contributing anything to the community: it's all "*take, take, take!*" Very depressing. [Sighs heavily] It's an area devoid of hope, it's an area devoid of investments. People don't come into Woodlawn.

Now the street's nickname has taken an ironic twist: it is a miracle for a business to survive on it. Not a single theater, bank, jazz club, or repair shop outlived the 1970s. The lumber yards, print shops, garages, and light manufacturing enterprises have disappeared as well. Fewer than 90 commercial establishments remain, most of them tiny eating places, beauty parlors, and barber shops, apparel, food, and liquor outlets which each employs at best a handful of workers.

Perhaps the most significant fact of daily life in today's ghetto, however, is the extraordinary *prevalence of physical danger and the acute sense of insecurity* that pervade its streets.[10] Between 1980 and 1984 alone, serious crimes in Chicago multiplied fourfold to reach the astonishing rate of 1,254 per 1,000 residents. Most of them were committed by and upon residents of the ghetto. A plurality of the 849 homicide victims officially recorded in Chicago in 1990 were young Afro-American men, most of them shot to death in poor all-black neighborhoods. With the wide diffusion of drugs and fire-arms, mortality in major inner-city areas has reached "rates that justify special consideration analogous to that given to 'natural disaster areas';" today males in Bangladesh have a higher proba-bility of survival after age 35 than their counterparts of Harlem (McCord and Freeman 1990). No wonder some analysts of the urban scene openly talk of young black males as "an endangered species" (Gibbs 1989). The combined availability of guns, durable exclusion from wage-labor, and pervasiveness of the drug trade have modified the rules of masculine confrontation on the street in ways that fuel the escalation of deadly assault. A former leader of the Black Gangster Disciples muses:

> See, back then, if two gang guys wanna fight, they let 'em two guys fight *one-on-one*. But it's not like that now: if you wanna fight me, I'mma git me a gun an' shoot you, you see what I'm sayin'? Whenever you got a gun, tha's the first thin' you think about – not about *peace treaties* an' let dese two guys fight and settle their disagreement as real grown men. It's *scary now* because dese guys, they don' have – [his voice rising in shock] I mean they don't have *no value for life* – *no value!*

Residences are scarcely safer than the streets. The windows and doors of apartments or houses are commonly barricaded behind heavy metal gates and burglar bars. Public facilities are not spared. Elderly ghetto dwellers nostalgically evoke a time when they used to sleep in municipal parks in the summer, rolled in mosquito nets, or on rooftops and balconies in search of relief from the summer heat. Nowadays, parks are considered "no-go" areas, es-pecially after nightfall; some are even off-limits to the youths who live in their immediate vicinity because they fall within the territory of a rival gang. Buses of the Chicago Transit Authority running routes from the downtown Loop through the South Side are escorted by special police squad cars to deter assaults and still register several hundred violent incidents per month. Several CTA train stations on the Jackson Park line have been closed to entry in an attempt to limit crime, at the cost of denying local residents access to public transportation. Insecurity is so deep that simply maneuvering one's way through public space has become a major dilemma in the daily life of inner-city residents, as averred by this comment from an elderly South Sider on a sunny day of late June: "Oh, I hate to see this hot weather back. I mean I do like warm weather, *it's the people it bring out I don't like*: punks and dope fiends, you're beginnin' to see them outa d'buildings now, on d'streets. This ain't no good."

Schools are no exception to this pattern. Many public establishments in Chicago's inner city organize parents' militias that patrol the school grounds armed with baseball bats while classes are in session. Others hire off-duty policemen to supplement security and use metal detectors to try to limit the number of guns and other weapons circulating on school grounds. A South Side elementary school on 55th Street briefly made the headlines after five youths were gunned down and killed within a few blocks in the course of a single year. Its students were found to be living in "numbing fear" of the gang violence that awaits them outside the school. Children "say they are afraid for their lives to go to school" confessed one teacher. "It seems like every year somebody's child loses their life and can't get out of 8th grade," added a mother. And the principal could only regret that the school security guards are unable to provide protection once pupils leave the premises (*Chicago Tribune* 1990).

Today's ghetto truly is "no place to be a child," as goes the title of a recent book comparing Chicago's inner city to refugee camps in war-torn Cambodia (Garbarino et al. 1991). Youngsters raised in this environment of pandemic violence experience enormous emotional damage and display posttraumatic stress disorders very similar to those suffered by veterans. A tenant of a South Side high-rise complex (cited in Brune and Camacho 1983: 13) concurs that Chicago "is no place to raise a family. It's like a three-ring circus around here during the hot weather. There's constantly fighting. They've been times when we had to take all the kids and put 'em in the hallway on the floor, so much gunfire around here." By age five, virtually all children living in large public housing projects have encountered shooting or death firsthand. Many mothers opt to send their offspring away to stay in the suburbs or with family in the South to shelter them from the neighborhood's brutality.

The incidence of crime in the ghetto is exacerbated by the racial closure of space in American cities. If so much violence is of the "black-on-black" variety, it is not only because inner-city Afro-Americans suffer extreme economic redundancy and social alienation. It is also that anonymous black males have become widely recognized symbols of danger (Anderson 1991: chapter 6) so that, unless they display the trappings of middle-class culture, they are routinely barred from bordering white areas where their skin color causes them to be immediately viewed as potential criminals or troublemakers: "You can't go over to the white community to do anything, because when you're seen over there, you're already stopped on suspicion. So you got to prey in your den, because you're less noticeable over there. You got to burglarize your own people" (cited in Blauner 1989: 223).

Depopulation, Economic Exclusion, and the Organizational Collapse of the Ghetto

Yet the continued physical and commercial decline, rising street violence, and ubiquitous insecurity of the ghetto are themselves but surface manifestations of a more profound transformation of its socioeconomic and institutional fabric. First, whereas the ghetto of the 1950s was overpopulated as the result of the swelling influx of black migrants from the South triggered by the wartime boom and the mechanization of Southern agriculture, the contemporary ghetto has been undergoing steady depopulation as better-off families moved out in search of more congenial surroundings. For instance, the core of Chicago's South Side lost close to half of its inhabitants, as the residents of Oakland, Grand Boulevard, and Washington Park decreased from about 200,000 in 1950 to 102,000 in 1980 – slipping even further down to an estimated 63,500 in 1990 according to early returns of the census. During those years, moreover, despite the construction of massive public housing high-rises, the number of housing units decreased by one third through arson (often perpetrated by absentee landlords seeking to collect insurance money) and the abandonment and destruction brought about by urban renewal programs that razed more dwellings than they built, so that overcrowding and inadequate housing are still widespread in the urban core.

But the most dramatic change in the demography of the ghetto has been the precipitous decline of the employed population caused by two mutually reinforcing factors: the continuing exodus of upwardly mobile black families and the rising joblessness of those left behind. In 1950 over half of the adults living at the heart of the South Side Black Belt were gainfully employed, a rate equal to that of the city as a whole. Chicago was still a dominant national industrial center then and half those employed blacks held bluecollar jobs. By 1980, the number of working residents had dropped by a staggering 77 per cent so that nearly three of every four persons over the age of 16 were jobless. In 30 years, the number of operatives and laborers crumbled from 35,808 to 4,963; that for craftsmen plummeted from 6,564 to 1,338, while the corresponding figure for private household and service workers fell from 25,181 to 5,203. And, whereas the black middle class multiplied fivefold citywide between 1950 and 1980, the number of white-collar employees, managers, and professionals living in the urban core was cut by half, from 15,341 to 7,394. A long-time resident of Woodlawn (who, ironically, recently moved to the city's North Side to shelter his children from the violence of the streets) complains about the disappearance of better-off families from his old South Side neighborhood:

> It [used to] be tonsa teachers livin' in d'neighbo'hood, but now they movin', *everybody move up* ... If you look at d'community, Louie, *it's decayin': ain't nobody here.* Ain't no teachers on 63rd Street, over here on Maryland, *ain't none*, know what I'm sayin'? Ev'rybody that's got a lil' knowledge, they leavin' it. If these people would stay in an' help reshape it, *they can reshape it.* Like teachers, policemen, firemen, business leaders, all o'em *responsible: everybody leavin' out.* An' they takin' the money with 'em.

How did this happen? At the close of the war, *all* blacks, irrespective of their social status, were forcibly relegated to the same compressed spatial enclave, and they had no choice but to coexist in it. As whites fled *en masse* to the suburbs with the blessing and help of the federal government, they opened up adjacent areas in which black families from the middle class and from the upper fractions of the working class could move to create new, soon to be solidly black neighborhoods. The deconcentration of the Afro-American community, in turn, dispersed the institutions of the ghetto and increased their class differentiation.[11] Simultaneously, in a systematic and self-conscious effort to maintain the prevailing pattern of racial segregation, the city was making sure that all of its new public housing was built exclusively in existing ghetto areas (Hirsch 1983), where only the poorest would soon tolerate dwelling. By the 1970s, then, *the urban color line had effectively been redrawn along class lines* at the behest of government, with the historic core of the Black Belt containing inordinate concentrations of the jobless and dependent while the brunt of the black middle and stabler working classes resided in segregated peripheral city neighborhoods.

The consequence of this threefold movement – the out-migration of stably employed Afro-American families made possible by state-sponsored white flight to the suburbs, the crowding of public housing in black slum areas, the expulsion of the remaining ghetto residents from the wage-labor market – has been soaring and endemic poverty. In Grand Boulevard, a section of the South Side containing some 50,000 people, half the population lived under the poverty line in 1980, up from 37 percent ten years earlier, and three of every four households was headed by a single mother. With a median family income below 7,000 dollars per annum (less than a third of the citywide figure), many families in fact did not even reach half the poverty line. Six residents in ten had to rely on one or another form of public assistance in order to subsist.

The social and economic desolation of today's ghetto is distinctly perceived by its inhabitants, as data from the Urban Family Life Survey show. [12] Asked how many men are working steadily in their neighborhood, 55 percent of the residents of Chicago's traditional Black Belt (South Side and West Side together) answer "very few or none at all," compared to 21 percent in peripheral black areas harboring a mix of poor, working-, and middle-class families. A full half also declare that the proportion of employed males in their area diminished over the preceding years. One adult in four belongs to a household without a working telephone (only one in ten in outlying black areas) and 86 percent to a household that rents its living quarters (as against about half among blacks in low-poverty areas); nearly a third reside in buildings managed by the Chicago Housing Authority (CHA), though the latter oversees only 4 percent of the city's housing supply.

It is abundantly clear that the urban core today contains mainly those dispossessed fractions of the black (sub)proletariat who are unable to escape its blighted conditions. Given a choice, fewer than one in four residents of Chicago's ghetto would stay in their neighborhood, as opposed to four in ten in low-poverty black tracts. Only 18 percent rate their neighborhood as a "good or very good" place to live, contrasted with 42 percent in peripheral black areas, and nearly half report that the state of their surroundings has worsened in the past few years. Not surprisingly, gang activity is more prevalent at the heart of the ghetto: half of its inhabitants consider gangs as a "big problem" in their area, compared to fewer than a third in low-poverty black precincts. As for its future, nearly one-third foresee no improvement in their neighborhood, while another 30 percent expect it to continue to deteriorate.

Today's ghetto dwellers are thus not only *individually poorer* than their counterparts of three decades ago in the sense that they have borne an absolute reduction in their standards of living and that the distance between them and the rest of society has widened – the federal poverty line represented half the median national family income in 1960 but only a third by 1980 (Beeghley 1983: 355). They are also considerably *poorer collectively* in several respects. First, they reside among an overwhelmingly deprived and downwardly mobile or immobile population, and therefore tend to be isolated from other components of the Afro-American community: as we saw above, the black middle class has both fled the urban core and grown outside of it.[13] Second, and as a consequence, they can no longer count on the nexus of institutions that used to give the ghetto its internal coherence and cohesion. The "Black Metropolis" of the mid-century so admirably dissected by Drake and Cayton (1962: 17) was a "distinctive city within a city" containing an extended division of labor and the full gamut of black social classes. The "proliferation of institutions" that made "Bronzeville," as its residents used to call it, the capital of black America enabled it to duplicate (though at a markedly inferior level) the organizational structure of the wider white society and to provide limited but real avenues of mobility within its own internal order.

By contrast, the hyperghetto of the late century has weathered such organizational decline that it contains neither an extended division of labor nor a representative cross-section of black classes, nor functioning duplicates of the central institutions of the broader urban society. The organizational infrastructure – the black press and the Church, the lodges and the social clubs, the political groups, the businesses and professional services, and the policy racket (or "numbers game") – that gave the classical ghetto of the 1950s its communal character and strength, and that served as an instrument of collective solidarity and mobilization, has by and large withered away, weakening the citywide networks of solidarity and cooperation typical of the communal ghetto (Mithun 1973). And, whereas, in the context of the full employment and industrial prosperity brought about by the Korean war, "the entire institutional structure of Bronzeville [was] providing basic satisfactions for the 'reasonable expectations' shared by people at various class levels" (Drake and Cayton 1962: vol. 2, p. xi), today the prevalence of joblessness and the organizational void of the contemporary hyperghetto prevent it from satisfying even the basic needs of its residents.

Oppressive as it was, the traditional ghetto formed "a milieu for Negro Americans in which they [could] imbue their lives with meaning" (Drake and Cayton 1962: vol. 2, p. xiv) and which elicited attachment and pride. By contrast, today's ghetto is a despised and stigmatizing locale from which nearly everybody is desperately trying to escape, "a place of stunted hopes and blighted aspirations, a city of limits in which the reach of realistic ambition is to survive" (Monroe and Goldman 1988: 251).

"Hustling" and Survival in the Informal Economy

The prevalence of chronic unemployment and underemployment among ghetto residents compels them to seek public assistance. The egregious inadequacy of public aid even for sheer survival, in turn, compels them to seek additional unreported or unreportable income-generating activities (Scharf 1987: 20). Most ghetto residents have little choice but to "moonlight" on jobs, to "hustle" money through a diversity of schemes, or to engage in illegal trades of various kinds (including the most dangerous and potentially lucrative of them, drug sale), in order to "make that dollar." The growth of the informal economy observed at the heart of most large cities in America can be traced directly to the combined weakness of low-skill core labor demand, the economic and organizational desertification of the urban core, and the failings of welfare coverage.

Survival strategies vary as a function of the social, economic, and cultural resources, as well as the composition, of poor households. When strapped without cash, as is frequently the case among welfare recipients whose monthly aid check is usually expended in full one or two weeks after receipt, a favorite strategy of solo women heads of households is to borrow small sums of money (from five to forty dollars in most cases) from parents, lovers, or close friends. For many, female kin networks are the most, if not the only, reliable source of financial support in case of emergency (Stack 1970). In the words of an unemployed mother subsisting on Aid to Families with Dependent Children (AFDC) with her four children: [14]

> If I get much down, then I can go to Mama, and my Mama, she help me a little bit. Can't do it too much, but she say to keep my kids from starvin', she help me a little. So now and then ... she help me out for a few days. Well, if it gets too much ... I tell her ... I tell her, "Well, we ain't got nothin' over here." So she try to get me somethin'.

Another prevalent option is to seek free food from a pantry, a church, or a governmental agency. In 1987, over 70 percent of the adults ages 18 to 48 living in Chicago's historic Black Belt had to call on such outside assistance to feed themselves and their kin. Soup kitchens run by churches on the South Side cannot keep up with demand and regularly turn away hungry families. Chronic malnutrition is a fact of life that is only too visible in the ghetto for those who care to look, notwithstanding government programs such as food stamps and the spotty free distribution of farm surpluses and dairy products unfit for commercialization. Many ghetto residents periodically pawn goods to raise the income needed to bridge a period of dearth, take in boarders, sell their food stamps, or dig into their meager savings if they have any. But 82 percent of adults in Chicago's ghetto had no savings account in the mid-1980s, and only one in ten could muster the means to maintain a checking account (Wacquant and Wilson 1989a: 22). Currency exchanges and pawn shops function as high-cost substitutes for the banks that do not exist (or that reject ghetto residents where they do), as this South Side mother of three indicates:

> I pawn my wedding rings and get a lil' money and when I get some money I go back and get my rings. They're gone now. I could have gone back and got them but I just forgot about them – I pawn them so much, I pawn them every month. The man at the pawn shop see me comin', he sees me, he knows me! Yeah, it's been like that for a couple of years now, he know what I'm bringing and he starts writin' it up before I even get there. And I get them out every month and pawn them every month. That's terrible. Twenty-five dollars is not that much. It can buy some cigarettes when I need it and that's a habit right there, definitely. It helps out a lot, a whole lot.

The mainstay of subsistence, however, is furnished by the odd jobs and marginal trades that have flourished in the past decade in the inner city. Some ghetto residents will baby-sit the children of neighbors, run errands for them, cut hair or grass, repair electrical appliances, shovel snow in the winter, collect pop cans for small sums of money, or "pick up junk outa the alley" for resale to those even less fortunate than they. Others yet become occasional street peddlers or vendors (Jones 1988), sell their blood, or go to day labor places in the hope of obtaining any kind of stopgap employment. "They go to Handy Andy. That's like a job, you can go up north and you get twenty dollars a day for working eight hours or something. That's what I did before but its not worth it, just temporary stuff," remarks a chronically unemployed single mother from the West Side.

One may also find irregular employ at an illegal "after-hours" club, operate a "gypsy cab," become a "jack-leg" mechanic or one of those "insurance artists" who try (especially when weather conditions are bad) to provoke auto or bus accidents in which they deliberately get injured with a view toward attempting to collect monetary damages. More hardened individuals may commit petty crimes for the express purpose of being incarcerated: jail is very violent and punitive but it offers a sure bed, three free meals a day, some medical care, and sometimes even work – all things that the outside world is hard-pressed to deliver for most inner-city poor. In this highly precarious setting ruled by unending economic uncertainty, children represent important resources and are under constant pressure to generate income at an early age. Thus, in the dead of winter boys eight to ten years of age can be seen at all hours of the day or night at gas stations on Chicago's South Side offering to pump gas or to wipe windshields for petty change, or waiting at the exit of supermarkets to carry grocery bags in exchange for a coin or some food.

The survival strategy of last resort involves a wide gamut of illegal activities, ranging from gambling and "mugging," street fencing and selling stolen ("hot") merchandise, to stickups, armed robbery, prostitution and drug dealing. Asked what people in her neighborhood of Grand Boulevard do to survive, a 47-year-old packer for a mailing company answers:

> Steal, knock old ladies down and take their pension checks. Like on the "El" [Elevated train] station there. Especially when they get their Social Security checks, *they be out there*, waitin' for them, grab their purses and everything. Lot of that happenin' around here ... They broke in on me when I first moved in here so I put bars in. They got my stereo. But I haven't any trouble since I put my bars up.

A 28-year old jobless single mother candidly adds: "Shit! Turn tricks, sell drugs, anything ... any and every thing. Mind you: everyone is not the stickup man, you know, but any and everything. Me myself, I have sold marijuana. I'm not a drug pusher, but I'm just tryin' to make ends ... I'm tryin' to keep bread on the table: I have two babies."

For individuals who are repeatedly rejected from the labor market or who resist being reduced to taking dead-end "slave jobs" that strip them of their dignity as they entail menial tasks paying poverty wages with no benefits attached, underground activities can easily turn into full-time employment. For them, predatory crime constitutes a form of petty entrepreneurialism in which they can put to use their only valuable assets, physical prowess and a working knowledge of the street world (Wacquant 1992a). Much of the attraction of gangs for young inner-city blacks has to do with the fact that gangs are, among other things, business concerns that increase one's chances of securing money and offer a modicum of financial security (Sanchez-Jankowski 1991: 40–1). In the void created by the absence of legitimate firms, illegal lines of work such as car theft and "stripping," robbery, and especially drug dealing can evolve complex organizational structures that almost mirror those of firms in the official economy. Besides, the drug trade is often the only form of business known to ghetto adolescents, and one which has the added virtue of being a genuine "equal opportunity" employer (Williams 1989; Sullivan 1989: chapter 7). In addition, unlike so many service establishments where one labors away for famine wages with little chance of a raise, drug employment promises immediate reward for those who display a good work ethic. A 34-year-old woman who shares a decrepit South Side apartment with her brother, a janitor, is considering this employment option for this reason: "The fellah told me: you make 250 dollars a week, okay – in this neighborhood, he's got so many people working for him for 250 dollars a week – and if you're good enough you might make 400 dollars a week."

Needless to say, the overall impact of the drug economy on ghetto communities is terribly destructive. Not only does it help sap the willingness of young men to work at low-level wages by offering apparently attractive, if risky, alternative economic opportunities – a skilled neighborhood dealer in East Harlem can generate weekly sales of $100,000; a "runner" on the South Side of Chicago commonly grosses several thousand dollars a week. [15] It creates an environment of poor health and high risk of death at an early age, strains family relationships, and severely weakens local social cohesion. And it causes rampant violence and a sharp decline in neighborhood safety (Johnson et al. 1990), which in turn accelerate the withdrawal of the wage-labor market and further isolate ghetto residents from the regular economy and society.

The *explosive growth of this underground economy* dominated by street-level drug trafficking thus helps make sense of the rise of the "culture of terror" that now engulfs many inner-city streets. Anthropologist Philippe Bourgois has shown that, in this economy, routine displays of violence are a business requirement: they serve to maintain commercial credibility and avert being taken over by competitors or being robbed by intruders and customers (or police, some of whom are not the last to partake of the trafficking). By extension, in a universe depleted of the most basic resources and characterized by a high density of social predators, trust is not a feasible option, so that all must protect themselves from violence – by being ready to wield it: "Inner-city street violence is not limited solely to drug sellers or to street criminals; to a certain extent, everyone living in the neighborhood who wants to maintain a sense of autonomy ...

finds it useful to participate, at least passively, in some corner of the culture of terror" (Bourgois 1989; 647).

THE ECONOMIC AND POLITICAL ROOTS OF HYPERGHETTOIZATION

Why have physical decay and interpersonal violence reached levels such that public space has nearly entirely withered away in the ghetto? Why are so many inner-city adults deprived of a secure foothold in the regular economy and forced instead to rely on a mix of underground and predatory activities and on the stigmatizing and flagrantly insufficient support of welfare to subsist? Why have public and private organizations declined so markedly at the core of the American metropolis? And what explains the bunching of poor blacks in these continually deteriorating enclaves?

The causes of the "hyperghettoization" of the inner city involve a complex and dynamic concatenation of economic and political factors unfolding over the whole post-war era that belies the simplistic, short-term plot of the "underclass" narrative. The most obvious, but not necessarily the most potent, of these causes is the mutation of the American economy from a closed, integrated, factory-centered, "Fordist" system catering to a uniform mass market to a more open, decentered, and service-intensive system geared to increasingly differentiated consumption patterns. A second, and too often overlooked, factor is the persistence of the near-total residential segregation of blacks and the deliberate stacking of public housing in the poorest black areas of large cities, amounting to a system of de facto urban apartheid. Third, the rentrenchment of an already miserly welfare state since the mid-1970s, combined with the cyclical downturns of the American economy, has helped guarantee increased poverty in the inner city. And, fourth, the turnaround in federal and local urban policies of the past two decades has led to the "planned shrinkage" of public services and institutions in the ghetto.

For the sake of clarity, I discuss each of these factors separately and *seriatim*, even though their full impact can be adequately assessed only by taking into account the interaction effects arising out of their changing synchronic and diachronic articulation. [16] I conclude by arguing that, on balance, it is not so much the impersonal workings of broad macroeconomic and demographic forces as the will of urban elites, i.e., their *decision to abandon the ghetto* to these forces as they have been politically (pre)structured, that best account for its virtual collapse in the 1980s and for its gloomy prospects for the remainder of this century.

Corporate Disinvestment, Polarized Growth, and the Racial Segmentation of the Low-Wage Labor Market

In the mid-1960s, beset by the saturation of domestic markets, intensifying international competition, and internal contradictions, the American economy entered a phase of transition to a new form of capitalist organization characterized by "flexible specialization," increased capital mobility, and decreased protection of wage earners (Scott and Storper 1986; Piore and Sabel 1984; Lash and Urry 1988). As the old economic system anchored in standardized industrial production, mass consumption, strong unions, and the corresponding "social contract" between large firms and their stable workforce progressively gave way to a new regime based on the dominance of service occupations, the bifurcation of financial and industrial capital, and the erosion of integrated regional economies, a sweeping reorganization of labor markets and wage structures took place.

During this period, a polarized labor demand, characterized by a widening gulf between high-wage, credentialed positions and variable-schedule, low-paying jobs, offering few benefits and no security, became a structural feature of the new American service economy (Thurow 1987; Sassen 1991). Thus, of the 23 million positions created between 1970 and 1984, a full 22 million were in the service sector, and today upwards of three-fourths of all employment is in the service industries. But nearly a third of all jobs generated in the 1980s were part-time positions and 75 percent of them were filled by people who would prefer to work full-time. Furthermore, many of these service jobs pay between four and six dollars an hour, a far cry from the hourly rate of $12 to 15 common in unionized, durable-goods manufacturing. Indeed, half of the jobs added between 1970 and 1983 paid less than $8,000 a year (Bureau of the Census 1985: table 40).

This change in the structure of labor markets was not driven by some inevitable, technologically preordained, change but resulted from the decisions of American firms to favor strategies of short-term profit and accumulation by way of reduction of their wage bill and operating costs. One study reported by Squires et al. (1987: 28) estimates that two-thirds of the 203,700 manufacturing jobs lost by the greater Chicagoland between 1977 and 1981 because of firm shutdown or "contraction" were in fact due to corporate disinvestment aimed at *transferring* activities to sites with lower land costs, cheaper labor pools, and low unionization rates, especially in the southern states and in Third World countries such as Mexico. Federal policies of government deregulation (in sectors such as transportation and communication) and high interest rates, together with the *laissez-faire* stance of the National Labor Relations Board in the last decade, assisted in this reorganization of the labor force by furthering the decline of unions and undercutting the protection of peripheral workers (Rosenberg 1983). This paved the way for the proliferation of contingent labor and subcontracting, as well as for the resurgence of homework and sweatshops. This development has been most significant for urban minority workers whose gains have historically come more from government policies than from the operation of the market.

Of these many crisscrossing forces that have reshaped the face of urban labor markets in the past 30 years, three are particularly relevant to the ghetto because they have converged to eliminate the function of reservoir of cheap, unskilled industrial labor that it assumed in the earlier state of the racial division of labor. First, the *sectoral shift* toward service employment has spelled massive cutbacks in those job categories traditionally most accessible to blacks and to the poor. Much like other major Northern cities such as New York, Detroit, Philadelphia, and Baltimore, Chicago saw its manufacturing base cut in half between the 1950s and the early 1980s. In 1947, the city had nearly 670,000 manufacturing jobs, or 70 percent of the region's total; by 1982, this figure had melted down to 277,000, representing only a third of the metropolitan total (Wacquant and Wilson 1989b). The disappearance of factory work accelerated as the decades wore on, rising from 52,000 jobs lost between 1947 and 1954 to 269,000 for the period 1967–82. Because inner-city blacks were overrepresented in factory work as late as the early 1970s, and because in addition they tended to be employed in the lowest industrial occupations and in the least protected firms of declining sectors (Stearns and Coleman 1990), they were disproportionately hurt by this sectoral reshuffling. And they continue to be primary bearers of the costs of deindustrialization in Chicago: a full 43 percent of the ghetto residents questioned by the Urban Poverty Project in 1987 reported that several or most of their friends had become unemployed owing to a plant shutdown in the previous few years (as against 31 percent in peripheral black neighborhoods). A 32-year old mother of three, laid off ten years ago from her job as an assembly-line worker, who now lives ill a South Side public housing project, reports: "There just ain't enough [jobs]. Used to be ... used to have the steel industry and all that. But they closed it down. Reagan closed that down and sent it to other states."

Secondly, the *spatial redistribution* of jobs correlative of the disagglomeration of the urban economy has also reduced the labor market options of inner-city minorities, as business moved out of central cities in search of tax breaks and cheaper labor. In the 1970s alone, while its suburbs gained employment in every occupational category, adding half a million positions on their payroll, the city of Chicago posted a net loss of some 90,000 clerical and sales jobs and of 119,000 blue-collar positions. The only categories in which it showed increases were those of managers, professionals, technical and administrative support personnel, that is, jobs requiring at least some college education (Kasarda 1989: 29) and therefore well beyond the reach of inner-city residents poorly trained by the crumbling public school system. The geographic shift of employment to the suburbs and exurbs has also impacted ghetto blacks harder owing to the gross deficiencies of public transportation. Blacks in Chicago are twice more likely than whites to use public transportation because the cost of owning and operating an automobile is beyond their means. But the underfunded public train and bus network is laid out in such a way that it isolates the suburbs from the inner city so that, "for all practical purposes, the jobs in the outer suburban areas are not accessible by public transportation from the high unemployment area" (Orfield 1985: 179).

Thirdly, the occupational shift to *higher-education jobs* has restricted the employment chances of ghetto residents because of the inability of public institutions – public schools, but also training programs and federal and local employment programs – to prepare them for this change. In Grand Boulevard, 65 percent of the adults 25 years of age and older have less than four years of high school and fewer than 3 percent have attended a four-year college. Only 16 percent of a cohort entering public high schools in the city graduate four years later at or above the national reading average. Yet, from 1970 to 1980, the number of jobs held by city workers with less than a high school education dropped by 42 percent and that held by workers who were high school graduates diminished by nearly one fifth. By contrast, the volume of jobs requiring some college education rose by 44 percent, and that of jobs mandating a college degree increased by 56 percent (Kasarda 1989).

A fourth critical factor in the economic marginalization of ghetto blacks is the *continued racial segmentation of low-wage labor* (Fainstein 1986–7; Bailey and Waldinger 1991, Waldinger and Bailey 1991). In the manufacturing and service sectors, most blacks are employed in specific "occupational niches" which contain heavy concentrations of Afro-Americans, and they are routinely excluded from others reserved to whites or even other minorities (especially Hispanics). In many service industries which have experienced rapid employment growth, such as restaurants and catering places, blacks tend to be segmented in the worst jobs and stacked in entry-level positions cut off from career ladders. Moreover, inner-city residents with low education, few skills, and scattered job experience have been pushed further down the job queue by the stepped-up competition of women and by the "new immigration," legal and illegal, which has flooded America's large cities with cheap, docile, unskilled labor as a result of the immigration law changes of the mid-1960s (Sassen 1989). A divorced mother of 38 with two children who works as a hotel cashier on the South Side complains: "Too many people, too few jobs. A thousand people go out and try for one hundred jobs. Machinery and computers are taking a lot of jobs."

Thus, at the bottom of the new postindustrial order, the growth of unskilled, service positions and downgraded manufacturing has largely bypassed inner-city blacks, as employers turned to other sources of pliable labor less likely to resist or protest superexploitative and unstable work conditions. And because the inner city has become ever more closely associated, in the public mind, with crime, depravity, and lawlessness, the mere fact of residing in the ghetto has become an additional handicap, a signal that some employers use to separate "good" (educated, middle-class) and "bad" blacks and to select ghetto inhabitants out of their pool of applicants. A 41-year-old nurse from the West Side complains: "I have been to jobs, and I have friends who have gone to jobs, and they asked them what neighborhood [they were from]. And as soon as they look at your address, they say "Wow! you live in this area!', you know."

The *stigma attached to ghetto residence* is yet another hurdle that inner-city blacks have to vanquish in the job search: "I think that if you have a decent address, it helps a lot," says an unemployed mother aged 37 living on the South Side. "Like when you apply to jobs, they see it's not the heart of the ghetto." [17]

All in all, the polarization of the occupational and wage structure, the downgrading of jobs, and the hardening of racial segmentation at the bottom of the labor market have effectively dried up the work options of ghetto blacks, pushing more of them into the only employment sector to which they readily have access: the irregular informal economy of the inner city.

Racial Segregation and the Concentration of Black Poverty via Housing Policies

But structural economic changes alone can hardly account for the accumulation of social dislocations in the ghetto. Racial segregation is the crucial intervening variable that explains how poor blacks have been severed from the new job openings of the decentralized service economy, and disabled from pursuing social mobility through spatial mobility. The continued residential segregation of poor blacks in the inner city is central to the decline of the ghetto because, in tandem with the suburbanization of whites (and, increasingly in recent years, of middle-class blacks), it underlies a distribution of employment opportunities, school chances, taxable wealth, and political influence that deprives them from all supports for socio-economic betterment (Orfield 1985). It thus operates in the manner of a "multiplier effect" that concentrates hardship in the urban core. Because recent discussions of the inner city have tended to gloss over the issue of race, sometimes to the point of total eclipse, as when "ghetto" is unabashedly equated with any high-poverty area irrespective of population and institutional makeup (e.g., Jargowsky and Bane 1991), it is not superfluous to reaffirm that *the perpetuation of the ghetto is first and foremost an expression of the persistence of the urban color line.*

Though it elected a black mayor in 1982, Chicago enjoys the dubious privilege of being the most racially segregated metropolis in America. As of 1980, over two-thirds of the city's 1.2 million blacks lived in tracts over 95 percent black. The segregation index has changed little since the 1950s; it even rose from 89 in 1970 to 92 in 1980 (out of a maximum of 100) as the proportion of blacks residing in all-black tracts grew slightly.[18] The "exposure index," another commonly used measure of segregation, reveals that the typical black person in the city lives on a block that is 4.5 percent white (though whites make up close to half of the city's population) while the block of the typical white resident is a paltry 2.6 percent black. Afro-Americans are virtually as separated residentially from other groups, including Hispanics, whose settlements tend to function as "buffer zones" between white and black neighborhoods (Squires et al. 1987: 111), as if they lived under a regime of legal apartheid. What is more, blacks are the only group to suffer such intense racial separation, as families of Hispanic and Oriental descent exhibit a comparatively moderate to low level of segregation. Thus, in the thirty largest US metropolitan areas, Latinos and Asians are more likely to share residence with whites than with their own group, whereas the likelihood of white–black contact based on residence rarely exceeds 5 percent (Massey and Denton 1987).[19]

It is important to stress that the unique residential isolation of Afro-Americans is not an expression of ethnic affinity and choice, for in both principle and conduct blacks overwhelmingly prefer to live in racially mixed neighborhoods (Streitweiser and Goodman 1983; Farley et al. 1978). Nor is it due to income differences between black and white families. Were that the case, the expansion of the black middle class since the 1960s would have been accompanied by a noticeable decrease in racial separation. In point of fact, if the Afro-American population were distributed in a color-blind, strictly income-driven housing market, the percentage of blacks per census tract in Chicago would range from a low of 10 percent to a high of 27 percent (Berry 1979: 9). Unlike other groups in US society, Afro-Americans who climb the class hierarchy do not experience a decrease in ostracization.

The color line is the result, first, of the persistent *dualization of the housing market along racial lines* (Foley 1973; Berry 1979). Forced racial steering by rental and sales agents, as well as bias in mortgage financing and informal white obstruction to the housing search process – all of them condoned by the reticence of Congress and the federal government to enforce existing Fair Housing laws – are still prevalent in large cities such as Chicago (Schlay 1987; Yinger 1987). Blacks who attempt to move out of the territory set apart for them encounter reticence, unease, if not outright hostility and violent resistance. While sizable majorities of whites agree on principle that people have a right to reside wherever they wish, this is a right that they continue to reserve for themselves: most whites would refuse to live in a neighborhood containing more than a small percentage of blacks and few support local ordinances designed to implement this principle (Massey and Gross 1991). [20]

A second major cause of continued racial segregation is the *housing and urban renewal policies* implemented by federal and municipal governments since the 1950s, which have intentionally trapped and packed poor Afro-Americans in the poorest all-black areas of the central city. The historical myopia of the contemporary debate on the "underclass" should not obscure the fact that the crumbling of today's ghetto is the tailspin of a downward spiral whose initial impetus was given some five decades ago by Washington's housing policies. [21] As Kenneth Jackson (1985: 219) shows in his authoritative history of American suburbanization, from the Wagner-Steagall Act of 1937, which legally established government responsibility to aid low-cost housing, to the present,

> the result, if not the intent, of the public housing program in the United States [has been] to segregate the races, to concentrate the disadvantaged in inner cities, and to reinforce the image of suburbia as a place of refuge for the problems of race, crime and poverty.

The state's approach for resolving the tensions of race and class in the struggle over scarce urban space and resources in the post-war era was indeed two-pronged. On the one side, the federal government underwrote the massive subsidization of *middle-class* housing in the suburbs through a combination of tax deductions, federal mortgage guarantees, and highway construction, while local zoning ordinances and racial restrictions enforced or "overlooked" by the Federal Housing Agency ensured that only *whites* would move out of the city. Until 1949, it was the official policy of the FHA to refuse to insure any unsegregated housing, and this agency did not require nondiscriminatory pledges from loan applicants until 1962. To this day, the Fair Housing legislation passed by Congress in 1968 has been given no enforcement apparatus. The Department of Justice has litigated but a handful of cases nationwide annually and even reduced requests for compensation under the Reagan administration.

On the other side, the state also embarked on a scheme of public assistance to low-income housing, but with two major differences. First, in sharp contrast with middle-class, white suburban construction, state help for housing blacks and the poor was remarkably stingy: from 1937 to 1968, 10 million middle- and upper-income private units sprang up with the backing of the Federal Housing Agency, while only 800,000 hastily and cheaply built public units were erected with federal housing subsidies (Kerner Commission 1989: 474). Second, because municipalities were granted discretion over whether or not to build public housing and where to locate it, federal projects invariably reinforced segregation, as peripheral white localities refused to create public housing authorities and white city neighborhoods ferociously resisted the penetration of blacks into their territory. In Chicago, white racial violence from below and white political manipulation from above converged to constrict the placement of CHA housing exclusively within the existing ghetto boundaries, "thus fixing and institutionalizing its borders like never before" (Hirsch 1983: 409). Nearly all public housing developed in the 1950s and 1960s was located squarely inside or immediately vicinal to the traditional Black Belts of the South Side and West Side. As of 1981, 95 percent of all Chicago Housing Authority family rental units were occupied by blacks. Instead of building low-density housing on cheaper and less congested land outside central cities, as western European countries did, the US government fostered the dumping of shoddy high-rises into the most poverty-impacted neighborhoods, making public housing over into a federally built and supported slum.

As early as 1968, the Kerner Commission (1989: 474) pointed out that "federal housing programs concentrate the most impoverished and dependent segments of the population into the central-city ghettos where there is already a critical gap between the needs of the population and the public resources to deal with them." This gap has done nothing but widen in the subsequent two decades as funds for public housing dried up and the city stopped building and even maintaining CHA units after it was found guilty of racial discrimination and put under court order to construct scattered-site public housing in racially mixed neighborhoods. To this day, the United States remains the only industrialized country in the world without significant public support of low-income housing, despite the obvious fact that private developers will not build for the poor – in 1980, publicly-owned housing represented about 1 percent of the American housing market, compared to some 46 percent in England and 37 percent in France. It is also the only advanced nation to have generated a state-enforced "vertical ghetto" doubly segregated on the basis of race and class. [22]

If poor blacks are so concentrated in the hyperghetto of the 1980s, then, it is first because the tolerance of government for the abiding, blatant racial segmentation of the housing market makes it harder for them to move out of the urban core by artificially raising the cost of home-ownership and rentals in peripheral Afro-American neighborhoods; and, second, because what meager and inferior low-income housing has been built by the state was deliberately put there.

The Retrenchment of America's Miserly Welfare State

The retreat of the welfare state during the 1970s and 1980s is another major political cause of the ongoing deterioration of the life chances of ghetto residents. Contrary to popular neoconservative rhetoric (Murray 1984), the past two decades have not been a period of expansion and generosity for welfare but one of blanket retraction. AFDC has become steadily less helpful to poor families since 1970 for failure to index grants on inflation and insufficient funding: program outlays peaked at 1.6 percent of the federal budget in 1973 and have declined steadily ever since. Not only has public aid been rationed via legal and bureaucratic restrictions on eligibility (Susser and Resnick 1987; Axinn and Stern 1988). The purchasing power of the average welfare grant has also been cut substantially. According to a study by the Center on Budget and Policy Priorities in Washington, DC (reported in the *Chicago Tribune*, August 16, 1990, p. 20), the real dollar value of the average cash grant to families on public aid in the state of Illinois has diminished by more than one-half since 1970. Presently, a family of three on AFDC receives, under the best of circumstances, a maximum of $645 a month, including food stamps, a sum barely equal to the rent of an average one-bedroom apartment in Chicago.

As a consequence of program changes and reductions in expenditures since the mid-1970s, *government cash transfers have ceased to play the compensating role they fulfilled* in the preceding decade, when poverty among ghetto blacks was slowly decreasing. Based on a detailed analysis of the rates of "effectiveness" of government welfare programs, that is, their ability to lift recipients above the poverty line, Axinn and Stern (1988: 102) contend that "the explosion of central city poverty was much more the result of declining program effectiveness than economic breakdown." Indeed, the effectiveness rate of government programs is lowest in the central cities where it has also decreased substantially over time: in 1983, 29.9 percent of their families nationwide were poor before transfer and 18.4 percent after, for an effectiveness rate of 38 percent, compared to a rate of 50 percent in 1973 when the corresponding poverty figures were 27.5 percent and 14 percent. If public programs had retained their limited effectiveness of the 1970s, they would have cushioned the effects of deindustrialization and polarized economic growth so that the poverty rate in cities would have grown by only one percentage point, from 14 percent to 15 percent. The deficiencies of American social policies becomes even more glaring when one contrasts the US with neighboring Canada – nary a world leader in welfare generosity. Economists Rebecca Blank and Maria Hanratty (1991) have demonstrated that if the United States adopted the Canadian system of anti-poverty transfer measures, the poverty rate for single-parent families would decrease from 43 percent to between 2 and 16 percent, depending on a range of assumptions about participation rates and labor supply. A genuine welfare policy would in effect nearly eradicate poverty among female-headed households, which account for an overwhelming majority of the ghetto poor today.

Those pushed out of the labor market have also been adversely affected by the *increased insufficiencies of social insurance*. In theory, the standard program for Unemployment Insurance is designed to meet cyclical needs and provides 26 weeks of coverage at about 40 percent of previous wages. However, in the face of persistent mass joblessness since the mid-1970s, the system has been bursting at the seams. Business lobbying and political concern with costs reduction have conspired to produce a severe tightening of eligibility and have multiplied administrative obstacles to benefit delivery. As

a consequence, the percentage of the unemployed covered nationwide declined from 50 to 30 percent of the jobless between 1975
and 1985. Again, this decline was particularly pronounced in large
cities and was especially detrimental to inner-city minorities who,
being confined in the lowest segments of the secondary labor market,
are more likely to have short work tenures and frequent employer
changes. In fact, most intermittently employed ghetto residents rarely
become eligible for unemployment benefits when they lose their jobs.

*The fiscal policies of the state and federal governments have also added
to the plight of the ghetto.* The adverse repercussions of Reagan's
federal tax policies on the poor are amply documented; less well
known is the fact that many states have evolved tax schemes that
further worsen the already precarious position of low-income families.
According to figures compiled by the advocacy group Voices for
Illinois Children, hundreds of thousands of such families in Illinois
pay a substantial portion of their meager income in state taxes.
Illinois has the second heaviest combined state and local tax burden
on the poor after Kentucky. As a result, the state's poorest 20
percent households pay nearly 11 percent of their yearly income
in state and local taxes, twice the percentage borne by the richest
1 percent. A preponderance of evidence thus suggests that public
neglect, not the emergence of an "underclass," explains rising poverty
and exclusion in the urban core.

Sacrificing the Inner City: "Planned Shrinkage" and the Political Marginality of the Ghetto

Public neglect does not stop at welfare policy but extends to the
whole gamut of urban services. In the 1950s and 1960s, the steady
expansion of the economy created a context favorable to oppositional movements, and black demands for a less unequal sharing
of urban resources were partially met by an expansion of federal
and local programs. The economic retrenchment of the 1970s and
polarized growth of the 1980s, by contrast, fueled a sweeping political
and business backlash against public efforts for the amelioration of
inner city. [23]

At the federal level, starting after Nixon's 1973 landslide re-elec-
tion, a sudden *turnaround in urban policies* was effected by the government that practically annulled and even reversed the modest gains
of the War on Poverty. Public housing funds were frozen and later
replaced with federal sharing grants controlled by local elites who
redirected them to the benefit of the real estate industry and property owners. A whole array of compensatory programs aimed at

keeping inner-city institutions viable, originally set up under the umbrella of the Great Society, were successively frozen, cut, and dropped. In the 1980s, federal resources directed at cities continued to erode with the termination of the CETA (Comprehensive Employment and Training Act) job training program, of General Revenue Sharing, and of Urban Development Grants. As urban machines and local parties were shunted from national politics and became electorally expendable, the system of intergovernmental grants that had cushioned the hardships of the urban poor across political boundaries was unhinged. The political isolation of cities, in turn, reinforced their role as entrepreneurs rather than providers of social services, further fragmenting the revenue base on which the financing of public institutions rests (Weir 1991).

At the local level, a coalition of business, banking, and commercial interests used the fiscal crisis of cities to press for the dismantling of social programs that sustained ghetto residents and their neighborhoods. They were joined by urban planners who saw in the rolling back of city services an efficient means of pushing the poor outside of the areas slated for revitalization. The result was what historian Robert Fisher (1984) has called *planned shrinkage* or "triage" of inner-city neighborhoods: the selective curtailment of public services such as schools, libraries, clinics, police stations, and firehouses, designed to goad the poor to leave the urban core and to free up resources for corporate and middle-class redevelopment in other neighborhoods. Thus, in Chicago, since the mid-1970s the location of public facilities and infrastructural outlays, land clearance decisions, and tax abatements have increasingly served to attract and boost private capital and to expand a new downtown dedicated to finance, management, and middle-class services. This diversion of resources has allowed but a trickle of public investment to flow into the ghetto neighborhoods of the West Side and South Side, leaving them in stasis and decrepitude (Squires et al. 1987).

Few organizations are more revealing of the degree of institutional abandonment suffered by Chicago's ghetto than are public schools. For they have in effect been reduced to *custodial* rather than educational facilities that serve more to ensnare the poor than to open an escape hatch out of the ghetto. Public schools are rigidly stratified by both race and income, with racial segregation unchanged and class segregation rising since the 1960s. Today's inner-city children attend class in establishments whose student body is generally entirely minority and over 80 per cent from families living below the poverty line. They are educated in the oldest, most overcrowded facilities, in larger classes led by teachers trained in the least selective colleges, and with fewer counselors than either suburban or private city schools. For instance, of the 601 pupils attending the Julia Lathrop School on the city's West Side in 1985, all of them blacks, 592 qualified for free breakfast and lunch. As of that year, the school had gone two decades without a library (books were left to gather mold in the lunchroom) and had no Parent Teacher Association. Many of its windows were boarded up or broken and its walls covered with graffiti; its basketball court had no hoops and its playground was littered with broken glass. Its teachers come from the outside and rarely venture into the community for fear of crime. Indeed, it is difficult to get substitute teachers to come at all once they find out the location and condition of the school: "When they see the building and the neighborhood," the principal laments, "they just keep on driving. You can't even get a taxi to bring you here" (*Chicago Tribune* 1986: 151–2).

The segregated public high schools of the city feed into a system of public community colleges that are also defined by race and poverty. And with drop-out rates soaring well above 50 percent (compared to 2.5 percent in the suburbs) and three in four schools unequipped to train students for entrance to a college requiring a reasonable scholastic level, higher education is out of the realm of the possible for the mass of ghetto adolescents. This leads Gary Orfield (1985: 176) to insist that they face

> a separate and unequal set of educational opportunities that continues throughout their schooling. One could easily argue that their educational experiences are not intended to and cannot prepare [them] to function in the same society and the same economy.

Because they serve a population that public officials consider expendable, ghetto schools are also on the front line of the budget cuts periodically imposed by a Board of Education perpetually strapped for funds. In the summer of 1991, the Chicago school superintendent announced plans to close down sixteen schools to try to reduce an unexpected $200 million revenue shortfall: fourteen of them were in poor black neighborhoods (*Chicago Tribune*, 5 July 1991). And parochial schools are no longer able to fill the gap created by the breakdown of public education: just a year earlier, the Chicago archdiocese had revealed plans to close down 17 establishments because of severe financial difficulties, 11 of them in poor black neighborhoods.

The degradation of public schools is matched perhaps only by that of public health facilities. In 1990 the Acting Health Commissioner of Chicago publicly acknowledged that the city's public health system "is a nonsystem ... that is falling short and close to falling apart" (*Chicago Tribune*, 16 January 1990). Because of low and tardy Medicaid reimbursements, a dozen inner-city clinics and hospitals have gone bankrupt in the past two decades. In 1987 Provident Hospital, the nation's oldest black hospital, founded nearly a century ago, closed its doors, leaving the South Side virtually without a hospital facility accessible to the poor. Four years later, local government has yet to fulfill its promise to put it back in operation.

Other than the excessively overburdened Cook County Hospital, no private health care provider in the Chicagoland area readily offers prenatal care to uninsured women. The "perinatal dumping" of ghetto patients is also a routine practice: poor women with no health insurance likely to have high-risk pregnancies are regularly turned away by private hospitals that do not hesitate to violate the law by transferring them to Cook County Hospital even during active labor (*Chicago Tribune* 1989). Inner-city residents clamor not for high-tech medical treatment but for the most basic care such as immunizations for children, Pap tests for women, high blood pressure and cholesterol screening, and nurses to visit poor patients. As a consequence of this "medical gridlock," whereas the infant mortality rate for whites in the state of Illinois stood at 9.3 per 1,000 births in 1985, the figure for blacks was 21.4 per 1,000 (*Statistical Abstract of the United States*, table 116). And in many ghetto areas, this rate has risen above 3 percent, exceeding that of Third World countries such as Costa Rica or Mali. Every year, over 1,000 newborns die in Chicago's ghetto and another 3,000 are born with brain damage and other serious neurological ailments.

Detailed ecological and medical research conducted in New York City on the synergistic pattern of increased health care inequality, violent death and homelessness, the spread of AIDS and substance abuse has established a direct causal relation between the urban desertification and social disintegration of ghetto neighborhoods on the one hand, and reductions in municipal services such as fire control, police protection, and sanitation to levels far below those needed to maintain urban population densities on the other (Wallace and Wallace 1990). Wherever city services have been cut or terminated, rates of morbidity and social dereliction have shot up, setting off a self-reinforcing cycle of urban decay and deadly violence sending entire neighborhoods into a spiral of deterioration.

The welfare system also interacts with landlords to aggravate the living conditions of ghetto residents and indirectly contributes to the profusion of substandard housing. Knowing that their tenants are a trapped clientele, slum landlords – including public housing authorities – charge high rents and neglect necessary repairs and services while receiving full rent for apartments that only welfare recipients would consider occupying (Susser and Krensike 1987: 57). Thus, in Chicago many public housing buildings are literally crumbling and nearly all of them have multiple violations of municipal housing codes They are commonly infested with roaches, rats, and maggots. High-rise projects such as the Henry Horner Homes on the city's West Side or Cabrini Green on the Near North Side have no entry halls and no security guards, broken elevators, walls covered with graffiti, and unlit, urine-stenched stairwells. Apartments on the first floor are generally abandoned and boarded up for lack of safety. Most units in Henry Horner have not seen a coat of paint since 1970 and are in such a state of disrepair that in June of 1991 the Henry Horner Mothers Guild filed a suit against the Chicago Housing Authority for overseeing a "de facto demolition" of their site: nearly half of the 1,760 units of the complex were vacant for lack of funds to renovate or clean them for rental.

The collapse of public institutions in the urban core and the sustained marginality of the ghetto population are thus the creation of a politics that has fragmented the public sphere, weakened black political capacities (Fainstein and Fainstein 1989), and stimulated exit into the private sector of all those who could afford it, leaving the poorest fractions of the Afro-American working class to rot in the social purgatory of the hyperghetto.

Concluding Notes

Alejandro Portes (1972: 286, emphasis added) remarks in a famous article on the shanty towns of Latin America that "*the grave mistake of theories on the urban slum has been to transform sociological conditions into psychological traits* and to impute to the victims the distorted characteristics of their victimizers." This is an apt characterization of the recent scholarly and public policy debate on the ghetto in the United States. By focusing narrowly on the presumed behavioral and cultural deficiencies of inner-city residents or on the aggregate impact of the consolidation of a postindustrial economic order without paying due notice of the historical structures of racial and class inequality, spatial separation, and governmental (in)action that filter or amplify it, recent discussions on the so-called underclass have hidden the political roots of the predicament of the ghetto and contributed to the further stigmatization and political isolation of its residents.

There is no room here to address the numerous analytical inconsistencies, grave empirical flaws, and policy dangers of the *demi-savant* concept of "underclass,"[24] including its internal instability and heterogeneity, which make it possible to redraw its boundaries at will to fit the ideological interests at hand; its essentialism, which permits a slippage from substantive to substance, from measurement to reality, leading to mistake a *statistical artifact* for an actual social group; its far-flung negative moral connotations and its falsely "deracialized" ring allowing those who use it to speak about race without appearing to do so. Suffice it, by way of conclusion, to highlight its built-in propensity to sever the ghetto from the broader sociopolitical structures of caste and class domination of which the latter is both a product and a central mechanism.

By reviving and modernizing the century-old notion that urban poverty is the result of the personal vices and collective pathologies of the poor, the rhetoric of the "underclass" has given a veneer of scientific legitimacy to middle-class fears of the black subproletariat and blocked an accurate, historically grounded analysis of the changing political articulation of racial segregation, class inequality, and state abandonment in the American city. It has diverted attention away from the institutional arrangements in education, housing, welfare, transportation, and health and human services that perpetuate the concentration of unemployed and underemployed blacks in the urban core. By omitting to relate the state of the ghetto to the breakdown of the public sector, it has absolved the urban, housing, and educational choices made by the federal and local governments of both Democratic and Republican stripes since the mid-1970s.

Yet it is this policy of abandonment and punitive containment of the black poor that explains that, one century after its creation and two decades after the country's aborted and ill-named "War on Poverty," the American ghetto remains, to borrow a line from the preface to the Kerner Commission Report (1989: xx) of 1968, "the personification of that nation's shame, of its deepest failure, and its greatest challenge."

NOTES

1 "The Ghetto," by Leroy Hutson, Donna Hathaway, Al Eaton, and Todd Shaw, copyright © 1990, Don Pow Music; administered by Peer International Music Corporation, all rights reserved; used by permission

(from the album *Short Dog's in the House*, 1990; Zomba Recording Corp.).

2 These lines were written before the South-Central Los Angeles events of April 1992, but the near-complete disappearance of the latter from public debate only weeks after their onset does not encourage me to revise this introductory statement. Indeed, most remarkable about this partially race-based outbreak of urban violence is how thoroughly it was assimilated to preexisting images and discourses on the ghetto (to the point of disfigurement since this erased its multi-ethnic composition as well as its class dimension) and how little impact it has had on policy and scholarly discussion on the nexus of race, class, and state in the city – as if it had been no more than a "reality show," if a particularly lurid and frightful one (Wacquant 1993b).

3 Thus research on "urban poverty" over the past decade has been fixated on issues of family, welfare, and deviance (in the realms of sexuality and crime in particular), at the cost of neglecting, if not obfuscating, both the deepening class disparities and racial division of American society and the political power shifts that have allowed a range of public policies (in education, housing, health, urban development, justice, etc.) to curtail life chances in the inner city. The issues of family structure, race, and poverty have become virtually confounded (Zinn 1989), as if some necessary causal relation obtained among them. Likewise, the question of urban decline and race have become thoroughly embroiled, so much so that the term "urban" has become a euphemism for poor blacks and other dominated ethnoracial categories (Franklin 1991: ch. 4).

4 Conversely, not all low-income areas are ghettos, however extreme their destitution: think of declining white industrial cities of the deindustrializing Midwest such as Pontiac, Michigan, rural counties of the Mississippi delta, Native American reservations, or entire portions of the United States in the 1930s. To call any area exhibiting a high rate or concentration of poverty a ghetto is not only arbitrary (what is the appropriate cut-off point and for what unit of measurement?); it robs the term of its historical meaning and empties it of its sociological contents, thereby thwarting investigation of the precise mechanisms and criteria whereby exclusion operates (discussions with Martin Sanchez-Jankowski helped me clarify this point).

5 Perhaps it was necessary, to produce this odd discursive formation, composed largely of empirically dressed moralizations and policy invocations, whose primary function is to insulate and shelter "mainstream" society from the threat and taint of poor blacks by symbolically removing them from it, for proponents of the underclass mythology to first studiously remove themselves from the ghetto in order to "theorize" it from afar and above, and only through the reassuring buffer of their bureaucratic research apparatus. One example: it is remarkable (and unfortunately rather typical) that, of the 27 authors who contributed to the lavishly financed and publicized collection of conference papers

pithily entitled *The Urban Underclass* (Jencks and Peterson 1991), only
one has carried out extensive first-hand observation inside the ghetto.

6 In an original yet regrettably often overlooked network analytic study,
Melvin Oliver (1988) provides a suggestive portrait of the urban Afro-
American community as clusters of interpersonal ties that directly belies
its common representation as a hotbed of social disaffiliation and pathologies. He finds in particular that the residents of Los Angeles's historic ghetto of Watts and of the newer segregated middle-class area of
Crenshaw–Baldwin Hills have quite similar networks (as characterized
by their size, relational context, spatial distribution, density, strandedness,
and reciprocity) and that extralocal ties with kin are equally prevalent in
both areas.

7 See Spear (1967), Philpott (1978), and Drake and Cayton (1962, vol. 1)
in the case of Chicago's ghetto, and Kusmer (1986) and Franklin (1980)
for a broader historical overview of black urbanization. It is not possible
here to give an adequate treatment of the historical roots of the trajectory of the dark ghetto in the *longue durée* of its lifespan. Suffice it to
point out that, even though its motor causes are situated outside of it,
the transformation of the ghetto is, as with every social form, mediated
in part by its internal structure so that a full resolution of its recent
evolution must start a century ago, in the decades of its incubation.

8 For instance, in 1930, at a time when the all-black South Side ghetto
already grouped over 90 percent of the city's Afro-American population, Chicago's "Little Ireland" was a hodge-podge of 25 "nationalities"
composed of only one-third Irish persons and containing a bare 3 percent
of the city's residents of Irish descent (Philpott 1978: 141–2).

9 Unless otherwise indicated, quotes from interviews and first-hand observations come from fieldwork I conducted on Chicago's South Side in
1988–91 in the course of an ethnographic study of the culture and
economy of professional boxing in the ghetto.

10 Violence is an aspect of ghetto life that is difficult to discuss without
immediately calling forth the willfully gory – and often grossly misleading
– images of stereotypical media descriptions of crime and lawlessness
that have become a staple of political and intellectual discourse on the
"underclass." Yet, based on my ethnographic fieldwork on Chicago's
South Side, I feel that any account of the ghetto must start with this
violence because of its experiential acuity and enormously disruptive
ramifications in the lives of those trapped in it. At the same time, I
want to insist, if only by way of prolepsis, first that inner-city violence
is, in its forms and organization, quite different from what journalistic
accounts reveal, in some ways not as horrific and in other ways much
worse, owing in particular to its routine and socially entropic character.
Second, this internecine violence "from below" must be analyzed not as
an expression of "pathology" but as a function of the degree of penetration and mode of regulation of this territory by the state – a response
to various kinds of violence "from above" and a by-product of the

political abandonment of public institutions in the urban core (Wacquant 1993b). I have tried elsewhere (see Wacquant 1992a) to offer a more nuanced account, from the inside, of the impact of systemic insecurity on the texture of everyday life in the ghetto, as seen through the eyes and survival strategies of a professional hustler who works the streets of Chicago's South Side.

11 To be sure, this class differentiation has existed in more or less attenuated forms since the origins of the Black Belt: the latter was never the *gemeinschaftliche* compact that analysts nostalgic of a "golden age" of the ghetto that never existed sometimes invoke. However brutal, the caste division imposed by whites never obliterated internal cleavages along class lines (partly convergent with persistent skin color differences) among Afro-Americans, as can be seen, for instance, in the spread of "store-front churches" in the face of old-line Baptist and Methodist churches in the 1920s (Spear 1967: ch. 9) or in the bifurcation of the "jook continuum" and the "urban-commercial complex" in the realm of dance and entertainment (Hazzard-Gordon 1990).

12 This survey was conducted as part of the Urban Poverty and Family Structure Project (directed by William Julius Wilson) at the University of Chicago. It consists of a multi-stage, random probability sample of residents of Chicago's poor neighborhoods (defined as census tracts with at least 20 percent poor persons in them in 1980) conducted in 1986–7. The survey covered 1,184 blacks, with a completion rate of about 80 percent, of whom a third lived on the city's South Side and West Side. The financial support of the Ford Foundation, the Carnegie Corporation, the US Department of Health and Human Services, the Institute for Research on Poverty, the Joyce Foundation, the Lloyd A. Fry Foundation, the Rockefeller Foundation, the Spencer Foundation, the William T. Grant Foundation, the Woods Charitable Fund, and the Chicago Community Trust for this research is gratefully acknowledged.

13 The fact that an increasing number of urban middle-class blacks have never experienced ghetto life firsthand (though, having generally lived in sharply segregated, all-black areas, they are fully acquainted with discriminatory and other racist practices) is bound to affect processes of black identity formation, individual and collective. The meaning that middle-class blacks attach to a range of ghetto idioms and expressive symbols (e.g., musical genres, hairdos and dress codes, linguistic demeanor) is likely to change when exposure to them comes from family lore or from secondary sources such as formal education and the popular media rather than through native immersion.

14 Interview excerpts in this section are drawn from data collected as part of the Urban Poverty and Family Structure Project (see n. 12 above).

15 But even such low-wage jobs are more often than not unavailable: another contrast between the monetary economy and the informal or illegal street economy is that the latter constantly offers *some* opportunity for "action" and income (especially since the expansion of mass drug

distribution) whereas the former periodically dries up. Thus the conventional relation between these two sectors of activity may be reversed: official employment is seen as irregular and unreliable while underground activities, taken collectively, appear regular and dependable: "You can *always* rack up somethin' off a back-alley and hustle some money on the street, Louie: *always*."

16 Thus, for instance, racial segregation, though nominally constant over the post-war era, operates variably both in the manner of a Keynesian "accelerator" amplifying the effect of external economic changes and as an enabling political precondition for the curtailment of public services in the urban core.

17 The two stigmata borne by ghetto residents on the labor market (and everywhere else), that of skin color and that attached to dwelling in a reviled locale publicly regarded as the breeding ground and epitome of "social pathology," are obviously not independent of each other. But neither are they confounded in their nature or identical in their effects. Racial markers are impossible to shed for nearly all African-Americans but their signification can at least be inverted and revalorized from within (according to the paradigm "Black is beautiful"). Residential taint may, in many situations, be shed by adept techniques of impression management. But having to hide one's place of residence from outsiders (including other blacks), especially when these are official agents of dominant institutions such as firms, schools, or government bureaucracies, who often have the means to uncover it at some point, constantly reactivates the sense of social indignity, and there is no way of effecting a reversal of the symbolic valence of ghetto dwelling (few today could effectively advocate "living in the ghetto is beautiful"). For a more detailed analysis of the logic of territorial stigmatization and its disintegrative impact on the structure of social relations in the ghetto, see Wacquant 1993a: 369–75.

18 The segregation index reaches 100 when racial groups are totally disjoint (i.e., when all city blocks are racially homogeneous, either 100 percent black or 100 percent white) and 0 when every block has the same black–white composition as the city as a whole. Other measures of segregation turn up the same pattern and reveal that Afro-Americans are unique in urban America in that they suffer extreme segregation in every possible dimension simultaneously: unevenness, isolation, clustering, centralization, and concentration (Massey and Denton 1989).

19 Of course, these populations themselves are not homogeneous in this regard. The category "Latino," for instance, is made up of different ethnonational and immigration streams that face widely varying conditions of entry and incorporation into America's social and physical space. The integration of Cubans, Mexicans, and Puerto Ricans differs notably, the situation of the latter being closer to that of African-Americans owing to the pronounced antagonism they encounter based on skin color – though, here again, the Puerto Rican urban community

is not cut of one cloth, as shown by Padilla's (1987) depiction of "Puerto Rican Chicago" and Rodriguez's (1989: esp. ch. 3) portrait of the "Rainbow People."

20 A survey of Detroit conducted in the mid-1970s found that 42 percent of whites would feel uncomfortable in a neighborhood comprising as little as one-fifth blacks, and fully half of the whites interviewed would be unwilling to move into such an area (Farley et al. 1978). There is no indication that more recent figures would differ greatly.

21 Most theories of the "underclass" go no further back than 1970 and focus on the seventies as the decade of its putative "emergence," largely for the reason that tract-level census data on poverty rates and associated variables are not readily available for previous years.

22 Owing to the rapid dwindling of federal funds, not to mention the shameless plundering of public coffers by high-level federal and local officials, most large cities are not only financially unable to ensure the upkeep of their already insufficient stock of low-income housing. Their oversight bureaucracies have also in many cases lost all control over the day-to-day management of their property. The ultimate hypocrisy and crowning act of abandonment consists then in proposing (as Bush's Secretary of Housing and Urban Development, Jack Kemp, did) that public housing tenants be "promoted" to ownership of housing that is so run down and unsafe that public authority cannot establish itself over it, save by means of a quasi-military occupation riding roughshod over the basic civil rights of tenants, as was done in a media-fashioned reaction to a series of killings in Chicago's infamous Cabrini Green project in the winter of 1992.

23 A full analysis of this backlash, its social roots and racial imagery, its political mediations, and its differential impact upon the various state programs and bureaucracies that serve (or control) diverse components of the ghetto population is needed here. I refer the reader to George Lipsitz's (1989: ch. 8) fascinating account of its onset in the city of St Louis for one case study, and to Edsall and Edsall (1991) for a suggestive discussion of the nexus between "race, rights, and taxes."

24 See Wacquant (1992b) for an analysis of the functions of the scholarly myth of the "underclass" in the intellectual and political-journalistic fields and of the sources of its social success. For a cogent discussion of its policy liabilities, see Gans (1991).

References

Anderson, Elijah 1991: *Streetwise: Race, Class, and Change in an Urban Community*. Chicago: University of Chicago Press.

Aschenbrenner, Joyce 1975: *Lifelines: Black Families in Chicago*. Prospect Heights: Waveland Press.

Auletta, Ken 1982: *The Underclass*. New York: Vintage.

Axinn June and Mark J. Stern 1988: *Poverty and Dependency: Old Problems in a New World*. Lexington: Lexington Books.

Bailey, Thomas and Roger Waldinger 1991: "The Changing Ethnic/Racial Division of Labor," in *Dual City: Restructuring New York*, ed. John H. Mollenkopf and Manuel Castells. New York: Russell Sage Foundation, pp. 43–78.

Beeghley, Leonard 1984: "Illusion and Reality in the Measurement of Poverty," *Social Problems* 31 (February): 322–33.

Berry, Brian J. L. 1979: *The Open Housing Question: Race and Housing in Chicago, 1966–1976*. Cambridge, MA: Ballinger.

Blank, Rebecca M. and Maria J. Hanratty 1991: "Responding to Need: A Comparison of Social Safety Nets in the United States and Canada," Center for Urban Affairs and Policy Research, Working Paper, Northwestern University.

Blauner, Robert 1989: *Black Lives, White Lives: Three Decades of Race Relations in America*. Berkeley: University of California Press.

Boskin, Joseph 1970: "The Revolt of the Urban Ghettos, 1964–1967," in *Roots of Rebellion: The Evolution of Black Politics and Protest Since World War II*, ed. Richard P. Young. New York: Harper and Row, pp. 309–27.

Bourgois, Philippe 1989: "In Search of Horatio Alger: Culture and Ideology in the Crack Economy," *Contemporary Drug Problems* (Winter): 619–49.

Brune, Tom and Eduardo Camacho 1983: *A Special Report: Race and Poverty in Chicago*. Chicago: The Chicago Reporter and the Center for Community Research and Assistance.

Bureau of the Census 1985: *Current Population Reports*, series P-60, no. 146. Washington, DC: Government Printing Office.

Chicago Tribune (Staff of the) 1986: *The American Millstone: An Examination of the Nation's Permanent Underclass*. Chicago: Contemporary Books.

Chicago Tribune 1989: "High-Risk Pregnancies Dumped on County Hospital, Study Finds," January 24.

Chicago Tribune 1990: "School Lets Out, Fear Rushes In: Gangs Terrorize Area after Classes," January 24.

Clark, Kenneth B. 1965: *Dark Ghetto: Dilemmas of Social Power*. New York: Harper.

Collins, Sharon M. 1983: "The Making of the Black Middle Class," *Social Problems*, vol. 3, no. 4 (April): 369–82.

Curtis, Lynn A. 1985: *American Violence and Public Policy*. New Haven: Yale University Press.

Drake, St Clair and Horace R. Cayton 1962 [1945]: *Black Metropolis: A Study of Negro Life in a Northern City*, 2 vols, rev. and enlarged edn. New York: Harper and Row.

Edsall, Thomas Byrne and Mary D. Edsall 1991: *Chain Reaction*. New York: Norton.

Fainstein, Norman 1986-7: "The Underclass/Mismatch Hypothesis as an Explanation for Black Economic Deprivation," *Politics and Society*, vol. 15, no. 4: 403–52.

Fainstein, Norman 1993: "Race, Class, and Segregation: Discourses About African-Americans," *International Journal of Urban and Regional Research*, vol. 17, no. 3 (September): 384–403.

Fainstein, Susan S. and Norman I. Fainstein 1989: "The Racial Dimension in Urban Political Economy," *Urban Affairs Quarterly*, vol. 25, no. 2 (December): 187–99.

Farley, Reynolds, Howard Schuman, Suzanne Bianchi, Diane Cosalanto, and Shirley Hatchett 1978: "'Chocolate City, Vanilla Suburbs': Will the Trend toward Racially Separate Communities Continue?" *Social Science Research* 7.

Fisher, Robert 1984: *Let the People Decide: Neighborhood Organizing in America*. Boston: Twayne.

Foley, Donald 1973: "Institutional and Contextual Factors Affecting the Housing Choices of Minority Residents," pp. 147–85, in *Segregation in Residential Areas*, ed. Amos H. Hawley and Vincent P. Rock. Washington: National Academy of Sciences.

Franklin, John Hope 1980: *From Slavery to Freedom: A History of Negro Americans*, 5th edn. New York: Knopf.

Franklin, Raymond S. 1991: *Shadows of Race and Class*. Minneapolis: University of Minnesota Press.

Gans, Herbert H. 1991: "The Dangers of the Underclass: Its Harmfulness as a Planning Concept," in *People, Plans and Policies: Essays on Poverty, Racism, and Other National Urban Problems*. New York: Columbia University Press, pp. 328–43.

Garbarino, James, Kathleen Kostelny and Nancy Dubrow 1991: *No Place to be a Child*. Lexington: Lexington Books.

Gibbs, Jewelle Taylor, ed. 1989: *Young, Black and Male in America: An Endangered Species*. New York: Auburn House Publishing Co.

Habermas, Jürgen 1984 [1981]: *The Theory of Communicative Action*, vol. 1: *Reason and the Rationalization of Society*. Boston: Beacon Press.

Hannerz, Ulf 1968: "The Rhetoric of Soul: Identification in Negro Society," *Race*, vol. 9, no. 4: 453–65.

Hazzard-Gordon, Katrina 1990: *Jookin': The Rise of Social Dance Formations in African Culture*. Philadelphia: Temple University Press.

Hirsch, Arnold 1983: *Making the Second Ghetto: Race and Housing in Chicago, 1940–1960*. Cambridge: Cambridge University Press.

hooks, bell 1992: "Loving Blackness as Political Resistance," in *Black Looks: Race and Representation*. Boston: South End Press, pp. 9–20.

Jackson, Kenneth T. 1985: *Crabgrass Frontier: The Suburbanization of the United States*. Oxford: Oxford University Press.

Jargowski, Paul A. and Mary Jo Bane 1991: "Ghetto Poverty in the United States, 1970–1980," in *The Urban Underclass*, ed. Christopher Jencks and Paul E. Peterson. Washington, DC: The Brookings Institution, pp. 235–73.

Jencks, Christopher and Paul E. Peterson, eds 1991: *The Urban Underclass*. Washington, DC: The Brookings Institution.

Johnson, Bruce, Terry Williams, Kojo A. Dei, and Harry Sanabria 1990: "Drug Abuse in the Inner City: Impact on Hard-Drug Users and the Community," in *Drugs and Crime*, ed. Michael Tonry and James Q. Wilson. Chicago: University of Chicago Press, pp. 9–67.

Jones, Yvonne V. 1988: "Street Peddlers as Entrepreneurs: Economic Adaptation to an Urban Area," *Urban Anthropology* 17 (Summer–Fall): 143–70.

Kasarda, John D. 1989: "Urban Industrial Transition and the Underclass," *Annals of the American Academy of Political and Social Science* 501 (January): 26–47.

Katz, Michael B. 1989: *The Undeserving Poor. From the War on Poverty to the War on Welfare.* New York: Pantheon.

Keil, Charles 1966: *Urban Blues.* Chicago: Chicago University Press.

Kerner Commission 1989 [1968]: *The Kerner Report. The 1968 Report of the National Advisory Commission on Civil Disorders.* New York: Pantheon.

Kusmer, Kenneth L. 1986: "The Black Urban Experience in American History," in *The State of Afro-American History: Past, Present, and Future*, ed. Darlene Clark Hine. Baton Rouge and London: Louisiana State University Press, pp. 91–135.

Landry, Bart 1987: *The New Black Middle Class.* Berkeley: University of California Press.

Lash, Scott and John Urry 1988: *The End of Organized Capitalism.* Madison: University of Wisconsin Press.

Liebow, Elliot 1967: *Tally's Corner: A Study of Negro Streetcorner Men.* Boston: Little, Brown and Co.

Lipsitz, George 1989: *A Life in the Struggle: Ivory Perry and the Culture of Opposition.* Philadelphia: Temple University Press.

Loewenstein, Gaither 1985: "The New Underclass: A Contemporary Sociological Dilemma," *The Sociological Quarterly*, vol. 26, no. 1 (Spring): 35–48.

McAdam, Doug 1981: *Political Process and the Development of Black Insurgency.* Chicago: University of Chicago Press.

McCord, C. and H. Freeman 1990: "Excess Mortality in Harlem," *New England Journal of Medicine*, vol. 323, no. 3: 173–7.

Massey, Douglas S. and Nancy A. Denton 1989: "Hypersegregation in U.S. Metropolitan Areas: Black and Hispanic Segregation Among Five Dimensions," *Demography*, vol. 26, no. 3 (August): 373–91.

Massey, Douglas S. and Andrew B. Gross 1991: "Explaining Trends in Residential Segregation, 1970–80," *Urban Affairs Quarterly* 27, no. 1 (September), 13–35.

Mead, Lawrence 1989: "The Logic of Workfare: The Underclass and Work Policy," *Annals of the American Academy of Political and Social Science* 501 (January): 156–69.

Mithun, Jacqueline S. 1973: "Cooperation and Solidarity as Survival Necessities in a Black Urban Community," *Urban Anthropology*, vol. 2, no. 1 (Spring): 25–34.

Monroe, Sylvester and Peter Goldman 1988: *Brothers: Black and Poor. A True Story of Courage and Survival*. New York: William Morrow.

Morris, Aldon 1984: *The Origins of the Civil Rights Movement: Black Communities Organizing for Change*. New York: Free Press.

Murray, Charles 1984: *Losing Ground: American Social Policy, 1950–1980*. New York: Basic Books.

Nathan, Richard P. 1987: "Will the Underclass Always be with Us?" *Society*, vol. 24, no. 3 (March–April): 57–62.

Oliver, Melvin 1988: "The Urban Black Community As Network: Toward a Social Network Perspective," *The Sociological Quarterly*, vol. 29, no. 4: 623–45.

Orfield, Gary 1985: "Ghettoization and Its Alternatives," in *The New Urban Reality*, ed. Paul Peterson: Washington, DC: The Brookings Institution, pp. 161–93.

Osofsky, Gilbert 1971: "The Enduring Ghetto," in *Harlem: The Making of a Ghetto. Negro New York, 1890–1930*, 2nd edn. New York: Harper, pp. 189–201.

Padilla, Felix 1987: *Puerto Rican Chicago*. Notre Dame: University of Notre Dame Press.

Pétonnet, Colette 1985: "La Pâleur noire. Couleur et culture aux États-Unis," *L'Homme* 97–8 (January–June): 171–87.

Philpott, Thomas Lee 1978: *The Slum and the Ghetto: Neighborhood Deterioration and Middle-Class Reform, Chicago 1880–1930*. New York: Oxford University Press.

Piore, Michael J. and Charles F. Sabel 1984: *The Second Industrial Divide: Possibilities for Prosperity*. New York: Basic Books.

Portes, Alejandro 1972: "The Rationality of the Slum: An Essay On Interpretive Sociology," *Comparative Studies in Society and History* 14.

Rainwater, Lee 1970: *Behind Ghetto Walls*. Chicago: Aldine.

Ricketts, Erol 1989: "A Broader Understanding Required (Reply to Steinberg)," *New Politics*, vol. 2, no. 4.

Ricketts, Erol R. and Isabell V. Sawhill 1988: "Defining and Measuring the Underclass," *Journal of Policy Analysis and Management* 7 (Winter): 316–25.

Rodriguez, Clara 1989: *Puerto Ricans: Born in the USA*. Boston: Unwin Hyman.

Rosenberg, Sam 1983: "Reagan Social Policy and Labor Force Restructuring," *Cambridge Journal of Economics* 9: 179–96.

Sanchez-Jankowski, Martin 1991: *Islands in the Street: Gangs in Urban American Society*. Berkeley: University of California Press.

Sassen, Saskia 1989: "America's 'Immigration Problem'," *World Policy* 6 (Fall): 811–32.

Sassen, Saskia 1991: "Internationalization, Informalization, and Economic Polarization in New York City's Economy," in *Dual City: Restructuring New York*, ed. John H. Mollenkopf and Manuel Castells. New York: Russell Sage Foundation, pp. 79–102.

Sawhill, Isabel V. 1989: "The Underclass; An Overview," *The Public Interest* 96: 3–15.

Scharf, Jagna Wojcika 1987: "The Underground Economy of a Poor Neighborhood," in *Cities of the United States: Studies in Urban Anthropology*, ed. Leith Mullings. New York: Columbia University Press, pp. 19–50.

Schlay, Anne B. 1987: "Credit on Color: Segregation, Racial Transition, and Housing-Credit Flows," in *Fair Housing in Metropolitan Chicago: Perspectives after Two Decades*. Chicago: The Chicago Area Fair Housing Alliance, pp. 109–88.

Scott, Allen J. and Michael Storper, eds 1986: *Production, Work, Territory: The Geographical Anatomy of Industrial Capitalism*. Boston: Allen and Unwin.

Son, In Soo, Suzanne W. Model and Gene A. Fisher 1989: "Polarization and Progress in the Black Community: Earnings and Status Gains for Young Black Males in the Era of Affirmative Action," *Sociological Forum*, vol. 4, no. 3 (Summer): 309–27.

Spear, Allan H. 1967: *Black Chicago: The Making of a Negro Ghetto, 1890–1920*. Chicago: University of Chicago Press.

Squires, Gregory D., Larry Bennett, Kathleen McCourt and Philip Nyden 1987: *Chicago: Race, Class, and the Response to Urban Decline*. Philadelphia: Temple University Press.

Stack, Carol 1970: "The Kindred of Viola Jackson: Residence and Family Organization of an Urban Black American Family," in *Afro-American Anthropology: Contemporary Perspectives*, ed. Norman E. Whitten and John F. Szwed. New York: Free Press, pp. 303–11.

Stearns, Linda Brewster and Charlotte Wilkinson Colenman 1990: "Industrial and Local Labor Market Structures and Black Male Employment in the Manufacturing Sector," *Social Science Quarterly*, vol. 71, no. 2 (June): 285–98.

Streitweiser, Mary, and John Goodman, Jr 1983: "A Survey of Recent Research on Race and Residential Location," *Population Research and Policy Review* 2: 253–83.

Sullivan, Mercer L. 1989: *"Getting Paid." Youth Crime and Work in the Inner City*. Ithaca: Cornell University Press.

Susser, Ida and John Kreniske 1987: "The Welfare Trap: A Public Policy for Deprivation," in *Cities of the United States: Studies in Urban Anthropology*, ed. Leith Mullings. New York: Columbia University Press, pp. 51–68.

Thurow, Lester 1987: "A Surge in Inequality," *Scientific American*, vol. 256, no. 5 (May): 30–7.

Wacquant, Loïc J. D. 1989: "The Ghetto, the State, and the New Capitalist Economy," *Dissent* (Fall): 508–20.

Wacquant, Loïc J. D. 1991: "What Makes a Ghetto? Notes Toward a Comparative Analysis of Modes of Urban Exclusion," paper presented at the MSH/Russell Sage Conference on "Poverty, Immigration and Urban Marginality in Advanced Societies," Paris, Maison Suger, May 10–11, 1991.

Wacquant, Loïc J. D. 1992a: "'The Zone': le métier de 'hustler' dans le ghetto noir américain," *Actes de la recherche en sciences sociales* 92 (June): 38–58.

Wacquant, Loïc J. D. 1992b: "Décivilisation et démonisation: la mutation du ghetto noir américain," in *L'Amérique des français*, ed. Christine Fauré and Tom Bishop. Paris: Éditions François Bourin, pp. 103–25.

Wacquant, Loïc J. D. 1993a: "Urban Outcasts: Stigma and Division in the Black American Ghetto and the French Urban Periphery," *International Journal of Urban and Regional Research*, vol. 17, no. 3: 366–83.

Wacquant, Loïc J. D. 1993b: "Morning in America, Dusk in the Dark Ghetto: The New 'Civil War' in the American City." in *Metropolis*, ed. Phil Kasinitz. New York: New York University Press.

Wacquant, Loïc J. D. and William Julius Wilson 1989a: "The Cost of Racial and Class Exclusion in the Inner City," *Annals of the American Academy of Political and Social Science* 501 (January): 8–25.

Wacquant, Loïc J. D. and William Julius Wilson 1989b: "Poverty, Joblessness and the Social Transformation of the Inner City," in *Welfare Policy for the 1990s*, ed. David Ellwood and Phoebe Collingham. Cambridge, MA: Harvard University Press, pp. 70–102.

Waldinger, Roger and Thomas Bailey 1991: "The Continuing Significance of Race: Racial Conflict and Racial Discrimination in Construction," *Politics and Society*, vol. 19, no. 3 (September): 291–324.

Wallace, Rodrick and Deborah Wallace 1990: "Origins of Public Health Collapse in New York City: The Dynamics of Planned Shrinkage, Contagious Urban Decay and Social Disintegration," *Bulletin of the New York Academy of Science*, vol. 66, no. 5 (September–October): 391–434.

Weir, Margaret 1991: "Urban Political Isolation and the Politics of Marginality in the United States," paper presented at the Working Conference on Poverty, Immigration, and Urban Marginality, Maison des Sciences de l'Homme, Paris, May 9–11.

Williams, Terry 1989: *Cocaine Kids*. Reading, MA: Addison-Wesley.

Wilson, William Julius 1987: *The Truly Disadvantaged: The Inner City, the Underclass and Public Policy*. Chicago: University of Chicago Press.

Wirth, Louis 1927: "The Ghetto," *American Journal of Sociology* 33 (July): 57–71.

Yinger, John 1987: "The Racial Dimension of Urban Housing Markets in the 1980s," in *Divided Neighhorhoods: Changing Patterns of Racial Segregation*, ed. Gary Tobin. Beverly Hills: Sage, pp. 43–67.

Zinn, Maxine Baca 1989: "Family, Race, and Poverty in the Eighties," *Signs: Journal of Women in Culture and Society*, vol. 14, no. 4: 856–74.

10

Emotions and Identity: A Theory of Ethnic Nationalism

Thomas J. Scheff

What, then, must be done? [To heal human separation between persons, men and women, classes, religions, and nations] ... turns out to be the most enormous question that has ever been asked.

Lionel Trilling, E. M. *Forster*

In this chapter I consider a vast sociological-political problem: the causes of interethnic conflict and cooperation. The ending of the Cold War has not led to peace. Instead, we see internecine and national violence continuing. I will use the phrase "ethnic conflict" to include violence between groups with different *cultures*, including differences based on language, religion, race, and class. Conflicts of this type include the highly visible (warfare in Yugoslavia, riots in Los Angeles, continuing tension between most of the countries in the Middle East), and the less visible, such as Indonesian suppression of Timor. Intractable differences between nations also seem to have a strong cultural component, such as the continuing tensions between Germany, Britain, and France that interfere with cooperation.

The urge to belong, and the intense emotions of shame and pride associated with it, may be the most powerful forces in the human world. When these forces are deflected or subverted, cataclysmic upheavals result. I outline a rudimentary theory of ethnic nationalism specifying conditions for four links in a causal chain: differentiation, sustaining processes, conflict, and integration, and the

This paper was presented at the Mini-Conference on Theory: ASA, Pittsburgh, August, 1992. It has benefited from comments on earlier drafts by Suzanne Retzinger, Don Brown, Gabrielle Hoffman, Michael Billig, and Craig Calhoun.

empirical indicators which signal these conditions. In the theory, I describe two different kinds of causal forces: *triggers*, causes of single events at the macro level, and *motors*, microsystems which continuously maintain stability and conflict.

The sources of ethnic conflict are much discussed in the current literature in the social sciences and humanities. The contemporary dialogue on this problem seems piecemeal and partial, however; it lacks a sense of a very large and coherent system of which ethnicity is only a part, and seems to omit crucial components of this system. These points could be illustrated with several valuable studies, but I will use two that have been recently influential as examples: *Imagined Communities* (Anderson 1983), illustrating concern only with parts, and *The Ethnic Origins of Nations* (Smith 1986), the omission of a crucial part.

In his study, Anderson (1983) makes a valid and important point, that the formation of ethnic and other cultural groups is based on an *idea*, an act of the imagination. The use of a common language, for example, doesn't necessarily lead to the formation of a cultural identity. In the world today, the groups which use English as their first language do not constitute a single coherent group. Similarly social class, race, and religion do not automatically lead to the formation of a group differentiated from other groups. For such differentiation to occur, the group itself, or its host group has to undergo a collective act of the imagination. This act is to imagine the specific group as an actual entity.

In his brilliant discussion of the cultural roots of nationalism (chapter 2), Anderson ties the rise of nationalism to the erosion of religions and religious certainty. He suggests that nationalism seems to provide its believers with the sense of continuity of life and the meaning of birth, suffering, and death that was earlier based on religion. But he fails to ground these ideas at the most general sociological level; a sense of continuity and meaning are only part of the feeling of *belonging*, of solidarity with a particular group. By introducing the concept of the quest for belonging, Anderson's whole analysis can be assimilated into the literature of social integration, solidarity, and alienation. I will return to this issue below.

To make sure that by criticizing Anderson's approach, I am not slighting his main idea, let me elaborate it further than he does. One of the most puzzling aspects of differentiation of cultural groups is why it is that one might feel more in common with people that one doesn't actually know than with one's neighbors, that is with persons one does know. This is the problem suggested by Anderson's formulation: under what conditions does one feel closer to unknown than known persons? Why is an imagined community chosen over an actual one?

This question leads to the heart of my problem; what is the nature of a community, and what are its variant manifestations? That is, what type of real community might lead some of its members to choose an imaginary community over the one in which they actually live? What types of social relationships would we expect to find in each? I appreciate Anderson's study, since it helps make this formulation vivid to me.

However, like many another helpful study, this one seems to deal with only a small part of the problem; it focuses on an *idea*. Anderson's approach is cognitive, saying little about feelings, perceptions, social interaction, social structure, and not much more about behavior. Moreover, even at the cognitive level, he deals only with *one link in what is probably a long causal chain*. Needless to say, it is an important link. The moment the idea of the imagined community comes alive in the minds and hearts of its members, and the subsequent moments when this idea is sustained, are near the core of ethnic differentiation. But Anderson provides neither concepts nor evidence concerning the forces which initiate or end these moments, the triggers and those that sustain them, what I am calling the motors.

Closely related to the issue of solidarity–alienation mentioned above is Anderson's treatment of the *attachment* of its members to an imagined community. He argues (chapter 8) that although most treatments of this attachment treat it as pathological, as in the case of jingoism and racism, it need not be. Anderson suggests that it can be a form of love. I grant his point hypothetically. But if the theory of pride and shame outlined here is accurate, then such attachments usually are or become pathological, even if they begin with love.

To understand this point, it is necessary to make a distinction between two kinds of attachment, love and infatuation. These affects appear similar only on the surface. On close examination, they are quite distinct. Infatuation rejects actual knowledge of the loved ones; it is based instead on *idealization*. Love, on the other hand, requires actual knowledge of the other, who is loved for both her or his good and bad traits. Anderson continually elides this distinction (p. 140): "It may appear paradoxical that the objects of all these [nationalist] attachments are "imagined" – anonymous, faceless fellow-Tagalogs [etc.]. But *amor patriae* [love of country] does not differ in this respect from the other attachments, in which there is always an element of fond imagining." The "always" in the last clause ignores the differences between infatuation and love.

In my analysis, infatuation is usually a crucial signal of pathologies in relationships and emotional expression. It signals a kind
of alienation which Bowen (1978) called engulfment, giving up important parts of the self to remain loyal to the relationship or group.
Infatuation also suggests the repression of shame: rather than dealing
with ones's own feelings of inadequacy, one hides them by fierce
attachment to an idealized person or group.

In our earlier work, Retzinger and I (Scheff 1990; Scheff and
Retzinger 1991) have traced the emotional dynamics of infatuation
in Goethe's novel *The Sorrows of Young Werther*. Our analysis of
the text suggests that Werther's infatuation with the heroine (Lotte),
and his attachment to Count C., his patron, are both shame-based
idealizations. The phenomena of hero-worship and "love" of one's
ethnic fellows in nationalism may often, if not always, proceed from
a similar dynamic.

The hypothesis that unacknowledged shame underlies infatuation,
if located in a broader theory of shame dynamics, might explain the
wide variations in the course of nationalist revolutions. I will return
to this issue after my discussion of overt and bypassed (unconscious)
shame, below.

The limitations I have described in the Anderson study seem to
apply to most other studies of ethnic nationalism. In his careful
review of earlier studies, Smith (1971) describes many of the same
flaws that I do. But in his own study (Smith 1976) he repeats some
of them. In particular, most of his analysis is focused on only one
part of one link, the generation of nationalist leadership. This is
an important part of a general theory, but it is only one part among
many others.

Smith's later (1986) study of the ethnic origins of nations is a
horse of a different color; it is a work of great historical scope and
depth. It certainly comes closer to including the larger social system
of which ethnicity is only a part. He examines the ethnic component in the formation and maintenance of an impressively large
number of nation states both in ancient and modern times. My
critique of this work concerns one clear issue, Smith's discounting
of emotions in ethnic differentiation, and a closely related but more
subtle difference of opinion about basic causes of differentiation and
integration.

According to Smith (1986: 3) the fundamental constituents of
ethnic identity are "myths, memories, symbols and values," which
he characterizes as "permanent cultural attributes." He contrasts
these permanent features with what he calls the "ephemeral dimensions of collective will, attitude, even *sentiment*, which make up the

day-to-day fabric of ethnic consciousness" (p. 3, emphasis added). Like most social scientists (Scheff 1992), he makes the *a priori* judgment that sentiments are ephemeral. As I indicate below, however, it is possible to construct a model which gives parity to day-to-day, even second-by-second process (the motor), and the gross forces which create large and dramatic changes in the macworld, the triggers.

A second issue is more subtle. As indicated in the Shibutani and Kwan (1965) passage quoted below, the model of ethnic formation which I propose suggests a single basic causal force which subsumes the micro and macro details. In this scheme, ethnic nationalism arises out of a sense of alienation, on the one hand, and resentment against unfair exclusion, whether political, economic, or social. By the same token, inclusion, justice, and fairness in these realms undercuts and defuses nationalism.

The issue of resentment is complex, because it concerns the *experience* of exclusion, which may be based on real events, or only imagined, or, most usually, a combination of the two. For an example of the interplay between actual and perceived injustice, Retzinger and I (1991) have proposed that Hitler's appeal to the Germans was partially based on gross insults and discrimination in the Treaty of Versailles, on the one hand, but also arose from the difficulties Germans had in managing shame. Elias (1989) has also proposed this latter point, as has Wurmser (1988).

Smith does not take up the issue of alienation, justice, and fairness explicitly; he seems to ignore it. Over the great historical span he examines, his treatment implies that ethnic differentiation is an inevitable part of human life, just as the differentiation of cells in living tissue is inevitable. I may be mistaken in this, but this book seems to relativize human history, treating the aspirations and actions of all groups, whether hosts or minorities, as equally valid.

If my explication of Smith's work is accurate, than my position is radically different from his. In my view, ethnic conflict is caused by the sense of alienation and injustice; in his it seems to be immanent in human nature. I return to this issue at the end of this chapter.

I will describe two directions for building a larger part of the causal chain. The first direction involves what I have called *part/ whole* thinking (Scheff 1990): trying to include all major components of a social system in a single model. This viewpoint is multidisciplinary and multi-level: society is being continuously created in every contact between persons and groups in every moment of contact. To begin to understand this vast and complex system, we must describe social process, make inferences about the meanings that it generates and the context in which it occurs. At the macro-level, the Shibutani–Kwan volume (1965) treats many of these issues.

The second direction involves a theory of social integration and the sociology of emotions: a way of including the relational and emotional aspects of ethnic nationalism that most current theories leave out. Such movements involve an intense and passionate quest for belonging. Descriptions of nationalist movements note the passion, indeed the very pages crackle with it. But these descriptions do little to conceptualize, analyze, or interpret it. In this chapter, I briefly outline a strategy for connecting the passion with the prose (to reverse E. M. Forster's dictum). These two directions, even if successfully followed, cannot begin to solve the whole problem, but they might be strategic for the present moment.

AN INTERPRETATION OF EUROPEAN ANTI-SEMITISM

Gordon Craig's (1982) treatment of the history of anti-Semitism in Europe gives an example of a description of ethnic differentiation fuller than Anderson's. It is only a single chapter in his book on the Germans, but it strikes an interdisciplinary note, interweaving economic, religious, and political strands.

To tell Craig's story in brief: In the Middle Ages in Europe, Jews were one of the few groups who were able to become bankers, since in their religion charging interest for loans was not a sin. For that reason, they become a very useful minority to the rulers, who were Catholic, and like their Catholic subjects, forbidden to take or give interest. At the same time, however, these rulers frequently used the bankers as a scapegoat for financial crises: "It was the Jews who did it." Whether the crises were due to a ruler's own peculations or were inadvertent, this strategy was usually successful, deflecting blame from the ruler to a small and powerless group. Anti-Semitism in Europe became the uneducated person's social science. It still survives with surprising virulence, given that the initial conditions which produced it, as described by Craig and others, have vanished.

Although Craig's analysis is more satisfying than Anderson's, it still seems quite incomplete. It does little to account for variations in the main story, those times and places where there was little anti-Semitism, even though the conditions were the same, or much anti-Semitism with different conditions. Craig's formulation has not been sufficiently grounded, to use Glaser and Strauss's (1967) apt term, documented in similar and contrasting circumstances. If we extend our gaze to the wide world, this limitation is striking. For example, the Chinese in Southeast Asia have long formed a merchant-banking class similar to the Jews in the Middle Ages, but with even more variants in their pattern of integration–differentiation than has been the case of the Jews.[1]

Further uneasiness with Craig's account is created by detailed biographical knowledge of actual actors in the drama of ethnicity. A recent account of the details of three notorious trials of Jews in nineteenth-century Europe (Lindemann 1991) is based on the biographies of the major figures in the case of Dreyfus in France, Beilis in Russia, and Frank in the United States. Lindemann shows that many of those who supported the Jews had anti-Semitic attitudes, and many who persecuted them had records of being neutral or even pro-Semitic. This study, like many earlier ones in the same vein, seems to deconstruct linear social science formulations; the ground quivers beneath our feet.

Social scientists have long known that the correlation between attitude and action is far from perfect, but there have been few vigorous attempts to study the deviant cases. Most actual empirical research in social science is still based on the assumption that attitudes cause behavior, period. The fact is that the findings repeatedly and monotonously suggest that attitudes (as they are measured in social science, at least) play only an infinitesimal role in actual behavior. (For a shocking case involving thousands of empirical studies of self-esteem, see Scheff, Retzinger, and Ryan 1989). Like the Sorcerer's Apprentice, the great machine of attitude research runs apace in laboratories and survey centers all over the world.

Two Directions

As Trilling (1943) asks, what needs to be done? My first suggestion is to expand our field of vision to include the whole system of which ethnicity is only a part, a system made up of tiny parts and huge wholes, the micro and macro worlds of human action. The Shibutani–Kwan volume (1965) provides macro-level theory and documentation under five main headings: (1) Identity and Status, (2) Differentiation, (3) Sustaining processes, (4) Disjunction, (5) Integration. The first heading states the problem, the rest describe stages of group formation, stabilization, conflict, and dissolution.

Even though Shibutani and Kwan do not attempt the micro level of analysis, they give what I now consider to be strong hints about how to conceptualize it. In an earlier article (1955), Shibutani suggested an answer to a question about *conversion* very similar to the question I asked about imagined communities: what is the type of relationship that the converted had with the original reference group or person, and the type with the new reference group or person? What kind of communities are we talking about here?

Shibutani's hypothesis is that conversion is sometimes less a matter of ideologies or interests, and more a matter of interpersonal relationships: conversion occurs when one has negative relationships with one's family, neighbors, etc., and positive ones with the cult or movement which one joins. This hypothesis seems to be supported by all of the conversions that I am personally acquainted with, and therefore might provide a starting place for understanding micro process in ethnicity.

This line of endeavor is further hinted at toward the end of the Shibutani–Kwan volume (1965: 585):

> The fundamental problem in the contact of peoples is the preservation of the individual's moral worth in his own eyes ... It is difficult to develop self-respect if one is not respected by others. Unless [human beings] can have self-respect, they will always be discontented ... [They] are willing to fight and even to die for it. Without it they can neither look themselves in the face nor stand before their children without a sense of shame.

Certainly this passage clearly concerns the micro level of analysis: the concepts employed are respect *between* particular persons, and self-respect and even an emotion (shame) *within* them. One difficulty, certainly in Shibutani's early hypothesis about conversion, is that the idea of negative and positive relations is a highly abstract gloss: the explanatory part of the hypothesis is insufficiently specified. This is less true of the 1965 formulation: respect in social interaction and certainly the emotion of shame are specific. Since the concept of self-respect has still not been conceptually defined, however, there is still muddle to be dealt with.

The use of concepts like respect, self-respect, and especially the emotion of shame leads into my second suggestion for the study of ethnicity, of introducing the sociology of emotions. Although there has been little current discussion of the emotional content in self-respect or self-esteem, Cooley may have come close to defining it in his discussion of the "looking-glass self" in terms of pride and shame (1922; for extended explication of Cooley's idea, see Scheff 1990: 81–4):

A self-idea of this sort seems to have three principal elements: the imagination of our appearance to the other person; the imagination of his judgment of that appearance, and some sort of self-feeling, such as pride or mortification."

In this passage he restricts self-feelings to the two which he seems to think are the most significant – pride and shame (considering "mortification" to be a shame variant). To make sure we understand this point, he mentions shame three more times in the passage that follows (184–85; emphasis added):

"The comparison with a looking-glass hardly suggests the second element, the imagined judgment, which is quite essential. The thing that moves us to *pride or shame* is not the mere mechanical reflection of ourselves, but an imputed sentiment, the imagined effect of this reflection upon another's mind. This is evident from the fact that the character and weight of that other, in whose mind we see ourselves, makes all the difference with our feeling. We are *ashamed* to seem evasive in the presence of a straightforward man, cowardly In the presence of a brave one, gross in the eyes of a refined one, and so on. We always imagine, and in imagining share, the judgments of the other mind. A man will boast to one person of an action – say some sharp transaction in trade – which he would be *ashamed* to own to another."

Cooley is suggesting that the emotional component of the social self, what we today would call self-esteem, is a kind of pride/shame balance. This idea also connects it closely with social status: gestures of respect lead to moment-by-moment indications of one's moral worth in social interaction.

Cooley's hint at the emotional component of self-esteem could be important because it gives us something observable to look for in social interaction. Retzinger (1991) has provided a procedure for coding cues to shame based on visual, verbal, and paralinguistic (loudness, emphasis, pauses, etc.) features in texts and verbatim transcripts. What she calls "hiding behavior," for example, concerns not only gross bodily movements like hiding the face with the hands, but also more subtle forms of hiding, like speaking too softly and/or quickly to be easily heard. *Withdrawal* from contact may be gross and flagrant, but it also can be subtle and disguised.

The specificity of Retzinger's lists of cues can be used to turn abstract terms like positive and negative, and muddled terms like self-respect or self-esteem, into clear concepts that can be applied to actual events. Retzinger and I (1991) have proposed that in *solidary* social relationships, a clear predominance of pride occurs in the pride/shame balance. In *alienated* ones, a clear predominance of shame or embarrassment occurs. Armed with this conceptual equipment, we may be ready to specify types of communities which lead to ethnic differentiation and integration.

The discussion of the theory of the pride/shame balance suggests the triggers for ethnic differentiation and integration, and the sustaining motor. The trigger and motor for conflict will require further theory. Since the relevant theory is simpler, I will first consider differentiation and integration.

The Shibutani–Kwan passage on moral worth and the idea of the pride/shame balance suggests a hypothesis about ethnic identity which links micro and macro levels. The motor of ethnic identification can be summarized as: *individuals and groups seek to increase their pride/shame balance, their moment-by-moment social status* (the pride/shame hypothesis). This proposition elevates social status from metaphor to concept, since it defines it operationally, moment by moment. Pride and shame signals can be used as an Ariadne's thread, to guide us through the arcanum of social status that was given its preliminary exploration by Goffman (1967).

At the macro level, the trigger appears at a single moment when an individual converts or an ethnic group coalesces into an imagined community. But in the microworld, the motor of one's awareness of relative status is always running, as Goffman was at pains to point out (1967). But the approach outlined here is broader than Goffman's, which focused on the microworld. My formulation includes gross disparities in cultures and interests as determinants of ethnic identity, since these also register as indicative of status. A complete picture, however, should include both micro- and macroworlds. It is said that by the beginning of the twentieth century the British had learned to rule India justly and effectively; they lost it for want of a smile.

My colleague and I have earlier (Scheff and Retzinger 1991: chapter 8) argued that the pride/shame hypothesis seems to explain the otherwise inexplicable appeal that Hitler had to the German people; the promise of ending Germany's shame after the Treaty of Versailles and raising its pride formed the core of virtually all of his speeches and writings. One of hundreds of examples of this practice: during his campaign for the chancellorship and after he gained power, Hitler never referred to the Weimar Republic, the government he succeeded, by its right name. Instead, with a fist banging the rostrum, he would shout "VIERZEHN JAHREN VON SCHMACH UND SCHANDE!" (Fourteen years of shame and disgrace!). This tirade always brought the crowd screaming to its feet. Hitler's appeal was that he promised that pride and community would replace shame and alienation.

The issue of pride, and by implication, shame, is clear in Billig's (1992) treatment of the attitudes in ordinary British families toward their royal family. He shows how they both talk about and disguise their own pride in British royalty (pp. 35–9). Particularly illuminating is his analysis of the way his interviewees seemed to view Britain from the imagined point of view of other countries, evoking imagined envy in other countries, and pride in their own (pp. 45–8). Retzinger and I (1991: 155–7) have shown how Hitler used the reverse strategy in his speeches and writings before he came to power, frequently imagining that other countries viewed Germany as weak and contemptible, which implies a shame state. Billig's study fleshes out in living people the abstract emotion dynamics of nationalism that Retzinger and I have described. Without commenting on his own method, Billig also shows how attitudes can be studied live (*in vivo*) in discourse, rather than hypothetically (*in vitro*) in experiments and surveys.

Since pride and shame signal the state of the social bond, the pride/shame hypothesis suggests a way of grounding what might otherwise seem to be a sociological truism: faced with a choice between solidarity and alienation, people usually choose solidarity. In the case of Hitler's Germany, the solidarity that Hitler promised depended on continually increasing alienation from other groups and countries, a social-political pyramiding scheme. To understand the triggers and motors in this system, it will be necessary to turn to another facet of shame dynamics, the generation of interminable conflict.

THE INFERNAL MACHINE

As many of the major commentaries on shame have indicated (Tomkins 1967; Lewis 1971; Izard 1977), it is the most social and reflexive of all the emotions. It always involves consciousness of self from the point of view of the other, which depends on the self viewing itself. This characteristic of shame gives rise to a dynamic which seems to be unique to this emotion, the generation of loops of shame of unlimited intensity and/or duration.

In his analysis of blushing, Darwin (1872) had noted the intense reflexiveness of shameful self-consciousness: persons prone to intense episodes of blushing seem to become progressively more embarrassed the more they become aware of their own blush. The runaway potentiality of shame loops is also implied in Elias's (1987) analysis of historical changes in shame thresholds in European civilization. Beginning in the late Middle Ages, his study of excerpts from etiquette manuals suggests that not only was there increasing shame about manners, the body, anger, and aggression, but also about shame itself (Scheff and Retzinger 1991: chapter 1).

In her moment-by-moment coding of emotion cues in psycho-therapy sessions, Lewis (1971) discovered shame sequences which involved both internal and external loops. She found that when patients interpreted comments by their therapist to be critical or rejecting, the patient and therapist frequently became entangled in what she called a "feeling trap," sequences of emotions which had both psychological and social components.

Patients in shame states rarely acknowledged shame or embarrass-ment; rather they appeared to slowly withdraw, or quickly become angry about being ashamed, then ashamed of being angry, and so on. This latter sequence usually was manifested as lengthy but only moderately intense chains of shame and anger which Labov and Fanshel later (1977) called "helpless anger." In Lewis's cases, this chain sometimes took a form which had a high level of both intensity and duration: she called it "humiliated fury."

In some of the episodes that Lewis described, the patient's shame and anger resulted in emotional "contagion": the patient's angry or sarcastic comments seemed to trigger shame and anger in the therapist. In one case, a therapist did not apologize after he missed an appointment. From this time on, through many sessions, the mood of the subsequent sessions changed. Although the preceding meetings had been productive, after the missed session much of the dialogue was argumentative, quarrels about who was right or wrong. In my earlier explication of this case (Scheff 1987) I proposed that a feeling trap involves three spiraling shame/anger chains (one within each party, and one between them). Like two adjacent burning embers, the anger from each party heats up both itself and the other.

Lewis (1971) noted a crucial characteristic of feeling traps. Al-though the therapist or the patient occasionally referred to the patient's anger, the patient's shame or embarrassment was rarely noted by either person. In Lewis's terminology, most shame goes *unacknowledged*. This idea suggests the decisive source of interminable conflict. If shame is acknowledged, it turns out to be an ordinary emotion, painful but bearable. But when unacknowledged, it becomes the fuel for an infernal machine, an insult-retaliation motor that can run forever.

Lewis noted that unacknowledged shame appeared in two different, seemingly opposite styles. The first style she called "overt, undifferentiated" shame. In this format, there appears to be intense awareness of emotional pain, since there is blushing, stammering and fluster, and unwanted physical symptoms, such as sweating and rapid heartbeat. However, shame in this form is seldom called by its right name. Instead a wide assortment of euphemisms are employed, such as feeling insecure, awkward, weird, etc., linguistic forms of denial or disguise. Although usually verbally disguised, this form of shame corresponds closely with our usual understanding, since feelings of shame are experienced in consciousness, even if the package is mislabeled.

UNCONSCIOUS SHAME

In the second format of unacknowledged shame, the painful feelings are not experienced in consciousness. Lewis referred to this form of shame as "bypassed." She noted that awareness of emotional pain, after a very brief initial wince or jolt, was entirely absent. Persons experiencing this type of shame instead report that they seem to have little feeling at all, or even feel blank or hollow.

Under these conditions, behavior takes on an obsessive quality, with rapid thoughts and speech which are at least slightly off-key, but may be flagrantly so. Under the whip of repressed shame, thoughts, speech and action are repetitive and compulsive. In a typical episode, patients will report obsessing about a scene in which they felt injured or ridiculed, or in error. They repeatedly replay the scene in their imagination, thinking about what they might have said and done. After many a replay, the issue may seem resolved intellectually, but the aftermath from the scene may still not subside. They are obsessed with the scene, and the obsession is compulsive; they cannot stop replaying it.

An example is provided by a male college student. He reported an incident to me which begins with his feeling pleased while attending a lecture that he had made a good impression on another student, a very attractive woman acquaintance, in a conversation he had with her just before class began. As he is remembering the conversation, however, he notices that this woman is sitting with a male student whom he had described to her as "an asshole." Seeing them sitting together, he realized that they were a couple, which he had known but forgotten. Up to this point, he had been intermittently listening to some of the lecture. But now, after a moment of feeling "like a complete fool," he becomes distracted, no longer hearing any of the lecture. Instead, he rehearses the conversation with the woman over and over, as it occurred and as he wished it had occurred. That evening, during dinner, his studies, and watching television, the scene keeps recurring to him. He is obsessed with it.

Although most of us are familiar with overt shame, the second type is a discovery of Lewis's. She found that a person can be in a state of shame, but not conscious of it. She reasoned that because all of the many instances of obsession and numbness to feeling occurred in shame contexts (real or imagined criticism or rejection by the therapist), obsession and feelings such as hollowness are outer cues to an inner state of shame, one that is so disguised as to be outside of awareness.

This is a new idea that takes some getting used to: one need not *feel* ashamed to be in a state of shame. One can be so habituated to defending against the painful feeling of shame by rapid thoughts, talking or acting that it becomes invisible to the bearer. Other defenses against shame, such as anger and infatuation, will be described below.

In Lewis's scheme, many affects are seen as disguises for shame or shame–anger sequences. For example, what is called social fear, social anxiety, or stage fright are all vernacular expressions for shame or shame loops. The most surprising outcome of Lewis's scheme is that seemingly basic affects such as guilt and resentment are seen as vernacular representations of shame–anger sequences: resentment (and hatred) is such a sequence, with the anger component pointed toward external targets; guilt, at one's self. In resentment, the anger component may be at least partly overt and conscious, but in guilt both affects are completely hidden from self. In Lewis's language, the feeling of guilt represents a complete bypassing of the component emotions.

Lewis explains that in guilt, the self feels intact, and even powerful; so powerful as to injure another, but also powerful enough to make amends. In shame, on the other hand, the self feels weak or impotent, at best. At the very worst, the self is felt as dissolving or evaporating, a waking nightmare. Lewis (1971) shows evidence in her verbatim transcripts how patients (and in one case, a therapist) defend against shame with guilt.

One implication of Lewis's work is that modern societies (as against traditional ones) can be seen as conspiracies to deny all shame by repressing it, beginning in the early years of childhood. This conjecture was arrived at independently by Elias (1939) and documented with extensive verbatim quotes from etiquette and advice manuals over the last five centuries. By analyzing excerpts from these manuals, he shows that the amount of shame implied by them has been steadly rising, but awareness just as consistently falling, a finding consonant with Lewis's idea of unconscious shame.

In order to understand the rest of this chapter, the reader should probably reread from the start of this section several times, since the idea of bypassed shame is counter-intuitive in our culture. In my opinion, Lewis should have used a term other than "bypassed" to describe this state. It would have been more forthcoming, I think, to call it unconscious shame. Where overt shame can come in different degrees of consciousness, what she called bypassed shame is always completely unconscious. This is not the place for further discussion of this issue, but the interested reader can consult the work of Lewis (1971, 1977, 1981, 1987), Retzinger (1991), Scheff (1990, 1992) and Scheff and Retzinger (1991).

The most dramatic cues for both overt and bypassed states of shame in social interaction involve gaze direction (Scheff and Retzinger 1991). Overt, undifferentiated shame leads to furtiveness, looking down or away, with only an occasional sidelong glance at the other. A normal gaze involves turn-taking, first looking at the other, then away. Finally, bypassed shame results in continuous looking at the other, attempting to stare them down. As will be described below, Hitler, perhaps the most shame-prone person who ever lived, was famous for his piercing stare.

Lewis's findings seem to correspond exactly to the distinction that was central to Adler's theory of personality (1956). He proposed that a child needs love at critical junctures in its development, or at least a secure bond with its caretaker. In the absence of such a bond, the child's development would proceed in one of two directions, toward an "inferiority complex," on the one hand, or "striving for power," on the other. Although he did not use the word "shame," Adler's descriptions strongly suggest two chronic shame states. The inferiority complex implies overt, undifferentiated shame; striving for power, bypassed shame.

The playing out of Adler's dynamic can be clearly seen in the case of Hitler's personality (Scheff and Retzinger 1991: chapter 8). Biographies furnish compelling evidence first that Hitler was openly humiliated virtually from birth by his father, and in an indirect, disguised way by his mother. Secondly, from early childhood Hitler was extraordinarily shame prone, alternating between feelings of inferiority and arrogance. As he grew older, however, especially after coming to power, the bypassed mode more and more predominated.

Although there is close correspondence between Adler's theory and Lewis's, the two are not at the same level of development. A theory and method for studying shame dynamics is not even implied by Adler, since he does not spell out moment-by-moment causal sequences, nor does he specify the observable cues for his concepts. A starting place for these steps is provided by Lewis (1971), however. She explicitly stated the dynamics of the feeling trap engine, and specified many of the cues to anger and both forms of shame. As indicated above, a comprehensive coding scheme for the visual, verbal, and paralinguistic cues to shame can be found in Retzinger (1991), based on the work of Lewis (1971), Gottschalk and Gleser (1969), Ekman and Friesen (1978) and Izard (1979). Lewis's work, and our subsequent expansion of it, has transformed Adler's conjectures into testable hypotheses.

The Adler–Lewis conjecture on the emotional sources of rage and aggression can be stated in the form of the following hypothesis: In a dispute between two parties, if *intense shame is evoked, but not acknowledged*, it may lead to an unending spiral of shame/rage and aggression, an irrational and interminable quarrel. The outward form involves a cycle of honor, insult, and retaliation by one party, which triggers the same cycle in the other, and so on, *ad infinitum*. Since unacknowledged shame and alienation go hand in hand, this proposition locates interminable conflict in civilizations in which relationships within and between groups are mostly alienated. Persons with zero bonds, if their alienation is completely unacknowledged, like Hitler, can go only one of three ways: madness, suicide, or homicide.

A verbatim text can be used to illustrate my main point, the structure of the unacknowledged shame–anger spiral, and how it leads to mindless aggression. I call this sequence the motor of interminable conflict. Referring to the Treaty of Versailles which ended the First World War as an instrument of "abject humiliation" of the Germans, Hitler wrote:

> How could every single one of these points [of injustice to Germany] have been burned into the brain and emotion of this people, until finally in sixty million heads, in men and women, a common sense of *shame* and a common *hatred* would have become a single fiery sea of flame, from whose heat a will as hard as steel would have risen and a cry burst forth: *Give us arms again!* (1927: 632, emphasis added)

The underlined words show the sequence (1) shame, (2) anger (hatred is itself a disguised shame/anger sequence), (3) aggression (Scheff and Retzinger 1991: 153–7). Note also how "a *common* sense of shame and a *common* hatred would have become a *single* sea of flame" promises solidarity and community three times in one clause. The promise to transform shame to pride and alienation to solidarity formed the basis of all Hitler's writings and speeches (Scheff and Retzinger: 143–4).

The shame–rage hypothesis suggests a motor for continuous conflict, an infernal machine which can run for the whole lifetime of an individual. It can also span generations, since shame–anger motors can be transmitted when parents teach their children to hate not only persons but whole groups. My colleague and I suggest such an explanation for the origins of the First and Second World Wars (Scheff and Retzinger 1991). The insult–retaliation cycle we examine begins with the defeat of France by Germany in the Franco-Prussian War, 1870–1. It cycles through the First World War, with France the humiliated party, and the Second, with Germany the humiliated party. Although some of the data seem to be still missing for evaluating this formulation, particularly some crucial details about the secret negotiations between the French, Russians, and Serbians in the year preceding the First World War, much of the required documentation is now available.

In the 1992 Los Angeles riots, the Rodney King verdict seems to have been only the trigger, the outward determinant of a violent shift in mood. The theory outlined here suggests that this shift could occur only because the underlying motor of shame–anger was running between the white middle-class majority and the race, class, and ethnic minorities.

TV networks had broadcast a videotape by a bystander of a defenseless black man being beaten to insensibility by four white policemen, while a large group of police looked on passively. A white jury found the four policeman innocent. Minorities may have experienced this verdict as a humiliating insult. The rioters, rather than acknowledging their shame and anger, acted it out in destructive violence.

Billig's (1992) methods, mentioned above, could be used to investigate interethnic (and interracial) conflict of the kind that generated the Los Angeles riots, to test my theory. His method could be used to disclose both attitudes and relationships in families, as required by the theory. Taking Los Angeles as an example, interviews of majority and minority families, and also (if possible) joint interviews involving dialogue *between* the members of a majority and a minority family might be used to test and extend the theory.

Dialogue within and between families concerning topics like the Rodney King verdict, and perhaps the causes of the riots, could be used to document the assumption that the motor which generates interminable conflict is continuously running.

For example, I noticed that for several weeks after the riots ended, when I asked minority residents of Los Angeles about their feelings concerning recent events, most of them assumed I was referring to the both the King verdict and the riots; white residents, on the other hand, assumed that I was referring only to the riots. Many of the latter made no connection whatever between the riots and the King verdict; instead they speculated about boredom among young people as a cause. Many of the white residents seemed not to be overtly prejudiced; their attitudes must be inferred by reading between the lines.

Hypothesis 1 concerns attitudes and emotions toward outgroups: *Prejudicial attitudes and shame–anger sequences directed at outgroups should be present, directly or indirectly, in all discussions of the other group, and in all contact between majority and minority and will be continuously reaffirmed within each group.* The theory proposes that shame–anger sequences cause and are caused by alienation. Discourse between family members about the King verdict and the riots could be used to determine the nature of the social bonds in each family, the extent to which they are secure, engulfed, or isolated (Bowen 1978). This idea is discussed further in the conclusion of this chapter, in connection with a general theory of social integration.

Hypothesis 2 proposes that prejudicial attitudes and feelings are caused by unacknowledged shame–anger and alienation: *The more secure the social bonds between family members, the more accommodating their attitudes toward the outgroup, and the fewer and shorter the shame-anger loops.* The theory also proposes that interminable and destructive conflict is generated by *unacknowledged* shame and alienation.

Hypothesis 3: The more direct the communication tactics, and the more the emotions are acknowledged, the less prejudicial the attitudes toward the outgroup, and the fewer and shorter the shame–anger loops.

These three hypotheses form the core of the theory presented here. They could be tested and/or modified with only a few interviews, since even a 30-minute interview generates a rich, vast body of evidence.

A study such as this one might extend our knowledge of intergroup relations by providing direct knowledge of the processes and emotions in social interaction within and between groups. The need for such studies is often voiced; for a recent example, see the critique (Stone 1992) of the studies in Jencks and Peterson's (1991) volume on the urban underclass.

A further issue concerns the symmetry or asymmetry of intergroup conflict. The theory proposes that all interminable and destructive conflict be at least partly symmetric; both parties are involved in reciprocal loops of unacknowledged shame–anger sequences, and in the social relationships within both parties, alienation (insecure bonds) predominates over solidarity (secure bonds). If the thoughts and actions of one of the parties to a conflict were not dominated by unacknowledged shame, anger, and alienation, it would be rational enough to either avoid the conflict (for example, by working out a mutually acceptable compromise) or quickly win it.

Our analysis (Scheff and Retzinger 1991: chapter 4) of the origins of the First World War suggests virtually complete symmetry between the contending parties. The major nations on the Allied side, France, Russia, and Britain and on the side of the Central Powers, Germany and Austria-Hungary, seem to have been quite close to being equally irrational in the motives, perceptions, feelings, and aggression that led to the war. This tragic war was avoidable in a way that the Second World War was not, since the conflicts of interests and differences in orientations among the major parties in 1914 were relatively minor. Our analysis suggests that the driving force underlying this war were conceptions of "national honor," which translated out of the language of denial means matters of pride and shame.

We (Scheff and Retzinger 1991: chapter 5) proposed that the Second World War was also generated by what I have called the infernal machine of shame–anger and alienation. But in this case, the symmetry was only partial. The orientation toward the world that was held by Germany's leaders and their supporters was vastly more irrational than the orientation that obtained within the Allied nations, and Germany was overwhelmingly the irrational aggressor. The irrationality of the Allies was shown not in reciprocating aggression, as was the case in the origins of the First World War. It was shown, rather, by irrationally discounting the immense threat of the orientation that was being displayed by the German government after Hitler came to power in 1933. Fortunately for the Allies, their fit of irrationality was of shorter duration than that of the Germans, lasting only until 1939.

Our analysis of French novels and military poetry in the period preceding the First World War, and Hitler's writings and speeches before the Second, provides support for that part of hypothesis 2 concerning shame–anger loops. The French materials and, to a much greater extent, Hitler's writing and speeches, are filled with evidence of unacknowledged loops of shame and anger preceding calls for aggression.

In support of hypothesis 3, concerning the role of alienation
in generating conflict, our study reports only partial and indirect
evidence for the German case before the Second World War: one
of the central themes of Hitler's speeches and writings was the
evocation of a national community (*Volksgemeinschaft*) under his
leadership, implying alienation among the Germans before his advent as leader. Retzinger and I (1991) found very strong evidence
in his biographies that Hitler himself had only the weakest of social
bonds as a child and adolescent, and had literally *zero* bonds for
his entire adult life. All of his biographers repeatedly make the
point of his complete isolation from others, *all* others (including
his mother, mistress and all of his associates). Since this material
documents only the bondlessness of the leader, but none of his
followers, it is incomplete as a test of the hypothesis.

To document hypothesis 3 directly, a historical study is required
that would compare levels of alienation in representative German
families and communities with those of France, Britain, and Russia
during the periods preceding the two World Wars. A similar study
comparing representative families and communities in Serbia and
Croatia might cast light on some of the features of the irrational and
interminable violence now evident in the former Yugoslavia. Serbian
terrorism and intransigence played a brief but significant role in the
instigation of the First World War: it was Serbian terrorists who
plotted the assassination at Sarajevo that triggered the war.

In the 1990s conflict in former Yugoslavia, it appears that Serbian
aggression and violence are the predominating cause, with the aggression of the other parties being at lower levels. The theory described
here proposes that we would expect to find more shame–anger
loops and alienation in Serbian families and communities than in
those of the Croatians and other parties to the conflict. Since this
case involves recent and current history, documentation relevant
to testing the hypothesis might be less difficult to find than in the
case of the two World Wars.

The direction that nationalist wars of liberation take may also be
determined by shame dynamics. Adler and Lewis considered only
two routes for unacknowledged shame, the route of overt shame
loops, which Adler called the inferiority complex, and the route of
bypassed shame and anger: striving for power, in Adler's terminology,
and the feeling trap of shame–anger loops, in Lewis's. Either of these
loops may begin or end with infatuation, however, a variant of
the overt shame route. One irrationally idealizes a person or group
because of one's own sense of unworthiness. Attachment to the
ideal is a way of denying ones's shame.

The "velvet revolution" in Czechoslovakia seemed to have a strong component of real love. Havel himself appears to be particularly free of infatuations, humiliated fury, and a sense of inferiority. In the origins of the Russian Revolution in the latter part of the nineteenth century, however, there were strong elements of infatuation (mixed with other sentiments) toward the Russian masses.

Both Dostoevsky and Tolstoy, whose thought fed the early sources of reform, both loved and idealized the common people of Russia. (My own grandfather was a local leader of the Revolutionary Socialist Party, whose program centered on a Tolstoyan campaign to teach the peasants to read.) Idealization of the working class was strong in the variant of Marxian theory followed by many of the Bolshevik, and later, Communist Party intellectuals.

As is the case with mutually infatuated individuals, infatuation in leaders and their followers in liberation movements is often followed by heartbreak and antipathy. Where love is clear-eyed about the other, infatuation is blind. Vast and unrealistic expectations are quickly followed by disaffection and depression, as has occurred in the new democracies in the former Soviet bloc.

The succession of leadership in liberation movements may also be dependent on shame dynamics. It is unusual that a leader like Havel was able to take power, since such persons are usually shunted aside or dispatched by leaders in the grip of hidden shame. In the early stages of the the rise to power, infatuated intellectuals and/or bypassed (power-oriented) persons become prominent. As power is consolidated, however, the latter type usually gain control. Although communist leaders such as Lenin, Bukharin, and Trotsky were not cold-blooded killers like Stalin, their biographies indicate that they were clearly power-oriented rather than infatuated types.

If these conjectures on the relation between shame dynamics and power struggles are accurate, they might explain why revolutions for ethnic or national liberation often end in bloodbaths and terror. Although neither Memmi (1957) nor Fanon (1952) use shame terminology explicitly, they use cognates (such as the feelings of inferiority of the colonized) to explain how wars of liberation can go wrong. (Catherine Silver pointed out this parallel to me.)

CONCLUSION

The theory of ethnic conflict outlined here is not only unproven, but also conceptually incomplete. The pride and shame dynamics emphasized in this essay can be seen as part of a larger theory of social integration, a theory which is only hinted at here. Pride generates and signals solidarity, shame is an indicator and cause of alienation. The emotions are the psychological sides of social relationships, just as relationships are the social aspects of the emotions.

To be of maximum use, however, it is necessary to further subdivide alienation into two basic types, which I have called engulfment and isolation, using Bowen's (1978) terms. Although Bowen never cited Durkheim's study of suicide, his distinction is parallel to Durkheim's. Isolation corresponds to what Durkheim called anomie-egoism, and engulfment to altruism-fatalism.

Although Bowen refers to the interpersonal level and Durkheim to the societal, both seem to imply the same thing. Social connections can be either too loose, isolating the individual, or too tight (engulfment), suffocatingly so. By implication, there also must be an ideal level of integration, neither too loose nor too tight. The Durkheim–Bowen approach implies an axis of integration with three main positions: isolation–solidarity–engulfment.

This idea runs through virtually all sociological theories, but has never been sufficiently explicated. One problem has been that theorists often focus on only two of the three positions. Durkheim had little to say about solidarity itself, even though he made an abstract distinction between mechanical and organic solidarity. Bowen also focused on the two types of alienated bonds, with almost no discussion of a secure bond.

Other theories of social relationships seem to ignore the engulfed type of alienation. Marx's ideas about alienation seemed to concern largely the isolated type. His remarks about solidarity are more diffuse and implicit; his discussion of communism implies an idea of solidarity. His scheme does not seem to include engulfment, however. Similarly, Buber's approach to personal relationships includes only two styles, which he refers to as I–thou (solidarity, secure bond) and I–it (isolation). In his terminology, engulfment would be represented by it–thou; one is loyal to the other to the point of subjugating one's self.

In addition to conceptual incompleteness, none of the theories of social integration go very far into definitions and empirical indicators. Perhaps it is for this reason that the testing of general theories has advanced so little. One promising exception to this critique is Elias's (1987) idea of the "I–We balance." This approach gives equal weight to all three positions of integration and suggests a possible empirical indicator: the ratio of first and second person to plural pronouns in discourse between individuals or groups.

Although Elias didn't apply his idea to actual discourse, his approach suggests a path to connecting abstract theory with empirical research. Discourse marked by a preponderance of I and YOU over WE, US, OURS would suggest isolation. The opposite ratio would suggest engulfment. A balance, finally, would suggest solidarity. Although not stated in theoretical terms, an earlier study of differing attitudes toward the Vietnam war by racial groups (Cramer and Schuman 1975) seems to support this approach.

My preliminary study of discourse within France and Germany in the period 1871–1914, prior to the First World War, suggests a double alienation within both countries, which I call *bimodal*: engulfment within, isolation without. That is, during this period there seems to be a steadily increasing blind loyalty within each country, engulfment, accompanied by spurts of animosity directed at the other country (isolation). Bimodal alienation would seem a necessary condition for irrational conflict.

This formulation would seem to mark an advance over those that are stated in terms of ethnocentrism. This concept by itself explains little. What is needed is knowledge of the intensity of ethnocentrism relative to contrasting impulses, such as xenophilia, the love of the exotic and foreign. Approaches which employ ethnocentrism also are usually static, as if degrees of attachment toward one's own group and other groups were fixed attributes of individuals or groups. A theory of social integration and its accompanying emotions would provide a dynamic analysis of complex currents of thought and feelings, one that could be tied to empirical indicators such as personal pronouns and pride and shame cues.

In my study of the origins of the First World War (Scheff 1993), I have applied this method to several of the emergency diplomatic exchanges between the heads of state of the major powers that immediately preceded the onset of the war. In a partial and preliminary way, my analysis suggests that the discourse of the Czar and the Foreign Minister of Britain shows bimodal alienation: engulfment within the nation, isolation toward nations outside. These marks are absent from the Kaiser's communications, but show up in the comments of his military advisors. These advisors prevailed upon the Kaiser to declare war.

For example, the dictum "Events take command!" was the slogan of the German General Staff during the crisis preceding the war. It implies that they, the generals, were not co-responsible for the onset of the war, a denial of their own responsibility, and projection on the outside world ("Events"). This kind of self-deception and denial is characteristic of engulfment in interpersonal as well as intergroup quarrels. These preliminary findings point toward the need for the development of a general theory of social integration.

As indicated, the theory proposed here is incomplete. But for the sake of closure, I will end by noting its implications for resolving interethnic conflict in both the short and long term. In contrast with the position that Smith (1986) seems to take, the theory suggests that ethnic conflict is a potentially soluble problem, since it arises out of alienation and a sense of injustice. I have suggested that interminable and senseless conflict is caused by an infernal machine, unacknowledged alienation and its associated triple spiral of shame and anger. If this theory turns out to be true, it is good news, since such a machine can be at least interrupted, and in the long run, perhaps dismantled.

For the immediate future, it seems to me that understanding of the nature of remedial social rituals needs to be explored. One need not have a duel or war if one has been insulted; there are remedial actions such as debates, lawsuits, and apologies that are available. Rituals of victim confrontation, restitution, apology, and repair of disrupted bonds between convicted criminal offenders and the community have been described in terms of shame dynamics by Braithwaite (1989).

Tavuchis (1991) has provided a general framework for such rituals in his discussion of the mechanics of offering and accepting apologies. His discussion is particularly applicable to ethnic conflict, since it encompasses reparative actions not only between individuals, but also between individuals and groups, and groups and groups. Such moves offer both psychological and social formats for ending cycles of insult and retaliation.

An example of a simple but effective remedial action is provided by a gesture of Willy Brandt's, when he was Chancellor of Germany in the 1960s. Although Germany had provided extensive reparations for Nazi oppression to surviving Jews in Israel, relations between the two countries were tense and distant. When Brandt visited the Warsaw Ghetto, however, he knelt and wept visibly, creating a new and more favorable climate between the two nations. According to Tavuchis (1991), the formula for a successful apology is that not only must you *say* that you are sorry, but it must be obvious that you actually *feel* sorry.

Underlying the Tavuchis formula, it seems to me, is the acknowledgment of shame. Although it's true that Brandt wept, which expresses sorrow or grief, the key ingredient might have been humbling himself, both by expressing emotion openly in public, and by kneeling. In our era, it is possible that the frozen stare and the stiff knee have caused more harm than high explosives. If that is the case, Brandt's gesture might show us one way of slowing down our descent into chaos.

In the long term, however, remedies that occur only after destructive acts will not be enough. How can interminable quarrels be prevented before they happen? This question may point toward needed changes in the basic institutions of our civilization. In particular, if the theory of the pride/shame balance is correct, fundamental changes would be needed.

1 Reduce the gross amount of humiliation of persons and groups that results in alienation and shame–rage loops. Perhaps one of the most important directions involves economic participation, since levels of wealth and poverty involve social status and honor. A right to livelihood and independence confers pride and honor, just as unemployment and poverty take it away. Changes in crime control policies and education would also be required. Both institutions at present are reacting toward subgroups based on race, ethnicity, and social class. This direction does not abandon shame as an instrument of social control, but changes the type of shaming, from what Braithwaite (1989) calls stigmatizing shaming to reintegrative shaming. He (1992) has described the reforms in this direction in delinquency control that are now taking place in New Zealand and Australia, reforms which originated in the traditions of an underclass, the Maori tribes in New Zealand.

2 Explore what steps might be needed in basic social institutions that would lead to more acknowledgement of shame and of human interdependency, and less denial and disguise. Such steps might require parental education for child-rearing, and educational institutions for children and youth that are student-oriented and participatory.

Merely to conceptualize such changes would require heroic efforts, let alone carrying them through. But to the extent that the theory outlined here is true, our survival might depend on such an agenda. This chapter started with the idea of imagined communities. I argued that persons choose imagined communities over real ones when they feel desperately humiliated. I have outlined what may be a new direction for the human sciences, imagining future communities that would speak a new language of interdependence and emotion, and would decrease humiliation to a bearable burden for humanity.

NOTES

1 For a description of the diversity of accommodations to the Chinese settlers, see Purcell (1965). For a reference to the Chinese as the "Jews of Asia," see Skinner (1957: 164 and passim).

REFERENCES

Adler, Alfred 1956: *The Individual Psychology of Alfred Adler*. New York: Basic Books.

Anderson, Benedict 1983: *Imagined Communities*. London: Verso.

Billig, Michael 1992: *Talking of the Royal Family*. London: Routledge.

Bowen, Murray 1978: *Family Therapy in Clinical Practice*. New York: Jason Aronson.

Braithwaite, John 1989: *Crime, Shame and Reintegration*. Cambridge: Cambridge University Press.

Braithwaite, John 1992: "Reintegrative Shaming and Recent Criminal Justice Reforms in New Zealand and Australia," paper read at the November meeting of the American Society of Criminology, New Orleans.

Cooley, C. H. 1922: *Human Nature and the Social Order*. New York: Scribner's.

Craig, E. Gordon 1982: *The Germans*. New York: Putnam.

Cramer, M. Richard and Howard Schuman 1975: "We and They: Pronouns as Measures of Political Identification and Estrangement," *Social Science Research* 4: 231–40.

Darwin, Charles 1872: *The Expression of Emotions in Men and Animals*. London: MacMurray.

Ekman, Paul and Wallace Friesen 1978: *Facial Action Coding System*. Palo Alto: Consulting Psychologists Press.

Elias, Norbert 1939: *The History of Manners*. New York: Pantheon (1978).

Elias, Norbert 1987: *Involvement and Detachment*. Oxford: Blackwell.

Elias, Norbert 1989: *Studien ueber die Deutschen* (About the Germans). Frankfort: Suhrkamp.

Fanon, Frantz 1952: *Black Skin – White Masks*. New York: Grove Press (1967).

Forster, E. M. 1927: *A Passage to India*. New York: Dutton.

Glaser, Barney and Anselm Strauss 1967: *The Discovery of Grounded Theory*. Chicago: Aldine.

Goffman, Erving 1967: *Interaction Ritual*. New York: Anchor.

Gottschalk, L. and C. Gleser 1969: *Manual for the Gottschalk–Gleser Content Analysis Scales*. Berkeley: University of California Press.

Hitler, Adolf 1927: *Mein Kampf*. New York: Houghton Mifflin (1943).

Izard, Carroll 1977: *Human Emotions*. New York: Plenum.

Izard, Carroll 1979: *The Maximally Discriminative Facial Movement Coding System*. Newark, NJ: University of Delaware, Office of Instructional Technology.

Jencks, Christopher and Paul Peterson, eds 1991: *The Urban Underclass*. Washington, DC: Brookings Institution.

Labov, William and David Fanshel 1977: *Therapeutic Discourse*. New York: Academic Press.

Lewis, Helen Block 1971: *Shame and Guilt in Neurosis*. International Universities Press.

Lewis, Helen Block 1977: *Psychic War in Men and Women*. New York: New York University Press.

Lewis, Helen Block 1981: *Freud and Modern Psychology*. New York: Plenum.

Lewis, Helen Block 1987: *The Role of Shame in Symptom Formation*. Hillsdale, NJ: Lawrence Erlbaum Associates.

Lindemann, Albert 1991: *The Jew Accused*. New York: Cambridge University Press.

Memmi, Albert 1957: *The Colonizer and the Colonized*. Boston: Beacon Press (1967).

Purcell, Victor 1965: *The Chinese in Southeast Asia*. London: Oxford University Press.

Retzinger, Suzanne 1991: *Violent Emotions: Shame and Rage in Marital Quarrels*. Newbury Park: Sage.

Scheff, Thomas 1987: "The Shame–Rage Spiral: Case Study of an Interminable Quarrel," in Helen B. Lewis, ed., *The Role of Shame in Symptom Formation*. Hillsdale, NJ: Lawrence Erlbaum Associates.

Scheff, Thomas 1990: *Microsociology*. Chicago: University of Chicago Press.

Scheff, Thomas 1992: "Rationality and Emotion," in James Coleman and Thomas Fararo, eds, *Rational Choice Theory: Advocacy and Critique*. Newbury Park: Sage.

Scheff, Thomas 1994: *Bloody Revenge: Emotions, Nationalism, War*. Boulder, CO: Westview.

Scheff, Thomas and Suzanne Retzinger 1991: *Emotions and Violence: Shame and Rage in Destructive Conflicts*. Lexington: Lexington Books.

Scheff, Thomas, Suzanne Retzinger, and Michael Ryan 1989: "Crime, Violence, and Self-Esteem," in Andrew Mecca, Neil Smelser and John Vasconcellos, eds, *The Social Importance of Self-Esteem*. Berkeley: University of California Press.

Shibutani, Tomatsu 1955: "Reference Groups as Perspectives," *American Journal of Sociology* 60: 562–9.

Shibutani, Tamotsu and Kian Kwan 1965: *Ethnic Stratification*. New York: Macmillan.

Skinner, G. W. 1957: *Chinese Society in Thailand*. Ithaca: Cornell University Press.

Smith, Anthony 1971: *Theories of Nationalism*. New York: Harper.

Smith, Anthony 1976: *Nationalist Movements*. London: Macmillan.

Smith, Anthony 1986: *The Ethnic Origins of Nations*. Oxford: Basil Blackwell.

Stone, Clarence 1992: "Unpacking the Urban Poverty Problem," *Contemporary Sociology* 21: 448–9.

Tavuchis, Nicholas 1991: *Mea Culpa: The Sociology of Apologies*. Stanford: Stanford University Press.

Tomkins, Silvan 1967: *Affect/Imagery/Consciousness*, vol. II: *The Negative Affects*. New York: Springer.

Trilling, Lionel 1943: *E. M. Forster*. New York: New Directions.

Wurmser, Leon 1988: *Die Zerbrochene Wirklichkeit: Psychoanalyse als das Studium von Konflict und Komplementaritaet* (A Broken Reality: Studies of Conflict and Cooperation). Berlin: Springer-Verlag.

11

Nationalism and Civil Society: Democracy, Diversity and Self-Determination

Craig Calhoun

In 1989, the self-declared "free world" reveled in the collapse of communism. Capitalism and democracy seemed simply and obviously triumphant. The Cold War was over. Everyone would live happily ever after.

Of course, there would be "transitional problems." Word came of fighting in Nagorno-Karabak. It crossed some minds that many residents of Soviet Central Asia might find fundamentalist Islam more appealing than American capitalism. Enthusiasm for Lithuanian nationalism was occasionally dimmed by memories of Lithuanian fascism and anti-Semitism. But in an efflorescence of faith in progress not seen since the nineteenth century, most western politicians and intellectuals confidently saw "excesses" of nationalism as at most minor detours on the road to capitalist democracy. Even thinkers on the left joined the enthusiasm and, embarrassed by seeming association with the losing side, hastened to forget the lessons of history and the need for serious analysis.

But 1989 imperceptibly gave way to 1992, and anxiety began to regain a little intellectual respectability. Still, it has taken quite

Paper presented to the American Sociological Association session, "The Future of the Nation-State," 24 August 1992. Earlier versions of this paper were presented to the conference, "Legacies of the Collapse of Marxism," George Mason and George Washington Universities, March 1992, and the Hungarian Sociological Association, June 1991. I am grateful for comments on both occasions, and for comments from and discussion with Lloyd Kramer, Pamela DeLargy, Lee Schlesinger, Michael Warner, Alan Sica, and Edward Tiryakian.

dramatic events, from Ethiopia to the former Soviet Union and especially Yugoslavia, to focus attention on the possibility that nationalism might be more than a passing problem. Serbian talk of "ethnic cleansing" brought shudders of recollection, yet many treated it – like the Nazi ideology it recalled – as a throwback to the pre-modern. It is no accident, however, that "ethnic cleansing" is the project of academics and technicians, not of peasants, just as Nazism was rooted in scientific discourse and technological dreams as well as old hatreds. Both are fundamentally and horribly modern. And if nationalism is a central problem of post-communist transitions, this is because it is a central way of organizing collective identity throughout the modern world.

Academics have repeatedly announced the death of nationalism, but like that of Mark Twain's demise, the reports have been greatly exaggerated. In one of the most recent waves of such assertions, analysts correctly observe that states are having difficulty organizing and controlling global markets, multinational corporations, large-scale migration flows and internal "tribalism." Yet these analysts seldom consider the possibility that, rather than spelling the end of nationalism, all these trends and difficulties are its occasion. All encourage the renewal and continuing production of nationalism because nationalism is the rhetoric of identity and solidarity in which citizens of the modern world most readily deal with the problematic nature of state power and with problems of inclusion and exclusion. Rather than following state-building in a neat correlation, nationalism is most an issue where the boundaries and power of a state do not coincide neatly with the will or identity of its members or the scale of action undertaken by other collective actors.

Nationalist claims are one genre of answers to the question of what constitutes an autonomous political community capable of "self-determination." These claims come in two main versions: one places crucial stress on the ethnic or cultural similarity of the members of a political community; the other on their common citizenship in a specific state (with its characteristic modes of political activity). But in both versions, nationalist answers to the question of what constitutes a political community underestimate the importance of the institutions, networks, and movements that knit people together across lines of diversity internal to nations and states; they underestimate, in other words, the specifically sociological problems of social integration.

Nationalism appeared in the post-1989 discourse on transitions to democracy – and in theories of democracy generally – primarily

as a hazard to be avoided, not as a central dimension of the
subject. Yet nationalism is directly and fundamentally involved in
questions about the social foundations for democracy. Leaving
nationalism to one side theoretically – and to often anti-democratic
activists in practice – the discourse on transitions did sometimes
take up the question of what social foundations enable a collectivity
of people to organize their institutions through popular political
participation. It did so most prominently under the rubric of "civil
society." This concept was invoked to account for the various resources outside direct state control that offered alternatives to the
state organization of collective life. In many invocations, thus, the
role of more or less self-regulating markets or processes of capital
accumulation was not distinguished from the roles of networks of
interpersonal relations, social movements, and public discourse.

The significance of this became apparent when the economic
challenges of post-communist transition began to compete with efforts
to increase democratic participation. Various different programs for
the rapid creation of "free-market" economies, thus, were all claimed
by their proponents to strengthen civil society, whether or not
they increased the capacity of ordinary people to join together in
associations and movements or otherwise to create a public sphere
capable of shaping social and political decisions on the basis of
rational-critical discourse. Many of these programs of economic
privatization, in fact, did relatively little to increase the extent of
popular participation in decisions regarding investment and economic
structure. While some did seek to increase opportunities for entre-
preneurship and the development of new small businesses, others
focused more on transferring large-scale state enterprises to "private"
owners. The link between the two was faith in the importance of
subjecting as much as possible of the formerly "administered" economies to the discipline of the market. The market, however, was
understood as an abstract, impersonal and self-regulating force, and
moreover one that either did or should transcend national and state
boundaries.

A tension was created, in short, between the pursuit of democratization and the pursuit of economic development. The former
was seen as essentially a matter of domestic institutions and actions
while the latter involved participation in an increasingly global
economy. The constraints and demands imposed by the effort to
compete in this global economy were and are frequently cited as
reasons for limiting or postponing the project of increasing democratic participation. Indeed, perhaps paradoxically, voters in the
new electoral democracies have even been persuaded on several

occasions that voting their pocketbooks meant voting against democratization. The prestige of the cadres of international economic consultants brought in to replace the cadres of communist central planners has often been placed behind such conclusions. The result often has been to replace the imperatives of party and state bureaucracies with the imperatives of impersonal market forces as interpreted by technical experts and politicians.

In confronting so dramatically the tension between economic globalization and the pursuit of democracy through domestic institutions, the ex-communist and newly independent states of eastern Europe highlight an issue faced much more generally in the contemporary world. A broad range of commentators and pundits have pointed to globalization and suggested that the era of the nation-state is at an end.[1] The mobility of capital and impossibility of containing economic activity within the bounds of state control allegedly suggest that states are no longer crucial units of organization and power. This misrepresents, however, the nature and significance of economically driven globalization. First, this is not an entirely new trend, but a continuation of the historical pattern of the whole modern era. Second, this economic globalization may reduce certain of the capacities of states, but it does not make them less important or imply that in general they are likely either to break up or amalgamate. Modern states have always existed and derived much of their significance from their contraposition to other states in a "world system" that has always been too large for any single state to control. States have existed in part to manage economic – and also military – relations that cross their boundaries. What is most distinctive about the current globalization is not that it creates a level of global integration that states cannot readily manage, but that it brings close to completion the process of continuously incorporating more and more parts of the world into the capitalist world system.[2]

The travails of eastern Europe reveal that incorporation into the global economy does not stop states from being crucial arenas of struggle. States remain the organizations of power through which democratic movements have the greatest capacity to affect economic organization. Given the current organization of the United Nations, states remain the highest level of institutional structure at which programs of democratization themselves can consistently be advanced. And states remain the most crucial objects and vehicles of efforts to achieve "self-determination" or autonomy as a political community. As states remain of crucial importance, so too does the ideology of nationalism. Characteristic of the whole modern era, this reflects the constitution of the modern world system as a system of states. The primacy of national identity is implicit in both sides of the eastern European transition. It is what gives force to the notion of using domestic institutions to attempt to position a people in the global economy. It is also what constitutes the most basic notion of a people capable of claiming rights over and against a government. This is equally the case whether the claims are those of secession or more simply of self-governance without change of borders. The definition of boundaries and constitution of a collective identity are crucial components of the constitution of a political community in the modern world system of states.

The problems of collective identity formation are commonly ignored by democratic theory. They are, however, endemic to modern political life. Nationalism, as the most potent discourse of collective identity, appears alike in projects of unity and division. It may be an irony of history, thus, but it is not a sociological contradiction that western Europe is pursuing the path of unification at the same time that eastern European countries are being rent by nationalist splits. By the same token, however, this reveals that nationalism is not itself an adequate explanation of such processes of integration or disintegration so much as it is a political rhetoric in which many of them are pursued.

Discussions of the idea of nation and of social integration need therefore to be joined. The theory of democracy needs to deal with both of the two senses in which they raise the question of how political communities are constituted. The first is the bounded nature of all political communities, and the embeddedness of all claims to constitute a distinct and autonomous political community in relationships of contraposition to other such communities or claimants. The second is the web of relationships that constitutes a people (or nation) as a social collectivity existing independently of common subjection to the rule of a particular state.

CIVIL SOCIETY

It is not mere coincidence that the opposition to totalitarian role and the transition to democracy have brought ideas about civil society to the foreground. The language of civil society – though often sociologically underdeveloped – has been the most prominent way in which claims to peoplehood and self-determination have been grounded in appeals to social integration. The events of 1989 catapulted this concern from academic circles to the broader public discourse. The phrase is now on the lips of foundation executives, business leaders, and politicians; it seems as though every university has set up a study group on civil society, and the phrase finds its way into half the dissertations in political sociology. Too often, the phrase is invoked without sorting out whether civil society means Milton Friedman's capitalist market policies or social movements like Solidarity or the sort of "political society" or "public sphere" beloved of thinkers from Montesquieu to Tocqueville and Habermas, and once thought to exist mainly in cafés and coffee houses. [3]

Two basic questions are raised in discussions of civil society. First, what counts as or defines a political community? Second, what knits society together, providing for social integration? There are several contenders in each case: state, market economy, cultural similarity (e.g., nationality), social networks, political participation by autonomous agents. The idea of civil society entered political philosophy and social theory as a way of describing the capacity of self-organization on the part of a political community, in other words the capacity of a society to organize itself without being organized by a state. If society had such capacity, then "the people" integrated in that society could better be seen as the source of political legitimacy rather than merely the object of rule. In some early uses – notably the Scottish moralists including Ferguson and Smith – the notion of civil society referred to all such non-state capacities for social organization. The economy was not only included, it provided a key example. To these early capitalist thinkers, the self-regulating character of markets demonstrated the possibility for social organization without the direction of the state.

As Charles Taylor has argued, however, it is crucial to distinguish two different branches of the discourse of civil society. [4] While one followed Ferguson and Smith in stressing the economic-systemic character of civil society, the other followed Montesquieu, Rousseau, and Tocqueville in stressing social relations entered into by autonomous agents. The eastern European discourse of the 1980s and much of the recent usage blurs important distinctions between the two. [5]

The issue is not solved by declaring that civil society must be kept conceptually distinct from capitalist economic organization. On the contrary, capitalism itself appears in both voluntary and systemic guises. On the one hand, capitalist ideology typically asserts that capitalist economic life *is* precisely the realm of free social relations. It offers a model of capitalist life as quintessentially the activity and relationships of owner-operators of small businesses and individual consumers. One might object that these are relations only among buyers and sellers, but one cannot deny that capitalism offers certain genuine freedoms. At the same time, capitalist ideology itself negates its proffered freedom by reference to the immutable "laws" of the market. It claims that the systemic character of markets dictates that interference from states or other collective actors (unions, social movements, etc.) must be kept to a minimum so that the capitalist system can organize itself. This kind of limit on free collective action is asserted by capitalist ideology itself, even when it refuses to recognize the salient distinctions between giant corporations and human individuals, or the inevitable dependence and mutuality between capitalist economics and certain forms of state support.

Nonetheless, capitalism *did* historically and can still play a special and crucial role in the growth of a civil society. The early growth of capitalist business relations provided essential support to the development of a sphere of political discourse outside the realm of state control. This is not to say that businessmen were the primary protagonists of the bourgeois public sphere. On the contrary, various state employees from ministerial clerks through university professors, and dependents of aristocratic sponsors played far more central roles in the eighteenth-century "golden age" of the public sphere. But the development of a public discourse in which private persons addressed public issues was made possible, in part, by both the policy issues posed by the growth of the non-state-dominated market activity, and the creation of settings for such discourse in coffee houses, journals, and other forums operated as businesses. [6]

It is crucial not to accept capitalist ideology uncritically, and therefore to imagine that capitalism is somehow by itself an adequate support for democracy or a viable alternative to state power. It is equally crucial not to ignore the role of certain kinds of at least quasi-autonomous business institutions in facilitating the development of a sphere of public discourse and capacity for social organization outside the immediate control of the state. Above all, we must look beyond capitalism (and more generally beyond the narrow realm of the economy as a putatively self-sufficient and self-regulating system) to seek (1) the extent to which societal integration can be accomplished through webs of interpersonal relations, and (2) the extent to which both these social relations and the more abstract ones of the economy can be organized voluntarily through public discourse. Only when these possibilities are addressed do we have a conception of societal integration that can serve as foundation to a theory of democracy.

In other words, from the point of view of democracy, it is essential to retain in the notion of civil society some idea of a social realm which is neither dominated by state power nor simply responsive to the systemic features of capitalism. The public sphere of civil society cannot be simply a realm in which representatives of state authority vie for attention with economists claiming to predict the economy like the weather on the basis of its reified laws. It must include an institutionally organized and substantial capacity for people to enter as citizens into public discourse about the nature and course of their life together. This capacity depends not just on formal institutions, but on civil society as a realm of sociability.

In this conceptualization, civil society must also be a realm of intermediate associations. Communities, movements, and organizations (from churches to political parties and mutual aid societies) are all potentially important. Though the nationalist impulse is sometimes to condemn these as intrinsically "partial," this needs to be affirmed as one of their major virtues. For it is precisely in such partial social units that people find both the capacity for collective voice and the possibility of differentiated, directly interpersonal relations. Such intermediate associations are also the crucial defenses both of distinctive identities imperiled by the normalization of the mass, and of democracy against oligarchy.[7]

Hidden in this discourse – in two centuries of public discourse as well as in the last few paragraphs – is the problem of identifying "the people" who may be members of a discursive public or a civil society. From its earliest instantiations, from classical Athens through revolutionary America or Enlightenment Europe, the democratic public sphere has been marred by exclusionary tendencies. Not just slaves, but non-natives, aboriginals, propertyless men and all women have been excluded at various points from both direct political participation (e.g., voting) and from participation in the discourse of the public sphere. Some other exclusions seem more justifiable, though the theoretical status of the justifications is complex: the participation of children, criminals, and the mentally incompetent is almost universally restricted. In short, "the people" have not all been citizens.

That democracy has always been restrictive has certainly been noticed. But there is an equally basic version of the question "who are the people?" which is less often posed. When we say, for example in relation to the breakup of Yugoslavia, that we believe in the right of "self-determination," just what self is involved? The notion of self-determination is basic to democracy, and yet both neglected by democratic theory and shrouded in illusions of primordiality. The problem of self-determination is that for every socially relevant self we can see internal divisions and vital links to others. There is no single, definite, and fixed "peoplehood" which can be assumed in advance of political discussion.

Moreover, as "no man is an island unto himself," no nation exists alone.[8] Each is defined in relation to others and exists within a web of social relationships that traverse its boundaries. Supposed historical autarky was never complete, and modern attempts to close borders have had only partial and temporary success.[9] Conversely, claims to indivisibility are always at least partially tendentious and often (as in the United States pledge of allegiance) recognitions of the successful application of force to preserve unity. In short, do we speak of Macedonians, Croats, and Serbs, of Yugoslavians, of Slavs, of Christians and Muslims, or of Europeans? The answers are obvious only from particular and partisan vantage points. Too often it is only forcible repression which makes us sure we see a true national identity. We lack a theory of the constitution of social selves which will give descriptive foundation to the prescriptive notion of self-determination. We are poorly prepared to talk about national identity or nationalism.[10]

NATIONALITY AND NATIONALISM

Ideologists of nationality almost always claim it as an inheritance rather than a contemporary construct. This is true whether the inheritance is conceived as a "primordial" identity, rooted deep in the mists of ancient history, or as deriving from a more recent founding moment like the French Revolution.[11] The notion of inheritance is not by any means simply false, for national identity is something that shapes individuals – a Durkheimian social fact, external, enduring, and coercive – not a matter of completely free individual choice. Claims to ancient origins and especially primordiality are, however, problematic. At the very least, they nearly always radically oversimplify the complexities of national identity and history. The issue is not just whether people are members of one or another nation, or whether a particular claimed nation has the right to self-determination, but what it means to be a member of that nation, how it is to be understood, and how it relates to the other identities its members may also claim or be ascribed.[12]

Such notions of primordial inheritance are among of the bases for the widespread illusion that somehow earlier traditions and identities can just be picked up and the communist era treated as an inconsequential interregnum. Among some groups in Russia, for example – and in a good deal of western discussion of Russia –

the idea is current that the "real" Russia is that of the czars. To some this means an ancient spiritual identity, preserved through long travails and waiting to flower again as beacon to all Slavs. To others, this means a political and cultural development, moving forward rapidly in the late nineteenth and early twentieth centuries, when Russia could aspire to European leadership. Protagonists of each interpretation imagine that somehow when the pall of communism is lifted, the Russians of the late twentieth century will begin to write like Tolstoy and pick up the torch of an interrupted political development. In this remembered history, the struggles against Orthodox religion, against czarist rule and rural landlords, and between *narodniki*, bourgeois democrats, and various stripes of socialists are somehow submerged, and communism becomes something both alien and accidental, not an outgrowth of national history.

In Hungary, it is easier to make the case that communism was something imposed from outside, but it is still not obvious that the nation can simply go forward in 1992 as a direct extension of that of 1945's imposed communism or 1921's repression of revolution. Is national identity simply ancient and timeless? Or has it been forged and remade in centuries of struggle? What is the relationship between the Hungary which struggled against Habsburg rule – and flowered under it, the Hungary which struggled to maintain independence and build a modern state in the early twentieth century, that of Nazi rule and resistance to it, that of communism, both domestic and imported, that of the Georg Lukács who lived in Budapest and the one who lived in Moscow, that of 1919 (just after collapse of the Austro-Hungarian empire), 1956 (rebellion against communism and its crushing), and 1989 (communism's collapse)? Different answers to these questions flow from different visions of what it means to be Hungarian. There are similar questions in every country's history, and they are central to the reasons why nationalism is always caught in an intimate but ambiguous relationship with history. Nationalist movements always revere martyrs and cherish sacred dates; they always give nations a history. But as Ernest Renan wrote in perhaps the most famous essay ever written on the subject, "Forgetting, I would even go so far as to say historical error, is a crucial factor in the creation of a nation, which is why progress in historical studies often constitutes a danger for [the principle of] nationality. Indeed, historical enquiry brings to light deeds of violence which took place at the origin of all political formations, even those whose consequences have been altogether beneficial. Unity is always effected by means of brutality ..." [13]

The issue goes further. History is problematic for nationalism and the tacit assumption of national identity because it always shows nationality to be constructed, not primordial. The history which nationalism would write of itself begins with the existence of national identity, continues through acts of heroism and sometimes struggles against oppression, and unites all living members of the nation with the great cultural accomplishments of its past. It is usually not a sociological history, of diversity forged into unity, of oppression of some members of the nation by others, of migration and immigration, and so forth. Precisely because it is not a socio-logical history, it allows all present-day Russians to identify with nineteenth-century novelists, and for the westernizing efforts of Peter the Great to make him now a nationalist hero. And even in cosmopolitan Budapest it encourages some Hungarian patriots to identify with Magyar horsemen, accept centuries of international influences, and yet think of Hungarian Jews as members of an alien nation.

So nationality is not primordial but constructed. It is, moreover, a construction specific to the modern era and to the emergence of a modern world system in which claims to statehood became crucial bases for standing in world affairs, and potentially for autonomy, and in which claims to statehood can be justified most readily by professions of nationhood. This does not make nationality or the sentiments of nationhood any less real. But by the same token, nationality is not *more* real than many other identities which people may claim, or feel, or reproduce in their social relations. The nationalist claim is that national identity is categorical and fixed, and that somehow it trumps all other sorts of identities, from gender to region, class to political preference, occupation to artistic taste. This is a very problematic claim.

It is not easy to define nationalism. There are important varia-tions where different cultures are at issue, where conquest has subordinated one group of people to another, where older ethnic groupings are being recast in terms of the idea of nation, and where an attempt is being made to forge a new unity out of previous diversity. It seems better to see nationalisms in terms of family re-semblances (following Wittgenstein) rather than to search for an essentialist definition of nationalism. When we speak of nationalism, thus, we speak of a somewhat arbitrary subset of claims to identity and autonomy on the part of populations claiming the size and capacity to be self-sustaining. For the purpose of any specific analysis we may want to include, say, the religious and political struggles in Northern Ireland or keep them distinct; there is no perfect boundary, no criterion of selecting nationalisms which includes all the familiar cases we are sure we want to consider without also including a variety of dubious outliers.

With more confidence, we can address the underlying factors which gave rise to nationalism and made it a major genus of identity claim and source of political mobilization in the modern era. Indeed, by noting these underlying factors we can see why in a strong sense only the modern era has produced nationalism. People have always been joined in groups. These groups have derived their solidarity from kinship and other forms of social (including economic) interconnection, from a common structure of political power, from shared language and culture. But in the modern era, cultural and social structural factors have converged to create and disseminate the notion of national identity and make it central.

Culturally, the most decisive idea behind nationalism (or national identity) is the modern notion of the individual. The idea that human beings can be understood in themselves as at least potentially self-sufficient, self-contained, and self-moving is vital. It is no accident that Fichte is crucial to the histories of both individualism and nationalism. For Fichte's notion of self-recognition, of the person who seemingly confronts himself (or herself) in a mirror and says "I am I" is inextricably tied to the notion of the nation as itself an individual. Just as persons are understood as unitary in prototypical modern thought, so are nations held to be integral. As Benedict Anderson has indicated, this involves a special sense of time as the history through which the nation as perduring and unitary being passes rather than as a differentiable internal history of the nation. [14] The process of individuation is important not just metaphorically, but as the basis for the central notion that individuals are directly members of the nation, that it marks each of them as an intrinsic identity and they commune with it immediately and as a whole. In ideology, at least, the individual does not require the mediations of family, community, region, or class to be a member of the nation. This is a profound reversal of the weight of competing loyalties from the pre-modern era (and much of the rest of the world). In this we see the sharp difference of nationalism from the ideology of honor of the lineage, and the chilling potential for children to inform on their parents' infractions against the nation. [15]

Nineteenth-century ideologists of nationalism emphasized a world-historical (or evolutionary) process of individuation in which the world's peoples took on their distinctive characters, missions, and destinies. Or at least the world's "historical nations" did so; others lacked sufficient vigor or national character; they were destined to be failures and consigned to the backwaters of history. Not surprisingly, this is typically how dominant or majority populations thought of minorities and others subordinated within their dominions. This was another conceptualization, in effect, of the Springtime of Nations. It was the period when France took on its "mission civilisatrice," Germany found its historical destiny, and Poles crystallized their Romantic conception of the martyr-nation.[16] Each nation had a distinct experience and character, something special to offer the world and something special to express for itself. "Nations are individualities with particular talents and the possibilities of exploiting those talents."[17]

It is no accident, thus, that philosophers like Fichte emphasized simultaneously the individuation of the person and of the nation. The two notions remain inextricably linked.[18] This very linkage, however, could create tensions. The great cultural geniuses of a nation's history were widely celebrated in the nineteenth century; the proliferation of individual geniuses was proof, especially for the Romantics, of the greatness of the nation. Though Norway had but recently gained an independent cultural status (and was not yet independent politically) her production of geniuses in the late nineteenth century, from Munch to Grieg to Ibsen, was proof enough of her standing even for the German intellectuals of the period. But being cast as the bearer of national identity was not always entirely comfortable for geniuses (or others) with their own individual identities. Writing to Ibsen on his 70th birthday in 1898, the Norwegian poet Nils Kjoer tried to recover something of the autonomy of the person from the demand for representation of national character: "But a people's individuality is manysided, sufficient to explain any peculiarity of the mind and therefore it explains nothing."[19] If recognized geniuses could feel a tension with the demand that they serve as icons of the nation, pressures of a much more troubling nature were (and are) brought to bear on cultural deviants and minorities.[20] Though nations are ideologically composed of individuals, they are not generally promoters of individual distinctiveness. In the formative phases of nationalism, heroic individuals – cultural as well as military and political heroes – figure prominently, but often in the established nation, conformity to the common culture becomes a central value. The character of nationalism is changed as it shifts from insurgent movement to dominant ideology, though even insurgents can be sharply intolerant of diversity. It is easier to admire heroes from afar, and easiest to claim them when they are dead.

The key structural change which makes it possible to conceive of the nation as unitary is the rise of the modern state. Previous political forms neither demarcated clear boundaries nor fostered internal integration and homogenization. Cities dominated hinterlands; sometimes particularly powerful cities dominated networks of others together with their hinterlands. The various kinds of military (and sometimes religious) elites we call "feudal" controlled substantial territories but with a minimum of centralization of power and limited ability to remake everyday life. Though empires could call on subject peoples for tribute and sometimes foster substantial interaction among diverse subjects, they posed few demands for cultural homogenization. Yet the rise of the modern state involved remarkable administrative integration of previously quasi-autonomous regions and localities. This was true both for purposes of military contest with other states and for internal economic activity and political rule.[21] Eventually, state power could be exercised at the farthest point of a realm as effectively as in the capital. Not only could taxes be collected, but roads could be built, schools run, and mass communications systems created. Linguistic standardization is a common measure of national integration, and historical research reminds us how recent such standardization was in most European countries. Most Frenchmen did not speak French before the second half of the nineteenth century.[22] Even demographic behavior – fertility rates, for example – which once varied from locality to locality, become strikingly uniform within nineteenth- and twentieth-century European nation-states.[23]

The capacity of states to administer distant territories with growing intensity was largely due to improvements in transportation and communications infrastructure, on the one hand, and bureaucracy and related information management on the other. It was part of a general growth in large-scale social relations. More and more of social life took place through forms of mediation – markets, communications technologies, bureaucracies – which removed relationships from the realm of direct, face-to-face interaction. In addition to facilitating state power, this growth in "indirect" and large-scale relationships directly facilitated nationalism. It encouraged, for example, increasing reliance on categorical identities rather than webs of relational identities.[24] This transformation was closely related to the growth of capitalism. In the first place, a growing division of labor and intensification of trade relations knit localities and regions together in relations of mutual dependence. Capitalism continually drove its agents out beyond local markets, established competitive pressures around the globe, and demanded coordination of ever-growing supplies of labor and raw materials – even before the generation of increasing consumer demand became an obsession.

Capitalism thus both depended on and continually increased the capacity for large-scale and indirect social relations. Because more and more of the activity on which lives and livelihoods depended was taking place at a distance from immediate locales, attempts to conceptualize the commonalities and connections among locales were increasingly important. Beyond this, connections established only through markets and the commodity form were especially prone to reification and representation in categorical terms. The nation became the domestic market, other nations international competitors or clients. [25]

Partly (though not entirely) under pressure of capitalist expansion, the entire world was divided into bounded territories. Every inch of land was declared the province of one state or another. No longer were there hinterlands in which people could follow their ways of life relatively undisturbed by pressures to conform to one or another state's dominant culture. Attempts to preserve local tradition now required active resistance. Where empires demanded mainly political loyalty, states imposed pressures for multifarious forms of cultural loyalty and participation. The opportunity for a people to be self-organizing was increasingly limited to those who could mount a successful claim to state sovereignty. Whatever the actual form of government claimants anticipated, from the moment that sovereignty came to be a claim from below, by the people, rather than from the rulers above, the modern ideal of the nation-state was born. Even Hobbes, in justifying the absolute sovereignty of kings, required first a body of citizens – a nation – capable of granting the right to rule in explicit or implicit social contract. And these citizens were, perforce, basically interchangeable as members of the nation.

This is a crucial contrast between the empire and the nation-state, or, as Weintraub has shrewdly noted, between the cosmopolitan city and the polis. The creation of a political community called for a new kind of interrelationships, and something more than a "live and let live" urbanity. In the cosmopolis or empire, since "heterogeneous multitudes were not called upon to be citizens, they could remain in apolitical coexistence, and each could do as he wished without the occasion to deliberate with his neighbors." [26] In both the polis and the modern nation-state, membership in a common polity requires more than tolerance and common subjection to an external sovereign. It requires mutual communication. This poses an impetus for erasure of differences among the citizens. One of the crucial questions of the modern era is whether meaningful, politically efficacious public discourse can be achieved without this erasure.

The claim to be a nation was a claim to be entitled to a state (or at the very least, to special recognition in the constitution of a state). Though the reciprocal claim was not logically entailed, it was common. By the nineteenth century it was thought not only that every nation deserved a state, but that each state should represent one nation. Nationalism, as Ernest Gellner writes, held that nations and states "were destined for each other; that either without the other is incomplete, and constitutes a tragedy."[27] One of the features of this new way of conceptualizing sovereignty was that it treated all nation-states as formally equivalent, whatever their size or power. It was no longer possible to conceive of derogated levels of partial or subordinate sovereignty − kings and dukes below emperors, autonomous cities under the protection of princes, etc. Either Burgundy was part of France or it was an alien state; if part of France, it was merely part and not nation in itself. In the mid-nineteenth-century United States, extreme claims to "states' rights" in a weak confederacy of strong subsidiary parts were not so much the claims of one or more alternative nationalisms as claims against nationalism itself. The "country" to which Confederate soldiers owed a duty was conceived from the immediate family and local community outward (and largely through a hierarchy of aristocratic connections, not laterally). It was not conceived primarily as a categorical identity, coterminous with a single polity and culture.[28]

Just as the spread of capitalism created a world system in which only capitalist competition could be effective, so the division of the world into states created a continuing pressure for the production of nationalisms. Claims for greater autonomy or greater unity could gain legitimacy primarily as claims to create a nation-state, that is, to create a new state to match a pre-existing nation. This is why the single term nationalism encompasses both fissiparous or secessionist movements and unificationist or "pan-"nationalist movements. Croatian or Ukrainian nationalism and pan-Slavic nationalism are dimensions of the same process. Programs for the unification of Europe draw on new histories which emphasize the commonality of the European experience and identity; the specificity of Europe is counterposed to the rest of the world, rather than the specificity of France being counterposed to Britain or the Netherlands. At the same time, fringe nationalist movements (and claims for regional autonomy) flourish within the European Community, while on its eastern border, the former Yugoslavia and perhaps other countries seem set to splinter into tiny nation-states. Indeed, nationalist struggles in eastern Europe reveal the continuing relevance of nationalism in a western Europe whose publicists had claimed it had moved beyond it. Divergent visions of the European Community and divergent interests have been brought out not just by German unification, but by fighting in former Yugoslavia and appeals from Poland, Czechoslovakia, and Hungary for community membership. Not least of all, east-to-west migration both results from nationalist strife (and nationalist protectionism which creates economic strife) and contributes to xenophobic nationalist responses.

Contrary to some over-glib journalism, there is no global reason for nationalism to be more integrating or disintegrating. The same rhetoric can as readily be deployed to claim unity across separate states (all Slavs or all Arabs) as to demand autonomy for a region of one (e.g., Slovakia or Ruthenia). But there are global reasons why nationalism remains the central form of identity in which people pose their claims to sovereignty. The most important of these is simply the creation of the world system as a system of states. Though some analysts predict the dissolution of such states in a postmodern welter of local identities and global corporations, the states do not yet seem to have given up the ghost. Nationalism remains important in part because claims to state sovereignty do matter – not least of all because states remain the central organizational frameworks within which democracy can be pursued.

Of course, as state administrative power was growing, and the world was divided into bounded territories, not all potential nationalisms thrived. [29] A variety of factors helped. One was simply the history and development of nationalist discourse itself. As Anderson points out, nationalist discourse was not simply a product of simultaneous invention around the globe. It was, at least in part, diffused; in his view it originated in certain colonial experiences and was exported to western Europe and thence re-exported. [30] The nationalist discourse has grown during the last 300 or so years; more is available as resource to latecomers. Within any putative nation as well, there may be greater or lesser history of nationalist discourse. There may be richer and more evocative discourses on national history and culture to provide particular content to nationalist aspirations. Specific experiences of external challenge or oppression may help to promote national consciousness, providing a clear and significant other for self-identification by contrast. It may be more or less possible to frame other discontents within the nationalist idiom. And other organizing bases, class above all, but also religious organizations, may be either absent, or congruent and supportive rather than competitive.

By the same token, not all nationalisms take the same form. They are shaped in different international contexts and from different domestic experiences. Some grow in response to histories of direct colonialism, others in response to present weakness in the world system without any specific colonial antagonist to shape them.[31] Some are elite, others democratic. Some seem to absorb an entire culture, claiming everything from language and literature through political practices and agricultural methods as specific to the nation. Others are more narrowly political movements, recognizing common participation in a broader culture. And last but not least, nationalist movements are shaped by the periods of their flowering: it was easier to believe in a happy fellowship of nations in the 1840s than it is today.

NATIONALISM AS SUCCESSOR IDEOLOGY

As recently as the early Gorbachev years of the mid-1980s, the leadership of the Soviet Union was still propounding a modified vision of the happy fellowship of nations. The condition of this fellowship was the elimination of the social antagonisms which set capitalist nations against each other and made nationalist conflicts an attractive distraction from class struggle. As a book in Novosti's series on "the Soviet Experience" put it, "as social antagonisms disappeared under socialism, so did national strife and racial inequality and oppression in every form ... The socialist multinational culture has been enriched through an intensive exchange of cultural and intellectual values. The socialist nations that have emerged in the USSR have formed a new historical community of people – the Soviet people. ... Today it would be no exaggeration to say that a feeling of being members of one family prevails among Soviet people."[32] On the one hand, such lines from a work entitled *How the Soviet Union Solved the Nationalities Question* seem laughably divorced from reality. On the other hand, a moment's reflection on the rapid return of nationalist conflict to what was once the Soviet sphere of influence reminds us why for so long Soviet ideology claimed the resolution of "the nationalities question" as one of the central accomplishments of communism.

Nationalism enters contemporary politics most strikingly in the wake of communist crisis and retreat. As obviously in Ethiopia as in eastern Europe, this has much to do with conditions which preceded (and sometimes coincided with) communism. Contemporary nationalism is, in part, a direct continuation of old struggles for autonomy from neighbors and stature among nations. This is accentuated in much of eastern Europe (and western or central Asia) by the extent to which communism appeared in the guise of Russian domination. But Russian nationalism is also resurgent, so this cannot be the whole story. Similarly, communism was in many cases imposed on people who had not made a commitment to it through struggles of their own. This too has probably made nationalism more likely as a successor ideology, but its effects should not be exaggerated, for the countries in which communism had most indigenous strength before becoming a Soviet-supported state ideology do not seem markedly less prone to nationalism than those for which communism was more clearly an external imposition.

Communist regimes were perfectly prepared to try to mobilize nationalist sentiments to bolster their legitimacy. The Romanian state made a massive enterprise of reproducing folklore in ways it could both claim and control.[33] The reconstruction of historical buildings was a major part of post-war rebuilding in both Poland and Hungary. Enormous resources and prestige were invested in production of international athletic successes. At the same time, communist states acted in ways which highlighted national identities in arenas where they officially denied or minimized their significance. Thus, Stalin sought to build "socialism in one country," and his Chinese counterparts still pursue "communism with Chinese characteristics."[34] Russia imposed its language as primary in the Soviet Union and secondary throughout the Warsaw pact. In Yugoslavia, the very stratagem of holding the country together by balancing national groups (and even making sure each nationally defined state contained regions with substantial members of other nationalities) reaffirmed infra-Yugoslavian national identities at the same time that it temporarily held nationalist rivalries in check.[35] Not least of all, the Soviet Army's occupation of much of eastern Europe could hardly fail to stir some nationalist resentment, especially when coupled with political interference.

Indeed, the most basic reasons for nationalism to flourish in the wake of communism have to do with political repression, not socialist – or statist – economics. Communist states repressed most forms of subsidiary identities and discourses on alternative political arrangements. Faced with pressures or opportunities for collective action, people were thrown back on preexisting bases for identification and collective action. This worked in two ways. First, when people chafed under centralized misrule their national identities were the most readily available ways to understand and respond to abuse. Second, when communism collapsed, nationalism was available to take its place. The latter was true especially where communism collapsed without the development of strong indigenous movements of resistance and counterculture. In Poland, Solidarity offered an alternative arena of cultural production and discourse – though of course Solidarity had a strong nationalist current of its own. In varying degrees other eastern European countries had both opportunities for cultural creativity and public discourse, and movements which both challenged the existing order and offered an alternative cultural discourse. In much of the Soviet Union, by contrast, repression was more severe, and insurgency from below less developed. One result was that in many settings – the Transcaucasus, for example – nationalism could emerge as the primary form of identity and the basic medium through which people expressed their aspirations for a better life. [36]

Communist states did not encourage the cultural creativity and free flow of discourse which could have both knit them together and opened a variety of bases of identity. This had several effects. It meant that in large and heterogeneous countries like the Soviet Union, only state-sponsored cultural productivity could work to unify the country as a whole. When the state lost its credibility, so did much of the cultural basis for unity at the largest level. Behind this suggestion is the general postulate that for populations to achieve some unity as citizenries, they need to be knit together by a common discourse. This does not mean that they are knit together simply by similarity of ideology. On the contrary, mere ideological similarity is a fairly brittle and easily fractured form of cultural unity, particularly when confronted with problems outside its familiar range. A shared discourse of problem solving provides a stronger foundation for confronting new challenges. More generally, culture is a stronger source of unity when it is open to rich and varied forms of creation and discussion. When discussion and creativity are foreclosed in order to maintain ideological conformity, it becomes difficult to achieve the manifold continuous cultural adjustments which are essential to both legitimation processes and sense of common membership in a political community. So, ironically, the very attempt to maintain complete conformity undermined identification with the whole, left it superficial and easily forgotten. [37]

At the same time, the absence of an open cultural sphere or political discourse meant that the development of multiple bases for individual identity was impeded. Outside the range of authoritarian rule and strong nationalism, it is common for people to gain their identities from a range of cross-cutting group affiliations (as Simmel suggested), and from membership in a variety of different salient cultural categories. Thus a woman in the United States may feel a strong sense of identity stemming from her occupation, her gender, her family, her community, her political activity, and her religion as well as and partially in competition with her nation. Though national identity may be a source of inspiration or pride, or of a sense of obligation to help others by pursuing the common good of the United States ahead of the general good of humanity, it is unlikely to be an identity which "trumps" all others. Of course, it is an open question how long this would last if the US ever came under severe external pressure, or wars were again fought on American soil. Nationalism comes to the fore under a variety of historically specific circumstances – like war – as well as per- haps being comparatively stronger in some cultural traditions than others. [38]

In the face of such pressure – and its immediate memory, as in eastern Europe – liberalism may seem a fairly thin ideology. Liberal capitalism is, however, the main ideological option offered by the West today. There is of course the Catholic Church, with its resurgent conservatism on the one hand (abetted by a Polish pope) and the remnants of liberation theology on the other. The Left remains relevant mainly by pursuing a variety of ameliorative reforms within the framework of welfare state capitalism, and defending various special interests of subordinated groups. But it is in disarray overall and no longer seems to offer a very compelling positive vision to complement its critique of liberal capitalism. Indeed, the western Left's failure of vision is directly related to the resurgence of national- ism in eastern Europe, as the Left has not been able to make much significant connection with advocates of a "third way" or a more robust notion of civil society. Westerners "on the Left" found East Germany's "New Forum" group appealing, thus, but were unable to connect with it in very deep or sustaining ways which would help to provide a viable electoral alternative to the vision of unity pro- moted by the Christian Democrats (largely because their own social democratic vision had been narrowed to a series of ameliorations of capitalist ills). The weakness of the western Left (not least its defensive posture in the US) helped to open the way to a discourse in which liberal capitalism and versions of nationalism are the main contenders for succession to communism. These contenders, as the German example reveals, are not as antithetical as has sometimes been thought. Many forms of nationalism can thrive quite happily on a capitalist foundation and put forward their claims in the rhetoric of liberalism. Indeed, liberalism's strengths run to the enun- ciation and preservation of certain liberties, not to the constitution of strong social or cultural identities. Nationalism can be its com- plement – rooted in the same individualism – as readily as it can be dissolved by liberalism's advocacy of the individual as the basic unit of analysis.

NATIONALISM AND DEMOCRACY

Nationalism is not an intrinsically "bad" ideology. It has been and remains an important source of inspiration. Any account of the political problems attendant on nationalism which does not recognize the achievements of poets, painters, and composers who were moved by nationalist sentiments misses an important part of the story. [39] Any account which imagines that citizens or human beings could be rational actors unmoved by cultural commitments and pre-rational identities loses touch with reality. In the political realm itself, nationalism is not intrinsically pernicious or antidemocratic. In the first place, there needs to be some culturally constructed identity behind the word "self" in the idea of self-determination. It is worth recalling too that in the 1840s nationalism often appeared as a progressive, liberal ideology in which a domestic push for democratic expression was coupled with a respect for other nations. Even more than respect, Romantics of the early nineteenth century were sufficiently inspired by heroic nationalist struggles to offer their own lives on behalf of alien nations. Yet even this phrase reveals a tension. To the strong Romantic humanist – to Byron, say – there were no alien nations, only many expressions of a common humanity striving for freedom and creative voice. Yet in extremes Romanticism (like its current postmodernist successors) had as much trouble making sense of difference as Enlightenment rationalism; neither grappled well with the problem of incommensurable practices, with the reasons why differences become hostilities. [40] And the exclusivity implied by the word "alien" is more common in the rhetoric of nationalism. Nationalism is all too often the enemy of democracy rooted in civil society.

In the first place, nationalism in power is very different from nationalist resistance to alien rule. Not unlike authoritarian regimes as I described them above, nationalists too often tend to promote the pseudo-democracy of sameness instead of the recognition and respect of difference. Ironically like communism, nationalism often stifles cultural discourse – not in the name of the state or even necessarily by the imposition of state power; it can work by a closure of the mind. Nationalism in power is often a repressive ideology demanding strict adherence to the authority of the official embodiments of national tradition – and very unlike nationalism in opposition, which is generally a strong stimulus to cultural productivity. The problems arise with the assertion that there is only one right way for any individual to be a Pole or a Russian, an Azeri or an American.

Repression is wielded not just against diversity of cultural expression but against the variety of alternative bases for personal identity which might compete with the nation. Thus the common antagonism of nationalists to autonomy and equality for women is not just a continuation of sexist traditions. Nationalism encourages this sexism by internal (and I think non-essential) cultural traditions – e.g., valuing the family as the source of the nation's continuity in time, and seeing men as future martyrs, women as mothers. Beyond this, however, nationalists resist women's movements because accepting the domination of male interests and perceptions merely perpetuates a taken-for-granted, monolithic view of the nation, while encouraging women to identify their distinctive interests and views opens claims that gender has autonomous status as a basis for personal identity which does not pale into insignificance before the commonalities of (male-dominated) nationhood.

In this sense, nationalism has totalitarian potential. It can be treated as a categorical identity more fundamental than other personal identities, even able to override them, and as fixed in both biographical and historical time. This is what I mean by saying that nationalism is used to "trump" other identities or values. [41] Nationalists often want the sentiment or sense of national identity to go beyond the feeling of being more at home in one place than another, beyond placing a special value on the traditions with which one grew up, beyond focusing one's attention more on one subset of humanity than on the whole. In its extreme forms, nationalism, like religious fundamentalism, often involves claims to monopolize the sources of legitimate identity. As Hannah Arendt wrote, we are apt since Tocqueville to blame conformism on the principle of equality, but "whether a nation consists of equals or non-equals is of no great importance in this respect, for society always demands that its members act as though they were members of one enormous family which has only one opinion and one interest." [42]

The decisive question about nationalism, therefore, is whether it can thrive with the nation open to competing conceptualizations, diverse identities, and a rich public discourse about controversial issues. These issues were faced in France in the late nineteenth century; in the Dreyfus affair, victory went to the forces of openness and heterogeneous civil society as the basis for democracy. There have been attempts to revoke the victory, notably by Second World

War era collaborationists and the contemporary radical right, under the leadership of nationalists like Jean-Marie Le Pen. But in central and eastern Europe there have been few such signal victories, and, as Adam Michnik has suggested, the issue is a very current one: "In both France and Poland the question was whether the nation was to be open and the state tolerant and multicultural, or whether the state was to be based on authoritarian principles and nationalistic doctrine. And I think this has been the central question ever since. Whenever the shadow of anti-Semitism arose in Polish public life, it was an unmistakable signal that people with antidemocratic, intolerant views were on the political offensive." [43]

It would be good, but not enough to say that tolerance should reign within states. Even multinational, multicultural states require more than simply tolerance among subsidiary peoples. They require public discourse. Citizens from different nationalities, as from different regions, religions, or occupations, need to be able and willing to engage each other in discourse about the social arrangements which hold them together and order their lives – in brief, about the common good. Moreover, the same is crucial within nationalities. There is no reason to accept monolithic conformity within any one nation or people (insurgent or in power). Not only may states be multinational or multicultural, nations themselves must – if they are to be allies of liberty – admit and encourage internal diversity whether they are coterminous with states or exist as subsidiary identities within states. It is necessary, in other words, that the nation be open to democracy and diversity, whether or not the close link between nation and state is severed. In power, extreme nationalists do not just repress other peoples, they repress the diversity and creativity of people within the very nation they cherish.

Without diversity, democracy is hardly distinct from a dictatorship of the mass. Indeed, it is hard to imagine how such a monolithic mass could be sustained beyond an ephemeral uprising except by means of centralized totalitarian power. Nationalism is benign only when it does not tend towards this pseudo-democracy of sameness. And this is where civil society comes in. Civil society is the locus of diverse groups and individuals and more importantly of their contact with each other. Division of labor and other sources of difference may arise within civil society or be brought into it from the family or other less public realms. But in civil society, the exchange not only of goods but of ideas can take place. Advocates of democracy in the late twentieth century are called upon to discover whether the virtues of diversity, sociability, and tolerance associated with the ideal of the cosmopolis can be combined with the self-governing political community of the polis. Can political arguments be considered on their merits, at least partially autonomous from the identities of the arguers? [44]

The *locus classicus* of such public life lay in European cities of the eighteenth century. It may be that current trends in Europe – especially the integration of the European Community but also perhaps the creation of small states in the east – may actually restore some of the early modern prominence of cities in public life and social organization. Links among cities and/or regions may partially replace those among states. But major improvements in the nature of modern public discourse cannot come about simply through direct interpersonal relationships in cities. They must happen also through television and newspapers. They must happen on the scale of millions of people in powerful states. Political parties with their patronage, bureaucracies, and public relations staffs will mediate the relations between groups as much as cafés with their intellectual arguments. [45] These parties must remain open to diversity for they are crucial means of achieving not consensus so much as reasonable compromises where consensus is impossible. If democracy is to flourish, nationalism must not become the enemy of difference.

The events of 1989 showed the power of mass media to further an internationalization of culture and politics. I was in Beijing that spring, and watched with amazement. Chinese students deliberately echoed Poland's Solidarity movement, and within days protesting students in eastern Europe marched with headbands and placards proclaiming their sympathy with the Chinese. And today Chinese democrats – and nationalists – look to eastern Europe for inspiration. The nationalism which figured centrally in these movements is an international phenomenon – as nationalism was in 1848. Not only is it shared through mass communication, it is driven by global processes that value and privilege nations as categories of identity between the immediately interpersonal and the local. It is often repeated that the twin tendencies of the present era are towards globalization and localization. This has an element of truth, but it is an overused mantra. It neglects the importance of states as arenas for democratic struggles, and as agents for contesting an economic power which has not ceased to be concentrated as it has become global. And it suggests that the division of the world into ever smaller units of putative internal sameness is the only way to achieve happiness in our immediate lifeworlds. It is as though someone decided that Durkheim's mechanical solidarity is the only kind that works.

Nationalism encourages the identification of individuals not with locality *per se*, not with the webs of their specific interpersonal relationships, but with an abstract category. This category of nation may be a helpful mediation between the local and the global. Indeed, I think this is one crucial reason why nationalism is unlikely to disappear any time soon. Globalization, where it occurs, is likely to call forth new and different nationalisms and more generally politics of identity. Far from producing a cosmopolitanism somehow antithetical to nationalism, the massive international migrations currently under way are apt to accentuate in both predictable and unpredictable ways the salience of cultural divides and identities in many people's everyday lives. Simply getting rid of nationalism is thus not a viable response to its disagreeable features.

Contrary to much received wisdom, I have argued that both states on the one hand, and nationalism and the discourse of national identity on the other, are likely to remain of central importance in an increasingly globalized world. Much of the question of how this will affect human life turns on the extent to which and manner in which institutions of civil society provide social foundations for democracy. Whether claims to national identity will be used to override other identities, either within or across national boundaries will be determined not just by the cultural content of nationalist ideologies or the choices of nationalist ideologues. It will be determined also by the presence or absence of cross-cutting social ties and mediating institutions.

Is it possible to build states and even confederations of states in which cohesion and self-rule are established through public discourse across lines of difference? Can we conceive the growth of a cultural unity within such states or confederations that does not devalue or demand the obliteration of other sources of personal and political identity? Or must we fall back on nationalism alone as our shelter in a world grown too frightening, or as the one immediately satisfying identity with which to confront the globalization of capital?

Notes

1 This has been one of the themes of postmodernism as well as of more conventional political economy. See the sympathetic but critical survey in David Harvey: *The Postmodern Condition* (Oxford: Blackwell, 1990).
2 Of course the related end to the political-military rivalry between the capitalist world system and communist countries is also significant. It is possible, but remains to be seen, that global integration is sufficient to prevent the emergence of a new state-capitalist military block that, like the Axis of the 1930s, seeks to carve an alternative world system to that built around capital accumulation through multilateral trade.

3 See the contrasting reviews and theorizations in Adam Seligman, *Civil Society* (New York: Free Press, 1992); Jean Cohen and Andrew Arato, *The Political Theory of Civil Society* (Cambridge, MA: MIT Press, 1992).

4 Charles Taylor, "Modes of Civil Society," *Public Culture* vol. 3, no. 1 (1991): 95–118.

5 This point is also made in a very different way by Jean Cohen and Andrew Arato, *Political Theory*. Cohen and Arato want to get away from a simple opposition of state to all other social organization (the sort of usage that resulted in a discourse of "society *versus* the state" in eastern Europe). They place an important stress on the role of social movements in democratic process and on "resources of solidarity" that enable individuals to join together in collective action to limit the power of state or economy (see ch. 9, esp. p. 472). Yet, drawing primarily on readings of Hegel and Habermas, they neglect both the Scottish moralists and the French tradition, treating social organization primarily in terms of notions of system integration developed by Talcott Parsons and Niklas Luhmann. Rather than calling attention to the reified and therefore anti-democratic nature of the description of social life as impersonally steered "system," they simply accept as given that much social life is so organized. Crucially, they accept without challenge the idea that power is a steering medium in the same sense as money. They also accept the Parsons–Luhmann understanding of economic life as simply a self-regulating functional system steered impersonally by money. They thus either neglect or reject the Marxian notion of the way in which capitalism structures not only the economy but the categories of economic understanding (1) so that money *appears* as the primary element in the economic system, (2) so that the centrality of capital accumulation is obscured, and (3) so that the system appears as necessary rather than transcendable. Such a view is elaborated in Moishe Postone, *Marx's Critique of Money, Labor and Time* (Cambridge: Cambridge University Press, 1993). Their sociological theory thus marginalizes the role of direct social relations – the kinds of structures studied, for example, under the rubric of social networks, and the basis of the communities, intermediate associations, and mediating institutions vital to democratic life – and thereby underestimates the capacities of actors to create and modify social institutions.

6 See Jürgen Habermas, *The Structural Transformation of the Public Sphere* (Cambridge, MA: MIT Press, 1989) and the various qualifications, extensions, and refinements suggested by the essays in Craig Calhoun, *Habermas and the Public Sphere* (Cambridge, MA: MIT Press, 1992).

7 This is a theme associated especially with Alexis de Tocqueville, *Democracy in America* (New York: Schocken, 1840–4) but also important to Durkheim, e.g., in the preface to the second edition of *The Division of Labor in Society* (New York: Free Press 1933) and a range of other thinkers since Montesquieu. See also Craig Calhoun, "Democracy,

Autocracy and Intermediate Associations in Organizations: Flexibility or Unrestrained Change?" *Sociology*, vol. 4, no. 3: pp. 345–61.

8 Even if one could point to completely self-contained island cultures somewhere in the South Pacific (and my reading of the anthropological evidence is that one cannot), these would not be nations in anything like the modern sense of the term, for that implies the definition of one by contraposition to others (as, indeed, do a variety of other forms of identity from lineage segment to clan to locality). Key to nationalist discourse is its rejection of any notion that identity is essentially fluid and shifting from one situation to another. National identity is commonly claimed to trump all others.

9 See especially R. Brubaker, *Citizenship and Nationhood in France and Germany* (Cambridge, MA: Harvard University Press, 1992) and G. Noiriel, *Le Creuset Français* (Paris: Seuil, 1988).

10 Perhaps the greatest single weakness of Habermas's *Structural Transformation of the Public Sphere* is his treatment of identity formation as essentially private and prior to participation in the idealized public sphere of rational critical discourse. A "politics of identity," therefore, could appear only as a degenerate intrusion into the public sphere, owing first to growing democratic inclusiveness and second to public relations manipulation. One result is that nationalism, a prototypical form of the politics of identity, and one broached crucially in the public sphere, did not figure significantly in Habermas's account.

11 It is common that a bit of each sort of claim is made. In France, histories trace French character back to the Gauls as well as anchoring national identity crucially in the Revolution and the distinctive notion of citizenship it brought forward. In China, national identity (a notion deriving in part from contact with the West) is at once seen as something extraordinarily ancient (and this with better claim than most of the world's other peoples) and as something given special purpose by the unification under the Qin dynasty.

12 Anthony Smith, esp. in *The Ethnic Origins of Nations* (Oxford: Blackwell, 1986), is the most articulate modern voice for the importance of ethnicity to nationalism, but see also the review and critique in Craig Calhoun, "Nationalism and Ethnicity," *Annual Review of Sociology* (1993).

13 "What is a Nation," tr. M. Thom, in H. K. Bhabha, ed., *Nation and Narration* (London: Routledge, 1990), pp. 8–22, quotation from p. 11.

14 Benedict Anderson, *Imagined Communities* (New York: Verso, 1983; rev. edn 1991).

15 National identity, thus, in its main western ideological form, is precisely the opposite of the reckoning of identity and loyalty outward from the family. Where the segmentary lineage system suggests "I against my brothers, I and my brothers against my cousins, I, my brothers and my cousins against the world," nationalism suggests that membership in the category of the whole nation is prior to, more basic than any such web of relationships. This suggests also a different notion of moral commit-

ment from previous modes of understanding existence. The prototypical discourse of nationalism carries the form even into non-western settings where kinship and communal bonds may figure more prominently or be claimed specifically against western individualism. See Partha Chatterjee: *Nationalist Thought and the Colonial World: A Derivative Discourse*, rev. edn (Minneapolis: University of Minnesota Press, 1993) and *The Nation and Its Fragments: Studies in Colonial and Post-Colonial Histories* (Princeton, NJ: Princeton University Press, forthcoming).

16 Hans Kohn: *The Idea of Nationalism* (New York: Macmillan, 1944); Andrzej Walicki: *Philosophy and Romantic Nationalism: The Case of Poland* (Oxford: Oxford University Press, 1982); Joan S. Skurnowicz: *Romantic Nationalism and Liberalism: Joachim Lelewel and the Polish National Idea* (New York: Columbia University Press, 1981); Friedrich Meinecke: *Cosmopolitanism and the National State*, tr. R. B. Kilmer (Princeton: Princeton University Press, 1970).

17 Fichte, quoted in Meinecke, *Cosmopolitanism and the National State*, p. 89.

18 William Bloom: *Personal Identity, National Identity and International Relations* (Cambridge: Cambridge University Press, 1990).

19 Nils Kjoer to Ibsen on the celebration of his 70th birthday (1898), quoted p. 7 of "Henryk Ibsen – Our Contemporary," the 1991 Ibsen Stage Festival in Norway, ed. Margrethe Aaby (Oslo, 1991).

20 See George L. Mosse, *Nationalism and Sexuality: Middle-Class Morality and Sexual Norms in Modern Europe* (Madison: University of Wisconsin Press, 1985).

21 See, among many general treatments, Anthony Giddens, *The Nation-State and Violence* (Berkeley: University of California Press, 1984); Charles Tilly, *Coercion, Capital and European States AD 990–1990* (Oxford: Blackwell, 1990); Michael Mann, *The Sources of Social Power*, vol. 2 (Cambridge: Cambridge University Press, 1992).

22 E. Weber: *Peasants into Frenchmen* (Stanford, CA: Stanford University Press, 1976).

23 Susan Cott Watkins: *From Provinces into Nations: Demographic Integration in Western Europe, 1870–1960* (Princeton: Princeton University Press, 1991).

24 See C. Calhoun, "Imagined Communities and Indirect Relationships," in P. Bourdieu and J. Coleman, eds, *Social Theory for a Changing Society* (Boulder, CO: Westview Press, 1991).

25 A relatively benign though potentially problematic aspect of nationalism in eastern Europe and the former USSR is the intentional deintegration of markets and division of labor. Rather than enhancing their cross-border relations, most formerly communist countries seem bent on developing their own individual relations with the West, and their own autonomous development plans. Economic integration seems to be experienced as a lack of national freedom, but this both forfeits comparative advantages in economic exchange and makes future conflicts more likely.

26 Jeff Weintraub, "The Theory and Politics of the Public/Private Distinction," paper presented to the American Political Science Association, 1990, p. 16; see Weintraub and K. Kumar, eds, *Public and Private in Thought and Practice* (Chicago: University of Chicago Press, forthcoming).

27 Ernest Gellner, *Nations and Nationalism* (Oxford: Blackwell, 1983), p. 6.

28 As Hobsbawm writes, "we cannot assume that for most people national identification – when it exists – excludes or is always or ever superior to, the remainder of the set of identifications which constitute the social being" (*Nations and Nationalism since 1780* [Cambridge: Cambridge University Press, 1990, p. 11]). But part of nationalist ideology is precisely the notion that national identity does "trump" other identities.

29 This point is made with some force by Eric Hobsbawm in *Nations and Nationalism since 1780* and Ernest Gellner in *Nations and Nationalism*. Both authors stress that this is not accidental, for "a world of nations cannot exist, only a world where some potentially national groups, in claiming this status, exclude others from making similar claims, which, as it happens, not many of them do" (Hobsbawm, *Nations and Nationalism since 1780*, p. 78).

30 Anderson's notion of "modular" nationalism may overstate the case to the point of denying creativity and indigenous roots to later nationalist discourses. See Partha Chatterjee, *Nationalist Thought and the Colonial World: A Derivative Discourse?* (London: Zed Press, 1986).

31 Resentments seem especially central to some nationalisms of central and eastern Europe. Some domestic religious traditions, like Russian and other "eastern" Orthodoxies, seem to encourage xenophobia beyond any influence of historical wrongs or current international threats. See Liah Greenfeld, "The Formation of the Russian National Identity: The Role of Status Insecurity and *Ressentiment*," *Comparative Studies in Society and History*, vol. 32, no. 3 (1990): 549–91.

32 Albert Nenarokov and Alexander Proskurin: *How the Soviet Union Solved the Nationalities Question* (Moscow: Novosti Press Agency Publishing House, 1983).

33 See Gail Kligman Calus: *Symbolic Transformation in Romanian Ritual* (Chicago: University of Chicago Press, 1984); Katherine Verdery: *National Ideology Under Socialism: Identity and Cultural Politics in Ceausescu's Romania* (Berkeley: University of California Press, 1991).

34 Communism has always been linked to nationalism in China, though the label "nationalism" was appropriated by its competitor, the Guomindang. In general, a kind of modernizing nationalism has often been part of communism's appeal, and it is no accident that communism has flourished especially in settings where people have felt cheated of their due stature by the capitalist world system (not in the advanced centers of capitalism as Marx predicted). As the case of largely ethnically homogeneous China illustrates, nationalist aspirations are not limited to the constitution of states or the alteration of their boundaries, but include

pursuit of a range of goals including regeneration, liberation, modernization, and power.

35 Ivo Banac: *The National Question in Yugoslavia: Origin, History, Politics*
(Ithaca: Cornell University Press, 1984); Walker Connor: *The National
Question in Marxist-Leninist Theory and Strategy* (Princeton: Princeton
University Press, 1984).

36 It was, of course, this same nationalism and this same weakness of
other cultural and movement forms which rendered the Transcaucasus
unable to sustain its federation after 1917, and unable to mount significant resistance to the Red Army's imposition of Soviet rule.

37 This is congruent with the suggestion of N. Abercrombie et al., *The
Dominant Ideology Thesis* (London: Allen and Unwin, 1984) that dominant ideologies are more effective in establishing cohesion among elites
than in enabling elites to "delude" or persuade the "masses."

38 On the connection to war, see Bryan Turner, *Citizenship and Capitalism:
The Debate over Reformism* (London: Allen and Unwin, 1986).

39 Similarly, it is analytically untenable to try to treat "nationalism" and
"patriotism" (or other labels amounting to "good" and "bad" nationalism)
as though they were fundamentally different ideological species. Artistic
inspiration, needed identity, will to power, and politics of repression
can be and often are bound inseparably together. The differences among
nationalisms come as much from the nature of international contexts as
from differences in internal form or content.

40 Practices are incommensurable when they are not only different but
impossible to combine within the same framework of understanding and
action – as for example one cannot play American football and soccer
at the same time. While some differences can be resolved by translation,
incommensurabilities cannot. Where they exist in important and competitive practices (like Chinese v western medicine) they remain sources
of tension unless overall frameworks of practice are transformed. See
Charles Taylor, *Philosophy and the Human Sciences* (Cambridge: Cambridge University Press, 1985); Craig Calhoun, "Culture, History and
the Problem of Specificity in Social Theory," in S. Seidman and
D. Wagner, eds, *Post-modernism and General Social Theory* (New York:
Blackwell, 1991), pp. 244–88.

41 Charles Taylor has argued that identity and moral commitment are
intimately intertwined, so that it is almost redundant to say "identities
or values." See *Sources of the Self* (Cambridge, MA: Harvard University
Press, 1989).

42 Hannah Arendt, *The Human Condition* (Chicago: University of Chicago
Press, 1958), p. 39.

43 "Poland and the Jews," *New York Review of Books*, May 30, 1991, pp.
11–12, quote from p. 11.

44 This is, of course, a core theme to Habermas's work from *The Structural
Transformation of the Public Sphere* to the present. One may accept the
centrality of the question without accepting quite the extreme of ab-

straction from issues of personal identity which is characteristic of Habermas's work.
45 See Craig Calhoun, "Populist Politics, Communications Media, and Large Scale Social Integration," *Sociological Theory*, vol. 6, no. 2 (1988): pp. 219–41.

Index